Contents

Part II: 9/11 as Narrative, Poetics, and Personal Stories

9/11 IN AMERICAN CULTURE

Crossroads in Qualitative Inquiry

Series Editors
Norman K. Denzin, University of Illinois, Urbana-Champaign
Yvonna S. Lincoln, Texas A&M University

ABOUT THE SERIES: Qualitative methods are material and interpretive practices. They do not stand outside politics and cultural criticism. This spirit of critically imagining and pursuing a more democratic society has been a guiding feature of qualitative inquiry from the very beginning. The Crossroads in Qualitative Inquiry series will take up such methodological and moral issues as the local and the global, text and context, voice, writing for the other, and the presence of the author in the text. The Crossroads series understands that the discourses of a critical, moral methodology are basic to any effort to re-engage the promise of the social sciences for democracy in the 21st Century. This international series creates a space for the exploration of new representational forms and new critical, cultural studies.

SUBMITTING MANUSCRIPTS: Book proposals should be sent to Crossroads in Qualitative Inquiry Series, c/o Norman K. Denzin, Institute for Communication Studies, 810 S. Wright Street, University of Illinois, Champaign, Illinois 61820, or emailed to n-denzin@uiuc.edu.

BOOKS IN THIS SERIES:

Volume 1: *Investigative Poetics,* Stephen Hartnett (2003)

Volume 2: *9/11 in American Culture,* edited by Norman K. Denzin and Yvonna S. Lincoln (2003)

Volume 3: *Turning Points in Qualitative Research: Tying Knots in the Handkerchief,* edited by Yvonna S. Lincoln and Norman K. Denzin (2003)

9/11 IN AMERICAN CULTURE

AltaMira
PRESS

A Division of Rowman & Littlefield Publishers, Inc.
Walnut Creek • Lanham • New York • Oxford

ALTAMIRA PRESS
A Division of Rowman & Littlefield Publishers, Inc.
1630 North Main Street, #367
Walnut Creek, CA 94596
www.altamirapress.com

Rowman & Littlefield Publishers, Inc.
A Member of the Rowman & Littlefield Publishing Group
4720 Boston Way
Lanham, MD 20706

PO Box 317
Oxford
OX2 9RU, UK

British Library Cataloguing in Publication Information Available

Library of Congress Cataloging-in-Publication Data

9/11 in American culture / edited by Norman K. Denzin and Yvonna S.
Lincoln.
   p. cm.
Includes bibliographical references.
  ISBN 0-7591-0349-6 (cloth : alk. paper)—ISBN 0-7591-0350-X (pbk. :
alk. paper)
  1. September 11 Terrorist Attacks, 2001—Miscellanea. I. Title:
Nine-eleven in American culture. II. Denzin, Norman K. III. Lincoln,
Yvonna S.

HV6432.7 .A13 2003
973.931—dc21   2002013165

Printed in the United States of America

⊗™ The paper used in this publication meets the minimum requirements of American
National Standard for Information Sciences—Permanence of Paper for Printed Library
Materials, ANSI/NISO Z39.48-1992.

*The Voices of Cultural Studies, Medicine and
Interpretive Social Science*

Acknowledgments

E ARE VERY FORTUNATE. Most authors and editors recognize the work—and faith—that their publisher has put into any book. We have the privilege of being grateful to two publishers. At AltaMira we thank Mitch Allen for making this project possible, and at Sage Publications we would like to thank Catherine Rossbach, our senior serials editor, for expediting the permissions process so that it was smooth and trouble free. We are also grateful to Grace Ebron at AltaMira for bringing coherence to it, and Richard Girazide for his patience and excellence in copyediting. We thank Ben Scott for gathering valuable information for the appendices and James Salvo for holding the Urbana office together and for his careful proofreading. Jack Bratich held the entire project together, and without him it would not have happened. Finally, we want to thank our contributors, who took time away from other projects to contribute to this volume. Their reflections, personal narratives, poems and political analyses add power and richness to the ongoing conversation about what 9/11 means.

Introduction
9/11 in American Culture

NORMAN K. DENZIN AND YVONNA S. LINCOLN

THE WORLD CHANGED ON 11 September 2001. For Americans, not since Pearl Harbor and Hiroshima (Hersey, 1946), had there been one global symbolic event of the force of 9/11 (see Baudrillard, 2001). The global repercussions of 9/11 are still being felt today, from the Middle East to Afghanistan to Washington, D.C.[1] Indeed, the 9/11 event is taking on the aura of history, an apocalyptic moment, a turning point in the history of America and its relationship to the world. The essays in this volume were written in crisis, literally within days and weeks of September 11.[2]

The immediacy of the writing is vivid. Together, these pieces register a variety of emotional responses and critical interpretations of the meanings of this world trauma.[3] There is a timelessness in the emotions, a timelessness that lingers after the memories of the tragedy begin to dim. Fear, trembling, doubt, anger, anguish, scapegoating, these are universal responses that dominate consciousness when humans are forced to live through a terrible atrocity. Events like 9/11 produce turbulent, volatile emotions, deep apprehension, and anxiety, a fearfulness that is increased when the future seems to hold only more violence and more terror (see Said, 2001, p. 1). This is a timelessness born out of dread and death, feelings of being powerless, of being a victim.

From the poetic to the personal, the theoretical to the historical, these contributions help us understand 9/11 in multiple ways, but always as an experience filtered through previous experiences: as a violent historical event of great consequence; as a set of stories; as a set of representations constructed in the mass media; as an experience interpreted by professors and by poets.

The attacks on the World Trade Center in New York City and the Pentagon in Washington, D.C., produced a horror, to quote New York City Mayor Rudolph W. Giuliani, that is (and was) more than the mind can bear. Confused, angry, depressed, full of grief, not knowing how to act, Americans watched their TV screens and read their newspapers, seeking direction from those who would bring meaning to this event.

We felt that the moment required critically informed responses from the academy. The academy has a moral responsibility to register intelligent, critical, reflective responses to crises like 9/11. To not do so is to turn the immediate interpretations of such events over to the journalists and the media. It is not, however, that the academy is necessarily prophetic in moments such as these. It is that informed responses and critical analysis can help frame and bring different meanings to these events and their aftermath. Furthermore, as editors and coeditors of two social science journals, we felt that such statements would help people recover meaning in the face of this senseless, brutal violence; a violence that continues to produce voiceless screams of terror and insanity; a violence and a horror punctuated by stories certain to become part of urban folklore. A young child awakens her mother: "Mommy can we use the cell phone to call Daddy in heaven?" (Tierney, 2001, p. A24).

So in response to the events following 11 September, we asked a number of leading cultural studies and interpretive qualitative research scholars to comment on this moment and its place in American culture. In some cases authors were given less than a week to prepare their remarks. Edited slightly, our invitation letter read thusly:

> In response to the events following 11 September, we are writing to invite you to contribute a short piece to be put into production as quickly as posisble. As you know we are open to many different perspectives, methods and paradigms circulating throughout interpretivist research. But we are also deeply committed to a socially conscious, ethically communitarian social science radically dedicated to social justice, and "read" through the struggles of race, class, gender, indigenous status, and culture.
>
> We are stunned, appalled and grieved by the attacks on the World Trade Center and the Pentagon, and sorrowing not only for the loss of life, but for the loss of opportunity, for the loss of love, and for the temporary loss of the ability of dialogue to work through problems of hatred and religious intolerance. We know that you grieve with us, and with those who have lost so much.
>
> We are also deeply concerned about the implications for an interpretivist social science which has left us with so little by way of understanding how or why this could happen. Our invitation to you is to join with us in a special theme issue in a brief contribution of your own to talk about the terror, about its implications for an intepretivist social science, and about ways in which a radically reformulated social science directed toward communitarian ethics and social justice might address our understanding of this horror, and perhaps our ability to resolve those issues which have seemingly created the circumstances which prompted this attack.
>
> We are not asking for long scholarly pieces. We are asking you to write brief works—2-6 printed pages, or 300-1000 words—which capture how you have worked through these issues, whether for yourself, or as a narrative to help you understand the issues, or in class, with students immediately following the attacks. We would need to have the pieces no later than November 12th, 2001.

We did not ask contributors to write from the perspective of a scholarly discipline.[4] Rather, we asked them to write from their own experiences, to speak from the heart. And they did.

This volume reflects an act of sharing: academics telling how they made sense of the tragic events of September 11, including what they thought the place of the humanities and the social sciences might be in an age of terror. In the pages that follow, they show us how they dealt with the shock and horror in their classrooms, on what the implications might be for their teaching. The lachrymal and elegiac tone of these short pieces will stay with many of us for years to come.

Those whom we asked represent a community for the two of us. Those in this community are special, in that their commitments to a radically reformulated social science responsive to social justice issues are clear in their writing. They are passionate about engaging issues of intolerance, injustice, hatred, discrimination and inequity wherever their inquiries have led them, and they bring this engagement to their work, whether in research, writing, or teaching.

Over 50 people responded to our invitations. Their powerful and moving interpretations are located in parts one, two and three of this book. We present them here with little interpretation. Although we do present a framework for reading them, they speak for themselves. These powerful and moving interpretations represent a shared grief, a sense of mourning, a sorrow which is almost unfathomable. It is a sorrow shared by millions, those who ache to understand that which cannot be understood, those who have suffered personal loss, and those who reach out to comfort those who have lost so much.

Policing the Crisis

Stealing a title from Stuart Hall and his coauthors (1978), it is necessary to police the present international crisis, to simultaneously create and sustain a critical dialogue focused on history and politics as they unfold in front of us. The starting point for this dialogue is painful. Jonathan Schell is correct, *"There is no technical solution to the vulnerability of modern populations to weapons of mass destruction"* (Schell, 2001, p. 5, italics in original). Terrorism may be abetted, but it cannot be stopped. No amount of money, no stealth system, no security system will stop violence. To think otherwise is to participate in an escalating self-destructive process that is guaranteed to produce destruction on a world-wide basis.

Starting with this fact, the dialogue must move in at least three directions at the same time. First, we must start with and always return to the personal and the biographical, the human tragedies following 11 September, and each person's intersection with this event. We need a critical, humane discourse that creates sacred and spiritual spaces for persons and their moral communities, spaces where people can express and give meaning to the tragedy and its aftermath. This project will work back and forth, connecting the personal, the political, and the cultural. Many of the contributions in part two do exactly this.

Second, a critical discourse must be launched at the level of the media and the ideological, including discourses on war, America, democracy, and the silences surrounding peace, human rights, and nonviolence. This discourse, as represented in the essays and poetry in parts one and three, calls for justice without war. These writers are asking for calm deliberations. They plead against rash actions, including hate crimes hidden behind flag-flying patriotism, acts of intolerance which erode human rights and civil liberties. They are asking, "Whose democracy? Whose America?"

We do not have a strong independent, critical press in America (McChesney, 2000, p. x). The materials located under "Media Matters" in part two criticize America's media and its treatment of 9/11. The writers in this section observe that we have a media which can instantly produce a sea of violent images, a media with a memory, but no critical history (Baudrillard, 1988, p. 126). Mainstream media have more or less uncritically adopted President Bush's rhetoric: We are at war; this is our Pearl Harbor; we were attacked by cowards; America's freedoms are under assault; an international war on terrorists and terrorism must be launched; if innocent citizens are killed, so be it.

The narrative is straightforward. Benign global techno-capitalism and the values of a free democratic world were attacked on dark Tuesday. Working from this premise, acting under the umbrella of an increasingly conservative, right-wing neoliberal agenda, President Bush and his National Security Advisers have moved quickly and decisively. The mythology of the Wild West is operative: "Osama bin Laden, Dead or Alive."

The "Dead or Alive" political logic works thusly. "Because America is a democracy . . . some democratic prerequisites might have to be abandoned. What might this mean? Increased domestic snooping by US law enforcement and intelligence agencies, ethnic profiling, another drive for a national ID card system" (Cockburn, 2001, p. 8). Congress promises to bail out the greedy airline industry. The lid is off Social Security. Within days of 9/11 thirty-five thousand National Guard troops were put on alert. Repressive, global corporate politics drive internal domestic policies.

The moral conservatives blame the event on homosexuals and the women's movement. The political conservatives say we have gone soft on national defense. The transition to a reactionary neofascist state is sped up. State-sponsored violence is taken for granted. The boundaries of personal democratic freedom are shrinking. The very foundations of our democratic institutions are under assault. And it all happened, it seems, in one week.

Third, there is a need for a critical national conversation on 9/11 and its aftermath, a coalition of voices across the political, cultural and religious spectrums, the socialist left, the green, peace, women's, gay, lesbian, African- and Asian-American, and Latino movements, libertarians, young, old, students, workers, the clergy and persons from all religions, as well as intellectuals. Every era must develop its own theory of radical politics and social democracy, so must ours (see Kellner, 1989, p. 227). We cannot allow the state and its officials to dictate the meanings of 9/11.

We must be vigilant against the forces of fascism and state-sponsored violence, and surveillance done in the name of freedom. We must question flag waving: "Whose flag is being waved, and what does it mean?" We cannot let democratic dialogue be eviscerated in a time of crisis. We cannot allow attacks on persons of color. We cannot let the political discourse be shaped by the needs and voices of multinational corporations (Giroux, 2000a, p. 13; 2000b, p. 15). We must ask, "Who is guarding our freedom?" and "What did America do to provoke this violence?"

These and other questions are raised in the commentary, essays and poetry which follow. Readers are invited to enter into this conversation about a practical, progressive politics, a radical discourse linking "ethics, politics, and power" (Giroux, 2000b, p. 25). America is indeed at a crossroads. The need to be radical, utopian and humane has never been greater. We demand a progressive road map for the future.

This will be a future grounded in human understanding, compassion and forgiveness. And there were powerful glimpses of hope and humanity underneath the violent images that circulated in the media during the week of September 11: A sea of photographs on walls and fences, pictures of human beings lost in the tragedy. Behind the faces pasted on handheld posters, there was a sense that we were a nation of people who felt deeply. Each photograph reached back to a tiny island of humanity, mothers, fathers, friends and coworkers, ordinary people who would never return home. A three year old asking her mother to call daddy in heaven. Beneath the flags and the tears, heartfelt emotion, a love and a humanity that transcended the horror of it all.

Reading 9/11

Of course, as the above commentary suggests, 9/11 was not and is not a single event. It is a sequence of experiences and discourses. Its meanings are constantly moving, unfolding, month by month, back and forth from the personal to the political; from stories in the media to political criticism from the right and the left (see appendices A and B).

Initial reactions, of course, were defined in response to the shock and loss of lives surrounding the collapse of the World Trade Center and the attack on the Pentagon. The heroic round the clock rescue activities of New York's police officers and fire department set the first stage of interpretation which was defined by grieving, terror, anger and bewilderment. The reflections in part one read 9/11 as an experience of enormous personal and political importance. Mary Weems, the poet, speaks of "Blood" and "Being under the World," "Aftermath," "One Face in the Crowd." Weems's words are sharply etched: "The woman's face is braided / white, dusted like fresh made rolls/ fear is a river."

Moving from this face in the crowd, critical theorists Denzin, Kellner, Giroux, McLaren, Bratich, Shepperson and Tomaselli attempt to make sense of the event. How did it happen? What is America's place in this archaeology of terror? Where does blow back fit in? What happens when war becomes imminent? What does war mean in this context? What happens to democracy in America under conditions of permanent terror?

Working from the standpoint of critical media analysis, these writers understand that the meanings brought to 9/11 and its aftermath are socially constructed through a process of signification. They also understand that there is no truth that lies beyond signification; there are no final meanings to 9/11. Giroux, Kellner, Bratich, McLaren, Shepperson and Tomaselli seek to create a critical consciousness about 9/11. This is a consciousness that intervenes in, challenges, and contests offical interpretations offered by the state. These scholars understand too that there "is a dialectic between specific US actions on the one hand and consequent attitudes towards America on the other hand" (Said, 2002, p. 3). And they ask a deeper question, namely, how it is that Americans find it so hard to believe that "in the Middle East and Arab world US actions as a state . . . are [so] deeply resented" (Said, 2002, p. 2). Reducing the attacks on America to the work of fanatics, or terrorists, dividing the world into those who are with us versus those who are against us is irresponsible. These are the issues raised in Part One.

Part Two begins with reflections by Patricia Clough and then presents poetry and personal stories. Fine and Lincoln register grief and mourning, the "mourning" after the event. They speak of tears on the faces of those who have lost family members, persons who cannot grieve, persons who keep the terror and loss inside. And alongside such emotions is talk of missile defense shields, antiterrorist legislation, confusion, exhaustion, the body as a carrier of social emotion. Joanne Robertson and Karen Staller listen to and mark the heartbeat of loss in New York City; Greg Dimitriadis offers thoughts on recovery; we must negotiate a new relationship with ourselves and with others; the world will never be the same again. Angharad Valdivia hears 9/11 through another set of personal traumas. Denzin asks, "What will we tell the children about this violence, this bombing, the death?"

America and the world learned about 9/11 through the media, the television screen, endless reruns of the planes hitting the Twin Towers and then the Pentagon. The world suddenly became small, and just like their parents, little children learned about 9/11 by watching television. Eight weeks after 9/11, America was in week four of its war against terrorists in Afghanistan. Halfway around the world smart bombs were bombing the fiercely proud people of a mountainous, rocky nation back into the Stone Age. Government officials tried to draw firm lines in a porous, fog-like space, and civil disobedience was alive and well in cyberspace. Americans were told to love the bomb and not ask questions. Indeed, to question the war on terrorism was to come to the aid and assistance of the terrorists. Soon an "Axis of Evil" would divide the world into an even smaller space, them against us, and us against them, and as this occurred the president extended his powers of war.

The world, it would seem, was coming apart at the seams in front of our eyes. Anti-Islamic discourse spread like wildfire across America. Joe Kincheloe observes that history lessons were forgotten, and America's history of violence in the Middle East was not addressed. We turned to Hollywood, Shirely Steinberg shows, to help us make sense of what was happening.

In the meantime we heard the stunned, angry voices of cultural studies, interpretive social science and medicine. Cameron McCarthy weaves his personal history, his thinking about the postcolonial, through this global event. Virginia Olesen seeks comfort in exchanges with friends and family, while Cary Nelson asks what it means to work in higher education in the aftermath of a defining moment of violence. Peter McLaren and Douglas Kellner criticize President Bush's "Axis of Evil," the infinite war, apocalypse now. Kenneth Gergen works through a poem to find a space to talk about the global implications of interpretive inquiry. Will Miller seeks a time for butterflies and salmon and Anton Kuzel says his patients are suffering from post-traumatic stress disorders, giving way to anxiety attacks about anthrax and bioterrorism. Mary Gergen asks that we change the ways of the world, or rather change our ways in the world. "Why do people hate us so?" she asks. Kathy Charmaz reads a hush of silence on the faces of her students, silent thoughts etched in sorrowful eyes, the tenets of terror. She asks how interpretive social science can help us find a space to battle the words that surround the rhetoric of patriotism, a rhetoric that mystifies the politics of power by drenching it in precious Middle Eastern oil.

Each person approaches an experience such as 9/11 through flashbacks, remembrances of previously experienced cataclysmic events. Davydd Greenwood returns to the assassination of John F. Kennedy in 1963, and to other events of violence. Greenwood, like others, resented the way that his experience and memory of 9/11 were being manipulated by politicians and the media. Shulamit Reinharz asks if we can educate ourselves and our students so that hatred can be reduced. Can Palestinians and Israelis, for example, find a common meeting place where understanding and compassion will flourish?

The poetry and reflections in part three address living in the present, dealing with the anger and the fear, saying prayers for small things. Staceyann Chin asks if we can get past war games. Lois Weis charts her fears on the day of 9/11, collapsing in tears when she learns her brother-in-law made it out of the Twin Towers alive. Being politically engaged, Weis reminds us, requires honesty and a commitment to speak out against what is wrong. Love survives, Arthur Bochner writes, etching memories of 9/11 in the days that led to the death of his mother. Carolyn Ellis writes of the racial and ethnic prejudices, and personal fears that circulated immediately after 9/11, and the need to take chances and trust strangers. Ivan Brady cries out for a signal, a sign of our humanness in this moment of violence. William Tierney maintains sanity by remembering an earlier time, a walk in an olive grove in Morocco.

Gerardo R. López comments on the excessive displays of patriotism following 9/11 and offers counter-narratives of his own, suggesting that the wounds and hatred Americans now feel and show toward dark-skinned others is not new. Historically, American patriotism has always needed to create enemies. H. L. Goodall, Jr., offers field notes from our war zone, suggesting that life in America, after 9/11, has not been easy, nor has it been easy to engage in the war on terrorism, when terrorism's target keeps changing.

Karen Scott-Hoy comes to doubt her taken-for-granted belief that the world is a safe place to live in. Tracy Lewis poetically marks the space where frauds wave the flag and sing an anthem, and someone steals "Happy," the scarecrow made by Patricia Geist Martin's eight-year-old daughter. "Happy" has been guarding their house since October 1. James Joseph Scheurich demands that the terror of 9/11 be connected to its larger global context, to sometimes murderous U.S. policy, now and in the past—death, bombing, bullet holes, suffering grenades, land mines, an aching sobbing hole.

Christopher Polous advises us on how to live in an age of anxiety: Can we find new ways of relating, of being with one another? Henry Giroux mourns for a lost democracy, the politics and cultures of fear in post-9/11 America. Gloria Ladson-Billings colors the past, offering another view of 9/11, another set of dates: pre–April 4, 1968, post–April 4, 1968, pre-summer of 1963 and post-summer of 1963. There is more than one history of violence in America, and she criticizes this penchant for fixing a point in time as the point in time for everyone. Stephen Hartnett ends our collection with a love poem for a hurt nation.

Critical Reflections

Hard questions are raised by 9/11; perhaps the hardest is the one suggested by many critics. As Americans we must take responsibility for the hatred others feel toward us and our nation (see Judt, 2002, p. 25). We cannot act as if these emotions do not exist.

We must look long and hard at America's past mistakes. We cannot be cajoled into a form of knee-jerk patriotism that divides the world into them versus us. Nor can we quietly go into that dark night of fascism, where our constitutional rights are trampled and our national standards of fairness and decency disappear (Dworkin, 2002, p. 44). We can no longer avoid taking responsibility for the injustices of democracy and capitalism, including poverty, ignorance, illiteracy and repression. Who among us has not manipulated the meanings of democracy, freedom and imperialism? Who among us has resisted the political rhetoric of war, and who among us has dared to imagine new forms of community, love, and international peace?

Too few of America's leaders have dared to ask these questions; too many have allowed the Bush administration to define the terms of this conversation. But we know that it is each person's duty to question the political order and the actions that are taken in the name of America as a nation. We know too that post-9/11 offered Americans an unprecedented opportunity to undertake a great project "that would strengthen America in some lasting way—a Manhattan project for energy independence" (Friedman, 2002, p. 15). This opportunity could have enlisted young and old alike, as well as science and industry, in a national movement for greater conservation, a crash effort to "produce enough renewable energy, efficiencies and domestic production to wean us gradually off oil imports" (Friedman, 2002, p. 15). But this opportunity has been squandered. And today America stands nearly alone in the world, refusing even to ratify the Kyoto treaty to reduce global warming.

Coda

The essays, reflections, poetry and criticism in this volume reinforce our belief that scholars have the moral responsibility to record and analyze such events as those of 11 September, and to do so for the benefit of future generations (Nelson and Parameshwar, 1996, p. 2). A genuine democracy requires no less. It is our obligation to make our voices heard (Giroux, 2000a, p. 15).

When you read these lines, well over a year will have passed since the original events of 11 September 2001. Far too many things have happened: an undeclared war in Afghanistan winds down, and in the American homeland, one multinational corporation after another collapses. The drums of war are beating in Washington and war in Iraq seems inevitable.

So this current moment gives us many new starting points. One is the Enron debacle and its scandals, the greed, the deception, and the thousands of former employees with unpaid mortgages and lost retirement accounts. Ties to people in power. The pain of the powerless concerns us here. But we must not lose sight of the global issues, global capitalism. Enron is about oil, wealth, power, energy, and deregulation. The undeclared war is also about wealth, power and pain, destroyed lives, violence. Critical inquiry inserts itself into these spaces, and helps us tell stories that move from the global to the local, ever keeping our eye on global captialism and its place in this big picture.

The mourning goes on. It is possible to spend a lifetime reflecting on what this means for our practice as scholars, and for our commitments to social justice and relief from oppression. Our readers will notice that while the reaction of the country was sorrow followed by anger, the voices here are not angry voices. Nor are they bitter voices. They are voices of concern, of commitment and recommitment to finding peaceful solutions, of genuine empathy for the Afghan people, many of whom are victims no less than those who died in the World Trade Center towers, in the Pentagon, and aboard Flight 99. In some instances, they are voices that wonder what to say next. We will be a very long time finding the answers, but in these pages are some of the hopes for that future.

Some Final Reflections, Part One

The 9/11 saga continues, moving in several different directions at the same time. Rebuilding at Ground Zero has started. Families still grieve for lost loved ones. A summer fuel shortage is likely, with higher gas prices at the fuel pump. One multinational corporation after another goes under, and it seems that last year's energy crisis in California can be traced directly to the White House. The CIA and the FBI fight over intelligence documents. President Bush asks Americans to trust him as he fights terrorism. And in the meantime civil rights are threatened. Anyone suspected of being a terrorist can be detained by the government. More and more, on a daily basis, life since 9/11 seems to be lived under the terrifying shadows of a violent, repressive, secretive fascism.

The nation has been in the grips of mass-mediated fear ever since 9/11. This is the dark side of 9/11. Clearly, as David Altheide recently noted (2002), the Bush administration has used the terrorist attacks to change long-standing policy about civil rights. Antiterrorist legislation passed since 9/11 has given broad surveillance and detention powers to the government. The passage of this legislation, with little protest from the left or from Democrats, serves to give the impression that the govenment is in control of the terrorist situation. The open-ended war on terrorism gives the administration further warrant to increase its detention powers. The same war emboldens our president as he launches his "Strike First" terrorist policy.

We must continue to ask, "Why do they hate us so much?" Killing those who hate us is not the answer. A loyal opposition must be created. This will be more than just an antiwar coalition. It will be a national presence that resists violence and the curtailment of civil liberties. Such a presence will direct us to explore and implement nonviolent forms of resistance and community formation. This must be a global movement, a peaceful, utopian movement that universally honors human rights, the sacredness of human life, and enhances social transformation.

Americans are trapped in a liminal space, somewhere between life before and life after 9/11. New terrorism alerts are experienced on a weekly basis. Just as everything seems back to normal, a new scare is discovered. America's undeclared war against terrorism continues. In the pursuit of terrorists we have now inserted ourselves in multiple national contexts. Israel and Palestine engage in a no-win war of mutual destruction. The Middle East, like the rest of the world, wait for the Bush administration to launch its first attacks against Iraq, which are expected before the end of 2002.

9/11 is like a lightning rod, a warning that all is not well in America. We are living under very threatening and terrifying conditions, but not the terror that Bush attacks. We are in danger of imploding from within if we do not seriously examine ourselves, our national dreams, our hopes, if we do not ask more of ourselves and our national leaders.

Invoking William Kittridge (1987, p. 87) the writers in this volume are struggling to revise the dominant myths that organize daily life in the many small worlds that proliferate and splinter under the nightmares of late capitalism after 9/11. Each writer seeks a new model of society, a new set of traditions, new stories which will bring the present in line with utopian dreams of liberation and freedom and justice, life without terror. Please join us in this project.

9/11 AS EVENT I

"Blood", "Under the World, 9/22/01" I

MARY WEEMS

Blood

The same bald-headed white man
gives blood. They re-run him like a
sad song, his arm moves in and out of the rubber
sleeve like a flip chart.

One-time the camera person makes a mistake
and rolls him backwards, the blood backs out
of his arm so fast it dyes the TV screen.

I wonder if Valentine's Day will ever come again,
if Christmas will be as red this year,
what hearts look like
flying through the air.

Under the World, 9/22/01

Everything smolders,
water seeps from brick, from stone,
from six open eyes.

They are not together and do not feel
the weather.

They can hear the crews saying prayers,
saying prayers, saying prayers.

A little girl inches.
Attached to her mother's death

she sucks breath. She folds her hand
over her mother's hand and gives her a kiss.
Rescue is the food she waits for, a trickle of
water hits her mouth, she drinks.

A father wears a battered Brooks' Brothers suit.
His head full of rocks, his body under blocks.
He wonders why he's awake and dreaming, if
his morning coffee is ready, if his secretary
washed his cup last night, why his cell phone
keeps ringing, whose voice that is, why he can't
feel his legs.

The infant moves protected by its mother's womb.
It doesn't know its sex, what sex is, what life is,
what that long cord is, what it's doing in this mess.
It knows to eat the food when it comes, that its space
is getting cold, that it hasn't felt its mother
in a long time.

Mary Weems is an African American activist, artist, and educator.

Terrorism and the Fate of Democracy after September 11

2

HENRY A. GIROUX
Penn State University

A tragedy of errors: nobody knows anymore who is who. The smoke of the explosions forms part of the much larger curtain of smoke that prevents all of us from seeing clearly. From revenge to revenge, terrorism obliges us to walk to our graves. I saw a photo, recently published, of graffiti on a wall in NYC: "An eye for an eye makes the whole world blind."

—EDUARDO GALEANO (2001)

IN THE AFTERMATH OF THE MONSTROUS EVENTS of September 11, there is a growing sense that history as we know it has been irrefutably ruptured. If politics seemed irrelevant before the attacks on the World Trade Center and the Pentagon, it now seems urgent and despairing. But history cannot be erased, and those traditional public spheres in which people could exchange ideas, debate, and shape the conditions that structured their everyday lives increasingly continue to appear to have little significance or political consequence. Already imperiled before the aftershocks of the terrorists attacks, democracy appears even more fragile in this time of crisis as new antiterrorist laws are being passed that make it easier to undermine those basic civil liberties that protect individuals against invasive and potentially repressive government actions.

As a result of the horrific events of September 11, civic engagement has reappeared in calls for unity and patriotism and in countless displays of compassion. But there is a dark side to this newfound call for unity. Notions of community are now organized not only around flag-waving displays of patriotism but also around collective fears and an ongoing militarization of visual culture and public space. Notions of democracy increasingly appear to be giving way to the discourse of revenge, domestic security, and war. The political reality that is beginning to emerge from this shattering crisis increasingly points to a set of narrow choices that are being largely set by the jingoistic right wing and fueled by the dominant media. One glaring example can be found in the constant televised image, "America Strikes Back," which frames much of the reporting used by CNN. Other examples can be found in the "America United" image used by the Fox News Network that is made concrete by an almost fever-pitched bellicosity that informs the majority of its commentaries and reactions to the terrorist bombings. Capitalizing on the pent-up emotions and needs of an angry and grieving public for revenge, both networks constantly frame their reportage of the terrorist attacks through the hyped-up language of war, patriotism, and retaliation. Similarly, conservative talking heads write numerous op-eds and appear on endless talk shows fanning the fires of "patriotism" by calling on the United States to expand the war against any one of a number of terrorist states. At the present moment, the language of indiscriminate revenge seeking seems to be winning the day, unconscious of its own dangerous refusal to acknowledge the important role that democratic values and social justice must play in a truly "unified" rational response so as to prevent the further killing of innocent people, regardless of their religion, culture, and place of occupancy in the world. Instead of seeing the current crisis as a break from the past, it is crucial for the American public to begin to understand how the past might be useful in addressing what it means to live in a democracy in the aftermath of the bombings in New York and Washington, D.C. At stake here is the need to establish a vision of society and a global order that safeguards its most basic civil liberties and notions of human rights. Any struggle against terrorism must begin with the pledge on the part of the United States that it will not target civilians and that it will rethink those aspects of its foreign policy that have allied it with repressive nations in which democratic freedoms and civilian lives are under siege.

President Bush and his cohorts caution the American public that a new kind of war has begun that will demand great sacrifices, including a rethinking of the relationship between security and civil liberties. As American troops are mobilized to occupy Afghanistan and potentially any number of Islamic countries that pose a threat to our interests, Americans are being asked in the name of patriotism and national sacrifice to give up certain civil liberties and to separate security from freedom, and these demands are most evident in the antiterrorism bill just passed by both houses of Congress. What is startling about this call to strengthen domestic security is that there is almost no debate in the dominant media about how the notions of freedom and security prior to the attack on September 11 had been taken up as part of a wider set of political, economic, and social interests that increasingly made it difficult for Americans to rely on the federal government to protect public goods, to translate private troubles into public issues, and to redefine freedom, in part, as a civic obligation of the American people to debate, participate in, and shape public policy. The delicate balance between freedom and security was already at risk before the shocking acts of terrorism brought the latter relationship back into focus.

I want to suggest that the ensuing debate that is emerging around the tension between freedom and security needs to be engaged as part of a wider conversation over the rise of neoliberalism and the collapse of the welfare state, the increasing militarization of public life, and the reduction of citizenship to the largely privatized rituals of consumerism. Lacking any sense of how citizen rights, public participation, and public freedoms have been shaped prior to the events of September 11 makes it all the more difficult to raise critical questions about the current debate regarding the balance between civil liberties and the imperatives of domestic security. Security and freedom prior to the September 11 attacks pointed to a very different notion of the social, one that had very little to do with democratic social relationships, compassion, and noncommodified values. Within the discourse of neoliberalism—which construes profit making as the essence of democracy and provides a rationale for a handful of private interests to control as much of social life as possible to maximize their personal profit—freedom was largely defined as the freedom to pursue one's own individual interests, largely free of governmental interference. Within this growing marketization and privatization of everyday life, democratic principles are either scorned as holdovers of an outmoded 1960s radicalism or equated entirely with the imperatives of capitalism. As Robert W. McChesney (1999) pointed out, Milton Friedman, the reigning guru of neoliberalism, captures and legitimates this sentiment in *Capitalism and Freedom*, arguing unabashedly that

> because profit-making is the essence of democracy, any government that pursues antimarket policies is being antidemocratic, no matter how much informed popular support they might enjoy. Therefore it is best to restrict governments to the job of protecting private property and enforcing contracts, and to limit political debate to minor issues. (p. 9)

Within neoliberal discourse, freedom is negatively reduced to the freedom from government restraint and the rights of citizenship translate into the freedom to consume as one chooses. In this instance, the welfare state becomes a threat to freedom, particularly the freedom of the market, as its role as guardian of the public interests is actively disassembled, although its powers are still invoked by dominant interests to ensure their own privileges (i.e., free trade agreements, government subsidies for business, and strike "negotiations"). But whereas neoliberals highlight the threat the state poses to the freedom of the market, the real threat comes from a state, which as it gives up its obligations to provide basic social guarantees is increasingly transformed into a repressive apparatus aimed at those individuals and groups who get caught in its ever-expanding policing interventions. As the United States is increasingly held hostage to capital and the laws of the market, a shift takes place from its "'popular democratic' features to its more authoritarian elements" (Aronowitz, 2001, p. 168). Under such conditions, not only does the state increasingly subject various populations such as youth, African Americans, and now Muslims to the full wrath of the criminal justice system, the courts, and various other repressive agencies, but the very public spaces available for Americans to dissent and offer resistance to what will surely be an attack on the most basic of civil liberties will be under siege.

This is a difficult time in American history. The American people have every right to demand to live in peace and call for forms of domestic security that protect human life from the evils of terrorism. The call for security, however, cannot be used to squelch those democratic freedoms that are already under siege. Democracy thrives on dissent, but dissent and critical citizenship cannot take place in a country marked by a widening gap between political democracy and socioeconomic capacities. A country that allows the power of transnational corporations to be exempt from rule of democratic law has already lost the battle between balancing civil liberties and national security. Any call for further giving up civil liberties suggests a dangerous silence about the degree to which civil liberties are already at risk and how the current call for national safety might work to further a different type of terrorism, one not marked by bombs and explosions but by state-supported repression, the elimination of dissent, and the death of the reality and promise of democracy. Terrorism comes in many forms, and if we are to be able as a country to affirm the principles of democracy it is crucial to fight the terrorism of religious fundamentalism and state repression. Increasing national security does not have to translate into giving the government more policing powers, particularly those that create a state marked largely by growing militarism. Terrorists who commit cowardly and inhuman acts must be brought to justice, but justice must be defined in ways that strengthen the resolve and principle of democratic societies. What happened in New York and Washington, D.C., is not simply a terrorist atrocity, but a crime against humanity, a political act, and should be dealt with through an international criminal court established by all of the democratic nations of the globe. The United States needs to work with other nations in providing the legal, economic, military, and intelligence networks to eradicate terrorism and to bring terrorists to justice. In the heat of the terrible attacks on the Pentagon and World Trade Centers, a sense of community has emerged in the United States that is mediated by a sense of compassion and revenge. Compassion can lead to understanding, to a national conversation that will allow us to address critically the conditions that produce terrorism and ways to resolve its threat. What is needed is an ongoing and critical public dialogue about the role American foreign policy plays in the world and how it contributes, in part, to the hatred felt by so many people worldwide because of its support for various totalitarian nations and its sometimes reprehensible policies. Noam Chomsky and Edward Herman reported as far back as 1979 that of the "35 countries using torture on an administrative basis in the late 1970s, 26 were clients of the United States" (Herman, 2001). The proclaimed government and media hype that the coming war is one of democracy versus terror rings hollow in the face of the U.S. funds and military equipment used by Israel to smash missiles into Palestinian homes, the United States's continuing sanctions on Iraq resulting in the death of more than half a million children, and its bombing of a crucial pharmaceutical plant in the Sudan while killing an estimated 10,000 people. At its best, patriotism means that a country does everything possible to question itself, to provide the conditions for its people to actively engage and transform the policies that shape their lives and others. At its worse, patriotism confuses dissent with treason, arrogance with strength, and brute force as the only exemplar of justice. Under such conditions, as Robert Fisk (2001) pointed out,

> It's OK to write headlines about "Islamic terror" . . . but it's definitely out of bounds to ask why the United States is loathed by so many Arab Muslims in the Middle East. We can give the murderers a Muslim identity: we can finger the Middle East for the crime—but we may not suggest any reasons for the crime.

Revenge, indeed, also shapes communities, and we see such communities emerging in the United States organized around indiscriminate attacks on Arab-Americans. Such acts are legitimated on a grand scale as the political conflict over terrorism is reduced in popular and state-sponsored discourse to a "clash of civilizations." This is the discourse of secular and religious fundamentalism, and fuels a version of so-called patriotism that requires obedience rather than citizenship and defines its relations with other nations through the arrogance of Western power, while unwittingly using the language of tyrants and terrorists.

At this time of national crisis, we need to recognize that the threat of terrorism cannot be understood apart from the crisis of democracy itself. It is all the more crucial, therefore, for educators, parents, artists, labor unions, and other groups to voice their dissent by joining with various demonstrators around the country to display solidarity with the victims and families of terrorists acts, to resist the strategy of fighting terrorism with more terrorism through the indiscriminate killing of innocent civilians and its escalating cycle of violence, and to struggle collectively to protect those democratic values whose absence make any talk about national security nothing more than an attack on democracy itself. Engaging terrorism demands more than rage and anger, revenge and retaliation; understanding why we need to confront it as a political act and a crime against humanity means raising questions about the shared obligations of human rights, social justice, and a meaningful sense of global democracy. Homi Bhabha (2001) summed up the challenge well:

> To confront the politics of terror, out of a sense of democratic solidarity rather than retaliation, gives us some faint hope for the future: hope that we might be able to establish a vision of a global society, informed by civil liberties and human rights, that carries with it the shared obligations and responsibilities of common, collaborative citizenship.

References

Aronowitz, S. (2001). *The last good job in America*. Lanham, MD: Rowman and Littlefield.

Bhabha, H. (2001, September 28). *A narrative of divided civilizations*. Retrieved from http://chronicle.com

Fisk, R. (2001, September 23). *How can the U.S. bomb this tragic people*. Retrieved from sysop@zmag.org

Galeano, E. (2001, September 21). The theatre of good and evil (J. Podur, Trans.). *La Jornada*. Retrieved from sysop@zmag.org

Herman, E. S. (2001, September 14). *Folks out there have a "distaste of Western civilization and cultural values."* Retrieved from sysop@zmag.org

McChesney, R.W. (1999). Introduction. In N. Chomsky (Ed.), *Profit over people* (pp. 7–16). New York: Seven Stories.

Henry A. Giroux is the Waterbury Chair professor in education at Penn State University.

September 11, Terrorism, and Blowback 3

DOUGLAS KELLNER
University of California, Los Angeles

MOMENTOUS HISTORICAL EVENTS like the September 11, 2001, terrorist attacks on the United States test social theories and provide a challenge to give a convincing account of the event and its consequences. They also provide cultural studies an opportunity to trace how the discourses of social theory play themselves out in media discourse, as well as to test how the broadcast and other dominant media of communication perform their democratic role of providing accurate information and discussion, and assume a responsible role in a time of crisis. In these remarks, I want first to suggest how certain dominant social theories were put in question during the event, how highly problematic positions generated by contemporary social theory circulated through the media, and how the media on the whole performed disastrously and dangerously, whipping up war hysteria while failing to provide a coherent account of what happened, why it happened, and what would count as responsible responses to the terrorist attacks.

Social Theory, Falsification, and the Events of History

Social theories generalize from historical experience and provide accounts of historical events or periods that attempt to map, illuminate, and perhaps criticize dominant social relations, institutions, forms, and trends of a given historical epoch. In turn, they can be judged by the extent to which they account for, interpret, and criticize contemporary conditions or predict future events or developments. One dominant social theory of the past two decades, Francis Fukuyama's *The End of History* (1992), was strongly put into question by the events of September 11 and their aftermath. For Fukuyama, the collapse of Soviet communism and triumph of Western capitalism and democracy in the early 1990s constituted "the end of history." This signified for him "the end point of mankind's ideological evolution and the universalization of Western liberal democracy as the final form of human government" (p. 4). Although there may be conflicts in places like the third world overall for Fukuyama, liberal democracy has triumphed and future struggles will devolve around resolving economic and technical problems and the future will accordingly be rather mundane and boring.

9

Samuel Huntington polemicized against Fukuyama's "one world: euphoria and harmony" model in his *The Clash of Civilizations and the Remaking of World Order* (1996). For Huntington, the future held a series of clashes between "the West" and "the rest." Huntington rejected a number of other models of contemporary history, including a "realist" model that nation-states were primary players on the world scene and would continue to form alliances and coalitions which would play themselves out in various conflicts, as well as a "chaos" model that discerned no mappable order or structure.

For Huntington, culture provided unifying and integrating principles of order and harmony and he delineated seven or eight different civilizations that were likely to come into conflict with each other, including Islam, China, Russia, and Latin America. I will argue that although Huntington's model seems to have some purchase in the currently emerging global encounter with terrorism, it tends to overly homogenize Islam and the West, as well as the other civilizations he depicted, and that his model lends itself to pernicious misuse, as I suggest in the following section. I will argue in a later section that Chambers Johnson's (2000) model of *blowback* provides a more convincing account of the September 11 terrorist attacks that more accurately contextualizes, explains, and even predicts such events, and also provides cogent suggestions concerning viable and inappropriate responses. First, however, I want to suggest how social discourses work themselves into the media, public policy debates, and can inform or legitimate certain practices.

Social Discourses, the Media, and the Crisis of Democracy

On the day of the terrorist attacks on the World Trade Center and Pentagon, the networks brought out an array of national security state intellectuals, usually ranging from the right to the far right, to explain the horrific events of September 11. The Fox Network presented former United Nations (UN) ambassador and Reagan administration apologist Jeane Kirkpatrick, who quickly rolled out a simplified version of Huntington's clash of civilizations, arguing that we were at war with Islam. In fact, Kirkpatrick was the most discredited intellectual of her generation, legitimating Reagan administration alliances with unsavory fascists and terrorists as necessary to beat Soviet totalitarianism. Her discourse was premised on a distinction between fascism and communist totalitarianism that argued that alliances with authoritarian or right-wing terrorist organizations or states were defensible because they were open to reform efforts or historically undermined themselves and disappeared, whereas Soviet totalitarianism had never collapsed, was an intractable and dangerous foe, and must thus be fought to the death with any means necessary. Of course, the Soviet Union collapsed in the early 1990s along with its empire, and although Kirkpatrick was totally discredited she was awarded a professorship at Georgetown and allowed to continue to circulate her crackpot views.

On the afternoon of September 11, Ariel Sharon, leader of Israel and himself implicated in war crimes in Sabra/Shatilia in Lebanon in 1982, came on television to convey his regret, condolences, and assurance of Israel's support in the war on terror. He called for a coalition against terrorism, which would contrast the free world with terrorism, representing the Good versus the Bad, "humanity" versus "the blood-thirsty," "the free world" against "the forces of darkness" who are trying to destroy "freedom" and our "way of life."

Curiously, the Bush administration would take up the same tropes, with Bush attacking the "evil" of the terrorists, using the word five times in his first statement on the terror assaults and repeatedly portraying the conflict as a war between good and evil in which the United States was going to "eradicate evil from the world," "smoke out and pursue . . . evil doers, those barbaric people." The semantically insensitive and dyslexic Bush administration also used cowboy metaphors, calling for bin Laden "dead or alive," and described the campaign as a "crusade" until he was advised that this term carried heavier historical baggage of earlier wars of Christians and Moslems. And the Pentagon named the war against terror "Operation Infinite Justice" until they were advised that only God could dispense *infinite justice* and that Americans and others might be disturbed about a war expanding to infinity.

Disturbingly, in mentioning the goals of the war, Bush never mentioned "democracy," and the new name for the campaign became "Operation Enduring Freedom" while the Bush administration mantra became that the war against terrorism is being fought for "freedom." But we know from the history of political theory and history itself that freedom must be paired with equality or things like justice, rights, or democracy to provide adequate political theory and legitimation for political action.

In his speech to Congress the following week, Bush described the conflict as a war between freedom and fear, between "those governed by fear" who "want to destroy our wealth and freedoms" and those on the side of freedom. Note that all of the dominant right-wing and Bush administration discourses are fundamentally Manichaean, positing a binary opposition between Good and Evil, Us and Them, civilization and barbarism. Such dualism can hardly be sustained in empirical and theoretical analysis of the contemporary moment. In fact, there is much fear and poverty in "our" world and wealth, freedom, and security in the Arab and Islamic worlds. No doubt that freedom, fear, and wealth are distributed in both worlds, so to polarize these categories and to make them the principle of war is highly irresponsible. And associating oneself with "good" while making one's enemy "evil" is another exercise in binary reductionism and projection of all traits of aggression and wickedness onto the "other" while constituting oneself as good and pure.

It is, of course, terroristic and theocratic Islamic fundamentalists who themselves engage in simplistic binary discourse. For certain Manichaean Islamic fundamentalists, the United States is evil, the source of all the world's problems, and deserves to be destroyed. Such one-dimensional thought doesn't distinguish between U.S. policies, people, or institutions while advocating a Jihad or Holy War against the American evil. The terrorist crimes of September 11 appeared to be part of this Jihad, and the monstrousness of the actions of killing innocent civilians shows the horrific consequences of totally dehumanizing an "enemy" deemed so evil that even innocent members of the group in question deserve to be exterminated.

Many commentators on U.S. television offered similarly one-sided and Manichaean accounts of the cause of the September 11 events, blaming their favorite opponents in the current U.S. political spectrum as the source of the terror assaults. For fundamentalist Christian ideologue Jerry Falwell, and with the verbal agreement of Christian Broadcast Network President Pat Robertson, the culpability for this "horror beyond words" fell on liberals, feminists, gays, and the American Civil Liberties Union (ACLU). Falwell said and Robertson agreed:

> The abortionists have got to bear some burden for this because God will not be mocked. And when we destroy 40 million little innocent babies, we make God mad. I really believe

that the pagans, and the abortionists, and the feminists, and the gays and the lesbians who are actively trying to make that an alternative lifestyle, the ACLU, People for the American Way—all of them who have tried to secularize America—I point the finger in their face and say, "You helped this happen."

In fact, this argument is similar to a right-wing Islamic claim that the United States is fundamentally corrupt and evil and thus deserves God's wrath, an argument made by Falwell critics that forced the fundamentalist fanatic to apologize.

For other right wingers, like Gary Aldrich, the president and founder of the Patrick Henry Center, it was the liberals who were at fault:

Excuse me if I absent myself from the national political group-hug that's going on. You see, I believe the Liberals are largely responsible for much of what happened Tuesday, and may God forgive them. These people exist in a world that lies beyond the normal standards of decency and civility.

For other rightists, it was all Bill Clinton's fault, and election thief manager James Baker blamed the catastrophe on the 1976 Church report that put limits on the Central Intelligence Agency (CIA).

On the issue of what to do, right-wing columnist and poster girl Ann Coulter declaimed, "We know who the homicidal maniacs are. They are the ones cheering and dancing right now. We should invade their countries, kill their leaders and convert them to Christianity." While Bush was declaring a "crusade" against terrorism and the Pentagon was organizing "Operation Infinite Justice," Bush administration Deputy Defense Secretary Paul Wolfowitz said the administration's retaliation would be "sustained and broad and effective" and that the United States "will use all our resources. It's not just simply a matter of capturing people and holding them accountable, but removing the sanctuaries, removing the support systems, ending states who sponsor terrorism."

Such all-out war hysteria was the order of the day, and throughout September 11 and its aftermath ideological warhorses like William Bennett came out and urged that the United States declare war on Iraq, Iran, Syria, Libya, and whoever else harbored terrorists. On the Canadian Broadcasting Network, defense commentator Frank Gaffney suggested that the United States needed to go after the sponsors of these states as well, such as China and Russia, to the astonishment and derision of the Canadian audience. And right-wing talk radio and the Internet buzzed with talk of dropping nuclear bombs on Afghanistan, exterminating all Moslems, and whatever other fantasy popped into their unhinged heads.

My point is that broadcast television allowed dangerous and arguably deranged zealots to vent and circulate the most aggressive, fanatic, and downright lunatic views, creating a consensus for the need for immediate military action and all-out war. The television networks themselves featured logos such as "War on America," "America's New War," and other inflammatory slogans that assumed that the United States was at war and that only a military response was appropriate. I saw few cooler heads on any of the major television networks that repeatedly beat the war drums day after day, without even the relief of commercials for three days straight, driving the country into hysteria and terrifying rational and sane citizens throughout the world.

This was one of the most disgusting and upsetting performances of U.S. broadcasting networks that I have ever seen. The unrelenting war hysteria and utter failure to produce anything near a coherent analysis of what happened and reasonable response to the terrorist attacks put on display the frightening consequences of allowing corporate media institutions to hire ideologically compliant news teams that are not competent to deal with complex political events and allow the most irresponsible views to circulate. I saw few, if any, intelligent and thorough presentations of the complexity of U.S. history in the Middle East, accounts of the origins of bin Laden and his network that discussed the complicity of the United States in training, funding, arming, and supporting the groups that became Islamic fundamentalist terrorists, nor did I see any accounts that went into the U.S. relations between the Taliban, the multifaceted U.S. role in Afghanistan, or the complications of Middle Eastern politics that would make immediate retaliatory military action extremely dangerous and potentially catastrophic. Such alternative information circulated through the media (including major newspapers) but rarely found its way into American television, which emerges at this point in our current crisis as a thoroughly irresponsible source of information and understanding.

Fortunately, there is a wealth of informed analysis and interpretation available in print media and the Internet, and in the following section I will argue that the causes of the September 11 events are highly complex and involve, for starters, the failure of U.S. intelligence and interventionist foreign policy since the 1980s and the policies of the Reagan, Clinton, and both Bush administrations. In other words, there is no one cause or faction responsible for the catastrophe but a wide range of blame to be ascribed. Yet I will argue that Chambers Johnson's (2000) model of blowback provides the most convincing account of how U.S. policy and institutions contributed to producing the worst terrorist crime in U.S. history with destructive consequences still threatening.[1]

The Bush Administrations, the CIA, and Blowback

In this section, I will argue that the events of September 11 can be seen as a textbook example of blowback because bin Laden and the radical Islamic forces associated with the al Qaeda network were supported, funded, trained, and armed by several U.S. administrations and the CIA. In this reading, the CIA's catastrophic failure was not only to have not detected the danger of the event and taken action to prevent it, but to have actively contributed to producing the groups who are implicated in the terrorist attacks on the United States.

The concept of *blowback* is developed in a book with this title by Chambers Johnson (2000), who wrote:

> The term "blowback," which officials of the Central Intelligence Agency first invented for their own internal use, is starting to circulate among students of international relations. It refers to the unintended consequences of policies that were kept secret from the American people. What the daily press reports as the malign acts of "terrorists" or "drug lords" or "rogue states" or "illegal arms merchants" often turn out to be blowback from earlier operations. (p. 8)

Johnson (2000) provides a wealth of examples of blowback from problematic U.S. foreign policy maneuvers and covert actions that had unintended consequences, as when the United States became associated with support of terrorist groups or authoritarian regimes in

Asia, Latin America, or the Middle East and its clients turned on their sponsors. In Johnson's sense, September 11 was a classic example of blowback, in which U.S. policies generated unintended consequences that had catastrophic effects on U.S. citizens, New York City, and the American and indeed global economy. As I suggest in the following analysis, U.S. policy in Afghanistan at the end of the cold war and to the present contributed to the heinous events of September 11. In the useful summary of Alexander Cockburn and Jeffrey St. Clair:

> In April of 1978 an indigenous populist coup overthrew the government of Mohammed Daoud, who had formed an alliance with the man the U.S. had installed in Iran, Reza Pahlevi, aka the Shah. The new Afghan government was led by Noor Mohammed Taraki, and the Taraki administration embarked, albeit with a good deal of urban intellectual arrogance on land reform, hence an attack on the opium-growing feudal estates. Taraki went to the UN where he managed to raise loans for crop substitution for the poppy fields.
>
> Taraki also tried to bear down on opium production in the border areas held by fundamentalists, since the latter were using opium revenues to finance attacks on Afghanistan's central government, which they regarded as an unwholesome incarnation of modernity that allowed women to go to school and outlawed arranged marriages and the bride price. Accounts began to appear in the Western press along the lines of this from the Washington Post, to the effect that the mujahiddeen liked to "torture their victims by first cutting off their noses, ears and genitals, then removing one slice of skin after another."
>
> At that time the mujahiddeen was not only getting money from the CIA but from Libya's Moammar Q'addaffi who sent them $250,000. In the summer of 1979 the U.S. State Department produced a memo making it clear how the U.S. government saw the stakes, no matter how modern minded Taraki might be or how feudal the Muj. It's another passage Nat might read to the grandkids: "The United States' larger interest would be served by the demise of the Taraki-Amin regime, despite whatever setbacks this might mean for future social and economic reforms in Afghanistan. The overthrow of the DRA [Democratic Republic of Afghanistan] would show the rest of the world, particularly the Third World, that the Soviets' view of the socialist course of history being inevitable is not accurate." (see Cockburn & St. Clair, 2001; see also http://www. counterpunch.org/wtarchive.html)

Thus, a highly problematic U.S. intervention in the late 1970s in a civil war in Afghanistan, which in retrospect appears as the last great conflict of the Cold War, helped create the context for the current crisis. As a response to U.S. intervention, the Soviet Union in 1978 sent in troops to prop up the moderate socialist and modernizing Taraki regime that was opposed by Islamic fundamentalists in the country. When Taraki was killed by Afghan army officers in September 1979, the Soviets invaded in force in December 1979 and set up a government to avoid a fundamentalist Islam and U.S.-backed takeover.

In the 1980s, the United States began more aggressively supporting Islamic fundamentalist Jihad groups, and the Afghanistan project was a major covert foreign policy project of the Reagan-Bush administrations. During this period, the CIA trained, armed, and financed precisely those Islamic fundamentalist groups who later became part of the al Qaeda terror network and those Islamic fundamentalist groups who are now the nemesis of the West, the new "evil empire."

In the battle to defeat Soviet communism in the Cold War, both the Saudis and the United States poured billions into Afghanistan to train "freedom fighters" who would overthrow the allegedly communist regime. This was a major project, with some estimates as high as $40 billion that went into training and arming radical Islamic groups who would emerge with a desire to fight other great wars for Islam. These groups included Osama bin Laden and those who would later form his al Qaeda network.

In 1989, Soviet troops left Afghanistan in defeat and a civil war continued for the next several years. At the time of the Gulf War in 1990–1991—another event that has generated yet to be fully perceived blowback—the Saudi government allowed the United States to position their forces in the holy land of Islam, angering bin Laden and more radical Islamic groups. When Saudi Arabia continued to allow the presence of U.S. troops after the Gulf War, bin Laden broke with his country and was declared persona non grata by the Saudis for his provocative statements and behavior. It was also reported at this time that Saudis put out a contract on bid Laden's life, supposedly with the assent of the earlier Bush administration (Weaver, 1996), although assassination attempts seemed to have failed.

In any case, by the mid-late 1990s, bin Laden established an organization of former Afghanistan Holy War veterans called al Qaeda. In February 1998, bin Laden issued a statement, endorsed by several extreme Islamic groups, declaring it the duty of all Muslims to kill U.S. citizens—civilian or military—and their allies everywhere. The bombing of U.S. embassies was ascribed to the bin Laden–al Qaeda network, and the Clinton administration responded by shooting 70 cruise missiles at a factory supposedly owned by bin Laden in Sudan that produced chemical weapons and at camps in Afghanistan that allegedly were populated by bin Laden and his group. The factory in Sudan turned out to be a pharmaceutical company and the camps in Afghanistan were largely deserted, producing another embarrassment for U.S. policy in the Middle East.

Meanwhile, as civil war raged in Afghanistan in the mid-1990s, Pakistani military and intelligence groups, with the support of the CIA, funded and organized one particularly fanatical Islamic group, the Taliban, which eventually took over control of much of the country in the mid-1990s, promising to stabilize the region and gaining recognition by the U.S. and Pakistan governments but not the UN and much of the rest of the world, which recognized the National Alliance groups fighting the Taliban as the legitimate representative of Afghanistan.

Although this is never mentioned in the mainstream media, the Bush administration was one of the largest financial supporters of the Taliban, providing more than $100 million this year in what they deemed "humanitarian aid" and providing an outright grant of $43 million in May 2001 for the Taliban's promise to declare opium production "un-Islamic" and thus to cut back on a potent source of the world's drug trade. Given the fact that the Taliban has allegedly been a major exporter of opium, which is Afghanistan's major cash crop, it raises eyebrows in knowledgeable circles as to why the Bush administration would have trusted the Taliban to cut back on opium production. Moreover, a story is circulating that the Bush administration was acting in the interests of the Unocal oil consortium to build an oil pipeline across Afghanistan, a project that had purportedly led the oil company to encourage the United States to support the Taliban in the first place because they were deemed the group most likely to stabilize Afghanistan and allow the pipeline to be built.

The Taliban, of course, were a highly theocratic and repressive fundamentalist regime that some have described as "clerical fascism" (Chip Berlet) or "reactionary tribalism" (Robert Antonio). Their treatment of women is notorious, as is their cultural totalitarianism that led to banning of books, media, and destruction of Buddhist statues. Like the Saudis, the Taliban practice a form of *Wahabism,* a derogatory term applied to a particularly virulent strain of Muslim fundamentalism also followed by the Saudis. The Taliban have also been the host of Osama bin Laden and the al Qaeda network since they were expelled from Sudan in 1996 at U.S. pressure and insistence. Although bin Laden and the al Qaeda were deemed enemies of the United States since their alleged involvement in a series of terrorist crimes, the Bush Administration continued to provide support to the Taliban group that hosted and protected them.

To summarize: The events of the September 11 terrorist attacks should be seen in the context of several U.S. administrations and CIA support for the perpetrators of the monstrous assaults on the United States from the late 1970s, through the Reagan-Bush years, to the present. This is not to simply blame U.S. policy in Afghanistan for the terrorist assault of September 11, but it is to provide some of the context in which the events can be interpreted. There are, of course, other flaws of U.S. foreign policy during the past decades that have helped generate enemies of the United States in the Middle East and elsewhere, such as excessive U.S. support for Israel and inadequate support for the Palestinians, U.S. support of authoritarian regimes, and innumerable misdeeds of the U.S. empire during the past decades that have been documented by Chomsky, Herman, Johnson, and other critics of U.S. foreign policy.

Still, although there were no doubt a multiplicity of contributing factors, the September 11 events can be read as a blowback of major policies of successive U.S. administrations and the CIA who trained, funded, supported, and armed the groups alleged to have carried out the terrorist attacks on the United States—and certainly all circumstantial and other evidence points to these groups. The obvious lesson is that it is highly dangerous and potentially costly to align one's country with terrorist groups, that support of groups or individuals who promote terrorism is likely to come back and haunt you, and that it is perilous to make Machiavellian pacts with obviously dangerous groups and individuals.

In addition, although I have used the term *bin Laden,* I think that it is a mistake to personalize the September 11 events or to contribute to the demonization of bin Laden, the flip side of which is deification—which no doubt is what he and some of his followers want. *bin Laden* is better interpreted as what Sorel called a "revolutionary myth," a figurehead for a network and movement to which his opponents ascribe great power and evil, whereas his followers ascribe wondrous effectivity and good to the name. In fact, there appears to be a worldwide radical Islamic theocratic network that has taken up terrorism and "propaganda of the deed" to help produce a Holy War between the East and West, and that consequently the problems of terrorism are not going to be solved by the arrest or elimination of bin Laden and members of his al Qaeda network.

It is also useful to make clear that the interpretation of Islam by this network goes against a mainstream reading of the Koran that prohibits suicide, violence against children and innocents, and that in no way promises sainthood or eternal happiness to terrorists. Islam, like Christianity, is complex and contested.

In arguing that the events of September 11 can be read as blowback against specific U.S. policies by specific individuals, groups, and administrations, I am not, of course, wishing to blame the victims, nor do I associate myself with those who inventory U.S. crimes during the past several decades and see the events of September 11 as a payback for these misdeeds. Moreover, I believe that some analyses that see the events as a logical response to U.S. policy and that call for changes in U.S. policy as the solution to the events are too rationalistic in regard to the perpetrators of the events and logical solutions to the problem.

First of all, the alleged terrorists appear to be highly fanatical and religious in their ideology and actions, of a sort hard to comprehend by Western categories. In their drive for an apocalyptic Jihad, they believe that their goals will be furthered by creating chaos, especially war between radical Islam and the West. Obviously, dialogue is not possible with such groups, but it is equally certain that an overreactive military response that caused a large number of innocent civilian deaths in a Muslim country could trigger precisely such an apocalyptic explosion of violence as was dreamed of by the fanatic terrorists. It would seem that such a retaliatory response was desired by the group that carried out the terrorist attacks on the United States and, thus, to overreact militarily would be to fall into their trap and play their game—with highly dangerous consequences.

Many critics and theorists of September 11 also exaggerate the rationality of the West and fail to grasp the striking irrationality and primitive barbarism involved in the immediate response to the horror by Western politicians, intellectuals, and media representatives—some of which I documented in an earlier section of this analysis. To carry out the military retaliatory response called for by high officials in the Bush Administration, crazed intellectuals, and many ordinary citizens, repeated endlessly in the media with almost no counterdiscourse, could risk apocalypse of the most frightening kind. Large-scale bombing of Afghanistan could trigger an upheaval in Pakistan with conceivable turmoil in Saudi Arabia and other Moslem countries, as well as a dangerous escalation of the Israeli-Palestinian conflict, already at a state of white-hot intensity, whose expansion could engulf the Middle East in flames.

Thus, although it is reasonable to deem international terrorism a deadly threat on a global scale and to take resolute action against it, what is required is an intelligent, multifaceted response. This would require a diplomatic consensus that a global campaign against terrorism is necessary that requires arrest of members of terrorist networks, regulation of financial institutions that allow funds to flow to terrorists, national security measures to protect citizens against terrorism, and a global criminalization of terrorist networks that sets international, national, and local institutions against the terrorist threat. Some of these measures have already begun, and the conditions are present to develop an effective and resolute global campaign against terrorism. There is a danger, however, that excessive military action would split a potential coalition, create perhaps uncontrollable chaos, and destroy the global economy. We are living in a very dangerous period and must be extremely careful in how we respond to the events of September 11. In this spirit, I want to conclude with some reflections on the concept of terrorism and the proper response on behalf of citizens, activists, and theorists to the September 11 events.[2]

Concluding Remarks

Thus, I would argue for a global campaign against terrorism and not for war or large-scale military action. Terrorists should be criminalized and international and national institutions should go after terrorist networks and those who support them with appropriate legal, financial, judicial, and political instruments. I would also suggest that another lesson of September 11 is that it is now totally appropriate to be completely against terrorism, to use the term in the arsenal of critical social theory, and to declare it unacceptable and indefensible in the modern world. There was a time when it was argued that one person's *terrorism* was another person's "national liberation movement" or "freedom fighter," and that the term was thus an ideological concept not to be used by politically and theoretically correct discourse—a position that Reuters continues to follow according to one report.

In terms of modern/postmodern epistemological debates, I am not arguing for absolutism or universalism. There were times in history when terrorism was an arguably defensible tactic used by those engaged in struggles against fascism, as in World War II, or in national liberation struggles that were arguably defensible, as in the American or various Third World revolutions against the oppressive European empire and colonialism. In the current situation, however, when terrorism is a clear and present danger to innocent civilians throughout the world, it seems unacceptable to advocate, carry out, or defend terrorism against civilian populations because of the lethality of modern weapons, the immorality of indiscriminate crime, and the explosiveness of the present situation when terror on one side could unleash genocidal, even speciescidal, terror as a retaliatory response.

It is therefore neither the time for terrorism nor military retaliation, but for a global campaign against terrorism that deploys all legal, political, and morally defensible means to destroy the network of terrorists responsible for the September 11 events. Such a global response would put terrorist groups on warning that their activity is not acceptable and will be strongly opposed, and that thus construes terrorism as a moral and political malevolence not to be accepted or defended.

To terrorism, I would append that progressives should be now, as previously, against fascism. The supposed perpetrators of the September 11 events were allegedly terrorists and fascistic Islamic fundamentalists who support a theocratic state that would abrogate human rights and employ torture and murder in the name of supposedly higher theological values. In the contemporary world, such fascism should be opposed and more democratic and progressive modern values and democratic politics should be defended.

I would be reluctant to defend, however, continuous U.S. military action against all countries that support terrorism in any way, as articulated in the "Bush doctrine," which could lead to an era of war and global devastation and that a global coalition against terrorism using all available political, legal, financial, and, if necessary, multilateral military forces be used, rather than unilateral U.S. military action on the grounds that the problem of terrorism is largely a global problem that requires a global solution through global institutions and not unilateral military action. Thus, whereas I would support allied, North Atlantic Treaty Organization (NATO), or UN military action against terrorism, especially the al Qaeda network, I would not trust U.S. unilateral military action for reasons laid out in this study of U.S. failures in the region and sustained history of supporting the most reactionary social forces. Moreover, one of the stakes of the current crisis and globalization itself is whether the U.S. empire will come to dominate the world or whether globalization will constitute a more democratic, cosmopolitan, pluralistic, and just world, without domination by hegemonic states or corporations. Now more than ever, global institutions are needed to deal with global problems, and those who see positive potential in globalization should renounce all national solutions to the problem of terrorism and seek global ones. Consequently, although politicians like Bill Clinton and Colin Powell have deemed terrorism "the dark side of globalization," it can also be seen as an unacceptable response to misguided and destructive imperial national policies that must be transformed if a world without terror is possible.

Notes

1. In addition to Johnson (2000) that I am utilizing to provide a conceptual overview of the September 11 terrorist acts, I am also drawing on a series of studies of U.S. foreign policy and Afghanistan, including Mary Ann Weaver (1996); a collection of articles contextualizing the events at *The Nation* Web site, especially Dilip Hiro, "The Cost of an Afghan 'Victory,' " at www.thenation.com; and articles collected at www.counterpoint.com. I am also grateful to Phil Agre's daily collection of articles on his Red Rock Eater list, collected at http://dlis.gseis.ucla.edu/people/pagre/rre.html.

2. I am editing this text in late November of 2001 when the Bush administration military action has dislodged the Taliban from control of most of the country, although Afghanistan's future is in question. I would argue, however, that continuing military action could aggravate problems with the Islamic world for generations to come and that a global coalition against terrorism rather than unilateral American action is the most efficacious way to proceed against terrorist networks.

References

Cockburn, A., & St. Clair, J. (2001, September 26). The price. Was it really worth it, Mrs. Albright? *Counterpoint.*

Fukuyama, F. (1992). *The end of history.* New York: Avon.

Huntington, S. (1996). *The clash of civilizations and the remaking of world order.* New York: Touchstone Books.

Johnson, C. (2000). *Blowback: The costs and consequences of American empire.* New York: Henry Holt.

Weaver, M. A. (1996, May). Blowback. *Atlantic Monthly.* Retrieved from www.theatlantic.com/issues/96may/blowback.htm

Douglas Kellner is the George Kneller chair in the philosophy of education at University of California, Los Angeles.

The Dialectics of Terrorism
A Marxist Response to September 11

4

PETER MCLAREN

> The law that authorizes torture is a law that says: "Men, resist pain; and if nature has created in you an inextinguishable self-love, if it has granted you an inalienable right of self-defense, I create in you an altogether contrary sentiment: a heroic hatred of yourselves; and I command you to accuse yourselves, to speak the truth even while muscles are being lacerated and bones disjointed."
>
> —CESARE BECCARIA (*On Crimes and Punishment*, 1764/1963, p. 1)

Part One: Remembering to Forget

WE HAVE ENTERED A REALITY ZONE already captured by its opposite: unreality. It is a world where nobody really wanted to venture. It is a world where order has given way to disorder; where reason has given way to unreason; where reality is compromised by truth; where guilt is presumed over innocence; where the once noble search for explanations has been replaced by a dizzying vortex of plastic flags, stars and stripes rhinestone belts, coffee klatch war strategists, Sunday barbecue patrioteering, militant denunciations of war protestors, a generalized fear of whatever lies ahead, xenophobic hostility, and point-blank outrage. Soccer moms in sports utility vehicles festooned with images of Old Glory park in dimly lit alleys and then slink into the local sex shop in search of red, white, and blue thongs for couch potato husbands strangely rejuvenated by daily doses of carnage, courtesy of CNN. Public school teachers across the country eagerly prepare new courses on Western civilization. Politicians sporting American flag lapel pins plan ways to purge domestic political dissent. Hollywood producers hunker down in their studios and plan new Rambo films. Retired generals shine in their new roles as political consultants, pronouncing the scenes in Afghanistan as invariably "fluid," which is a giveaway that they do not know much more than their interviewers, and probably less. Harvard Law School Professor Alan Dershowitz basks in the national limelight again, this time advocating the use of "torture warrants" in specified circumstances when the issue of "time" is crucial. Their reason paralyzed by fear and replaced by the logic of mob fury, American citizens eagerly give up their right of habeas corpus for government assurances that terrorists will be tracked down and killed, or if they are captured, for assurances that they will be tried by secret tribunal and *then* killed. Once the war on terror was announced, some doyens of the establishment right must have been so thrilled at the prospect of limitless political opportunity that they were driven mad, especially after the consentaneity of the public was secured, federal dragnets for rounding up suspicious Arabs were launched across the nation, wiretapping without warrants was put into effect, and a move to reverse a decades' old ban on government assassination signed by Gerald Ford in 1976 was floated by the Bush administration through Congress. I can imagine Henry Kissinger in his living room, wickedly brandishing a Clockwork Orange codpiece emblazoned with stars and stripes and dancing La Macarena in Imelda Marcos's ruby slippers. Go for it, Hank!

The world has been transformed into pure intensity where to seek refuge in the sanctuary of reflection is to engage in an act of unpardonable treason, where previously silenced realities are now guaranteed never to be heard. It is truly a world turned, in the words of Eduardo Galeano (2000), "upside down." It is a looking-glass world that "rewards in reverse: it scorns honesty, punishes work, prizes lack of scruples, and feeds cannibalism. Its professors slander nature: injustice, they say, is a law of nature" (p. 7). Within this looking-glass world, that world that exists upside down, there exists the "looking-glass school" that "teaches us to suffer reality, not to change it; to forget the past, not learn from it; to accept the future, not invent it. In its halls of criminal learning, impotence, amnesia, and resignation are required courses" (p. 8).

A disquieting incongruence has arisen between democracy and freedom. It is the reverse mirror image of the democracy that we thought we knew, a democracy for which many had fought and some had died. The United States as the global steward of benevolence has dropped its mask of civil comity to reveal its spectral Dorian Gray smile. The retreat of civil liberties is understood not as something imposed by a proto-fascist administration that has rehired many of the participants in the Iran-Contra scandal of Bush *padre*, but as something "natural" like the self-regulation of the stock market. Henry Weinstein, Daren Briscoe, and Mitchell Landsberg, staff writers at the *Los Angeles Times*, explain it to the public this way:

> American civil liberties are as fixed and steady an influence in national life as the stock market—and every bit as elastic. Like the market, the rights enjoyed by U.S. citizens have grown to an extent that the Founding Fathers probably never imagined. But in times of danger, civil liberties have shrunk, suffering what market analysts might call a correction. (2002, p. A1)

Using the same market logic, Bush is looking towards more deregulated, technology-driven wars (i.e., employing "adaptive" nuclear capabilities, bunker-busting mini-nukes, and nuclear weapons that reduce "collateral damage") to ensure the United States' geopolitical dominance, so the country can feel secure enough to reverse the contractions in civil rights investment that occurred after September 11 and bounce back from our current civil rights recession. But the problem is, in an era defined as one of perpetual danger, as one of permanent war, will we ever regain the rights that we have lost?

We can now put aside our fin de siècle existential anxieties about individual mortality and our financial worries about stock market investments and lose ourselves in the sheer adrenaline rush of watching the daily carnage that only a new war can bring. As families across the country break out their beer and barbecue chips and sit concupiscently enthralled in front of their television sets watching bombs drop, rockets fire, and buildings explode, approvingly nodding their heads when the newscaster details (with the aid of computerized illustrations) how the BLU-82 "daisy cutter" bomb incinerates everything in its path while sucking up all the oxygen so that nothing can survive its wrath, thousands of Afghan refugees die ignominious deaths from hunger, freezing weather, and "collateral damage." Following the war coverage on television is like watching a 24-hour infomercial produced by the U.S. Army, where images of death and destruction are accompanied by voice-over editorials that legitimize them as the regrettable but necessary price of freedom. And it is not as though our unqualified enthusiasm, rapt attention, and untempered bloodlust go educationally unrewarded. We are generously repaid, for instance, with technical knowledge. We learn that the ordnances we are dropping on frontline troops defending the poorest country in the world are the size of Volkswagen Beetles—even bigger than those deployed by our most famous ex–Gulf War veteran, Holy Ghost warrior, and domestic militia movement patriot:

> The BLU-82 combines a watery mixture of ammonium nitrate and aluminum with air, then ignites the mist for an explosion that incinerates everything up to 600 yards away. The BLU-82 uses about six times the amount of ammonium nitrate that Timothy McVeigh used in the bomb that blew up the Oklahoma City federal building in 1995. ("Response to Terror," 2001, p. A10)

Imagine the limitless opportunities now available for high school science teachers to capture the interest of their freshmen chemistry students.

While publishers in Alabama are stamping 40,000 biology textbooks with warning stickers, reminding students that evolution is a controversial theory they should question; and while President Bush pushes for faith-based programs (what he calls "armies of compassion") to provide social services and for tax breaks and other benefits for religious charities that would entitle them to be the recipients of billions of dollars of government funding; and while Christian talk show hosts prone to lachrymose sermons on the goodness of America continue to bless the war on terrorism "in Jesus' name," one realizes that the United States functions as a covert theocracy.

Those disappointed that the apocalypse was not ushered in at the millennium's end are making up for it in their razor-edged celebration of the war on terror. History has been split down the middle as if it had been sliced by a Taliban cane soaked in water. On the one side, modernity houses the transnational ruling class, whose dreams remain unbounded, rewinding time. On the other side, the transnational working class takes refuge in modernity's refuse heap of time unraveled and dreams dehydrated. Understanding how this mighty division has been prepared by capital is the skeleton key that unlocks the bone yard of reason where truth can be found amid the charred ruins of civilizations past and those yet to come.

We have entered a world where the concinnity between democracy and justice has been irreparably fractured. The events in the United States since September 11 despairingly record not only what John Powers (2002) called the "Trumanizing of George W. Bush" (p. 24) but also the remorseless widening of powers by hard-liners, revanchists, and hawks over the average citizen, following in the wake of a constitutional coup d'etat in the form of the USA Patriot Act. Regrettably, the "vestigial spine" (Powers, 2002, p. 24) developed by the Democrats has done little to stem the tide of resurgent fascism. Bush *hijo* stands under the cover of popular political support that is as sturdy as an Augustan arch. His gee-whiz-I'm-just-folks bipartisan style has become cruelly calcified in tandem with the autocratic character that his presidency has now assumed. His Enronesque ideology of loathing the little guys who can be squeezed like wet-rag dolls if it can wring more profits from their labor power has permeated the culture of the White House. John Powers noted,

> Nobody wants to say it during wartime, but the cozy yet ruthless Texas business culture that produced Enron also produce[d] our president. Bush takes pride in working like a CEO, and if you study his behavior, you find him duplicating, almost exactly, the culture of Enron. He displays the same obsession with loyalty (his number one virtue), the same habit of dishonest, short-term accounting (think of his lies about those tax cuts), the same blithe disregard for ordinary workers (his post-September 11 economic proposals all aimed at helping corporations) and the same pitiless certainty he's on the side of the free-market angels. (p. 17)

The smooth-shaven smile of the impish fraternity brother has given way to the permanent jaw-jutting sneer of the dictator. Bush's increasingly Nixon-like penchant for secrecy, his arrogant attempts to keep his and his father's presidential papers from public scrutiny, and his creation of drumbeat courts vitiate the very notion of the "open society" he was wont to celebrate before the unforgiving and unforgivable events of September 11. His aw-shucks dyslexic humor and light-minded reveries have given way to preternatural jingoism, to imperial declarations of war against all those who oppose his definition of civilization (i.e., whatever economic, legal, foreign, or domestic policies the United States chooses to undertake). As Donald Freed remarked, "He [Bush] looks taller when you are on your knees" (Mikulan, 2001, p. 23). What was once thought to be Bush's political autism when it came to foreign policy has now been reevaluated as political psychosis. We have seen him mutate from an *übermensch* raised on political junk food to a smirking avenging angel growing mean on a diet of corporate swindle served up at Enron executive lunches. As Bernard Weiner (2002) notes, "The Bush Administration is like an Enron alumni reunion, with officials in charge of investigating Enron formerly working for Enron" (p. 6). Bush is our American Werewolf in Kabul, lapping up the lifeblood of the Afghan people—oil—with the approval of Hamid Karzai, chairman of the interim administration and former consultant for Unocal, the oil company.

It has become dangerous to think, to ask too many questions, or to look beyond the face value of whatever commentary is served up to us by our politicians, our military, and our so-called intelligence agencies, summarized daily in the infantilizing screeds of daily media columnists who have disingenuously become their Beverly Hills lap dogs. Not only has dialectical thought been lamentably undervalued and shamefully underpracticed by these media commentators, but political propaganda in the name of Western truth has been accorded supercelestial status.

It is a world where it is safer to engage in rehearsed reactions to what we encounter on our television screens. After all, domestic dissent has now acquired a police state translation that equates it with terrorism. It is safer to react in ways that newscaster/entertainers big on acrimonious scapegoating and short on analysis define for us as patriotic: Applaud all actions by governmental authorities (especially those of the president) as if they were sacerdotal or morally apodictic. CNN has already declared that it is "perverse" to focus on civilian suffering (some reports have already placed the number of civilian Afghan casualties from U.S. bombing raids at 3,500), exercising a racist arithmetic that deems civilian casualties in the United States to be more important than those of Afghan civilian dead. Death and destruction have become as faceless as a smoldering turban on the side of a dirt road.

Fox Television commentator Bill O'Reilly—his mind rarely burdened by a dialectical thought—berates with autocratic homilies those few guests he invites on his show who dare offer an explanation for the events of September 11. He enjoys sparing his audiences insight and lifting from them the burden of comprehension, preferring instead a spectacle of self-congratulatory belligerence and Stygian anger. The majesty of O'Reilly's self-regard is propped up by a stubborn conviction that unsupported opinions presented in a mean-spirited fashion are preferable to complex analysis. Proud of his simple patriotic (i.e., war-mongering) advice to kill the enemy because the enemy is evil, he admonishes anyone offering critical analysis as giving evil credibility and as comforting our enemies. On a September 17 segment of his show, *O'Reilly Factor*, our "no-spin" host Bill put forth a plan for action if the Taliban did not hand over bin Laden:

> If they don't, the U.S. should bomb the Afghan infrastructure to rubble—the airport, the power plants, their water facilities and the roads. This is a very primitive country. And taking out their ability to exist day to day will not be hard. Remember, the people of any country are ultimately responsible for the government they have. The Germans were responsible for Hitler. The Afghans are responsible for the Taliban. We should not target civilians. But if they don't rise up against this criminal government, they starve, period. (Hart, 2001, p. 8)

O'Reilly also went on to say that the infrastructure of Iraq "must be destroyed and the population made to endure yet another round of intense pain" (Hart, 2001, p. 8). He also disembarrassed himself from any humanitarian sentiments by calling for the destruction of Libya's airports and the mining of its harbors, crying, "Let them eat sand" (Hart, 2001, p. 8). There is no spectacle of suddenly vanishing competence here, for his reasoning is as inexorably puerile as it is predictable. He is effectively asking for millions more Iraqi children and civilians to die at the hands of the United States (as if the U.S.-imposed sanctions have not killed enough), not to mention the millions of civilian casualties that would result from the kind of utter destruction of the infrastructure that he so perversely calls for. So savage was O'Reilly's call for acts of terror to be rained down on Afghan civilians by the U.S. military, one wonders if he received his political education in the caves of Lascaux. We have heard this kind of advice before. It is underwritten by the same logic that spikes the Taliban's advice to their own followers. It is the logic of fascism, only this time it is our fascism sweetened and made more palatable by the nationalist arrogance and righteous indignation betrayed by O'Reilly and those of his stamp.

By and large, the U.S. media has treated Afghan civilian deaths as part of a propaganda war. The notion of journalistic impartiality has been thrown out the window, along with any sense of human dignity. Fox News chair, Roger Ailes, proclaimed in the *New York Times*, "We don't sit around and get all gooey and wonder if these people have been misunderstood in their childhood. What we say is terrorists, terrorism, is evil, and America doesn't engage in it, and these guys do" (Hart & Naureckas, 2002, p. 9). Fox TV's lead anchor, Brit Hume, was quoted in the *New York Times* as saying, "The fact that some people are dying, is that really news? And is it news to be treated in a semi-straight-faced way? I think not" (Hart & Naureckas, 2002, p. 9). Credit Dan Rather for taking the public relations war over civilian deaths to a higher level when he introduced a David Martin CBS report by exclaiming: "Afghanistan's Taliban leaders may be growing so desperate they may kill Afghan civilians just to blame the United States" (Coen, 2002, p. 8). And the American public wonders why most of the Islamic world still believes that Arabs were not involved in the September 11 attacks? American media audiences should examine the propaganda machines operating in their own living rooms before passing judgment.

It is not as if the flat-footed storm troopers have already arrived. It is more as if shimmerings of fascism have crossed our political landscape. Ghostly coruscations of negative energy are slowly crystallizing into holograms of Joe McCarthy hovering ominously over the White House. We are living in the moist flaps of Richard Nixon's jowls, drowning in the yellow ink of Steve Dunleavy's pen, sleepwalking on a Pirandello stage, discovering ourselves as Ionesco characters in a Rod Sterling nightmare. Unlike *The Twilight Zone*, the horror of the human condition will not disappear when we turn off our television sets. Bill O'Reilly's kerosene tongue will always be there, wagging obscenely on our television sets or disguised in the mouths of everyday God-fearing folk.

The sword of Damocles that hangs over the American way of life glows blood red. The act of patriotism has been shamelessly downgraded by making it compulsory. According to novelist John le Carre (2001),

> it's as if we have entered a new, Orwellian world where our personal reliability as comrades in the struggle [against terrorism] is measured by the degree to which we invoke the past to explain the present. Suggesting there is a historical context for the recent atrocities is by implication to make excuses for them. Anyone who is with us doesn't do that. Anyone who does, is against us. (p. 15)

Edward Said echoed a similar sentiment:

> What terrifies me is that we're entering a phase where if you start to speak about this as something that can be understood historically—without any sympathy—you are going to be thought of as unpatriotic, and you are going to be forbidden. It's very dangerous. It is precisely incumbent on every citizen to quite understand the world we're living in and the history we are a part of and we are forming as a superpower. (Barsamian, 2001)

James Petras (2002) perhaps said it best when he argued that we inhabit a veritable police state, at the cusp of a totalitarian regime. He wrote,

> One of the hallmarks of a totalitarian regime is the creation of a state of mutual suspicion in which civil society is turned into a network of secret police informers. The Federal Bureau of Investigation (FBI) soon after September 11 exhorted every U.S. citizen to report any suspicious behavior by friends, neighbors, relatives, acquaintances, and strangers. Between September and the end of November almost 700,000 denunciations were registered. Thousands of Middle Eastern neighbours, local shop owners, and employees were denounced, as were numerous other U.S. citizens. None of these denunciations led to any arrests or even information related to September 11. Yet hundreds and thousands of innocent personals were investigated and harassed by the federal police. (p. 10)

As long as we live in an unthinking world where nations follow shallow ideologues and their corporate overworlder sponsors into the killing fields of last resort, there is not much hope for social justice and world peace. As Steve Niva (2001a) noted, "Terrorism's best asset, in the final analysis, is the anger and desperation that leads people to see no alternative to violence" (p. 2).

Those stubborn enough to break away from the media's unvarnished boosterism and to insist on understanding world events and their connection to the terrorist attacks of September 11 are implored to submit to the explanations provided by carefully chosen "experts" hired by our corporately owned and controlled media if for nothing else than fear of public humiliation via media-speak homiletics (author Susan Sontag and left-libertarian talk show host Bill Maher being two prominent examples that most readily come to mind, although in the case of Maher I acknowledge the insight of a *New Times* reader that "Maher isn't Voltaire at the court of the Sun King; he's a corporate lackey who forgot what he did for a living") (Tryferis, 2001, p. 7). It is a world best left to the television journalist experts to figure out. After all, who are we to question the people who, after all, must "know things" that we do not—like CBS anchorman Dan Rather? Or Fox TV's bullet-dodging Geraldo Rivera? Who are we to argue with *Newsweek's* Jonathan Alter when he suggests that the U.S. consider subjecting terror suspects to torture? But should we use only legal forms of psychological torture at home or transfer selected suspects to our "less squeamish" allies for the testicle slicing and eye gouging (see Rendall, 2002, p. 17)? Should we nod our heads approvingly when four out of five panelists on the McLaughlin Group's November 9 show endorse torture? Should we follow the advice of *National Review* editor, Rich Lowry, and send suspects to be tortured by "Filipinos" or should we follow the sage advice of McLaughlin himself and send them to "the Turks" (see Rendall, 2002, p. 18)? According to recent reports (see Campbell, 2002), the U.S. military has not yet followed Lowry or McLaughlin's advice. So far, the choice of countries has been Jordan and Egypt. It is already the case (see Campbell, 2002) that the U.S. has been secretly sending prisoners suspected of al-Qaeda connections to countries where torture during interrogation is allegedly legal (the process of seizing suspects and taking them to a third country without due process of law is known as "rendition"). Prisoners who are transported by the U.S. to countries such as Egypt and Jordan can be subjected to torture and threats to their families to extract information sought by the U.S. For example, one suspect was taken from Indonesia to Egypt on a U.S.-registered Gulfstream jet without a court hearing after his name appeared on al-Qaeda documents. At the time of this writing, he is still in custody in Egypt and has been subjected to interrogation by intelligence agents. A Yemeni microbiology student has been flown from Pakistan to Jordan on a U.S.-registered jet. Other cases have been reported. U.S. intelligence agents allegedly have been involved in a number of these interrogations.

Attempts to link September 11th to the crisis of global capitalism are left solely in the hands of a few leftist editors whose publications are marked by outlawed academics such as Noam Chomsky and Edward Herman but also modest and diminishing circulation numbers, whereas the mainstream media is mining the entrails of academia for more comforting oracular theories such as those offered by well-heeled Harvard professor Samuel Huntington. Huntington (1996) argues that the world is moving from a cold war bipolar division to more complex multipolar and multicivilization divisions with greater potential for conflict. Here, Islamic cultures conveniently collide with Western ones with the force of tectonic plates. John Pilger (1999) has appositely noted that "Huntington's language relies upon racial stereotypes and a veiled social Darwinism that is the staple of fascism. It is a vision of global apartheid" (p. 36).

Against this explanatory backdrop, readers can find conscionable the mirror image, either-or choice between Bush and bin Laden, both of whom betray a profound contempt for the masses that helps to support each other's position.

Does the comfort of easy binary-based explanations sound familiar? Isn't this part of the willful compliance to the conservative status quo that we were taught so well in schools? In fact, the American Council of Trustees and Alumni (ACTA) (founded by Lynne V. Cheney) has released a report condemning the response of many university professors to the September 11th attacks (ACTA claims Senator Joseph Lieberman as a cofounder, but Lieberman says he was only a supporter). Titled "Defending Civilization: How Our Universities Are Failing America, and What Can Be Done About It," the report itemizes 117 incidents that allegedly reveal a treasonous refusal of the professoriate to defend civilization and a stubborn willingness to give comfort to its adversaries through statements of moral relativism and opposition to the U.S. war effort. In other words, some professors have the gall to be critical of Bush's war on terrorism. Comments condemned in the report included the following: "We have to learn to use courage for peace instead of war"; "war created people like Osama bin Laden, and more war will create more people like him"; "it is from the desperate, angry and bereaved that these suicide pilots came"; and "we must acknowledge our role in helping to create monsters in the world, find ways to contain these monsters without hurting more innocent people and then redefine our role in the world" (these comments were uttered, respectively, by an Oberlin freshman; former U.S. ambassador at large to Russia, Strobe Talbott, currently at Yale; and Arun Gandhi, the grandson of Mahatma Gandhi, speaking to a crowd at the University of North Carolina at Chapel Hill) (see Scigliano, 2001). ACTA lashed out at a Penn State vice provost for telling a faculty member that his Web page advocating military action against terrorists was "insensitive and perhaps even intimidating." The faculty member in question had quoted and endorsed an editorial by Leonard Peikoff of the Ayn Rand Institute that read, "We must now use our unsurpassed military to destroy all branches of the Iranian and Afghani governments, regardless of the suffering and death this will bring to the many innocents caught in the line of fire" (Scigliano, 2001, p. 16).

Manning Marable (2001b) declared that "we will inevitably see 'dissident profiling': the proliferation of electronic surveillance, roving wiretapping, harassment at the workplace, the infiltration and disruption of anti-war groups, and the stigmatization of any critics of U.S. militarism as disloyal and subversive" (p. 8).

Today, it is imperative that we understand why developing countries regard the United States with increasing cynicism and its role as the world's "peacekeeper" as janiform and opportunistic. Although on one hand the United States seeks cooperation from the world in its war on terrorism, it often refuses to cooperate with other nations unless it is in the direct interest of the United States to do so. As Dean Baker (2001) asserted, more than 35 million people in the developing world are HIV positive. To address this problem, the United States pledged $200 million, which amounts to 6 hours of the Pentagon budget. At the same time, those countries that provide low-cost drugs (such as drugs to combat HIV) by ignoring the patents of U.S. pharmaceutical companies are threatened with severe trade sanctions by the U.S. government. Most of what official aid does get distributed (approximately 0.15% of GDP) goes to reward political loyalty, with Israel and Egypt being the two largest recipients (Baker, 2001). Marable (2001a) captured some of the root causes of this cynicism when he asserted,

> The United States government cannot engage in effective multilateral actions to suppress terrorism, because its behavior illustrates its complete contempt for international cooperation. The United States owed $582 million in back dues to the United Nations, and it paid up only when the September 11 attacks jeopardized its national security. Republican conservatives demand that the United States should be exempt from the jurisdiction of an International Criminal Court, a permanent tribunal now being established at The Hague, Netherlands. For the 2001 World Conference Against Racism, the U.S. government authorized the allocation of a paltry $250,000, compared to over $10 million provided to conference organizers by the Ford Foundation. For three decades, the U.S. refused to ratify the 1965 United Nations Convention on the Elimination of Racism. Is it any wonder that much of the Third World questions our motives? (pp. 1-2)

One event that is particularly illustrative of the hypocrisy surrounding the U.S. war on terrorism occurred when Bush *padre* telephoned Nelson Mandela after he was released from a South African prison after 28 years—that same prison where he was placed after the CIA (under the directorship of *padre* Bush) provided information regarding Mandela's whereabouts. Once labeled a terrorist by the U.S. government, Mandela is now touted internationally as a hero.

In the face of the particularly fierce hawkish administration of Bush *hijo*, and in the midst of widespread apprehension about the motives behind the U.S. war on terrorism among Third World peoples, it is an especially urgent time to call for rethinking the role that the United States plays in the global division of labor. The recent events of mindshattering world-historical dimensions, the sudden unfolding nightmare that saw death and destruction unleashed on thousands of innocent and unsuspecting victims in Washington and New York City, such that the gates of hell appeared to have been blown open, have made it difficult for many U.S. citizens to comprehend why their familiar world has suddenly turned upside down. Those of us who practice critical or revolutionary pedagogy take a strong position against terrorism. Acts of terrorism are as backward and horrific as acts of capitalist-driven imperialism, and under no circumstances can they be justified.

And although I will discuss some of the horrors of U.S.-driven imperialism in the pages that follow, I would like readers to keep this thought in mind. Critics of U.S. capitalism—and world capitalism, for that matter–and I count myself as one of them, should be careful in listing all the horrible acts of imperialism engaged in historically by the United States (a long and bloody list, to be sure) as a rationale for why these terrorist acts occurred. To do so is irresponsible and leads to a "chickens have come home to roost" scenario that reduces the dialectical character of historical events to a simple Newtonian reflex and adventitiously gives fuel to those who would dismiss the radical left as "America-hating" zealots. The terrorist attacks occurred without reason, demand, or proclamation (Hudis, 2001). But it is never the less extremely important to examine the history of U.S. imperialism and the crisis of global capitalism to understand the historically specific backdrop against which hatred of America incubates and terrorism sprouts.

The practices of U.S.-backed regimes in the Middle East such as Egypt, Algeria, Jordan, Israel, and Saudi Arabia, who are waging brutal campaigns of violence against their Islamic opposition, certainly provide a backdrop against which we can begin to analyze—but not justify, rationalize, or legitimize—the events of September 11. I do not think that we should uncritically proclaim that U.S. actions were the direct cause of the attacks, because such a position is undialectical. For instance, the North Vietnamese, who suffered the tragic loss of millions of dead at the hands of the United States, did not attack the U.S. populace in retaliation (Hudis, 2001). The terrorist attacks required a certain willful "agency" that served to generate the terrorism. Terrorism does not work on the basis of operant conditioning and is not teleologically inscribed in history as a reaction to U.S. foreign and economic policy. But it is surely the case that U.S. involvement in the Third World in general and the Islamic world in particular has created—and continues to create—the background conditions that are likely to lead to terrorism. The taproot of terrorism surely lies in the fertile soil of imperialism—both military and economic. It is nourished by the transnationalization of the productive forces and fertilized by the defeated dreams of the vanquished poor. The terrorism of September 11 was rhizogenic—its roots and filaments interlaced with U.S. foreign policy and practices. To say this is not to take a "hate America" position as it is to take a "wake up America and don't be misled by your leaders" position. We cannot divorce the recent acts of terrorism from their historical context.

Although clearly U.S. policies and practices are a factor in creating an environment for terrorism, it is also clear that other factors are involved, such as anti-Semitism, anti-Americanism—as against genuine anti-imperialism—a reaction against the dimensions of "Western society" that every leftist should support: workers rights, feminism, gay rights, and so forth (Hudis, 2001).

Peter Hudis (2001) is bracingly forthright in asserting that it is wrong to believe that bin Laden was simply responding to the same injustices as radical leftists, except that he used a method leftists would never condone and would find utterly abhorrent. Bin Laden loathes the masses, whom he is willing to use as canon fodder in the name of his "holy" war. Steve Niva (2001a, 2001b) has rightly pointed out, for instance, that bin Laden's small, violent, and socially reactionary network—influenced by the socially reactionary Wahhabi school of Islam practiced in Saudi Arabia and the conservative Pakistani Islamist Party, Jamaat-i Islami—is roundly antagonistic to social justice and differs in important ways with the wider current of Islamic activism in the Arab world and more globally. The wider current of Islamic activism does have a social justice agenda on behalf of the poor and dispossessed, is more involved in party building and mass mobilization, and largely rejects the simplistic Islamic doctrines promoted by bin Laden's network. Moreover, Niva stressed that bin Laden's organization is disconnected from wider Islamic activist movements in that they do not locate their struggle in a national context but rather in a global war on behalf of Muslims worldwide. It is problematic therefore to locate the attacks on September 11 in a natural reflex reaction to U.S. policies and practices. It is much more complicated than that.

The previous point deserves repeating. Although it is important to understand how U.S. foreign policy historically has helped create conditions that breed terrorism, it is not useful or correct—in fact, it is morally repugnant—to argue that we are now repaying in blood what we have done to other countries via Osama bin Laden's intercivilizational war. There is a difference between saying that the United States helps to foster conditions in which terrorism thrives and saying that the terrorist acts of September 11 were a causal reflex of U.S. foreign and economic policy—like billiard balls in a mechanical Newtonian universe. U.S. imperialism creates the potential for and probability of terrorist attacks, but it does not ensure that they will occur. To say that U.S. imperialism caused the terrorist attacks skips over the notion that acts of terror are often the outcome of an irreducible plurality of causes and overlooks the fact that some forces, such as the terrorist factions of Osama bin Laden, are as regressive as anything done in the service of U.S. imperialism (Hudis, 2001). It forgets that there exists a great array of crimes that can be linked to world capitalism that go beyond the participation of the United States. In fact, it is important to point out that Islamic fundamentalism (what Samir Amin calls political Islam) is, itself, an adaptation to world capitalism. As Amin (2001) noted, political Islam is in fact not a reaction to the abuses of secularism and little more than an adaptation to the subordinate status of comprador capitalism. He wrote that political Islam's

> so-called "moderate" form therefore probably constitutes the principal danger threatening peoples concerned since the violence of the "radicals" only serves to destabilize the State, impeding the installation of a new comprador power suitable to the designs of the "moderates" beloved by the West (those of Iran are a good example). The constant support offered by the pro-American diplomacies of the Triad countries (U.S., Europe, and Japan) toward finding this "solution" to the problem is absolutely consistent with their desire to impose the globalized neoliberal order in the service of dominant transnational capital. (p. 4)

Furthermore, it is important to recognize that the September 11th acts of terrorism were not acts against U.S. capitalism, imperialism, or injustice but were demonic crimes against working people and crimes against humanity as a whole (Hudis, 2001). For instance, hundreds of workers from all over Latin America and the Caribbean were killed in the attacks, including those who worked at Windows on the World, in the office cafeterias, cleaning services, and delivery companies, and little media attention has so far been paid to them (Anderson, 2001, p. 1). And although we can gain a deeper and more nuanced understanding of these events by recognizing how the United States is implicated in a long history of crimes against the oppressed throughout the world—including interventions in post–cold war theaters—this history in no way justifies the terrorist attacks. These attacks were, in the words of Peter Hudis (2001), "the reverse mirror image of capitalism and imperialism" and not the opposite of capitalism and imperialism. I think this is a good description. Such attacks have been propelled by reactionary religious fundamentalist ideology—that could more accurately be called Islamism—that represents only a small and fanatical number of followers of Islam. As Edward Said (2001) remarked,

> No cause, no God, no abstract idea can justify the mass slaughter of innocents, most particularly when only a small group of people are in charge of such actions and feel themselves to represent the cause without having a real mandate to do so.

Terrorism is one of the most repulsive and contemptible acts of political retribution imaginable, and the recent attacks of September 11 certainly qualify as a crime against humanity.

These attacks follow the terrorist killing of 239 U.S. servicemen and 58 French paratroopers in Beirut in 1983; the 1998 bombings of U.S. embassies in Kenya and Tanzania in which hundreds were killed; the 1996 car-bomb attack on a U.S. barracks in Dhahran, Saudi Arabia, that killed 19 Americans; the 1995 car-bomb attack on an American national guard training center in Riyadh, Saudi Arabia, that took four lives; and, of course, the 1993 World Trade Center truck bombing that killed six people and injured more than a thousand others. And there was the more recent attack on the *U.S.S. Cole* in Aden that killed 17 sailors. Terrorism is always abhorrent, and this time it was captured by the media in Washington and New York City in such a spectacular fashion that the images of New York City during and after the attack will permanently be implanted in the structural unconscious of U.S. citizens. What is less clear is if the country's structural unconscious will ever become receptive to the fact that those who carried out the attacks of September 11 were the ideological twins of those who had been recruited by the CIA in its support of the Jihad against Communism, were those who had been proclaimed "heroes" in the U.S. press before 1989, were those whose extremism and fanaticism were encouraged by the U.S. military, were those, like bin Laden, who held accounts in the Bank for Credit and Commerce, the same bank the CIA used to finance its own covert operations (Gibbs, 2002).

Peter Hudis (2001) has noted that in the midst of this antihuman destruction, the light of humanism did shine in the hundreds of workers and citizens who flocked to "ground zero" in New York to help clear rubble, save victims, and provide medical aid to those who had been bloodied and battered in the attack. Construction workers rushed to save office workers, Black youth assisted elderly Jewish people to get out of the area—events like these became commonplace. Hudis reported on new forms of solidarity that emerged that included prisoners at Folsom Prison, most of them Black, who collected $1,000 dollars to aid victims of the disaster. However, these humanist expressions of solidarity are being quickly and shamefully silenced by Bush's effort to use the attacks as an excuse to militarize America, restrict civil liberties, and achieve militarily what Washington has long sought: a permanent U.S. presence in central Asia and the Caspian Sea region. Hudis remarked that in just one single day, the terrorists succeeded in totally shifting the ideological ground and handed the far right one of its greatest victories.

Terrorists All

The recent congressional statement by the Federal Bureau of Investigation (FBI) (2001) defines both international terrorism and domestic terrorism. Most threatening to critical educators is its definition of domestic terrorism as

> left-wing groups [that] generally profess a revolutionary socialist doctrine and view themselves as protectors of the people against the "dehumanizing effects" of capitalism and imperialism. They aim to bring about change in the United States through revolution rather than through the established political process. (p. 3)

It cautions that its investigations of terrorist groups "are not predicated upon social or political beliefs; rather FBI investigations are based upon information regarding planned or actual criminal activity" (p. 2). In such a with-us or against-us moment, the press has been deputized to weed out fifth columnists, as leftist critics are being run out of town like cattle rustlers on a *Bonanza* episode. In the span of one week, New York State's terrorism law made terrorism a new crime with a maximum penalty of life in prison. And given the shifts undertaken by the U.S. government in recent years with respect to who is a terrorist and who is a freedom fighter, this new law should send a shiver down the spine of anyone who supports liberation movements worldwide. Marable (2001b) warned,

> Anyone convicted of giving more than one thousand dollars to any organization defined by state authorities as "terrorist" will face up to 15 years in a state prison. When one reflects that, not too many years ago, that the U.S. considered the African National Congress as a "terrorist organization," and that the Palestinian Liberation Organization is still widely described as "terrorist," the danger of suppressing any activities by U.S. citizens that support any Third World social justice movements now becomes very real. (p. 6)

When White House Press Secretary Ari Fleischer insisted that people now have to "watch what they say, watch what they do," it was not, as some have claimed, a flippant remark. Interestingly, but not surprisingly, Cuba is listed as a country that exports terror internationally. Since September 11, some members of Congress have tried to have Cuba removed from the terrorist list, but the Cubans in Congress stopped this move in its tracks. Even though Fidel Castro roundly condemned the terrorist attacks on September 11, and offered to cooperate with Washington in combating terrorism, the State Department put

forward an unconvincing case against Cuba by noting that Cuba harbors Basque separatists. But the truth of the matter is that that they are there as the result of an agreement
between the Spanish and Cuban governments and are not engaged in terrorist activities of
any kind (Kawell, 2001). The State Department can put forward specious reasons for putting Cuba on the list of countries that harbor terrorists but remains adept on ignoring its
own local swamp for terrorist infestation: Florida. As John Pilger (2001a) noted, "There
is no 'war on terrorism.' If there was, the Special Air Service would be storming the beaches
of Florida, where more terrorists, tyrants and torturers are given refuge than anywhere in
the world" (pp. 2-3). Bertell Ollman echoed similar sentiments to those of Pilger when he
wrote,

> I'm still waiting for [Bush] to declare war on Florida. Miami is a haven for terrorists, it's the
> terror capital of the world. All these Latin American and Cuban terrorists go there to refresh,
> to retire, to conduct their business. If Bush wants to make a war on terror he should start by
> bombing Miami and arresting the governor of Florida, even if he is his brother. . . . And
> after he's successfully done away with terrorism in Miami, then we'll talk about the next step.
> (quoted in Monchinski, 2001, p. 8)

It is difficult to deny that the United States has a calculated penchant for ignoring its
own terrorists (groups and individuals who have been trained and financed either directly
or indirectly by the U.S. military), not just the "gusano" mafia in Florida (see McLaren &
Pinkney-Pastrana, 2001) but also fundamentalist Christian mass murderer General Efrain
Rios Montt of Guatemala, Savimbi and Renamo in Angola and Mozambique, and the
Nicaraguan Contras.

The Broader Picture

There has been sporadic media debate around the issue of what some perceive to be the
current assault on civil rights but little explanation of what reporters often refer to as "the
broader picture" and what academics frequently describe as the "larger geopolitical or sociopolitical context" surrounding the appalling events of September 11. At the present
time, U.S. citizens are still trying to cope with newfound feelings of vulnerability, as well
as understandable anger and rage against an unseen enemy. But they have also displayed a
willingness to give up one of the hallmarks of U.S. democracy—civil rights—as long as
it is the civil rights of "other people" that are sacrificed.

Many people reject the idea that the United States exports terrorism. Some no doubt find
it difficult to understand why a powerful nation such as the United States would need to employ what are generally considered to be the weapons of the weak. Klare (2001) asserted that

> throughout history, the weapon of those who see themselves as strong in spirit but weak in
> power has been what we call terrorism. Terrorism is the warfare of the weak against the
> strong: if you have an army you wage a war; if you lack an army you engage in suicide bomb-
> ings and other acts of terrorism. (Remember: this is exactly what the American Revolution
> looked like to the British, the strong force in 1775.)

Chomsky (2001) took issue with this view of terrorism. He explained that far from being a weapon of the weak, terrorism is primarily the weapon of the strong:

That is the culture in which we live and it reveals several facts. One is the fact that terrorism works. It doesn't fail. It works. Violence usually works. That's world history. Secondly, it's a very serious analytic error to say, as is commonly done, that terrorism is the weapon of the weak. Like other means of violence, it's primarily a weapon of the strong, overwhelmingly, in fact. It is held to be a weapon on the weak because the strong also control the doctrinal systems and their terror doesn't count as terror. (p. 11)

Eqbal Ahmad (1998) made the point that the moral revulsion in response to terrorism is highly selective. He wrote that "we are to feel the terror of those groups, which are officially disapproved. We are to applaud the terror of those groups of whom officials do approve" (p. 3). Ahmad notes that when President Reagan said, "I am a contra," he was, in effect, identifying with a U.S.-sponsored group of vicious terrorists. Ahmad writes that U.S. policy during the Cold War period sponsored all sorts of terrorist regimes such as those of Somoza, Batista, and Pinochet, to name just a few.

Did You Pass Terrorism 101?

In this context, it is impossible not to question seriously the odious role of the Western Hemisphere Institute for Security Cooperation, or Whisc, based in Fort Benning, Georgia (until January this year, Whisc was called the School of the Americas, or SOA). Since 1946, SOA has trained more than 60,000 Latin American soldiers and policemen. Its graduates constitute a veritable rogues' gallery of the continent's most notorious torturers, mass murderers, dictators, and state terrorists.

How can the United States condemn other countries for human rights abuses and acts of terror and not recognize that it houses, educates, and graduates some of the most notorious butchers in the Americas? If the United States really believes that supporting terrorists makes you as guilty as the terrorists themselves, then it would have to put on trial most of its military and political leadership over the last handful of administrations—and more. Alexander Cockburn reported that in recent years, the United States has been charged by the United Nations and also by human rights organizations such as Human Rights Watch and Amnesty International with tolerating torture in its prison system. Methods of torture range from putting prisoners into solitary confinement in concrete boxes, 23 hours a day, for years on end, to activating 50,000-volt shocks through a mandatory belt worn by prisoners. The United States began serious experiments in torture during the Vietnam War. One experiment involved three prisoners being anesthetized and having their skulls opened up. Electrodes were planted into their brains. They were revived, given knives, and put in a room. CIA psychologists activated the electrodes to provoke the prisoners to attack one another, but the prisoners did not respond as expected. So the electrodes were removed, the prisoners shot, and their bodies burned (Cockburn, 2001).

By all reckoning, George Bush and his administration have enjoyed a very successful war. The reengineering of the globe is proceeding apace, and the sustained conquest of other parts of the globe is (at the very least) in its planning stages. But Bush and his hawk-headed advisors are really part of the larger political will of global market agents and the logic of transnational capital. It is not surprising to read in a 1995 *Harper's* roundtable discussion titled "A Revolution, or Business as Usual?" Wall Street editorialist David Frum arguing that the government should "get rid of " Medicare, Medicaid, and all other social programs for children, the poor, the elderly, and the racially or otherwise disadvantaged "overnight" if possible, at the same time as media "neoconservative" William Kristol is railing against the Roosevelt New Deal and proclaiming that "you cannot have a federal guarantee that people won't starve" (*Harper's Magazine*, March 1995, p. 42, as cited in McMurtry, in press). It is as if the transnationalization of the productive forces and the emergence of the transnational capitalist class carry an ethnocidal logos, shaping the collective will of the ruling elite, triggering the killer instinct of its political servants, and provoking them to retreat into their cave like Cacus, the Roman mythological figure who was half man–half beast. Whereas Cacus stole oxen and dragged them backwards into his lair so that their footprints made them appear to have emerged from the cave, the ruling elite has stolen the labor-power of the poor by making it appear as if the working class was fairly compensated. Bertell Ollman notes that after quoting Luther's account of Cacus, Marx exclaimed: "An excellent picture, it fits the capitalist in general, who pretends that what he has taken from others and brought back to his den emanates from him, and by causing it to go backwards, he gives it the semblance of having come from his den" (Ollman, 2001, p. 61).

It is important to see the events of September 11 within the context of the transnationalized fractions that have gained a powerful hold over most nation states worldwide. The global capitalist historical bloc is attempting to consolidate its social compact but is riven with contradictions and competing forces (see Robinson, 2001a, 20001b, 2001c, 2001-2002; Robinson & Harris, 2000). This is not the same thing as arguing that global capitalism is free floating. Because capitalism was formerly organized in geographically bound national circuits, and today these circuits are becoming less geographically anchored to the nation state, this does not mean that nation states are irrelevant sites for commandeering capital or, for that matter, sites for resisting the "capitalization" of the life world. But I do agree that the social configuration of space within transnationalized circuits of capital can no longer be conceived solely or mainly in nation state terms (Robinson, 2001b, 2001c). We have to think more in terms of what Robinson (2001–2002) described as uneven accumulation denoted for the most part by social group rather than differentiation by national territory. Nation states and national production systems no longer mediate local, regional, and global configurations of space the way that they used to before the move toward a transnationalization of the productive forces. But the truth of the matter is that many of those social groups most severely exploited by the forces of transnational capital are located within Islamic populations. We need to renew our commitment to anti-imperialist struggles, not in the narrowly defined sense of being anti-Western, but in the sense of supporting class struggles inside the Arab world, and everywhere that capitalism hacks it way throughout the globe, dragging imperialism in the wake of its impersonal law of social domination (see Hudis, 2002).

As Bush moves toward the creation of a permanent war, the left is faced with powerful challenges. One of these is to move beyond a narrow anti–U.S. imperialism and to get on with the crucial business of class struggle against monopoly capitalism. As Peter Hudis (2002) importantly remarked, we need to move beyond the limitations of an anti–U.S. imperialism and get back to the principled anti-imperialism displayed by Lenin during World War I. In this sense, we need to move away from an anti-Westernism and get on with the task of supporting class struggle in the interests of creating a new human society. Remaining critical of U.S. foreign and economic policies is important, but in our practice of criticism, we need to avoid falling into a reactionary anti-Americanism. Instead, it is important to set our sights on the struggle against monopoly capitalism, which is, after all, at the root of imperialism. As Hudis noted, imperialism is an outgrowth of a state-monopoly capitalism writ large on the world stage. There is a philosophical foundation for rejecting the left's focus on the current perniciousness of George Bush's political acts, particularly in advocating the importance of a Marxist-humanist response to the war on terrorism. In Hegelian terms, we need a *concrete particular* that can show an internal connection between Marxist-Humanism and anti-imperialism (remembering that using an *abstract* particular renders the Syllogism contingent with regard to its determinations.) As Hudis (2002) notes, in focusing only on Bush's imperialism, we abstract one element out from a wealth of particulars, masking the need for a second negation. We must not only negate Bush and his administration but also focus on the need to negate its opposite such as bin Laden, Al-Qaeda, and all other narrow and reactionary "anti-imperialisms" (Hudis, 2002).

Embracing a Marxist humanism means avoiding entrapment in concrete abstractions and focusing our efforts on the concrete particulars that face us in the objective conditions of our historical struggle against the hydra-headed beast of capital. This means a concerted effort to resist simultaneously Bush's policy of permanent war, the political Islam of bin Laden and his supporters, and the politics of neoliberalism that are ravaging the world's poor and powerless. If it is true that the transition from the nation state to a new global phase of capitalism involves the necessary transnational integration of national production systems, as Robinson suggested, this means that we need to organize the increasingly transnationalized fractions of the working class. This does not suggest, of course, that competition and conflict among capitalists are coming to an end or that the nation state is disintegrating. But, as Robinson noted, intercapitalist conflict is no longer coterminous with interstate conflict. Consequently, it makes sense to wage a global counterhegemonic struggle against transnational capital and at the same time a struggle for a socialist alternative to capital.

What will be the outcome of the current imperialist rivalries, the "hot conflagrations" and the fiercely contending blocs of capital occurring with the expansion of the traditional axis of exploitation between capital and labor? Will they, as Nick Dyer-Witheford asks, exceed the scale of twentieth-century holocausts? Dyer-Witheford comments:

> As David Harvey chillingly reminds us, there is no better solution to an accumulation crisis of the sort now building in a world market than mass destruction of excess capacity. It would mark the return of what E.P. Thompson, in some of the most fraught years of the U.S.–Soviet confrontation identified as the dynamic of "exterminism." The failing discipline of the Global Factory may be replaced by the command of Global War. This draws a dark, scorched line across the horizon of the future towards which so many radical rivulets and transformative tributaries are flowing. It would be an answer to the crisis of capital's value system that risks the violent devaluation and decomposition of all

its subjects. It is a prospect that may take all the internationalist, combinatory powers of today's movements to avoid. (2002, p. 28)

A Marxist humanism that springs from the tension between free production and unfree history, one that is centered around a struggle against the expropriation of subjectivity by an identification with capital's law of value and a subsumption of living labor by abstract labor, needs to look toward the building of internationalist struggles that will take human society beyond both the global factory and the social universe of capital in which it is housed.

References

Ahmad, A. (2000). A task that never ends: Bush proposes perpetual war. Unpublished manuscript.

Ahmad, E. (1998, October 12). *Terrorism: Theirs and ours.* A presentation at the University of Boulder, Colorado, Association of Tamils of Eelam & Sri Lanka in the United States. Available from http://www.sangam.org/ANALYSIS/Ahmad.htm

Amin, S. (2001, Winter). Political Islam. *Covert Action Quarterly, 71,* 3–6.

Anderson, K. (2001). Immigrant victims of the WTC attack. *NACLA Report on the Americas. XXXV*(3), 1–2, 4.

Baker, D. (2001, November/December). From new economy to war economy. *Dollars & Sense, 238,* 7, 39.

Barsamian, D. (2001, November). Edward Said interview. *The Progressive.* Available from http://www.progressive.org

Beccaria, C. (1963). *On crimes and punishment* (H. Paolucci, Trans.). New York: Macmillan. (Original work published 1764)

Campbell, D. (2002). U.S. sends suspects to face torture. *The Guardian.* Retrieved March 11, 2002, from http://www.guardian.co.uk/bush/story/0,7369,665940,00.html

Chomsky, N. (2001, October 24). The new war against terror. *Counterpunch.* Available from http://www.counterpunch.org/chomskyterror.html

Coen, R. (2002, February). See no evil. *Extra!,* 15(1), p. 6–8.

Cockburn, A. (2001, December 24). Sharon or Arafat: Which is the sponsor of terror? *The Nation,* 273(21), 10.

Dyer-Witheford, N. (2002, January). Global body, global brain/global factory, global war: Revolt of the value-subjects. *The Commoner.* Retrieved March 2002 from http://www.commoner.org.uk/03dyer-witheford.pdf

Federal Bureau of Investigation. (2001, May 10). *Congressional statement.* Available from http://www.fbi.gov/congress/congress01/freeh051001.htm

Galeano, E. (2000). *Upside down: A primer for the looking-glass world.* New York: Metropolitan Books.

Gibbs, D. (2002, February). Forgotten coverage of Afghan "freedom fighters." *Extra!,* 15(1), pp. 13–16.

Hart, P. (2001). No spin zone? *Extra!,* 14(6), 8.

Hart, P., & Naureckas, J. (2002, February). Fox at the front. *Extra!,* 15(1), p. 9.

Hudis, P. (2001). Terrorism, Bush's retaliation show inhumanity of class society. *News & Letters,* 46(8), 1, 10–11.

Hudis, P. (2002, January 20). *The power of negativity in today's search for a way to transform reality.* Presentation to the Expanded Resident Editorial Board of Chicago: News & Letters.

Huntington, S. (1996). *The clash of civilizations and the remaking of world order.* New York: Touchstone Books.

Kawell, J. (2001). Terror's Latin American profile. *NACLA Report on the Americas, XXXV*(3), 50–53.

Klare, M. T. (2001, September). *Asking "why." Foreign policy in focus.* Available from http://fpif.org/commentary/0109why.html

le Carre, J. (2001). A war we cannot win. *The Nation,* 273(16), 15–17.

Marable, M. (2001a, November). The failure of U.S. foreign policies. *Along the Color Line.* Available from http://www.manningmarable.net

Marable, M. (2001b). Terrorism and the struggle for peace. *Along the Color Line.* Available from http://www.manningmarable.net

McLaren, P., & Pinkney-Pastrana, J. (2001). Cuba, Yanquizacion, and the cult of Elian Gonzales: A view from the "enlightened" states. *International Journal of Qualitative Studies in Education,* 14(2), 201–219.

McMurtry, J. (in press). *Value wars: Moral philosophy and humanity.* London: Pluto Press.

Mikulan, S. (2001). A small universe of people. *LA Weekly,* 24(2), 22–23.

Monchinski, T. (2001). *Capitalist schooling: An interview with Bertell Ollman.* Available from http://eserver.org/clogic/4-1/monchinski.html

Niva, S. (2001a, September 14). Addressing the sources of Middle Eastern violence against the United States. *Common Dreams News Center.* Available from http://www.commondreams.org/views01/0914-04.htm

Niva, S. (2001b, September 21). Fight the roots of terrorism. *Common Dreams News Center.* Available from http://www.commondreams.org/views01/0921-06.htm

Ollman, B. (2001). *How to take an exam and remake the world.* Montreal, Canada: Black Rose Books.

Petras, J. (2002). Signs of a police state are everywhere. *Z Magazine,* 15(1), 10–12.

Pilger, J. (1999). *Hidden agendas.* London: Vintage.

Pilger, J. (2001a). There is no war on terrorism. If there was, the SAS would be storming the beaches of Florida. *New Statesman,* 14(680), 16.

Pilger, J. (2001b, October 29). This war is a farce. *The Mirror.* Available from http://mirror.icnetwork.co.uk/printable_version.cfm?objectid=11392430

Powers, J. (2002a). Davos, American style: The state of global protest. *LA Weekly,* 24(11), 24, 26, 28.

Powers, J. (2002b). Rank and yank at Enron, or, the fine art of bankruptcy. *LA Weekly,* 24(3), 11–17.

Rendall, S. (2002, February). Pro-pain pundits. *Extra!,* 15(1), 17–18.

Response to terror: In brief. (2001, November 16). *Los Angeles Times,* A10.

Robinson, W. (2001a, August 18-21). *The debate on globalization, the transnational capitalist class, and the rise of a transnational state.* Paper delivered at the 2001 meeting of the American Sociological Association, Anaheim Hilton, Los Angeles.

Robinson, W. (2001b). Response to McMichael, Block, and Goldfrank. *Theory and Society,* 30, 223–236.

Robinson, W. (2001c). Social theory and globalization: The rise of a transnational state. *Theory and Society,* 30, 157-200.

Robinson, W. (2001–2002). Global capitalism and nation-state-centric thinking—What we don't see when we do see nation-states: Response to critics. *Science & Society,* 65(1), 500–508.

Robinson, W., & Harris, J. (2000). Towards a global ruling class? Globalization and the transnational capitalist class. *Science & Society,* 64(1), 11–54.

Said, E. (2001, September 16). Islam and the West are inadequate banners. *The Observer.* Available from http://www.observer.co.uk/comment/story/0,6903,552764,00.html

Scigliano, E. (2001). Naming—and un-naming—names. *The Nation,* 273(22), 16.

Tryferis, A. (2001, December 6-12). Bill's blather. *New Times,* p. 7.

Weiner, B. (2002, March 3). The OEWar on terrorism for dummies. *Counterpunch*. Retrieved March 3, 2002, from http://www/counterpunch.org/weinerdummies.html

Weinstein, H., Briscoe, D., & Landsberg, M. (2002, March 10). Civil liberties take a back seat to safety. *Los Angeles Times*, A1, A28–A29.

Peter McLaren is a professor in the Division of Urban Schooling, Graduate School of Education and Information Studies, University of California, Los Angeles.

Cultural Studies, Immanent War, Everyday Life

5

JACK Z. BRATICH
University of New Hampshire

September 24, 2001

IN RECENT DAYS, "America's New War" has been given an official name: "Operation Infinite Justice." On one level, this name is itself an injustice. I think of Levinas here, whose notion of justice is an inexhaustible responsibility to the other, where any repayment of debt only multiplies obligation. In this sense, the horrors of 9/11 are "ours" and "not ours" at the same time, and this singularity needs to be remembered. This militarization of justice, then, is an infinite response without responsibility. On another level, it is this very conceptual injustice that gives us a sense of what is to come in this new war. For this is not merely America's next war, not another war in a series of wars. Even the military experts are alerting us to the new form of war that we are about to witness.

Or maybe we won't witness it: Many are asking what this war will "look" like. Whereas spectacular news and entertainment media are indispensible, also crucial is what Guy Debord calls the spectacle's complement—generalized secrecy (in *Comments on the Society of the Spectacle*, 1998). We have already been assured that this war will be unprecedented in its secrecy. This is a secret war against a shadowy enemy, and citizens have been publicly informed of this secrecy. Generalized secrecy has become public, but secretly.

This new form of war requires a new form of home front as well. In the past few days, the Office of Homeland Defense was established to coordinate homeland security. On one hand, this is a bolstering of national security infrastructure (tightening national borders, increased air patrols, and detention of immigrants). On the other hand, "homeland" becomes more than a territory to be defended against outside attacks. This affect-laden term signifies the dense terrain of biopolitical production—it refers to the mundane habits of everyday life and the plurality of micropractices that make up life itself. Homeland is more terrain than territory—a field of forces that needs to be reconstituted from the inside, as a generalized and diffuse turning of the inside against itself.

We can see that the attack on September 11 was a turning of the inside on itself. Some of the hijackers learned how to fly planes at U.S. pilot training schools, and the attacks themselves turned the everyday practice of travel into a horrific weapon. This in-volved at-tack set the stage for the "homeland's" constitution. In other words, both the attacks and the war response to them have become immanent to everyday life.

What does this mean? According to professor of information studies Philip Agre (2001), what is happening is an institutionalization and normalization of warfare into everyday life. The U.S. home front itself is as much of a theater of war as the foreign lands where the special forces and cruise missiles wreak devastation (although the deadly toll will be unequal). The importance of the domestic is not just as the imagined ideological space of a unified nation; it is the material, diffuse reorganization of everyday life. "Temporary inconveniences" at isolated sites (airports, government buildings, national monuments) in the name of security may well become mundane habit in the indefinite future. It is in this way that "infinite justice" translates into "permanent war," where an unspecified enemy can always potentially arise, giving an indefinite time to a state of permanent exception.

We can see early calls for this domestic state of war in the seemingly paradoxical state-ments, "Americans will never be the same" and "Americans should get back to their rou-tines and normal lives." Repeated, sudden announcements of vague threats interrupt com-monplace routines (e.g., "Rumor of New Attacks Leave Cities on Edge: Officials Urge Normalcy Despite High Alert"; see Connolly & Eggen, 2001). Homeland defense is tak-ing on both forms of security that Agre describes: (a) taking infrastructures as they are and increasing their boundary protection, and (b) redesigning the basic components of in-stitutions and subjects in everyday life. The first type may be seen as corresponding more with disciplinary forms (enclosures, visible boundaries, and logics), whereas the second more to what Gilles Deleuze calls control societies (marked by a generalization of insti-tutional logics across social space, rapid communications, continuous info flows and their monitoring, and imperceptible maneuvers). But it is in this second type of security, as Agre argues, where political and democratic forces can affect the redesigning of infrastructure. Culture itself is part of this recomposition.

Already in the span of a few days, as popular culture begins to "get back to normal programming," we can see this redesigning at work. Professional football announcers have refrained from using war metaphors in their coverage, the host of a television news satire program has announced that for the time being there will be no jokes at President Bush's expense, and a late night comedian has already had to apologize for calling cruise-missile warfare "cowardly" (in fact, his program, significantly titled *Politically Incorrect*, is currently under threat of cancellation because of it). And among the barrage of images represent-ing the current crisis regarding civil liberties and security is a chilling Associated Press photo depicting a security guard searching an older, White woman's handbag, with both figures turned to the camera and smiling.

With this new war, then, new parameters and conditions of critique also arise. As I write this, George W. Bush is about to release an executive order that lists numerous ter-rorist organizations and delineates what is meant by "support" for terrorism. Will "intel-lectual support" be a criminal act, even treasonous? We can look to the Italian politics of terror in the late 1970s and the imprisonment of Antonio Negri for "intellectual leader-ship" of terrorism as a warning sign (for a reflection on those times, see the Semiotext(e) issue on Autonomia [Lotringer & Marazzi, 1980]). And how have the attacks overdetermined possible antiglobalization positions (as Yann Moulier Bouteng has argued)? If homeland security requires a generalized deterrence of dissenting thought, then the work of cultural studies is indeed imperiled.

But in saying this I am not trying simply to predict a dystopic future (although because this issue will come out a few months from now I am caught up in writing in the future anterior—"it will have been that"). Making war immanent to everyday life, if these are the conditions we as cultural analysts and practitioners are facing, may be precisely where cultural studies becomes useful. For the new context has not been settled, and this, as numerous others have argued on the *cultstud* listserv, is where cultural studies may be effective. What conditions of possibility are there in these societies of war-control?

Faced with the logic of "we need to destroy liberties to save them," who will speak to and about the parameters of critique? The recomposition of everyday life is being done in the name of democracy, which itself may be contestable. Even the flag and patriotism are insecure and up for articulation, as numerous cultstud posters have argued. For the time being, collective patriotism is resettling on military might and religious crusading, but done in the name of freedom and democracy (just after I wrote the first part of this piece, the name of the military operation was changed from Infinite Justice to Enduring Freedom). The terms of debate, although certainly constrained, are also being foregrounded as *stakes* in the debate, which renews and expands their contestability.

If September 11, 2001, marks the end of a U.S. fake "holiday from history" (as Slavoj Zizek put it), how will the specifically American return to the world stage as a historic actor take place? And how can the Left and cultural studies make its impact on this global moment not through fear, but with a vigilance coupled with creative and productive interventions?

References

Agre, P. (2001, September 14). Imagining the next war: Infrastructural warfare and the conditions of democracy. *Red Rock Eater New Service*. Available at http://dlis.gseis.ucla.edu/pagre/

Connolly, C., & Eggen, D. (2001, September 22). Rumors of new attacks leave cities on edge: Officials urge normalcy despite high alert. *Washington Post*, p. A21.

Debord, G. (1998). *Comments on the society of the spectacle*. London: Verso.

Lotringer, S., & Marazzi, C. (Eds.). *Italy: Automania* (Vol. 3, No. 3). New York: Capital City.

Jack Z. Bratich is assistant professor of communication at the University of New Hampshire.

What Relevance Cultural Studies Post–September 11th?

6

ARNOLD SHEPPERSON
KEYAN G. TOMASELLI
University of Natal, South Africa

"Bully With a Bloody Nose Is Still a Bully." This kind of headline appeared in the South African press following September 11, 2001. This press, however, was quick to unreservedly condemn the attacks. Few here were really surprised, though all were shocked at their scale and audacity. The United States went into panic. Greyhound terminated its services for 24 hours when, 3 weeks later, a madman slit the throat of one of its drivers.

For us Third Worlders, it is déjà vu. Thanks to the superpowers' surrogate strategies of the cold war, a litany of international excesses punctuated our lives. People daily confronted acts of terror, potential assassination, and torture, from the right, the left, officialdom, and madmen of all kinds. We lived—and many still do—under regimes of authorized violence, authorized by the regimes themselves and by the superpowers' spook agencies. Let us not forget that the CIA shipped Nelson Mandela to the apartheid police, that Dick Cheney opposed Mandela's later release, and that it was the United States that supported the Bin Ladens, the Saddam Husseins, and the Manuel Noriegas in the first place. This is the myopic and self-destructive foreign policy of a country that, though in the world, conducts itself separately from it, mostly against it, and then wonders at the consequences: "Why do they hate us so?" asked a bewildered George W. Bush shortly after September 11.

Our approach to cultural studies in Africa has had two objectives: first, to return to the terrain of real struggle, not just the sanitized "popular" as a form of writing as it has largely become, and second, to remind the academic enterprise that the majority of the world's people are hungry, angry, and resentful of International Monetary Fund structural adjustment programs that utterly fail to address pressing social conditions.

In the tradition of Hobbes and Von Clausewitz, violence is not violence if it is authorized, lawful, and perpetrated by the state whether against individuals within states or targeted against other states. Hence, Tomaselli's 13-year-old daughter learned at a Michigan high school in 1998 that all the wars in which the United States had been engaged were to "bring democracy" to those countries. When she suggested that Vietnam was more about U.S. hegemony, she was asked to leave the lesson: Coming from Africa, that cauldron of instability, revolution, and disease, what could she know? When she admitted that monkeys live in her garden, thus ineluctably associating "Africans" (and herself) with primitivity, she vainly tried to recover the moral high ground by explaining that "monkeys are to Durban what squirrels are to East Lansing." But the Hollywood image of diseased monkeys/apes threatening the health, wealth, and stability of the United States remained. Now, an extremist Islam is taking over this role. "The war against terror," "them versus us," has been rekindled. But who is the "them," and where do we locate the "us"—ourselves?

"They" plant bombs, hijack aircraft, conduct massacres, and sponsor acts that result in injury or death of U.S. civilians. "We" bring democracy and peace via surrogate governments. September 11 in the United States, and the beginning of the Chechen uprising in Russia, reversed the location of the terror. But this excludes instances such as the Columbine High School massacre and the Oklahoma City bombing. There is no comparable surrogacy apparent in cases such as these, yet the constitution into victims of citizens doing their business remains the same.

The act of constitution is, therefore, something that can occur independently of the Hobbesian state or the Clausewitzian conception of "policy." As acts, they are necessarily done and completed, whether they are the outcome of private conspiracies or state policies. As such, semiotically, they are fully determined in the sense of C. S. Peirce's conception of the symbol. But as such, as a final instance of interpretation, they are nevertheless different because of their context of action and the origins of their origination. Peirce's distinctions in the modes of being of symbols, the distinction between tone, type, and token, are useful here. If a single act of political terror is a symbolic representation, it is therefore a token symbol. Given the variations on this theme, we can then examine what type-symbol and tone-symbol characteristics apply to different acts.

One familiar pure political-type symbol is nationalist: the Irish Republican Army, Palestine Liberation Organization, Polisario Front, and the Basque ETA, among others, all claim responsibility on the basis of a national freedom charter (as did the African National Congress in South Africa). The religious-type claims are found in groups such as Hamas and Hizbollah in the Middle East, the Lord's Resistance Army in Uganda, Abu Sayyef in the Philippines, among various abortion clinic bombers, and so on. Ethnic-type claims may also be discerned in the actions of the Interahamwe of Rwanda, the Tigers of Tamil Eelam in Sri Lanka, and the Moro Liberation Front of the Philippines. This becomes relevant to cultural studies when these types can (although not necessarily) originate in the tone symbol "is cultural."

Al Qaeda's attacks demonstrated that the predicate cultural is not benign. The term *cultural* becomes very much a "real vague" (Peirce, 1998, p. 395) that can have indefinitely many consequences. The idea of culture is not in itself malign, but experience demonstrates that it can be mobilized as a predicative tone symbol alongside nationalist, religious, and ethnic type symbols as a justification for acts that will earn the token symbol "terrorist." But a concept's capacity to generate indefinitely many symbolic outcomes in a wide range of action classes means that it is also a political concept. Examining the modern meaning of culture as a political concept suggests some lines of cultural studies inquiry into questions of value arising from globalization.

Raymond Williams (1958) traced the ways that the idea of culture developed, firstly in parallel with English social progress and secondly in parallel with the technologies of symbolic reproduction. The problem for non-British readers is that the accompanying political history remains unclear without additional reading. The texts Williams chose to illustrate his thesis in *Culture and Society* mostly relate to the political issue of extending political rights and representation to previously excluded classes. Wordsworth, Coleridge, Burke, and Cobbett at the beginning of the 19th century, and T. E. Hulme, T. S. Eliot, and George Orwell in the 20th century, all confronted one principal issue mobilizing English cultural theory, analysis, or criticism: The admission of excluded groups into the representative processes of state and government raised the need for a parallel intervention that would mitigate the social disturbances that accompanied this process of inclusion.

Impulsive policy responses to September 11—"if you are not with us, you are against us," for example, and the attempt to label the counterterror operation "Infinite Justice" and as a "crusade"—have stretched the developed world's intellectual resources in seeking to mitigate them. Academics are supposedly the last formal bastion of critical, principled, and hopefully independent thinking. However, the role of culture as a mobilizing concept in the era of globalization can no longer be identified with the issues it was intended to solve one or two centuries ago. The Twin Towers and Oklahoma City bombers fit neither the type symbols of European working-class problems nor the later anthropological types associated with the Dervishes of Omdurman. They are, or were, technically educated men who turned the institutions of national states against its citizens. They are, those still out there, almost universally opposed to states in general.

Despite all this, the response to date has been largely conceived around nationally based alliances, governmental transitions, and policies. What Al Qaeda did, as did Timothy McVeigh, was to take the criminal token symbol into a realm over which national states can claim no jurisdiction. Al Qaeda is not an international terror group: It is the flip side of globalization, and as such the response to its actions and strategies needs to be globally conceived. Cultural studies must begin to consider its subject matter in global terms but not merely as a function of "Disneyfication" (although the new media pretty well did just that). Culture has to be seen as having type symbols that empower affirmative global token symbols in the form of restitutive acts. These include the extension of representative institutions in the realms of economics, media, and health, among others, such that no citizen of the globe need suffer to the extent that an alien observer might believe that Earth's humanoid animals are composed of two separate species, one of which lives twice as long as the other (Honderich, 1989, p. 5).

References

Honderich, T. (1989). *Violence for equality*. London: RKP.

Peirce, C. (1998). *The essential Peirce: Selected philosophical writings—1893–1913* (Vol. 2). Bloomington, IN: Peirce Edition Project.

Williams, R. (1958). *Culture and society*. Harmondsworth, UK: Pelican.

Arnold Shepperson is a researcher based in the Graduate Programme in Cultural and Media Studies, University of Natal, Durban, South Africa.

Keyan G. Tomaselli is a professor based in the Graduate Programme in Cultural and Media Studies, University of Natal, Durban, South Africa.

9/11 AS NARRATIVE, POETICS, AND PERSONAL STORIES

II

MARY E. WEEMS

One Face in the Crowd

The woman's face is braided
white, dusted like fresh made rolls.
Fear is a river.

I want to know her name. Lucky
to carry her life away like a last meal.

I wonder if she dances, sings, tells
co-workers a joke over an outside
cigarette.

I let blood
wet the ground,
like friends who pour wine
on the dirt.

Aftermath

Media blitz: daze, blaze, ash.
W wages war.

Propaganda re-runs, re-runs, re-runs . . .

CNN, BBC, TV land.

One of my Palestinian male students, 18, beat-down
in a bar by a 35-year-old white male.
His performance text "I sing America, too."

One of my Palestinian female students 19, performs
with doll and Palestinian flag—stops.

Flags come out like bandages.
Candlelit vigils for democracy.
People tatoo, shout, sing, paint cars, faces
places deep red, deep white,
deep blue.

Scam artists knock, make calls,
start websites for their favorite charity.

My neighborhood talks about A-rabs.
I ask why? Pray. Breathe differently.

9-16 I Imagine 9-11:

Cell phone lifelines, sky-blood, burn,
faces flying, brown eyes blinking,
20,000 empty hands, afraid
an open mouth.

Help; night-hush;
heart-pulse
nobody
sacred
ground.

Mary E. Weems is a Black activist poet.

Posts Post September 11

PATRICIA TICINETO CLOUGH

E-mail September 13, 2001

YES I AM OK. THANKS for thinking about me and asking how I am. I must say, it gets worse here each day, as it does elsewhere if differently. There is the horror of the emptied space against the sky that becomes a place of zero grounding, a place one smells and sees with inward senses that fail to memorize. It is traumatic. But even more, as I am sure you know, I am feeling lost in this nation, in a sea of people screaming for war. What can they be thinking that I don't understand any of them? And you must feel that too—the deep concern.

much love, patricia

E-mail September 21, 2001

I was so sad that last night's meeting ended with heavy hearts, as I think each of us felt, if not in different ways. I was full of confusion. I have often felt that I could not bear doing the kind of politics being done at the meeting: their slowness without the subtlety of our own conversations about the struggle between a peace movement and movement against international racism and policing. They say "workers and class action" and seem to silence what we could hardly say to each other just the night before as we planned to meet with them. And the only one of us who is a person of color was bent in pain throughout the meeting, bodily offended by the language of those seemingly on our side. I could see her and it hurt me too there in the middle of my body. I have thought so many times as I left some group, left off some identification, "Just let me be a teacher." But I also realized that politics always is like the meeting was. But maybe this time it is not just a repeat (not one without difference). The difference, I think, is that we know that each of us has suffered differently the past days. And the differences bring each of us back to other past sufferings. These past sufferings are pressing on us as they slowly hurt each of us differently, even as we try to act together. If I let any one of you down last night by not speaking up as I think you hoped I would, I am sorry. I couldn't locate myself well, but I did feel your hurt, if not the same as my hurt, then one near to mine, your hearts next to mine close. I want you to know I am so glad to have had time with all of you of late. I needed it and need it. I see that clearly, if nothing else, and please know how much we mean to me when we are we. And I hope we can keep trying to be.

much love, patricia

E-mail September 23, 2001

Class tomorrow will be in the old room where we first met, which now seems so long ago. Thanks for all the e-mailing back and forth, and I look forward to seeing you all and embracing you all. I hope we can talk and console each other. I look forward to teaching again but know not what form the differences I feel will take. I thought it sadly ironic or maybe flatly disturbing that we began our course this semester with work on thermodynamics and the economics of information starting with the 1973 oil crisis—that crisis which more often has come to be referred to as the crisis of capitalism in the arrival of postmodernity. Even as I watched those icons of world trade crumble before my eyes, I could not help but think that the analysis was so close at hand, even if my hand seemed numbed to the tips of my fingers. But since then I have heard those close-at-hand analyses from the lips of those closest to me politically and I have found that they are not exactly right for me; they are not exactly the analysis that began to etch itself in my mind as I watched the TV-screened collapse of the World Trade Center. There is the one analysis that knows that we should have expected this terror, given the lack of economic justice in global capitalism. Although economic justice is a necessary cause to endlessly promote, should we have expected "this" as an inevitable effect of economic injustice? What of this expectation and that expectation of which the others, those on the right, speak of the "uncivilized," of "their" envy of "our" modernity, of "our" technology, of "our" wealthful freedoms? I worry about the bond of similarity between these two expectations. What does this bond necessarily exclude? What of the silenced differences that make power, economics, and hateful desire discontinuous? And there are the other analyses that underscore the lack of knowing and publicize the need for learning histories and cultures in other worlds than "ours." There is no doubt that many have allowed the powerful position of the United States to dumb them; indeed we all are dumbed and complicitous in the horrible use of U.S. power, and it should not remain the case. But what of the questions about knowing, of knowledge formations and authority, questions that were being discussed about the opposition of the "occident" and the "orient" and the answers to which questions might allow us to follow this media/mediated language of networks and webs of terrorists/ interpol and through that web, the creation, in ways we on the left surely had not wanted, of an internationalism beyond the nation state? Is the event of terrorism at the World Trade Center to put an end to the questioning? Just when these unfinished debates about knowledge and authority are being materialized and institutionalized as such through militaristic and policing assemblages, are we to think that returning to histories or anthropologies of so-called "ancient" cultures and "premodern peoples" like the erection of missile defense shields, the development of space weapons, and the passing of antiterrorist legislation will somehow secure our/the nation-state? If instead the world order of nation states territorially based is displaced by the web/network of power, peoples, capital, and violence, with the circuits now being hard wired, then what has this energy crisis that we now are suffering already wrought and do we have what we need to be with the forces of life? For all that and all these words carrying my thoughts to you, I remain confused, strangely exhausted, and so looking forward to seeing you.

patricia

Patricia Ticineto Clough is a professor of sociology, the director of the Center for the Study of Women and Society, and the coordinator of the Women's Studies Program at The Graduate Center/City University of New York.

The Mourning After

9

MICHELLE FINE

12.September

YOU CAN TELL WHO'S DEAD or missing by their smiles. Their photos dot the subways, ferries, trains, and Port Authority Terminal, shockingly alive with joy, comfort, and pleasure. They died before they could know what we now know. The not-dead travel on subways and trains filled with hollow eyes; no smiles; shoulders down. Five thousand dead and still counting, and that's without the undocumented workers whose families can't tell, the homeless men and women whose families don't know. Each evening, millions of nightmares startle and awaken, alone and dark, throughout the metropolitan area.

The air in the City chokes with smoke, flesh, fear, memories, clouds, and creeping nationalism. My niece, a bus driver on Wall Street, describes the plume of smoke "chasing me down the street" as she abandoned her bus. Now a flood of flags, talk of God, military, and patriotism chase us all. Searching for an icon of meaning—the flag worries, it feels like draperies for war. The globe doubles as globalization. Even the dove and peace symbol, my students tell me, feel like generational imperialism. We blanket this terror with Vietnam, just to make it familiar to those of us who remember the '60s.

Comforted and humiliated by loving e-mails from friends in Northern Ireland, Gaza, Australia, Israel, and New Zealand, I recognize that, of course, I don't e-mail them every time a bomb goes off in their country. How much do I/we collude in the imperial calculus of whose body/whose tragedy/whose land counts more?

And still, a student's husband is gone; neighbor boys are orphaned; children waited at school for parents who never showed up; cars sit idle, still, in commuter parking lots.

We've learned the vulnerability of isolation. Bush and colleagues walked out of the environmental meetings in Kyoto, the racism meetings in South Africa. *Isolated and privileged*, a dangerous combination. The Fantasy of Invulnerability—one more product made in the U.S.A.—in ruins.

Agoraphobia—unfamiliar to me—is a warm buddy.

As in the streets, the air in the academy is getting thin. To raise questions about the horrors of terrorism and U.S. imperialism in the same breath morphs into a betrayal of patriotism, a disregard for those who sacrificed life. Many work to separate grief and critique, as though we can't mourn as we consider critically what the U.S. might have done to contribute to the mass hatred that surrounds.

What counts as dissent has swollen beyond recognition. Censoring spawns mild and bold. Japanese internment, McCarthy, and Vietnam haunt. A timely e-mail from the Black Radical Congress—brilliant and powerful— was passed around with scores of others. This one provoked a protest. Complaints to the Provost, followed by more e-mails about academic freedom. A speak out at City College of New York, followed by nasty newspaper coverage, followed by pressure for us all to rally around America.

The air is getting thinner. Intellectual surveillance constricts narratives and talk. Maybe this is the work of meaning for the radical democratic possibilities of social science. To make sure there is discursive air to breath, to reimagine, to critique, and to construct other stories of what could be.

14.September

The Path train stopped. In a tunnel. No apparent reason. I couldn't breathe. Anxiety replaced my more typical early morning obsessive review of what I must do for the day. "Is there no air on this train?" I am afraid to ask the man who stands so close behind me I can feel his breathing on my neck. Beads of sweat populate my forehead. "Will I faint?" I check out my neighbors, my "self" splitting rapidly into two and then three: "Come on, everyone else is breathing." "In fact, they are *reading*." "Are you *really* reading?" I say nothing.

Back to Michelle-as-hysteric—"Is this an okay way to die? Will it happen fast? What will happen to Sam and Caleb (my sons), David (my partner)? Mom?" I channel surf my selves. I hear a calming voice, "Focus on anything else. Check out the public service announcements: A woman is beaten every 7 minutes. A woman discovers breast cancer every 13 minutes. Sell your eggs for $5,000 and help a loving couple have a child! Women's bodies are everywhere. "You're being hysterical." I reassure (or traumatize) myself.

A sign for Christopher Street—we're through the tunnel.

Interpretive Social Science as Critical Democratic Engagement in Times of Terror

Yvonna and Norman asked us to be useful, to provoke a conversation from the fog about critical interpretive social science. And so from the rumble of my ramblings, I extract a series of questions in the undertow; challenges the mourning after that awaken me to my work, research, teaching, activism, being a mother, and being a daughter.

I must say that writing on our work still feels too fast, like turning our back on the dead or even more recently, a retreat from the terror. I despair when people wrap this tragedy in a package from which we can glean lessons, learn something, generate insight out of trauma.

That said, I worry that a suffocating "consensus" is choking democracy and hope, in some small way that critical social scientists can carve out spaces before the narrative of war freezes solid as the only acceptable position to assert. That is, it seems useful to consider interpretive social science as the blood donations, the Visine contributions, of public intellectuals; a fan dispersing democratic contradictory consciousness; a strategy to keep the oxygen circulating. So, contradicting my disdain for "insight out of trauma" narrative, in the following I write—in pencil—a set of lessons we might gather for interpretive social science as critical democratic engagement.

Lives and Politics; Grief and Analysis

Those of us in New York seem to be having trouble writing, talking, or holding in our minds at the same time thoughts of lives lost, families and communities devastated, and the political and economic relations of terrorism, U.S. politics then and now, racial profiling, and anxious worries about what's coming next. It's not easy for people to talk together or even within ourselves.

My first, tentative lesson. Death, ghosts, orphans, analyses of U.S. imperialism, Middle East politics, and the fears of what's yet to come sit in the same room and need to sit in the same text. That said, tears can't trump analysis, but so too analysis can't evacuate emotion. In fact, the binary of grief and analysis must collapse. Even further, because we challenge what has been U.S. foreign and domestic policy does not release us from the responsibility to critically examine this assault. The intellectual, political, and ethical task of interpretive social science—of living and working ethically on projects of meaning—is to join the contradictory genres of writing and coping, to seek evidence, and to ask *Why and What next* through the streams of tears.

The significance of why. Since September 11, mainstream media have covered—albeit partially—who, what, how, where, and when (at least when "they" attacked, less so when "we" did). The coverage, however, rarely enters the dangerous territory of *why*. Why us, why now, why those buildings, why the mass hatred? Why terrorism, why mass destruction, why this form of international assault?

Lesson 2. Descriptive research, I worry, will no longer do. In our research we are now obliged to interrogate *Why*, assuring that analyses of history and justice are joined; discussions of what "is" are yoked to "what has been" and "what must be." *Why* raises hard questions, negotiated genesis stories, contentious histories. Given the shrinking community of people who are allowed to speak, the scripts for public intellectuals must grow correspondingly bold.

The stretchy capillaries of surveillance surrounding public talk require that intellectuals dare to speak, dare to frame, and dare to analyze critically when so few will—or can. Muslim cab drivers try so hard to convince that they are loyal, good citizens. An Indian shopkeeper has handwritten a sign explaining to potential customers, "Please, we are Indian not Arab." A national hyperbole of patriotism drums out dissent, discourages collective self-reflection. Edward Said (2001) clarified when he wrote, "Peace cannot exist without equality: This is an intellectual value desperately in need of reiteration and reinforcement" (p. 28). French theorist Erika Apfelbaum (2001) wrote on the intellectual's need to hear and to translate—*the dread.*

Lesson 3. We must seek the words of dread and speak them back in ways that interrupt the dominant script. To do so, we may have to turn, more creatively, to talk and bodies that survive beneath dominant ideologies.

Studying Beneath Ideologies

Mik Billig (1995) wrote on Banal Nationalism, the everyday practices by which we in America learn to be patriotic. He argued that these social practices operate just below the surface of consciousness, seeping into mind, body, and soul, slipping under the skin with depth, intimacy, and automaticity:

> Ideology comprises the habits of behavior and belief which combine to make any social world appear to those who inhabit it, as the natural world. Thus, nationalism is the ideology by which the world of nations has come to seem the natural world—as if there could not possibly be a world without nations . . . the banal reproduction of nationalism in established nations depends . . . upon a collective amnesia. . Not only is the past forgotten, as it is ostensibly being recalled, but so there is a parallel forgetting of the present . . . reminders of "flaggings" are so numerous and they are such a familiar part of the social environment that they operate mindlessly, rather than mindfully. (pp. 37-38)

Catherine Lutz (2001) wrote on aggressive ideologies that structure the accepted stories of American history taught in schools and justify the accepted practices of American foreign policy implemented in the name of global peace keeping:

> We have already been in a permanent state of war since the late 1930s. Mainly outsourced to the global south since 1945, this war has now come home to roost. . . . While this long war has sometimes drawn on elevated ideals like antifascism, more often it has been carried on in the name of stability for any regime that would don an anticommunist mantle and allow American business access, hiding a rotten core of systematic terrorism against its own people, often with our weapons and training. Those terrorists were labeled realists and the long reign of nuclear terror by the Soviet Union and the United States—who together took aim at millions of people in skyscrapers and hovels—was called defense, or even peace. Its architects were called men of honor. (p. B14)

Both Billig (1995) and Lutz (2001) help us see the long reach of ideology bleeding into conscious and unconscious thought and talk. You can't be in New York, New Jersey, the United States without hearing personal testimonies wrapped in thickly accepted nationalist discourse. It is as though the nude and shivering terror embodied in the American people steals warmth and comfort from the flag and religion. These ideological robes, however, protect as much as they falsely unify the varied perspectives percolating within the America (un)conscious.

Lesson 4. Critical interpretive social science needs methods and theories that allow us, invite us, force us to crawl under the laminated discourses that refuse complexity and enable us, instead, to reveal the cacophony and dissent (Carney, 2001). Perhaps we can exhibit our most bold and radical democratic presence by refusing the freezing of conversation and imagination, revealing the fractures in the rapidly cementing ideological architecture of the state and the media, prying open the contradictions inside national consciousness, complicating the views of violence while still holding accountable those who have terrorized, and by retelling stories that challenge hegemonic narratives of the "peace" of war (see Kitzinger, 2001; Scott, 1992; Wilkinson, 2000). Recognizing that no one is "uncontaminated," to find material beneath the ideologies, we have to search for complexity, evidence, those who stand alone and peer, more explicitly perhaps, into the messages carried not only in words but in bodies.

The World Splits Open When Girls and Women Speak

For years, so many of us traded e-mails, petitions, and articles about women living under the Taliban suffering massive, intolerable oppression. Yet somehow, even within the leftist feminist community, these devastating accounts were framed, almost dismissed, as a gender issue. Significant but not the same as national oppression. We now know, across research projects, that we can no longer confuse the demographics of who speaks with the *structures and politics of who/what is being spoken about.*

Lesson 5. Girls and women narrate national and global injustices; we live in the tucked away underbelly of dominant talk and often know the lies being told about unity, culture, consensus, and harmony. Not that girls and women are unaffected by or incapable of mouthing the dominant script; only to say that the critique that some girls and women do dare to speak needs to be heard as profound and structural, not as whimper from those in pink (see Smith, 2001).

The Power of Those Who Stand Alone

> With grief horror and anger over the WTC and the Pentagon carnage gripping the nation, the drums of war beat ever faster and louder from the highest office in the land to street corner apostles shouting, "Bomb them back to the Stone Age." Amid this emotional milieu, it takes a lot of political courage to stand up against a precipitous rush toward military vengeance and only one member of Congress found the temerity to do so. That person is the House representative from the Ninth District of California, the Honorable Barbara Lee. (Beal, 2001)

Barbara Lee speaks of the fear of being alone and the power of speaking for so many who wouldn't speak:

> It never dawned on me that I would cast the only vote against this resolution. Many members asked me to change my position. They were friends and they said, "You do not want to be out there alone." I said, "Oh, no don't worry. There will be others." When there weren't I said, "Oh my God." . . . I think that, when I cast that vote, I was speaking for other people in Congress and outside Congress who want a more deliberative approach. (Nation, October 8, 2001, p. 5)

Lesson 6. In critical interpretive social science, using numbers or words, we need to find and foreground those *who speak alone for many.* In statistics, these "cases" are called the "outliers," and in qualitative analyses, these are cases that stand apart from the others. This means we cannot only report those who fall along the slope of the majority of cases; we cannot only document those themes that emerge most frequently.

It is important to understand that majorities and "consensus" don't represent well the bandwidth of popular consciousness. By presenting a social science of consensus, we not only distort variation in the "common sense," but we may consolidate that very frozen, solid group that believes they speak for all. As in looking for the case that dares to stand alone, another site for getting beneath the ideologies, for encountering "counter stories" (Harris & Fine, 2001), may be the body.

The Body as a Carrier of Social Emotion

As we dig through the rubble, searching for words, I am struck by the common reaction in so many different bodies walking the streets of New York: the hollowed, empty eyes, refusing contact, the dark shadows beneath, the sweaty hands and heads, the feverish reading, the dreams. These are data, empirical material, floating through, contained in, and performed by bodies—particularly forbidden emotions, thoughts, and fantasies.

Lesson 7. A critical interpretive social science deserves methods for excavating and collaborating with the body (see Roberts, 2001) as the body creates, suppresses, and performs the material of identity, consciousness, contradictions, politics, and action. I'm not sure how we can do this, although my student, Rosemarie A. Roberts, is beginning to reveal the knowledge located in the micro-moves of Black dance as resistance in motion. I only know that we must. This knowledge may be most concentrated inside the bodies, or the body politics, of historically marginalized communities.

The Knowledge of Global Oppression Inside Historically Marginalized Communities

Patricia Hill Collins (1991) wrote beautifully on the wisdom and critique percolating in persons situated at the bottom of social hierarchies. Building on her theoretical work on standpoint, men and women living on the bottom of the class, race, and ethnic stratifications called America know "more" because they experience, see, care for, anticipate, and have to study those with privilege. These men and women, particularly men and women of poverty and/or of color in the United States, are also profoundly and perversely dependent on the very systems that (try to) cannibalize their bodies and minds. They know too intimately how (and on whom) the "system" operates (Morrison, 1992).

By now, September 25, working-class students, particularly students of color, are the ones who report to me that brothers have "gone away"—to Pakistan? the Gulf? Afghanistan? "They call but can't say where or how they are." Undergraduates in ROTC, high school students in JROTC, are "on deck." Usually poor or working class—White,

African American, immigrant, Latino, Asian—they are typically trying to pay for an education, secure an extra income, support too many people with too little. I find myself in distasteful humor, wondering if now we will have prison reform. Who else are we going to send to fight but the 2,000,000 men and women whom we have locked up in prisons (see Fine et al., 2001)?

Lesson 8. Women and men in historically marginalized communities know in their bones, nightmares, and around the dinner table, the moves of the State.

I worry that if we don't ask why, don't listen to girls and women, don't seek evidence of outrage and imagination in the outliers, in the bodies that reveal pain and courage, in the stories whispered under the fabric of the flag, that in silence and despair . . .

We will watch our students in ROTC disappear, with only tears because we can't imagine that others would also resist;

We will come to accept racial profiling as a necessary evil;

The academy will mutate toward self-censorship, compromised as a site for full freedom of expression;

We will document, and thereby constitute and assure, "consensus";

We will try to "return to normal" and forget that "normal" for us was oppression for most of the globe, and for many in the United States;

We will forget that dissent is at the heart of democracy, and

We will write about the apocalypse rather than organize to resist. . . .

References

Apfelbaum, E. (2001). The dread: An essay on communication across cultural boundaries. *International Journal of Critical Psychology, 4*, 19–34.

Beal, F. (2001). *Barbara Lee speaks for me.* Retrieved September 24, 2001, from PortsideMod database.

Billig, M. (1995). *Banal nationalism.* Thousand Oaks, CA: Sage.

Carney, S. (2001). *Analyzing master-narratives and counter-stories in legal settings: Cases of maternal "failure-to-protect."* Unpublished dissertation proposal, City University of New York.

Collins, P. H. (1991). *Black feminist thought: Knowledge, consciousness, and the politics of empowerment.* New York: Routledge.

Fine, M., Boudin, K., Bowen, I., Clark, J., Hoyton, D., Martinez, M., et al. (2001, in press). Participatory action research: From within and beyond prison bars. In P. Camic, J. Rhodes, & L. Yardley (Eds.), *Qualitative research in psychology: Expanding perspectives in methodology and design.* Washington, DC: APA Publications.

Harris, A., & Fine, M. (Eds.). (2001). Under the covers: Theorizing the politics of counter stories. *International Journal of Critical Psychology, 4*, 183–199.

Kitzinger, C. (2001). Resistance in women's talk: Thinking positively about breast cancer. *International Journal of Critical Psychology, 4*, 35–48.

Lee, Barbara. (2001, October 8). *The Nation,* p. 5.

Lutz, C. (2001, September 28). Our legacy of war. *The Chronicle of Higher Education,* p. B14.

Morrison, T. (1992). *Playing in the dark: Whiteness and the literary imagination.* Cambridge, MA: Harvard University Press.

Roberts, R. A. (2001). *Pedagogy, encounter and critical consciousness in African derived dance.* Unpublished dissertation proposal, City University of New York.

Said, E. (2001, September 17). The public role of writers and intellectuals. *The Nation, 273*(8), 27–33.

Scott, J. (1992). Experience. In J. Butler & J.W. Scott (Eds.), *Feminists theorize the political* (pp. 22–40). New York: Routledge.

Smith, L. T. (2001). The earth splits open: When youth speak in community tribunals. *International Journal of Critical Psychology, 4,* 167–182.

Wilkinson, S. (2000). Women with breast cancer talking causes: Comparing content, biographical and discursive analyses. *Feminism and Psychology, 10,* 431–460.

Michelle Fine is a professor of social psychology, urban education, and women's studies at the Graduate School and University Center, City University of New York.

Grief in an Appalachian Register 10

YVONNA S. LINCOLN

OR TWO WEEKS NOW, WE have watched the staggering outpouring of grief, shock, and horror as a nation struggles to come to terms with the attacks on the World Trade Center towers and the Pentagon. We have seen a courageous widow sit quietly as a president, addressing the nation, pointed her out for her husband's solemn decision to retake a plane rather than have thousands more die. We do not know where that plane was bound when the terrorists rerouted it. We can guess that it was an equally grisly target, destined to maximize the loss of unsuspecting civilian life. We have all seen the faces of boneweary firemen and policemen as well as rescue workers as they struggled with a mountain of unyielding debris in the fading hope of finding someone, anyone, whom they might rescue and whose rescue would have made the staggering effort worthwhile. And indeed, some were rescued. But we have also had to come to terms that many will not only not be rescued but will simply never be found—crushed to small pieces beneath the weight of steel and hatred. We have seen torrents of tears as survivors, family members, and others who joined with them across the country shared their sorrow and the inconceivability of this senseless set of attacks.

And I too have sat numb with shock, glued to the television screen, struggling with the incomprehensibility of these acts, overwhelmed by the bewildering worldview that could have led people to commit such atrocities. But I have been numb for another reason, and it will be important to see my reasons as another part of the phenomenon that has struck so deeply at the heart and soul of the United States. I sat numb because my reactions to grief are always usually private. They are always delayed.

My people—my family (of English and Dutch and Scottish stock)—now live in urban areas of the South. But they were born and raised, as were their parents before them, in the southern Appalachian Mountains. My mother's people came over before the Civil War, in which the men of age fought. My father's people came over with Oglethorpe and were said to be good horse thieves. My mother's people settled in the foothills of the Georgia Appalachians and eventually came to rest between Rabun Gap, Toccoa, and

Lincolnton. My father's people took to the mountains north and west of Florence, South Carolina, but eventually moved near Waycross, where they pieced together a small, hardscrabble, red-clay, subsistence freehold sold only when my father died and when my great-aunt, who lived on and worked the place into her 90s, died also. But none of them were originally red dirt farmers. They were mountain people.

Mountain people are often the same everywhere. Perhaps it is the very close feeling one gets in the mountains. Perhaps it is the inability to see either the sunrise or the sunset, depending on which side of the mountain you settle on. Maybe it has to do with how problematic it is to get in and get out, especially in the spring and fall when streams and creek beds rise up and devour dirt roads. Perhaps it is the loneliness of those towering pines that eventually settles into the skin and bones so that a person finds it easier to talk to the trees, to the squirrels, to the bobwhites and partridges than to other humans.

Whatever it is, eventually the whole genetic structure changes, and the silence gets bred in the bones. I am never more at home than when driving home on some two-lane byway through the loblolly and slash pine. When I drive alone, I often sing all the old mountain songs my grandmother used to sing when she played her dulcimer. Sometimes, I forget the words. But the feeling is there, and I can hear her voice still.

[*And she was a typical mountain woman: mean, tough, like Poke Salat Annie, a "straight-razor totin' woman."*]

Mountain people are clanny. They are closed to outsiders. They are warm and free with kith and kin but withdrawn and silent and wary with strangers. They keep their emotions to themselves, especially those of a most private nature. Grief is one of those private emotions. Love and caring are others. Grief belongs back at the homestead, not in the public arena of church or town.

[*At family funerals, my mother would grasp my wrist in that handcuff fashion my parents used to keep small children with them and say, "Shush. We don't cry here. You can cry later. Don't let these people*]

These people? Members of our church? Family friends? Neighbors?

[*. . . see you cry!" My mother sat through funerals stoic and silent. My father, clearly grieved but bred not to show emotion in public*]

Which carried, finally, over into not being able to show emotion at all.

[*. . . would sit on the pew, unmindful of anyone, lost in his silent grief, and sometimes shake his head imperceptibly from right to left, as though he were trying to comprehend the mysteries of death. I watch him, the elegant, aristocratic profile chiseled into stoic emotional control which must have cost him dearly, from a slight turn of my head and a sharp cast of eye. When he catches me, he comes to himself and whispers, "Listen to the minister! Turn your face forward," and I obey.*

The ceremony at the cemetery is worse, for now we are standing. My parents and all our kin stand with their long legs slightly apart, staring off into the distance.]

It is only many years later that I realize this is to keep their bodies from swaying as they watch the casket lowered into the ground. To steady themselves much as servicemen move into the "at ease" position.

Over the years, we have lost them all: grandparents, beloved uncle, crabby uncle who always seemed to have silver dollars for us on birthdays, beautiful aunts, competent and cheerful great-aunts and uncles, and with them, the fall butchering, the women cleaning intestines and stuffing sausage, the peach cobbler bubbling over an open-hearth fire—with peaches from the trees in the chicken run—my father's stand of popcorn and his Morgans and matched mules and buckboards, and the surrey, and the hand-sheller for the popcorn, and everyone's barns, the fireplaces and dogtrots, the family reunions, the smokehouses with great salty hams, the tobacco curing sheds, the hateful cows kept in the closest pasture for milk for the children and cooking, the cool draw wells, the tidy and clean farmhouses, the warm smell of hay and horses, and most of all, swapping lies—the great, long, rainy afternoons with Great Uncle Pat whittling and the men trying to outdo each other with tales more fanciful than the last, and each sworn to be the "God's own truth."

But never a tear.

I am certain that there was much reason for tears. Neither my mother's family nor my father's were ever rich. And there were stories, late at night, about the hard, mean years of the Depression when there were cows to sell but no buyers and corn but no one could afford to get it to market. When my father, who hated killing deer, would hunt to have meat for his family.

[*My father taught me to shoot. He never, ever hunted with a rifle or shotgun. He thought it "un-sporting." My father hunted all his life with a Colt .22 automatic pistol ("Count your ammo, Sister. Eight bullets in the clip, one in the barrel. Count every time you fire, Girl. Don't lose track of where you stand with bullets. You never know when you'll need to know."), a gun I cherish now—even though I never shoot with it—and occasionally take out just to handle and remember our days down at the pistol range. I was 6 the first time I picked up this gun, 25 when we last went target shooting together.*]

Somehow, these people saved grief for another time, for some time in the future. The end result, I have come to realize, is a human being who lives with his or her grief for all their days. The future, like tears, never comes. The griefs, which should have been shucked, come to live permanently in the hearts and on the faces of those mountain folk. Over time, all but the most relentlessly cheerful fall into a great yawning silence, brought on by old griefs and the uncontrollably aching heart.

These are the people who have not come to terms with the events of September 11. They are not necessarily Appalachian, but their responses are the same. Trained to refrain from public displays of emotion, their sorrowing comes later. Privately. In the long morning shower. In a moment of some other disappointment or secret vulnerability. In the afternoon of having found oneself alone. Over a cooking pot or some gardening project. This kind of grief cannot accept the release of sharing, of communal mourning. Born to the flinty rectitude of public restraint, this kind of anguish breeds a solitary melancholy loosened only in isolated and clandestine bursts.

As the nation returns to its common lives, we should be remembering those who could not afford the lapse into public tears. Some of us will only begin to deal with this much later, our reactions delayed, withheld, cloistered from public eyes, perhaps even from ourselves. A second wave of grieving will come from those who could not afford the tears in a time of crisis. Many Americans will confront their grief and move to reengage their lives. Others, however, will have delayed reactions—private grief, eked out over days, months, years. For them, the long national keening of shock and sadness and disbelief, the consolation of loss shared, will have moved on, and once again, they will face sorrow alone. We ought to remember that lamenting goes on long after the television cameras have left and the world has returned to the work of rebuilding.

[*If you picked at him, my father would have talked about this tragedy*] But he did not, thankfully, live to see it . . .

[. . . *only in distant retrospect, some years later, when he could describe the emotions without emotion, as though he witnessed them in another man. My mother is already saying, "It is sad, I know. But life goes on." I wait for the hideous enormity to break across me. I am my parents' child. The mountains are in my bones.*]

Yvonna S. Lincoln is Ruth Harrington Chair of Educational Leadership and University Distinguished Professor of Higher Education at Texas A & M University.

Listening to the Heartbeat of New York 11
Writings on the Wall

JOANNE ROBERTSON

Introduction

Strong Spirits Never Break

I T IS UNUSUALLY WARM THAT FIRST day of the semester, September 9, 2001. As I drive west on Canal Street, I think about the ways I might introduce the course to my university students.[1] I want to familiarize them with qualitative and quantitative research methodologies, and encourage them to critically view data that minimizes the complexity of literacy and learning. Student empowerment is essential, for it will assist my students to re-envision their role in this inquiry process. The morning session is productive, and we leave class feeling optimistic about co-constructing new understandings together. None of us, however, can foresee that two days later our worlds will be irrevocably changed; for, a mere ten blocks from our campus, the World Trade Center will lay in smoldering ruins.

I Pray

As we try to make sense of a senseless act, we become a new community of learners, transformed through the discourses that permeate, influence, and redefine our conversations. We expand our notions about the types and uses of literacy,[2] chronicle what new literacy practices[3] evolve over the next eight weeks, and form understandings about the ways people use reading and writing to support and sustain one another.

> "America is a good cahte ."
> "God Bless amrica"
> "Dear New York I hope you feel be t ter. Big kiss."
> (kindergartners' writing on red construction paper hearts)

Shadings and Hues

The shape, texture, and form of an ethnographic portrait "takes on the shadings and hues of our own palette" (Sullivan, 1996). Attitudes and belief systems determine the ways we re-present[4] the realities of others. My interpretations of the "writings" are solidly grounded in sociocultural theories of literacy and learning. In accordance with this view of discursive and textual practices, community and family literacies are multiply and uniquely configured by the contexts in which they occur. Literacy practices can neither be decontextualized nor studied autonomously. Language processes are both social and communicative in nature, and are embedded within social, political, and historical contexts.

Denzin (1998) states, "The Other who is presented in the text is always a version of the researcher's self." Krieger (1991) adds, "images of 'them' are images of 'us.'" Indeed, this is the case, for my rendering of the events and shared experiences of 9/11 is value-laden and culturally mediated. I make no claims to objectivity; I am a New Yorker and a member of the community I describe in this narrative. Therefore, in order to make apparent the ways in which I frame, layer, and encapsulate this moment in time, I must make apparent my emic perspective, conceptual framework, and emotive stance in relationship to the events of 9/11.[5]

And yet—Look at all this *LIFE*.

Constructivism and transactional theory are foundational to my understandings of language processing, as are my ideas about "interpretive interactionism" (Denzin, 1998). Rosenblatt's (1978) notions about the transaction between "the reader, the text, and the poem," Dewey and Bentley's (1949) writings about the "knower, knowing, known," and Peirce's theory of "sign, object, and interpretant,"[6] reaffirm my belief that meaning making or understanding results from the interaction and transaction of separate but unified components that mutually condition, constitute, and transform one another in the construction of new knowledge. With this theoretical understanding, I watch the landscape of Lower Manhattan transfigure itself each week, as more and more people strive to bear witness to 9/11. I expect to be transformed through my interactions with my students, the literacy events and artifacts, and the research context. Yet, I will not understand the depth of this transformation or "ephiphany" (Denzin, 1998) until several months later.

We will not be defeated! Our thoughts and prayers are with you.

Literacy to Bear Witness

As the weeks pass, it appears that no freestanding wall space or structure is devoid of signage, text, or artwork. These texts become the objects of analysis, as they represent a defining moment in time; a writing culture is evolving. Solitary, yet communal, the writings on the walls speak to shared values, attitudes, philosophical beliefs, and spiritual issues, as well as man's role in the universe.

Even heroes cry.

Photo taken by a rescue worker at the site.

From the ashes we will rise and become even stronger.

Tell Your Story to the World

Language has long been considered to be a human birthright. Whether mankind is "hard-wired"[7] for this process is debatable. However, the need to communicate symbolically appears to be deeply ingrained in the human psyche.[8] Perhaps this can explain why scribbled messages on post-it notes and index cards, handwritten letters on bits of stationery or notepaper, commercial and homemade greeting cards, drawings from children, yellow ribbons, slogans written boldly in capital letters, pictures and descriptions of loved ones placed in makeshift memorials, and prayers in many languages begin to cover every inch of the exterior wall space of the University's Varrick Street Campus. Someone has carefully covered all of these texts with sturdy, transparent plastic sheets, duck-taped securely into place. These messages snake around the corner and make their way up Canal Street, to a temporary shelter and restaurant for firefighters and police officers.[9] Layer upon layer of message boards are stacked there, and replenished as countless passersby stop to add their thoughts. The common denominator appears to be a need to transcribe their feelings into writing.

America = Unity
Unity = Life

Look teacher, the birds are on fire!

A week after classes resume, I receive an e-mail from a colleague requesting books for Shelly Harwayne's children. In the note, she quotes Harwayne, who is the superintendent of School District 2 in Lower Manhattan. Four of her eight schools were evacuated on 9/11. Shelly describes the lasting impressions of that day, as her teachers valiantly usher every child to safety. Thick black smoke, ankle deep soot, and blaring sirens do not deter them from their responsibilities. As I read the e-mail, I am in awe of their courage, dedication, and selflessness.[10] Not one teacher leaves a child unattended, or puts personal safety above the needs of the school community.

Shelly relates that as one primary teacher is evacuating her class, she instructs everyone to hold hands, to not be afraid, and to keep moving forward. However, one student glances upward and exclaims, "Look teacher, the birds are on fire!" The child is referring to the people who either fell or jumped to their deaths from the World Trade Towers. I can only imagine the horror of that moment for both the teacher and her class.

This story, however, makes me realize that in so many ways my students' "birds are on fire" as well. They are so fragile, many have lost close friends and family members; they are so young, most in their early twenties. Their world is splitting at the seams, as are their students' worlds. I want to usher them to a safe place where they will not be touched or harmed. Once there, I can help them be strong for their children, as I need to be strong for them. This is the impetus for the ethnography of communication project I envision. I hope that through reading, writing, and dialoguing about the "writings," I can create and bring us to that space.

My students reading the "writings" by Nemo's on Canal Street.

A Cloud over the City

We venture forth on our first field trip; the air is acrid and our eyes begin to tear. The cloud over the city is both literal and figurative. I notice how my students stay close to me as we walk down Varrick Street. Not everyone opts to join our small band of ethnographers, stating they're just "not ready"; I respect their right to decline my invitation. Later, some recant and join us as we make our way to Nemo's. I reassure them that it will be all right. I chat briefly with a police officer; he tells me the area has become a "Dead Zone." As I jot down his words, I wonder if I am making the right decisions for my students. I feel dizzy; the context seems alien and surreal. We find ourselves drawn to the "writings," experiencing a sense of kinship to those who have left them behind. Who are the people who have stopped to jot down a quick phrase or word of encouragement? Have they lost someone?

> We believe in life. We are living for life. They're preparing for death and sacrifice. They're reading the Koran in two ways.

What can I learn from the authentic texts produced in response to this tragedy? Such strong emotions pour forth from their writings. The heartbeat of their words resounds strongly, albeit a broken heart, but optimism and renewal are represented in their scribings. It is evident that a desire to be part of this writing culture is gaining momentum, as is a need to use writing to memorialize the shared experience of this tragic event. My student writes in her reflective paper, "When I walked outside I felt desolate. Sadness pervaded the air. The once bustling area was quiet and subdued. I felt like an outsider peeking into a world that has been mortally wounded. The notes posted all over reflected this sadness, yet within the sadness was hope and strength. When we are stripped of our complacency, we see that we are all essentially good. People are good, strong, and hopeful."

I am reminded of Richardson's (1998) "crystal" analogy, to describe the interpretative or "crystallization" process by which researchers analyze qualitative data. The ethnographer, like a crystal or prism, "reflects externalities and refracts within themselves" (p. 359), dependent upon their angle of repose. My student perceives people as "good, strong, and hopeful." I am not so sure. We each "transact"[11] in our own ways to the writings on the walls. The quotes we select to copy are different, as we make personal connections to the words and our worlds. Later in class, we combine our multiple perspectives to achieve macro-understandings about this literacy event, the intersection of public and private lives, and the opportunities this knowledge provides for critical praxis.

Hate the enemy—the enemy is hate.

The Function and Purpose of the Writings

Photography becomes an ethnographic tool to further scrutinize the context of the writings. As we "transact" and make our own associations, we begin to notice that the messages embedded within these texts infinitely surpass the immediacy of the moment. The words mean far more than they denote; multiple languages, cultures, and realities seem to speak collectively. For me, this strong, coherent, living, and breathing voice rises powerfully towards the sky like a shimmering skyscraper. It becomes the inspiration for my class discussions about literacy, learning, and life. We begin to identify the purposeful ways in which New Yorkers use language to convey their innermost thoughts and sentiments. The writings on the wall become our touchstone to explain the ways in which people use stories to define their experiences and to name their worlds. It becomes our task to gather the individual threads of each story to weave the larger tale. We learn about the ways we project our own identities into this process.

My name is Marc and my friend Joey worked on the 105th floor of No 1 WTC. After 9/11, I put his "missing" flyer all over the streets of this changed city, choosing spots as if I were painting graffiti, looking for the best light, the easiest places to see my friend's face.

At 26th St & Lex, next to the Armory, strangers were nice to me saying, "I hope you find your friend." I just thanked them & kept looking for more places where Joey's smile would catch people's eyes. It felt good to be doing something, not just sitting and mourning.[12]

Photo by Laura Hanney.

My student writes in her journal, "Reading the writing from the WTC makes you 'see' the stories. Individuals come to life even though you have never met them. Each word takes on such weight and importance you can't help but get emotional. The writing and reading has been a healing process. Listening to eulogies (the power of 'story-telling') at memorials has given life to lives that are lost." A second student writes, "There were many different languages though it seemed as if it were one voice." Others students' comments about "one voice" reflect what Fine (2000) describes as "the hyphen at which Self-Other join in the politics of everyday life, that is, the hyphen that both separates and merges personal identities with our inventions of others" (p. 70). Fine encourages qualitative researchers to "work this hyphen." My early writing about 9/11, however, is distinguished by a "thin signature" (Clandinin and Connelly, 1998). I deliberately distance myself from the analysis so as to give prominence to the writings. In doing so, I silence my own voice.

Street (2002) describes critical reflexivity as a way for researchers to "take hold of knowledge" and make their "claim on how things are patterned."[13] Framing, he states, is always "problematic." For frames shift, overlap, and sometimes merge. Cultural boundaries are not fixed, and are best marked with "dotted lines." Street asserts that writing is at best a "rhetorical activity" or "conduit" to present a heuristic for looking at the world in a particular way. "Put it up," Street says about cognitive grids, "then shoot it down. Take hold of the knowledge." It is with this mindset that I suggest the following "ways with words"[14] and notion of "spaces,"[15] as a conduit to re-present the significance of the "writings." I am fully aware that my own sensibilities are intertwined, connected, and sustained by this representation.

Ways of Seeing—Spaces to Think

My graduate student tells me, "Writing for me during this time of tragedy is very comforting and plays a role as a stress reliever. I have experienced the loss of a very close friend on that day, Sept. 11, 2001. I was able to express many of my emotions by writing in my journal. I also found it comforting to send personalized e-greetings to many of my friends."

I feel so SAD. There's an emptiness in my soul. WE WILL SURVIVE—THANK YOU ALL FOR HELPING.

Only within the historical and social context of Downtown Manhattan can the function and purpose of the writings be explored, for so many individual pieces seem communally linked in theme and intent. Many of the notes reflect people's desires to gain clarity or to make sense of the tragedy. The walls become places where both readers and writers take time to think, construct new understandings, and share their thoughts by posting a message.

One of my students, a young policewoman, tells me about the children's notes that are taped to the walls of her station house. "We're always reading the children's letters, they warm up the place and make us laugh. You need that, you know." She giggles nervously. I notice that she has lost weight and is very pale. She tells me she isn't sleeping well. "A lot has been going on," she explains, but adds that she is not at liberty to tell me more. I have empathy for her predicament. I too experience hyper-vigilance, am eating less, and seem to find the nights interminably longer. Every evening I listen to the fighter jets patrol the skies above our Long Island home. I try to block out the noise by leaving the TV on, but invariably more scenes and commentary about 9/11 arouse me from my sleep. I am living in a war zone. There appears to be no respite from the continual bombardment of my senses, and I crave the space I define for myself in this piece. I write and rewrite sections of my field notes, make graphic organizers, and piece together data on conceptual maps. I am desperate to make sense of it all. The initial drafting process supports my transitions as I concretize my thinking and resolve inner conflicts.

> Dear NYC
>
> I was born here. I grew up here. I moved to Chicago but you always remained a part of me and now I know why – this is still the most special place on earth. I am so proud of you for taking care of each other, and getting through with style. I miss you and love you more than ever.
>
> From J

Another one of my students describes her feelings and transactions. "So much has changed for all of us in light of the events of September 11th, not only emotionally but also in how I view many aspects of life. I have always known how important literacy is to the world, but in taking this class during such a traumatic time in history, I can see literacy in a whole new light. While so many people posted their thoughts and feelings on the wall for all to read, I couldn't find the right words for myself to post. Instead, I felt more comfortable in reading others' words and connecting to complete strangers who were feeling similar emotions to myself." I relate to her comments, for when I am offered a paper and pen from a volunteer, I decline to post a note. Instead, I rummage through my purse for a donation. I seem to have no language for the events of 9/11.

Ways of Acting—Spaces to Reclaim Territory

Feelings of vulnerability and fear are freely acknowledged; however, sentiments of renewal, territorialism, and optimism are equally reflected in the ways people posted their thoughts. "It's like they're tagging!" my student exclaims in class. We talk about issues of power and control, and decide that the writings might mirror people's desire to reclaim lost territory. We talk about the permanence of the written word, and its role as testament in a time of impermanence. We marvel at the ways in which people attempt to clothe the barren and sooty walls of New York with language that is fertile with images. One student brings in a picture taken by a firefighter beneath the ravaged Trade Towers.

We compare this still life to photographs we've seen of interior sections of the submerged *Titanic*. Time has stopped in this photo. We note the ways New Yorkers have etched more writing into the soot covered storefront signage. These writings, including gang logos, are further testament to the ways New Yorkers declared their "territorial rights."

The spirit of the World Trade Center is giving us the energy to rebuild this great city. Thank you!

The postings reflect both personal and shared ownership of ideals and emotions. It is a space where past and present intersect. These writings become the touchstone for defining the worldviews and literacy practices of New Yorkers. In this process, we redefine ourselves.

Tough Times
Never LAST
Tough People
DO

Ways of Visiting—Spaces That Give Life to Lives That Were Lost

Certain locations become grieving sites known as "walls of prayer," that is, where family members post flyers with pictures and descriptions of loved ones for rescue workers to review. As was the case with other writings, many were meticulously wrapped in plastic overlays to protect them from the elements.[16] Firefighters, police officers, and passersby visit and spend time reviewing these flyers every day.

Greg—You live in your children's eyes.

The photographs and accompanying messages are the most difficult for the class and myself to process and understand. There are so many pictures of young people, faces beaming with vitality and optimism, beckoning to us from the walls. A reciprocal dialogue evolved; this is too close to home, this could be my son, my daughter, my husband, my father, my friend. For some of my students, this is indeed the case.

Every time I have Irish money I'll think of you.

Denzin (2001) speaks of the way an ethnographer might "embed the self in stories of histories, of sacred places." My students help me to understand how I am moving "outward and backward" as Denzin writes, experiencing, internalizing, and transforming my thoughts through introspection and conversations with my students and the texts of 9/11. I realize that my main purpose for writing is to give this piece life. For, it represents the transactions of multiple shared realities, and has become an entity in its own right.

Ways of Knowing—Spaces to Identify What It Means to Be "American"

It's no(t)w our war!

Another student writes, "The field trip made me proud to be an American because the writings showed us how we as a people really pulled together. Literacy is very powerful." Indeed, the writings seem to convey in one pluralistic voice, this is who we are and what we see ourselves becoming. Resolve and determination are repeatedly expressed, as the writers' stories are transformed through their telling and our reading of their texts.

America—"Like A Rock"

A second student writes, "I found the quotes to be very moving and powerful. They helped me to feel safe, to know that I was not alone with my feelings. Many people share the same fears and concerns. It is what joins us together as a people and as Americans."

LOOK! You've only caused us to unite.
Our country is now stronger than ever.

Agar (1994) writes, "Words aren't just things you memorize whose meanings fit neatly into a dictionary. Words go well beyond that. They channel you into a way of seeing, of thinking, of acting. Words are the surface of culture" (p. 79).[17] He terms this notion "languaculture"; that is, the necessary tie between language and culture.[18] Agar helps me understand the way I frame the "writings" beyond the narrow parameters of the printed text, to the individual, social, ideological, and historical functions they serve. Behavior and thinking are always embedded within relationships of power.

Furthermore, as Anderson and MacCurdy (2000) state in *Writing and Healing: Toward an Informed Practice*, "As we manipulate the words on the page, as we articulate to ourselves and to others the emotional truth of our pasts, we become agents in our own healing, and if those to whom we write receive what we have to say and respond to it as we write and rewrite we create a community that can accept, contest, gloss, inform, invent, and help us discover, deepen, and change who we have become as a consequence of the trauma we have experienced" (p. 7).

No one takes away the spirit and courage of NY & the USA

Flags may change, but we all wear the common flag of humanity. This was a blow against this humanity, and so we all must show our patriotism as *humans*, as *beings*, as existing entities.

Spiritual and Philosophical Ways—Spaces for Introspection

I begin to realize that making visible what I consider to be extraordinary is complicated. The modes of representation produced in response to 9/11 are multiple and constantly evolving. Writing on the wall is now a socially valued practice in Lower Manhattan. However, my attempts to describe the reasons for these literacy practices are at best snapshots of a phenomenon in motion. The spaces I define seem inadequate, as I reclarify and extend my original understandings through dialogue and interactions with others. The photographs now take on an inter-animated quality, as the students and I speculate about their significance. My documentation of this unprecedented event is a highly subjective process. I seem to highlight patriotic and spiritual aspects, as well as children's unique transactions to the events of 9/11.

Senseless, BUT NOT IN VAIN. We love you all. God Bless!

Wisdom first—force later.

Dios lo bendiga a todos y lede el descanso externo y perdon a los terroriste que no sabia lo que hacia en la tierra todo rezemes par ustedes.

[God bless you everyone and give you rest and forgive the terrorists that did not know what they did to our land and we pray for you.]

The writings appear to be a conduit for expressing closure and optimism about the future. In many drawings, angels or just their wings (as in the photograph below) are depicted. Children draw multicolored, lively angels with smiling faces and expansive golden

haloes, sailing above the Trade Center or walking on the sidewalk in front of them. What a shame that as we grow older we no longer see these angels. The prayers and blessings offered by New Yorkers of all ages reflect sentiments of transcendence.

> May you all live life. Whether on Earth or Some Where else . . . All are in my Heart & soul . . . My love to all who Died & lived through this all . . . We will fight & we will win in your honor.

> Love. All my prayers go out to [picture of a heart] those who lost their loved ones. We will always remember their love, and we must continue to love so that no one else on [picture of a heart] this earth should lose a [picture of a heart] child, a parent, or wife or husband in this tragedy of people killing people.

Standardized and Sanitized Ways of Teaching Children to Write

We miss you and even if we don't know you we miss you.
(sixth grader)

A student notes, "This class made me think about literacy in a different way. I have become more aware of how people use forms of literacy to express themselves." Another writes, "I also found that I started noticing things that were happening in my school, that were not effective in teaching literacy." A third reflects, "I have become more aware of how people use forms of literacy to express themselves." A fourth writes, "We learned a great deal about our vulnerability and feelings."

> Dear Rescue Workers,
> I hope that you find more people! Every night I pray for the people who got hart and that you find more people. *God Bless America *
> Love,
> Meghan
> (first grader)

We problematize how writing and reading instruction are federally mandated at the state level, and how our understandings of literacy factor into this agenda. We question state assessments that stress writing formulas. We critique a mechanistic view of the writing process, focusing solely upon syntax and grammar. We review the purposeful ways New Yorkers moved beyond the sentence level of writing, to voice personal and social sentiments to a universal audience. Within this theoretical framework, we discuss the ways "schooled literacies"[19] are disconnected from the authentic literacies of our students' worlds. We question the belief systems that drive current instructional reform movements. We begin to engage in critical literacies, as we question curriculum and "high stakes" tests that ignore students' cultures, identities, interests, and questions. We find no easy answers to our questions. We start to conceptualize ways to prepare students to master statewide writing exams, while staying faithful to our notions about the nature of reading and writing, the role of motivation, voice, and purpose in the process, and the validity of assessments that are decontextualized from real world literacies.

Dear Rescue Workers,
   Hi. I am a third grade student at P.S. 102 in Elmhurst Queens. You are doing a wonderful job keep on working. I think you are nice trying to save our world. I am proud of you when the Twin tower broke and you saved many people. Try to find more people. Do not give up saving people. Thank you for saving people.
   Your
   Friend,
   Warren

   Wood Ray (2001) speaks about the need for students to develop writing identities and understandings of the conventions that enable them to effectively communicate to a global audience. However, she cautions, "We need to be careful not to lose sight of why understandings about language conventions are important. They serve a specific purpose—they aren't ends in themselves. If students aren't finding audiences who are important to write for, then we've got no business teaching them the 'skills' writers use to prepare writing to go into the world. If our students aren't learning to write with style, voice and focus and a strong sense of craft, what difference does it make if their subjects and verbs agree and everything is spelled correctly? Who would want to read it?" (p. 39)

   God Bless You! Thank you for working so hard to save the people. Do you think they will build new twin towers? I think we should build smaller ones. (third grader)

   I'm not scared because you rescue workers protect everyone. (second grader)

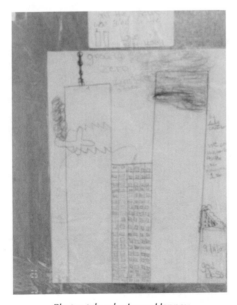

Photos taken by Laura Hanney.

Teaching Critical Literacies

My student writes, "We connected the September 11th events with literacy and the need for humans to communicate. Literacy goes far beyond just learning how to read!" Comber (2001) defines critical literacy as "people using language to exercise power, to enhance everyday life in schools and communities, and to question practices of privilege and injustice" (p. 1). Critical literacies, Comber continues, involve "an ongoing analysis of textual practices." Comber's comments enable me to suggest ways my teachers might guide their children to acquire and develop these literacies, and to help them take critical stances about how texts work, who produces them, and under what circumstances readers connect to them.

I share a draft of this article with another class, and as a result of our conversations about making time for children to share their stories in order to make sense of their worlds, one of the teachers provides time for her third graders to write and draw.[20] One child begins her " I Do Not Understand" poem very differently from its ending.

> I do not understand why the Mets didn't make the playoffs this year.
> I do not understand why schools aren't closed on Halloween.
> I do not understand why third graders have to take four city tests.
> I do not understand why Mrs. Suraci gives a lot of homework.
> But most of all, I do not understand why the Twin Towers are not standing tall and pretty anymore.
> I do understand that Mayor Guiliani is working hard to rebuild our city since the tragedy on September, 11, 2001.

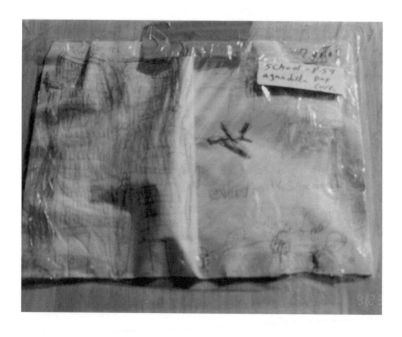

In similar fashion, I make time for my students to reflect upon their semester's work, one writes in her final paper, "Losing one of my best friends has changed/shaped my life forever. Talking about HOPE I don't see that right now I only see SADNESS! I had to make the flyer for Jenn so I see that side of how people let their emotions out! At the time of the flyers I put my heart to the side and let my mind take over. To write MISSING was the hardest part and to describe her. But I feel the worst part is seeing her constantly around the neighborhood with MISSING on top—Is this my friend, are these my words—Is this real?"

All Gave Some,
Some Gave All.
For Engine Company 4

Implications for Critical Praxis

I realize that at every level of academia, teachers need to acknowledge and validate what students bring with them to the classroom and to their literacy tasks. Variation is not an abnormality. Culture is not a deficit. Family histories and national tragedies become part of the curriculum, as diverse communities of learners come together to construct, negotiate, and reconstruct their understandings. Too often, "healing" stories are marginalized in traditional school settings, as more formal ways of reading, writing, and testing are privileged. In doing so, students' voices and lives are silenced. We must reconsider this stance, and reinvent reading and writing programs that allow for the ebb and flow of life, literacy, and learning. This type of literacy curriculum enables teachers to feel the pulse of their students' words and worlds, which facilitates communication, understanding, and learning.

Do not give up trying to save people. (third grader)

Continuing Conversations

The writings of 9/11 continue to evolve, as letters, poems, and iconography on the Internet become yet another way for people to use reading and writing to communicate thoughts and emotions.

A candle loses nothing by lighting another candle.*

∧
( )   This candle was lit on the 11th of September, 2001.
_   Please pass it on to your friends & family so that it
[ ]   may shine all across America.
[ ]
[ ]
[ ]
[ ]
_

---

*The icon and message received from an anonymous sender, America Online, December 4, 2001.

However, the true "touchstone" of the ways writing is used to express support, strength, and courage comes in the form of a 12-by-18-foot American flag donated to the Police Department two weeks after the tragedy. It proudly draped the ravaged skeleton of 2 World Financial Center, until it was necessary to sheathe the buildings with protective netting. The flag, however, is destined for another noble purpose.

> To all the boys, Heaven has one hell of a team.
> Message inscribed on the flag by police officer Glenn O'Donnell

Chen writes in the *New York Times*, "No one is exactly sure how the flag started, or who wrote what first. . . . But once someone scribbled a tribute to the New York City police officers who died on Sept. 11 . . . it was hard to stop. On the red stripes, friends, relatives and colleagues etched personal correspondence. . . . On the white, they offered sentiments such as 'God Bless America,' and defiant pledges such as 'We didn't ask for this fight but we will finish it now.' . . . On the starry field of blue, they spelled out the names of the deceased, one per star, in boldface letters."[21]

> For my sons . . . Joe and John Vigiano. They gave their lives doing what they loved —helping others. God bless them and all their 'brothers.'
> An unsigned note by the parent of Police Detective Joseph Vigiano, 34, and Firefighter John T. Vigiano II, 36.[22]

Chen writes, "As news of the flag spread, some people drove 20 or 30 miles out of their way to sign it. . . . Eventually it became so popular that the area was roped off for crowd control." With the well wishes of the New York City Police Department and the assistance of the United States Marine Corps, the flag is shipped to the 26th Marine Expeditionary Unit in Afghanistan. It now flies over the Kandahar Airport. The director of the Marine Corps public affairs office states, "It's going to bring closure to a lot of people who wrote on the flag. That in itself is poetic; it's going to come full circle."[23]

> We will not be intimidated. We will be strong in love.

Writing History or Writing Ideologies?

In conclusion, there can never be one authentic, verifiable version of any historical event. Each writer brings ideologies, biases, memories, and "heartbeats" to bear upon the process of re-presenting reality. Furthermore, these constructs are never inert, but continually reconstructed and redefined through dialogue and interactions with others. Every story is an unfinished story, for the author is unfinished. It is nearly six months later, and I find myself crying as I rewrite, "Look teacher, the birds are on fire!" Unfinished history. I think of the voices I have purposefully excluded from the narrative. My "angle of repose" (Richardson, 1998) in relationship to the events of 9/11 influences the way I structure and craft the writing. My student makes this point: "The writings on the walls cannot be extrapolated from who and what I know. I know my heart breaks with words of despair; people longing for those who will never be held again; those who want war or want to recreate peace. I cannot separate the past reactions to devastation with these. . . . My God," she continues, "we must look at things as inextricably bound by history, by hearts. We must look to see what this representation means. Do we know of others' pain in other lands? Do they have these words on the wall? Did we care before it was 'no(t)w our war'? Yes, there is hope abounding out there on the walls. But, for me, it is about what is not being said—or hasn't been reflected upon before." Unfinished history.

Bibliography

Agar, M. (1994). *Language shock: Understanding the culture of conversation.* New York: William Morrow and Company, Inc.

Anderson, C. M. & MacCurdy, M. M. (2000). *Writing & healing: Towards an informed practice.* Urbana, IL: National Council of Teachers of English.

Bahktin, M. M. (1986). *Speech genres and other late essays.* Austin: University of Texas.

Barton, D. & Hamilton, M. (1998). *Local literacies: Reading and writing in one community.* New York: Routledge.

Chen, D. W. (November 26, 2001). "Flag to carry sentiments from Ground Zero to Afghanistan," B1 and B6, *New York Times.*

Chomsky, N. (1965). *Aspects of a theory of syntax.* Cambridge, MA: MIT Press.

Clandinin, D. J. & Connelly, F. M. (1998). Personal experience methods. In N. K. Denzin & Y. S. Lincoln (eds.). *Collecting and interpreting qualitative materials.* (pp. 150–178). Thousand Oaks, CA: Sage.

Comber, B. (2001). Negotiating critical literacies. *School talk,* 6 (3), 1–2.

Denzin, N. K. (1998). The art and politics of interpretation. In N. K. Denzin & Y. S. Lincoln (eds.) *Collecting and interpreting qualitative materials* (pp. 313–344). Thousand Oaks, CA: Sage.

———. (2001). Two-stepping in the '90s. *Qualitative inquiry,* 5 (4), 568–572.

Dewey, J. & Bentley, A. F. (1949). *Knowing and the known.* Boston: Beacon Press.

Fine, M. (2000). Working the hyphens: Reinventing self and other in qualitative research. In N. K. Denzin & Y. S. Lincoln (eds.) *Handbook of qualitative research.* (2nd ed.), (pp. 70–82). Thousand Oaks, CA: Sage.

Krieger, S. (1991). *Social science and the self: Personal essays as an art form.* New Brunswick, NJ: Rutgers University Press.

Meek, M. (1991). *On being literate.* Portsmouth, NH: Heinemann.

Richardson, L. (1998) Writing: A method of inquiry. In N. K. Denzin & Y. S. Lincoln (eds.) *Collecting and interpreting qualitative materials* (pp. 345–371). Thousand Oaks, CA: Sage.

Rosenblatt, L. M. (1978). *The reader, the text, and the poem.* Carbondale: Southern Illinois Press.

Street, B. (2002, February). *Higher education in the new work order: Implications for student writing, reading, and representation.* Keynote address presented at the National Council of Teachers of English, Assembly for Research Association, Midwinter Conference, New York, NY.

Sullivan, P. A. (1996). Ethnography and the problem of the "other." In P. Mortensen & G. Kirsch (eds.), *Ethics and representation in qualitative studies of literacy* (pp. 97–114). Urbana, IL: NCTE.

Taylor, D. & Dorsey-Gaines, C. (1988). *Growing up literate: Learning from inner city families.* Portsmouth, NH: Heinemann.

Wood Ray, K. (2001). *The writing workshop: Working through the hard parts (and they're all hard parts).* Urbana, IL: National Council of Teachers of English.

Notes

1. "Literacy and Research," Adelphi University (Manhattan Campus), Fall Semester, 2001.

2. *Growing Up Literate,* Taylor & Dorsey-Gaines.

3. *Local Literacies,* Barton & Hamilton.

4. I believe that it is impossible to represent the realities of others. Instead, we re-present the impressions we formulate from observations in the research site.

5. The term "9/11" has just been added to *Webster's Dictionary,* and will therefore be used throughout the article.

6. I became familiar with C. S. Peirce, as well as William James's notions about the "experiential reservoir," when Louise Rosenblatt cited them in *The Reader, the Text, and the Poem,* as influential upon her conceptualization of the transactional theory related to a literary experience. The transaction, or "poem," happens "during a coming-together, a compenetration, of a reader and a text" (p. 12).

7. Chomsky's notion of a "language-acquisition device."

8. The cave art of the Cro-Magnon man, as exemplified in the drawings in Lascaux, France.

9. Nemo's clothing store was transformed into a temporary restaurant and shelter for police officers and firefighters.

10. The teachers and administrators of School District 2 were publicly acknowledged and honored at the National Council of Teachers of English, Assembly for Research Association, Midwinter Conference, Feb. 22–24, 2002, in New York City.

11. *The Reader, the Text, and the Poem,* Louise Rosenblatt.

12. Note found on a subway wall by a student.

13. Brian Stret's keynote address, "Higher Education in the New Work Order: Implications for Student Writing, Reading, and Representation." National Council of Teachers of English, Assembly for Research Association, Midwinter Conference, Feb. 22–24, 2002, New York City.

14. Shirley Brice Heath's term, used in *Ways with Words.*

15. Brian Street speaks of contested notions of literacy and what counts as knowledge. He suggests that we look at writing practices in terms of power relations. Contested spaces, Street believes, help to constitute the formative aspects of that literacy (NCTERA, Winter Conference, 2002).

16. Nearly five months after the World Trade Center attack, these "walls of prayer" still existed in Penn Station and other locations.

17. *Language Shock: Understanding the Culture of Conversation.*

18. Ibid., p. 60.

19. Margaret Meek.

20. Leonora Suraci is a third grade teacher and graduate student in St. John's University.

21. "Flag to Carry Sentiments from Ground Zero to Afghanistan," November 26, 2001, David W. Chen, B1.

22. Ibid., B6.

23. Ibid., B1.

Joanne Robertson is assistant professor of reading in the Literacy Department at St. John's Univeristy's School of Education.

Relationships–Responsibilities, Once Removed and Ever Connected

KAREN M. STALLER

Filtering the News

ON THE MORNING OF SEPTEMBER 11, 2001, I was aloft on a Northwestern Airlines flight bound from Detroit to Amsterdam and investing, foolishly, in a romantic relationship destined for failure. Less than 24 hours earlier, I had taught my first class as a newly hired, freshly installed assistant professor at a university ranked at the top of my field. Presumably, it is not the kind of institutional environment where playing hooky is condoned so, ridden with self-imposed guilt, I found myself engaged in a stealthy act of truancy, responding to a personal desire to fuel the flames of a floundering romance. I anticipated a couple of carefree days on the French Riviera before returning to serious academic business, undetected, and well before my next scheduled academic appearance.

I landed in Amsterdam to bedlam. In a transit hub where masses of humanity generally flow with purposeful direction people were uncharacteristically stalled. A disembodied female voice on the public address system, echoed in every outpost of the terminal, endlessly repeating the same incomprehensible announcement, "Due to the closure of U.S. aerospace, all flights to the United States have been cancelled." Meaningful words that made so little sense to me, my mind obsessively fixed on how odd the word "aerospace" sounded, incapable of absorbing the larger import of the message. It would take hours before the public address voice provided useful direction by urging people to gather in a baggage claim area for additional information.

In the meantime, incoming jetliners discharged fresh batches of passengers, hundreds at a time, adding to the growing swell of baffled wanderers. American travelers swamped the pay phone islands that dotted the airport and promised easy global communication, frustrated because not one phone was accepting credit cards. In this information age, there was precious little information to be had. Scraps of news about hijacked planes—more than one, maybe three or four—passed among us like the child's game of telephone. We were, individually and collectively, severed from homes and homeland but united in our confusion and concern.

I turned out not to be as stranded as some. International flights around Europe were still moving. As I negotiated my plane ticket from Amsterdam to Nice, the ticket agent shook her head sadly and said, "It's so sad about the World Trade Center being gone." The words confused me. Missing towers, closed aerospace, hijacked planes, I couldn't produce a coherent picture from these informational shards. Only later, right before my plane departed for Nice, were the airport TV monitors turned to CNN and the horrific images began to link puzzle pieces.

I was stranded in France well beyond my intended stay. Days of canceled flights created a backlog of bumped passengers. The airlines tried to clear out travelers sleeping in airport lobbies before permitting those of us safely nestled in hotels to file in behind. Of course, complaining about being stranded on the Riviera is unseemly. Yet toward the end, I found myself alone in Cannes, already abandoned by my friend who had eagerly headed home at his first opportunity answering to more important priorities than me.

I wanted to use my bonus time wisely, but I was distracted and found myself wandering the streets aimlessly. One afternoon I took a sightseeing boat ride but sat far removed from a group of boisterous German tourists. Rather than take in coastline sights with the others, I stared absently at a vast expanse of ocean and wept silently. Evenings, I watched CNN as if being assaulted by the same video clips over, and over, and over again would produce meaning eventually.

Mostly, as I walked or stared, my mind ran through lists of names. I had left New York City two years earlier for my first academic teaching post, but the city had been home for my entire adult life. So I churned through the name of every person I could think of I had ever known. The list included sprawling networks of people: classmates, work colleagues, apartment neighbors, health club acquaintances, and others who populated relationships I had cultivated over 15 years. I calculated the possibility of each one being in the geographic vicinity of the World Trade Center that morning, no matter how improbable the chance. It was a futile act, in light of the dearth of concrete information, yet since I was alone and isolated, it served as a mental activity that connected me with home and event. Besides, New York is a big city, but not so big when you begin to break it down.

There was one group I worried about a lot. Police officers I knew who were employed by the Port Authority Police Department (PAPD). The NY/NJ Port Authority was a cooperative, if not always amicable, joint venture between the neighboring states of New York and New Jersey. It was responsible for securing all ports of entry: airports, bus stations, train stations, tunnels, and bridges. It had outpost offices around the city but its New York headquarters was in the World Trade Center. I focused my worries on one veteran PAPD police sergeant. He was an ex-colleague and old friend. Given the opportunity, I knew he would be first in line to respond to crisis.

Working through the Filters

On the day I returned home, I stopped to empty my university mailbox of its accumulated contents. Amongst the flyers for lectures and candlelight vigils already passed, was an envelope from *Qualitative Inquiry* and a note urging me to finish revisions on a manuscript, submitted eons earlier, and lying inexcusably dormant. The letter made me shudder. The study was of a youth services unit within PAPD and had been facilitated by my friend, who I dubbed in the manuscript "Sgt. T." I had spent the last week consumed with worry about whether Sgt. T was dead or alive. Now I faced an eerily timed invitation, in my academic capacity, to revisit our personal and professional pasts.

Call me a coward, but I was emotionally incapable of placing the simple, direct, phone call that would have answered my most immediate question about Sgt. T's well-being. I could have called his home, but wondered if I would find the right words if his wife or daughter answered the phone. Alternatively, I could have called the office but convinced myself that the police were far too busy with serious business to be fielding such calls. In my heart, I knew what was stopping me. It was that at very best a conversation with the unit would be about *whom* was lost and not *whether* there were casualties. The truth was, I wasn't ready to know.

Manuscript Filters

Interpretation and Representation: Temporally and Spatially Contexualized. Manuscript in hand, I wrestled with questions both personal and professional. Could I face the revisions now? Did I have the courage to go back and re-read, re-remember, the material? If so, should I revise the manuscript according to suggestions offered by helpful reviewers in the world before September 11th as though nothing had happened? The study had been completed, interpreted, and written up, long before September 11th. Yet proceeding as though nothing was different seemed dishonest. However, locating the essence of that difference was not easy. Did it reside in me, in my relationship with my characters, in my understanding of their world, or in my understanding of my world? In short, what should my representation look like?

At the heart of my dilemma was the matter of timing. Denzin argues interpretation, an act of both art and politics, bridges field and text (Denzin, 1998). The writer "transforms" the statement into a "public document, which embodies the writer's self-understandings, which are now inscribed in the experiences of those studied" (Denzin, p. 316). Certainly that is true, but what about lag-time infused with calamity? When does interpretation take place relative to observations and publication? What happens when an event occurs within the scope of your field, but not while you are observing? What if it alters you profoundly? What if it isn't just a localized event but is so big that it captures global attention and changes the course of world history? How and when should you freeze-frame a changing world for public examination and call it scholarship? I couldn't find textbook guidance on what should happen when a cataclysmic event crashed into the center of my study and sent debris spewing into every space I subsequently wandered.

In the end I left the study mostly unaltered but tried to put it in post–September 11th political context. Recently, however, I received a note from *Qualitative Inquiry*, informing me publication is delayed until next fall to accommodate reflections on September 11th. There is some irony that a study conducted a year before September 11th, written up in the immediate emotional aftermath of September 11th, will appear in print October '02, a full year after September 11th. Of course, the intersections between interpretation, representations, and timing have many variations.

Politics and Ethics of Disclosure. Timing was not my biggest manuscript dilemma. There was a more troubling question of disclosure. Convention suggests that identities and location of research sites should be concealed (Punch, 1998). Should I disclose the site of my research? Did it matter that it was New York City?

Practicing qualitative researchers are quick to point to the folly of confidentiality mandates. Ellis (1995) courageously addresses the problem of assuring confidences in communities too intimate not to see through the charade. Punch (1998) points to the "painstaking" work of Holdaway (1982) in using "pseudonyms for his research police station" only to refer "in his bibliography to publications that make it plain that he studied the Metropolitan Police of London" (Punch, p. 176). Punch continues by asking, "How do you disguise research conducted in readily identifiable cities such as London, New York, or Amsterdam?" (1998, p. 176). Pushing that question further, I ask, *must one try?* Certainly, I would not be fooling my friends, my colleagues, my students, or any stranger with the slightest desire to determine what city had hosted my work. More importantly, was the location now critical information?

I consulted others. The advice I received from colleagues was mostly of the highly safe variety. Don't reveal the site of the research but go ahead and make general references; don't reveal the identity of the individuals, give them pseudonyms. It was advice from a research community that believes in arm's length engagement. Research is never personal. Big numbers reveal useful truths of some sort, I guess, and they guarantee individual anonymity. In fact, individuals matter mostly because they add bulk to findings. In my work, individuals matter. Should my readers know my primary character, Sgt. T, worked as a cop in New York City? Should they be concerned, along with me, about whether he survived September 11th?

Over the last decade the "autonomy and rationalist presumptions of canonical ethics," as offered by my colleagues, has been challenged by "social and feminist" ethicists (Christians, 2000, p. 142). A new orientation, dubbed "feminist communitarianism," rests on the philosophical underpinning that "situates the moral domain within the general purposes of human life that people share contextually and across cultural, racial and historical boundaries" (Christians, p. 142). In this worldview, "moral agents need a context of social commitments and community ties for assessing what is valuable. What is worth preserving as a good cannot be self-determined in isolation" (Christians, p. 144). At its heart, this is an orientation that accommodates relationships, in multiple spheres and spaces, in their full complexity. It accepts the fact that uniform rules must give way to moral reasoning which can only exist in the context of "reciprocal care and understanding rooted in emotional experience" (Christians, p. 145). "The challenge," notes Christians, is not to limit moral perspectives to codes of ethics, "but to understand ethics and values in terms of everyday life" (p. 147). That became my challenge. It involved understanding my personal, professional, and human responsibilities as an integrated whole and not parceled into separate categories in my life. For me that also means coming to terms with my responsibilities as they exist in a new context of shared community grief.

Personal Filters

The answer to one dilemma was unexpectedly delivered on September 25th, with a predictable thud to my driveway, via the morning paper. It caught me off guard. That was the day the Port Authority of NY & NJ published a full-page announcement in the *New York Times* (2001, Sept. 25, p. A17). It read, in part:

> On Tuesday, September 11, the Port Authority lost 74 of its own. Plus thousands of its friends, neighbors, and colleagues. The agency also lost its home.
>
> With the towers gone, it is the memory of people that stands tallest in the hearts and minds of the Port Authority staff. Our deepest sympathies go out to the families of all the victims.

There was an image of the Twin Towers, portrayed as unfurled American flags, standing side by side. Next to the towers was a list of the names, an announcement of the dead, all seventy-four, in alphabetical order.

I flew through the list, scanning the second half for Sgt. T's name. It wasn't there. I felt an enormous wave of relief. As my heart returned to its normal rhythm, I went back to the list and scrolled through the names more slowly. In spite of everything, what I found was as unexpected as it was inevitable. The name of someone I did know. Not a best friend like Sgt. T, but an acquaintance. I had met him, in passing, on more than several occasions. Sgt. T and his unit had spoken of this man with love and respect for years. His name had been in my life vocabulary for over a decade, a player in my shared world through Sgt. T and his unit.

I pondered a weird question: Would he have known my name as I knew his? I think so. More significantly, why did this matter to me? Is it because I would like to think if I suddenly died, there would be an extended community that cared? Or is it because I needed to be tied to this tragedy in some sort of tangible way? Perhaps it granted me the social license to grieve the way I was craving to grieve. It connected me to September 11th, so I could claim a personal right to a bigger share of national grief. Even more selfishly, however, perhaps it opened publicly acceptable space to legitimize my mourning for a series of private losses as well. It allowed me to grieve for a failed romance, for friends and family left in New York, for a social support network left behind at another university, and to acknowledge the strange sense of homelessness I felt in this first semester in a new and unfamiliar hometown. I felt painfully alone at a time when everyone was searching for connections. Perhaps having an individual I could grieve allowed me to tuck all those layers of loneliness, loss, and sadness under one big, but legitimate, shroud of depression.

Infiltrating Filters

I heeded the advice of my colleagues by not disclosing the site of my research in my manuscript submission, until today, when I wandered into a more dangerous space, where we can struggle to give meaning to our lives and this tragedy by asking questions that connect the personal and individual with the political and the cultural.

I am haunted by an image in my mind's eye of a huge obtuse triangle frozen in time and space. One point rests in my plane approaching Amsterdam, a second in another plane hurdling directly toward the Trade Center, and the last is in a friend, alive, at the bottom of one of those enormous towers. In a stunning second later that triangle implodes in a tangled mass of new realities and relationships.

Perhaps I need my work to stand as tribute and memorial to all those new realities and relationships. Perhaps I'm using this public space to ask the scholarly community to share my grief. Perhaps there need to be footnotes in historic records, archived in scholarly journals, that provide the raw material for a next generation to make sense of September 11th and the scholarship that surrounded it. Perhaps I'm using personal disclosure for my own closure. In the moment, all I know for sure is that I want to say good-bye. Not through a generalized message to the thousands of souls lost on that pivotal day, but to just one.

Chief James A. Romito-
-Jimmy-
may you rest in eternal peace
d. 09-11-01

References

Christians, C. G. (2000). Ethics and politics in qualitative research. In N. K. Denzin & Y. S. Lincoln (eds.), *Handbook of qualitative research* (2nd ed.) (pp. 133–155). Thousand Oaks, CA: Sage.

Denzin, N. K. (1998). The art and politics of interpretation. In N. K. Denzin & Y. S. Lincoln (eds.), *Collecting and interpreting qualitative materials* (pp. 313–344). Thousand Oaks, CA: Sage.

———. (2002). Cultural studies in America after September 11, 2001. *Cultural Studies—Critical Methodologies*, 2, 1, 9–14.

Ellis, C. (1995). Emotional and ethical quagmires in returning to the field. *Journal of Contemporary Ethnography*, 24,1, 68–98.

Holdaway, S. (1982). "An inside job": A case study of covert research on the police. In M. Bulmer (ed.), *Social research ethics* (pp. 59–79). London: Macmillan.

Punch, M. (1998). Politics and ethics in qualitative research. In N. K. Denzin & Y. S. Lincoln (eds.), *The landscape of qualitative research* (pp. 156–184). Thousand Oaks, CA: Sage.

United We Stand. *New York Times* (September 25, 2001). The Port Authority of NY & NJ. A17.

Karen M. Staller is assistant professor at the University of Michigan School of Social Work.

Some Thoughts on Recovery 13

GREG DIMITRIADIS

I HAD DINNER 2 WEEKS AGO with a friend who recently entered a 12-step program for alcohol abuse. A well-known ethnomusicologist, he tells me of his now preeminent personal struggle—the struggle to find the right "fit" in and with the world. What's the right size in the here and now? What's too big? What's too small? How to avoid speaking from everywhere? How to avoid speaking from nowhere? "How can I be just the right size for you, Greg, the way you need me to be, right here and right now?" I try to sort out my own thoughts and feelings about September 11. What's too big and what's too small? What's appropriate right here and right now—September 19?

I have family and friends in New York City. Immediately after the attack, I hear a rumor that a low-level nuclear bomb was finally what brought the towers down. Someone else e-mails me, reporting an acrid smell around Columbia University. Was it poison gas? Anything seems possible. My father tries walking home from midtown Manhattan to the North Bronx. He doesn't have his blood pressure medicine. He panics. He is convinced that all traffic has stopped and plans to simply walk up the middle of the West Side Highway. We are out of touch for more than 4 hours. A long story, but he's now home.

CNN reports an ever-rising and near incomprehensible death count. They also offer intensely personal stories about those dead, those missing, those who survived, those who helped. I hear the phrase, "putting a human face on the tragedy" several times. None of it computes. Someone must be shielding us from something larger, I think—the horror of the final death count? Of what it might be like below 14th street in Manhattan? Almost everyone I know compares it to a movie with an unbelievable plot. I'm numb.

Posters for the film *The Last Castle* are removed from city buses because they feature an upside-down American flag. This is a signal of distress. The release date for Arnold Schwartzenagger's film *Collateral Damage* is pushed back. The proposed *War of the Worlds* film has stopped production and may cancel. Posters and trailers for the forthcoming *Spider-Man* movie are pulled because they feature the World Trade Center. Editors will airbrush them out of the final film print. The Web site has been taken down and will be redone.

Alcoholics have an extraordinary capacity for fantasy and denial, my friend tells me. His own moment of clarity, his own epiphany, came reading an old diary. He realized, he told me, that he'd been telling himself the same story about his drinking for 20 years. A perpetual present of political and personal grandiosity, followed quickly by political and personal despair, followed again by personal and political grandiosity. His life is now, he says, about finding just the right fit, wherever he finds himself, with whomever he finds himself. America is now beyond its own capacity to imagine itself. We must negotiate a new relationship with ourselves. We must negotiate a new relationship with others. The world will never be the same again, people tell me. What they really mean, of course, is that America will never be the same again. Anything seems possible.

Greg Dimitriadis is an assistant professor in the Department of Educational Leadership and Policy at the University at Buffalo, The State University of New York.

What Is Over? Ruminations From One Who Has Already Lived Through Another September 11

14

ANGHARAD N. VALDIVIA

IT'S SEPTEMBER 11, 1973, AND MY MOTHER COMMENTS, "It's over." The planes have flown in and bombed La Moneda, the presidential palace in downtown Santiago, Chile. Within hours, democratically elected President Salvador Allende is dead—it is still unclear whether he shot himself or he was shot. It is a little clearer that the United States had direct and indirect influence in the concerted effort to destabilize the Chilean economy as well as in the military and funding processes that fomented, trained, incited, and abetted the military coup that ended Allende's presidency and Chile's long-term standing as a democratic nation. Pinochet, as a member of the junta and then as self-declared president, the winner of an election with only one candidate and no opposing party, a so-called plebiscite, stayed in power until 1990. His legacy in terms of the rewritten constitution and his own personal standing as senator for life still lives on.

We were then in Kettering, Ohio—part of the large diasporic group of Chileans who left the country in fear of what Allende might do (not to be confused with the later group who left in fear of what Pinochet might do). "I have to get my family out of this communist circus," my father is often quoted as having said before he took us all out of Chile for our own ideological safety. We, the children, of course had no say in this matter. We are packed; we are moved; we follow the parents. Farewell parties, grandmothers crying, and house packed up, past the wailing family group on our way to the departure lounge. We didn't know what was over then, and we are no closer to it on September 11, 1973. Are we going back to Chile? Can we see abuelita again? Is the Allende period all that is over? For my mother, whose political sympathies do not necessarily match my father's, maybe the socialist hope is over. For certain, her professional career is over, as she lost it when she crossed the border. Much of her independence is behind her as is her agency in terms of political choice. For my dad, the circus is over. For us kids, we don't know what is over. We did not understand then what moving meant. We thought we'd go back. We did not know we would never see some of our family and friends again. We could not have anticipated that our "voluntary" exile would soon be followed by a forced exile of friends and relatives from the socialist part of the family. We would not grow up knowing our cousins for they also would be in places such as Mozambique, Cuba, Austria, and Argentina before being able to return to Chile. We also did not anticipate that when we finally got to visit Chile again, we'd face soldiers with machine guns sporadically dispersed throughout the streets of Santiago, Valparaíso, Concepción, and so forth; an increased state of surveillance so that people only dared to talk politics in the middle of a field somewhere out in the countryside; growing indices of alcoholism as those who stayed behind had no occupational future and no space to voice their demands; and an incipient neoliberalism that not only immediately wiped away most of Allende's social policy but went much farther back to erasing much of the little accomplished during the presidencies of Frei and Alessandri. By 2001, a trip to Chile was a trip to two Chiles: On one hand, there is Providencia, Las Condes, and other upper crust neighborhoods in Santiago and elsewhere, where one can engage in a sanitized cosmopolitan environment with clean streets, English-names establishments, and most of the latest commodities available to those of us living in the geopolitical North; on the other hand, there is the Chile that was and that remains, the one most Chileans still live in, the one with high unemployment, low standards of living, where most of our relatives still reside.

Back in the United States, 28 years after the Chilean coup, I am dressing my toddler, getting a few minutes of CNN in between "Elmo's World" in Sesame Street and the drive to the child care center. It's September 11 again, and I am thinking of Chile as I always do on this date. Decades of living here and a citizenship away, I still think of Chile all through September. You see, September includes the coup and independence day, the parades, the parties, the national holidays, the beginning of spring, my birthday—how can I forget all of that? But this day, CNN has a long, fuzzy shot of one of the World Trade Center towers. They do not really know what happened, something about a plane or maybe a fire. Then the second plane flies into the screen and right into and through the second tower. The message is quite clear: We are under attack. I hear my mother's words again: "It's over."

What is over? So much as it turns out. Of course, my trip to New York City in 2 days is over. Without flights and in a state of emergency, it's out of the question. So is any type of carefree air travel. The armed troops checking out my luggage, my body, and my passport are only the most visual and palpable reminders that the world has changed. I look at everyone in the airport suspiciously. I feel suspiciously analyzed myself—after all, my Hispanic origin is bound to include at least some Arabian elements, Spain having been so influenced and composed of Moorish populations. It is not an altogether new feeling. It reminds me of visiting Chile for the first time after the coup and encountering a militarized country, where soldiers with machine guns stood in the street corners of Santiago. They gaze on you, and their weapons follow their gaze. Once inside the plane, I try to figure out who is/are the air marshal(s) and what type of weapons she or he carries. A friend is afraid that if she or he has to shoot, it'll depressurize the cabin. I figure their weapons have to be more sophisticated than that. But then, the terrorists apparently used box cutters. We both had one of our nail files and nail clippers confiscated on boarding. I notice later that there is another nail clipper in my purse, and they missed it. I wonder how many other things they missed. The whole sense of security that I took for granted is gone. Now I can add this to my increasing fear of flying.

What does the attack mean? Surely it cannot be justified. Despite the nearly iconic meaning of those two towers and the Pentagon, the fact remains real working people died in the debacle—janitors, waiters, secretaries, fireworkers, police, and clergy. Very wealthy and powerful people who worked in the financial world also perished by the hundreds as well as the unnamed workers in the secret CIA office stashed away somewhere in the towers and the undocumented workers whose death will also be undocumented. Left behind are children, grandparents, and husbands but also, most important, in terms of media representation and nation building, widows and mothers.

Out of the ashes and stench of Ground Zero and the challenged national identity of a nation who thought of itself as unattackable and secure the mythical sign of woman once more carries the meaning of loss, victimhood, and nation. Just as the mothers participated in the marches of the pots and pans in the streets of Chile; the mothers of the disappeared demonstrated in the Plaza de Mayo in Buenos Aires, Argentina; and the widows of heroes and martyrs (both of the Right and the Left) organized in Nicaragua, we experience the power of the gendered sign here in the United States. The attack can most visibly and forcefully be symbolized through the broken security that the United States can provide its women and children. Widows represent both familial and national loss; weeping mothers make very good news. The whole nation identifies with these widows and mothers, despite the fact that many of them led lives that few of us could ever dream of. It is significant that whereas most of the mothers and widows in Chile, Argentina, and Nicaragua were working—or barely middle class—in the United States, our sympathies go to investment banker widows, whose troubles include the burial of a loved one and figuring out how to file taxes on a million dollar plus estate. But death and gender are universalizing factors. These women can demand a meeting with the mayor and have the luxury of yelling at him for more than an hour. Going against official decisions, they ask for a memorial place instead of a rebuilt trade center. They do not want the steel from the buildings recycled through the used commodities market. Needless to say, they demand restitution, monetary and symbolic. They argue among themselves as to who is a more worthy victim and, therefore, deserves more compensation. They are the only ones who actively can participate in this division of the spoils as nobody else dares to contradict a mother or widow at this point in time. They set the tone of both the memory and the reconstruction. The attack means, partly, that women can rise out of the ashes and grief and guide the nation through some sort of ethical self-reflection. This gendered pursuit may influence the course of politics and history, though there is not guarantee that it will be pacifist in character. Certainly, this seems to be one of the fissures among the widows and mothers—should we respond in kind or turn the other cheek? Our leaders and representatives have resoundingly made the former decision. It is unclear whether the widows and mothers will unswervingly support this trend. If anyone can back the political wisdom of the day, it's them. Here, even I root for these women, seeing them as one of the few sites of hope out of this hyper-militaristic moment. Of course, I also know that there are plenty of these women who fully support the military juggernaut. We ask the women for meaning like I asked my mother that September 11 more than 28 years ago. Gendered and outright sexist expectations of a more humane response from the women lead us to hope greater things from them than from our political leaders. Women have historically been left behind like my abuelita, my nana, and my tía Lucy. They have waited, in vain, for either those who left and did not come back or may have returned after the women died.

Many of the issues that precipitated the Chilean coup remain unresolved. Pinochet is a senator for life. A civilian government lives under the shadow of the military and of the military written constitution. There is still great inequality in Chile. The so-called economic miracle involves a small component of the population. Transnational capitalism benefits the few at the expense of large numbers of impoverished Chileans. What could have been done differently? How does a nation or its people resolve issues of poverty and inequality? Will we be looking back 28 years from now with as many questions as we now have regarding this second 9/11 tragedy? If we rest back and allow the debate to continue without our dedicated input, a long and unresolved conflict is totally within the realm of possibility. Many people will continue to perish, we will become used to our reduced civil rights (or, at least, we will get used to not resisting their loss), and we will forget the urgency to find ways out of the conflict and the root causes of global wars. I don't know if my mother cried when the planes bombed La Moneda, but she must have had the same gut feeling I had when the towers came down: gather my loved ones around me so I can at least hold them if not protect them. Yet as an active human being, a critical scholar, and a diasporic survivor of a previous 9/11, I cannot believe that that's all I can do. Writing this piece both allows me to put some of this in writing and glaringly reminds me that I have to formulate a strategy of analysis and resistance. Critical studies, especially when infused with and through transnational feminism, urge us to examine the interconnected layers of difference and oppression as well as the unexpected opportunities for ruptures, agency, and intervention. We are at a moment when we can, against nearly all odds, attempt to direct our energies, solidarity, and focus to a more just and peaceful world, one that respects difference rather than develops hierarchical modernist models to catalog it and therefore subjugate entire populations. It would be much easier to give up by succumbing to that stylistic "post-9/11" jaded sense of identity. Call me a romantic, idealist, or dreamer, if you want, but I have to believe that it will take our constant effort as human beings, citizens, scholars, and family members to avoid the tendency to lethargy and acquiescence so overdetermined by the U.S. government and mainstream news coverage, to keep previous 9/11s in mind and remember not just the ruptures, the losses, the deaths, and the closing of possibilities but also the responsibility, indeed the unavoidable duty, to forge a democratic and humane response to this latest and horrific crisis. I want to remember the women in this and previous crises so they can continue to fuel, through memory, my efforts to support and sustain a more peaceful and just world where our mobility is not marked by exile but by possibility and solidarity.

Angharad N. Valdivia is a research associate professor at the Institute of Communications Research at the University of Illinois.

What Will We Tell the Children?   15

NORMAN K. DENZIN

RITING 2 DAYS AFTER SEPTEMBER 11, 2001, on first hearing of the airplanes and the towers, Laurel Richardson (2002) asked, "What will the children be told?"
She answered her own question.

> And then, I see that the children are being told, as the adults are, through television cameras and media voices. The children are seeing the airplane and the second tower, and the airplane/tower, airplane/tower over and over until it's All Fall Down. And All Fall Down again and again. (Richardson, 2002, p. 25)

The next day, she called her grandson's mother who reported that he was afraid an airplane would hit his school.

What Will We Tell the Children?

What can we tell our children when we are all being told the same thing they are? Do we tell our daughters and sons that if you challenge the pictures and the stories on TV you are betraying President Bush? Do we tell our grandchildren that those who raise doubts may be traitors? Do we tell them that peace protesters are challenging President Bush and threatening America's mission in this war, a war that is still unofficial? Do we say that it is unpatriotic to seek the goals of peace and justice? Do we teach them that in a democracy there can be no dissent? What if they answer that a genuine democracy requires opposition and criticism? Must we remain silent?

On September 12, writing from New York City, Michelle Fine (in press) reported that

> you can tell who's dead or missing by their smiles. Their photos dot the subways, ferries, trains and Port Authority Terminal, shockingly alive with joy, comfort and pleasure. They died before they could know what we now know. The not-dead travel on subways and trains filled with hollow eyes; no smiles; shoulders down. Now a flood of flags, talk of God, military and patriotism chase us all.

What Will We Tell the Children?

What will we tell the mothers, the fathers, the wives, and husbands, those with hollow eyes, no smiles? Yesterday, a New York City widow killed herself. Her husband died on September 11.

Yvonna S. Lincoln (in press) spoke for those for whom the expression of grief does not come easily. For persons, like herself, raised to hide their sorrow, "the end result, I have come to realize, is a human being who lives with his or her grief for all their days. The future, like tears, never comes."

What Will We Tell the Children?

Do we allow our children to grieve? What are they grieving for? What are you grieving for? I'm grieving for a lost democracy. So, what does grief mean in a time like this? For whom and for what are we grieving?

Two days ago, the *New York Times* ran a picture of an Afghan mother and her 10-day-old daughter huddled under a blanket in an earthen cave outside Kandahar. Bomb craters surrounded the earthen structure. Mountain peaks hovered in the distance. A clear-white jet trail cut the vivid blue sky in half, as a U.S. bomber returned to base. What will this mother tell her daughter, if they get out of this mess alive? Will she tell her that the Americans came to Afghanistan to free women from the Taliban? Or will she say that the Americans with their planes and their bombs are on a mission to destroy terrorism?

The earth is a living thing. Of course, we all know this. The earth is more than a set of coordinates on a map; it is more than a physically bounded geographical site. The earth is a living thing. The earth and its places ought not be transformed into bomb sites. When we allow language to do this, we turn people into military targets. The earth and the people who make up the country called Afghanistan have been turned into targets for America's war machine. They are already dead, even before the bombs hit the ground.

Invoking, and paraphrasing, William Kittridge (1987, p. 87), in America today, in the brutally cruel cold days since September 11, we are struggling to revise our dominant mythology. Just who are we as Americans? What story about ourselves do we want to inhabit? Who are our storytellers, whose stories will we accept? Which laws will we allow to control our lives?

We want laws designed to preserve a model of a radically peaceful democratic society, a society that is nonviolent. We want laws and courts based on a post–September 11 mythology. We want a new mythology for America. We must reimagine our myths. Only then can we coherently remodel our laws and hope to keep our society in a realistic relationship to our utopian democratic ideas. Then we will know what to tell the children.

References

Fine, M. (in press). The mourning after. *Qualitative Inquiry*, 8.
Kittridge, W. (1987). *Owning it all*. San Francisco: Murray House
Lincoln, Y. S. (in press). Grief in an Appalachian register. *Qualitative Inquiry*, 8.
Richardson, L. (2002). Small world. *Cultural Studies-Critical Methodologies*, 2(1), 24–26.

Small World

16

LAUREL RICHARDSON

Spring 1942

A VISITOR COMES TO OUR FIRST GRADE Sunday school class at Anshe Emet Synagogue on Chicago's North Side. Our regular teacher, Mrs. Goldberg, tells us we are to listen carefully to what the Visitor tells us.

The Visitor speaks with an odd accent, heavy, fast, and angry. I am trying to listen, but I have trouble understanding her.

"Jewish boys and girls just like you are having their skins made into lampshades," she tells us.

I think the children would be very cold and not look very pretty without their skins.

"Nazi doctors are experimenting on children. They break their bones and set them wrong."

I had something like that happen to me, too, I am thinking, because my father wouldn't let my first broken arm get set and it healed wrong, so the doctors had to break it and set it right. But why would doctors set them wrong on purpose? Are they against medicine, like my father? I am confused.

"Nazi doctors give Jewish children diseases and make them sick."

My mother put me in bed with my brother when he had the measles and when he had the chicken pox, so I would get them and be sick, too. Is my mother a Nazi?

"Jewish men and women are separated. Men go to one room, women to another. They have to get naked. Then they are brought naked into showers. But the showers have bad gas in them and it kills all the Jewish men and women."

July 1942

On a very hot Chicago day, my parents drop my brother and me off at a large, public pool on the West side of Chicago. I have never been at a public pool before.

My brother and I are separated. A woman, dressed in a gray uniform, tells me to strip naked. She looks me over, puts my clothes in a metal basket, gives me a key, and tells me to get my suit on and go into the showers. I have never been in a shower. I have never even seen one. Water is coming from the ceiling and the walls. I run through the showers into a narrow passage. The floor is ankle high in a strong smelling green liquid. I run out to the pool. A different gray uniformed woman puts me into a metal bin, where purple light streams over me. I try to run away. I collapse.

"She's had heat stroke," I hear a gray-uniformed woman say.

"Are her parents here?" a man asks.

"We've not located them."

I don't know what a "heat stroke" is, and I don't know if the green liquid and purple light have taken off my skin or whether my parents have sent me to the showers or whether they are in the showers, too. I think I see my brother. I want to sleep.

Days, Weeks, Months, Years

I don't like to shower when I am home alone, and even when there is someone in the house, I'm in and out of the shower as quickly as possible. I had thought my shower activity was just one of my quirks—a way not to waste time, energy, or precious skin oils. But it is not a quirk. Rather, my behavior, I am realizing, is how my unconscious deals with learning about horrors I was too young to understand.

September 11, 2001

The above is what I was writing on the Eve of September 11. It is the beginning of a longer autoethnographic essay exploring how knowledge of trauma begets trauma; how innocence is lost; how vulnerable is the child. Learning at young ages about unspeakable crimes against children and families deeply affects one's life. My life—from showers to career to politics to arenas I have yet to explore—has been constructed to avoid and/or control the unfathomable.

When I hear of the airplanes and the towers, my first thoughts are—the children. Oh, the lives of the children! What is happening? What will the children be told? What can they understand?

And then, I see that the children are being told, as the adults are, through television cameras and media voices. The children are seeing the airplane and the second tower, and the airplane/tower, airplane/tower over and over until it's All Fall Down. And All Fall Down again and again.

I call my children. I call my stepchildren. I call my grandchildren. My granddaughter, Shana, an anthropology senior at Kenyon College, is angry with me. She thinks I'm insufficiently pacifist, but I think we're on "the same page." I listen to her pain and compassion, but I'm not doing a very good job of listening to her ideas. My 6-year-old grandson, Akiva, won't talk to me about the "towers," but he hates first grade now, and he doesn't want to talk about that either.

My heart breaks for the children whose lives are broken: And I am thinking about Every Child. Our global village. Our small world.

September 19, 2001

Norman Denzin asks some of the editors of *Cultural Studies Critical Methodologies* to write something for the journal about the events of September 11, in the next couple of days, if possible.

What can I say? What can anyone say? My e-mail listservs are repositories for quick fixes, ideological purity, liberal talk. I can't join the discussion. I refuse to intellectualize, analyze, or academize. I don't have any answers.

As I write this, my husband's jazz band is practicing in the next room. The singer is a member of the International Peace Committee (or some such title) at the Unitarian church. She says everyone is signing the "international law/ human rights petition," but secretly they're not convinced. "Let's fall in love," she sings. And the band plays on.

I call my dear friend, Marilyn. She's a hospice volunteer. That's where she was when the towers collapsed. She cried. Then went into a patient's room to change his sheets. The head nurse chastised her for "not seeing the Big Picture." "I guess I live in a small frame," Marilyn said.

I call my dear friend Betty. She is Jewish but wishes she had insisted that her 4-year-old grandson be taken to Quaker meetings. I wonder if she thinks it's too late, but I don't say anything. She tells me that the young children interviewed on television are of one accord: Are airplanes safe?

I call my grandson's mother to see how Akiva is doing. She tells me that he was afraid an airplane would hit his school, because it is a big building. Akiva and his friend Olivia are the only two children in his class who have not seen the television. The teacher is not allowing the students to talk about what they saw because of Akiva and Olivia. She is sending healing and peace to everyone. It helps her overcome her grief.

On Rosh Hashanah the rabbi said, "Choose Life." Choosing life I gather up clothes for the Kidney Foundation. I pet Maxwell the cat. I go to physical therapy. I send a "Get Well" bouquet to my brother-in-law. I e-mail Carolyn and Art to find out how their ill mothers are doing. I admire my friend Merry's new paintings. I send a sympathy card to my friend, Pat, who put her dog of 20 years to sleep on the 11th, and feels guilty about her grief. I tutor. I talk to my stepdaughter in Lebanon. I give thanks for another day of life. I follow my granddaughter Shana's e-mail request to support Project Open Hand's HIV-AIDS initiatives. I meditate on our small world. I pray. I write this piece.

Laurel Richardson has multiple attachments to The Ohio State University—and to the World.

Week Four   17

NORMAN K. DENZIN

WEEK FOUR OF THE WAR. Newspaper headlines: U. S. planes bomb Taliban artillery near a rebel artery. Mr. Rumsfeld cautioned that rooting out terrorism is a difficult task that will take time and patience. Coordination between American air strikes and the battlefield remains problematic. Twice in two days American bombs were dropped on Red Cross headquarters. Efforts to calm the nation's fears over the anthrax threat spin out of control. We are days away from Ramadan, Islam's sacred month of fasting. But wars rarely pause for holy days. Secretary Rumsfeld informs us that Muslim nations have often made war on one another during Ramadan. God is on our side.

The War goes on. Bahawalpur, Pakistan. October 28. At 8:50 a.m. on this bright sunny autumn Sunday morning "three young men with Kalashnikov rifles walked into St. Dominic's Roman Catholic Church. . . . A group of 35 Pakistani Protestants . . . were just preparing to go home. . . . The intruders opened fire . . . blood everywhere" (Burns, 2001, p. A1). Sixteen people died.

The theory, uncontested, shared by Christians, Muslim clerics, and Hindu sadhus, was that the killers "were acting to avenge the American bombing of Afghanistan. 'The Americans are attacking Afghanistan, and we are Christians, and America is mostly a Christian country, and so it is a matter of revenge,' said Elizabeth David, a nurse at the railway hospital" (Burns, 2001, p. A1). Her husband, an engineer, elaborated, "The trouble started when President Bush called America's war on terrorism a crusade . . . that means the revival of history . . . East against West, Islam against Christianity, and in Pakistan it means Muslims against Christians . . . and that means jihad" (Burns, 2001, B5).

Week Four. The War goes on. "America on Alert." The FBI has arrested 900 suspects, exactly zero have been criminally charged. It took the Bush administration at least a week to realize that a second attack on America was underway. Following administration directives, the major networks now censor the news about the war. A growing peace movement takes shape across America and is barely reported on by the media. Patriotism is the national watchword. The American flag waves everywhere.

Game 2, World Series. Last night in Phoenix, Arizona, Ray Charles sang the American anthem. His piano was on the baseball field, which was covered by a huge American flag. High above the stadium, the Stars and Stripes waved in the wind. Last night, Ray Charles sang the anthem like only he can sing the blues, shades of St. James Infirmary. It was slow and painful, drawn out, like a funeral march. He wailed in the high notes. His voice was full of pain, sorrow, and suffering. It was as if he felt the blues for America, as if he were singing at America's funeral. And in that moment I was taken back to June Jordan's (1998) jazz prose poem, "Good News' Blues," a poem written around Billie Holiday and her version of the blues:

> In Billie's land
> It's never mind
> about the prosecutors
> and the INS
> and the po-lice politicians . . .
> and never mind
> Apache helicopters
> carrying a war load
> cost more than it cost to build
> 2 hospitals
> 4 schools. (p. 194)

No "Good News' Blues" in America today.

Annie Dillard (1974) said that divinity is not playful, that the universe was not made in jest but in "solemn incomprehensible earnest. By a power that is unfathomably secret, and holy and fleet" (p. 270) and violent. I choose to believe this.

In the "Peace of Wild Things," Wendell Berry (1981) said that when

> Despair for the world grows in me . . .
> I go and lie down where the wood drake rests in his beauty on the water, and the great heron feeds.
> I come into the peace of wild things . . .
> For a time I rest in the grace of the world and am free. (p. 180)

Noon, September 15: Mattis Lake, Champaign, Illinois. Fishing pole in hand, I parked and walked over a small hill to Mattis Lake, which is near my home. The lake is not large. It is surrounded by walking paths and small picnic areas. An apartment complex is located nearby. Reeds, rushes, and willows grow in its corners and along its banks. Two tall maples shade the water where I stop. Rocks butt out into the water, bull rushes sway in the wind, grasshoppers sun themselves on blades of green grass, the noon sun dances off of the water, and waves ripple as the wind comes over the hill. I bait my hook with a dried-up earthworm and cast my line into the water. Just as my red-and-white bobber settles on the surface, a tall sand crane makes a delicate landing on the grassy shoreline. As if on stilts, this elegantly awkward bird walks in an easterly direction, head darting back and forth and up and down, looking for I know not what.

My line is tugged sharply; I jerk my rod upward. A large bass jumps in the air. It jerks its head and then dives down into deeper water. I set the hook and begin to reel in the line. The bass comes back to the surface, drawing near to me. I reach down and touch the fish, it must be over 12 inches long and weigh over a pound. I cradle the fish in my palm, and holding it in the water, I reach over with my other hand and remove the tiny hook from its jaw. I then put the fish back in the water, and with a violent twist of its body, it disappears into the depths.

As I stand to catch my breath, the sand crane, which has been watching me, flies off in haste, and on the distant shore, ducks glide quietly into the hidden waters beneath a regal oak tree.

In his antiwar anthem, Bob Dylan asks, "How many miles must a wild duck sail, before she sleeps in the sand?"

In these times I seek the peace of wild things; wild ducks, sand cranes, geese flying south, and bass who swim in shallow waters. I accept a power that is unfathomably secret and holy and fleet. But as part of the bargain I seek a serenity that allows me to rest in the grace of the world. I seek the self-awareness that will tell me when I must place myself in the presence of wild things. I want to live in a world where there are wild things who do not tax their lives with grief and violence, wild things who do not have a god who is on their side when they go to war.

References

Berry, W. (1981). The peace of wild things. In W. Berry, *Recollected essays, 1965–1980* (p. 180). New York: Farrar, Straus and Giroux.

Burns, J. F. (2001, October 29). Gunman kills 16 Christians in church in Pakistan. *The New York Times*, pp. A1, B5.

Dillard, A. (1974). *Pilgrim at Tinker Creek.* New York: Harper & Row.

Jordan, J. (1998). A good news' blues: A jazz prose-poem. In *Affirmative acts: Political essays* (pp. 182–200). New York: Doubleday.

Norman K. Denzin is assistant professor of communication at the University of New Hampshire.

Drawing a Line in the Fog

18

JACK Z. BRATICH

December 13, 2001

WHEN ATTORNEY GENERAL JOHN ASHCROFT recently told a congressional committee that his critics are giving "new meaning to the term 'fog of war,'" he invoked a well-worn, almost "naturalized" metaphor (Gullo, 2001). Often attributed to Clausewitz (somewhat erroneously, see Kiesling, 2001), the phrase refers to the uncertainty and unreliability of information that a battlefield commander has during decision making. By using fog of war to refer to "uninformed" and mystifying critics, Ashcroft himself was giving the phrase new meaning, one that although clouding the critics' arguments also gives us an insight into the tactics of this indefinite "new war." The haze of undecidability lifts from the ground of battle to enshroud the very form of the new war—a "fog war." We can see this in the oft-asked, though not completely new, question, "Are we at war?" whose official answer depends on the circumstances—no (if this means following domestic or international law) and yes (if this means suspending laws and trampling civil liberties). The uncertainty of facts and information in war becomes the uncertainty of war itself.

In addition, the U.S. war on terrorism employs a strategy of "organized insecurity" against an "unspecified enemy" (Deleuze & Guattari, 1987, pp. 422, 467; Massumi, 1993, pp. 10-11). Although occasionally accruing a concrete content (at this moment, Bin Laden, Al Qaeda, and the Taliban), the unspecified and diffuse enemy can potentially take on infinite examples. The fogginess of the enemy is accompanied by a boundaryless terrain of war, an immanent war (see my previous piece, pp. 41–43) that takes place in the "biopolitical context" of everyday life (Hardt & Negri, 2000). As a swelling confluence of chemical, biological, and even agri-terrorism, the unspecified enemy of terrorism operates through disrupting everyday life (a normalized state of high alert). A war on terrorism, naturally, has to follow this enemy on this mundane and ubiquitous field, or atmosphere. Its immanence, amorphous constitution, and vague enemy mean that this new war itself is redefining the fog of war.

But we cannot merely expand the metaphor fog of war to shroud a totalizing space of war, for this would erase the differentiations and power dynamics that compose this state of emergency. Instead, we need to move to a more active expression, one that foregrounds the spectacular production of obscurity, uncertainty, and secrecy. We can call it the fog machine of war, in which both dimness and clarity are deployed, producing the distinctions that mobilize and justify this new war.

These distinctions take on a new tenor in a fog war. Even while the battles in Afghanistan invoke the Gulf War, we will not hear Bush II reiterate Bush I's infamous dictum to "draw a line in the sand." When war is deterritorialized from particular spaces, lifting from the ground to be fought virtually anywhere, lines have to be drawn in this amorphous space. The U.S. administration makes these purifying separations (good/evil, us/them, civilized/barbaric, American/enemies) but deploys them in a boundaryless terrain and for an indefinite duration. The fog machine of war is a hybrid of boundaries and boundarylessness, of distinctions and ambiguities—in fact it is marked by a management of anxiety and certainty.

The very phrase *war on terrorism* already tries to manage this hybridity. It separates the two terms, untangling the network that links U.S. foreign policy and its recent enemy, both in form (especially the incorporation of civilians into military action) and content (the blowback thesis elaborated by Kellner, McLaren, and others in this volume). The current Hollywood blockbuster *Spy Games* is an example of this futile untangling. Whereas it glamorizes the adventures and moral integrity of spies, its narrative includes a CIA-sponsored bombing in Beirut by one terrorist group on the leader of another. "War on terrorism" conceptually betrays the "terror/war" hybrid that composes global violence, be it a network of strong states or a network of weak nonstate actors battling for domination.

Given this perspective that examines the war time management of lines and fogs, we can also rethink the exhaustive attempt by Bush and others to distinguish terrorism from Islam. Although to equate the two would of course be a grave injustice, we cannot explain it away as the all-too-rare enlightened stance of the Bush administration. For one thing, distinguishing Islam from terrorism decreases the hostility by Muslim people and nations toward the United States and allows for a coalition that includes Islamic nations. For another, it gives the United States the ability to detach "terrorism" from Islam and reattach it to other kinds of groups, political values, and activist tactics. The State Department lists almost 30 terrorist organizations in its pre–September 11 report on terrorism (including Islamic fundamentalists, Irish and Basque separatists, and Colombian, Philippine, Japanese, Turkish, Peruvian, and Spanish Marxist insurgents), and the list can grow indefinitely (http://www.state.gov/s/ct/rls/pgtrpt/2000/index.cfm?docid=2450). In this war against an unspecified enemy, the capacity to produce distinctions can create the very authority to produce future articulations.

Looking at the production of hybrids, distinctions, and hazes brings us to a more fundamental division—between those who are given the right, authority, and capacity to produce and those who are not. We see this usurping of productive capacities when G. W. Bush, under the right to invoke war, calls for the widespread use of military tribunals. In addition, he gives himself the right to decide on a case-by-case basis who will be brought to trial. Obviously, not everyone has the capacity to exercise authority in this war. If so, Cuba could legitimately declare war on the United States for providing support for Cuban exiles who for 40 years have been involved in violent anti-Castro activities (often with U.S. military and intelligence support). Or take Vietnam, which defines the Free Vietnam organization as a terrorist group involved in bombings over the past few years (Martelle & Tran, 2001). For that nation to declare war on terrorism would mean sending troops to Los Angeles, the headquarters of Free Vietnam. These are absurd scenarios only because the United States has internationally appropriated the right to produce meanings, generalize them, and take action based on them.

Domestically, one could argue that the capacity to produce suspicion, rumors, secrecy, and even humor have all been quickly appropriated by official organs, whereas more popular, ground-level versions are problematized, if not criminalized. Even the meanings of democracy, patriotism, freedom, and dissent seem to require an Office of Homeland Security press release to achieve proper definition. In sum, the capacity to create antagonism (us/them) and associations (e.g., "We the People") is increasingly being hijacked in the name of fog war.

But as authority is becoming concentrated, so the capacity to produce is being challenged and brought into public discussion. We can see the cracks in popular and elite consensus around the military tribunals, precisely because Bush wants to usurp the right to define justice, war, peace, democracy, and the "American." This excessive appropriation of power without responsibility, accountability, and reversibility may engender a backlash that calls into question that very power. Jean Baudrillard (2001) argued that at the symbolic level, the September 11 attacks themselves were a singular response to a system that monopolizes power: "By taking all the cards to itself, it forces the Other to change the rules of the game." Certainly, we can imagine a way to confront this concentration that does not rely on ghastly murder. Perhaps one confronts the "constituted power" of the new war with the "constituent power" of the democratic and popular subjects in whose proper name this war is fought (Hardt & Negri, 2000).

This would mean producing alternative hybrids, associations, and distinctions (why is it that the statement "with us or against us" currently belongs only to the state?). We can see this in the postal workers who publicly refused to be sacrificed as casualties of biowar while state executives were safely shielded from anthrax dangers. We can also see this new alliance in the thousands of Ground Zero firefighters who protested mayoral cutbacks of their recovery efforts. They walked the streets in November chanting "They took the gold out!" while Giuliani sent in the police to arrest dozens of them. We can see in these actions, along with the inexhaustible Ground Zero spirit of mutual aid and cooperation, a form of association outside of its exploitation by a war state. These are refusals of the fog machine of war, and they draw their own lines.

References

Baudrillard, J. (2001, November 2). The spirit of terrorism (R. Bloul, Trans.). *Le Monde*. Available from http://slash.autonomedia.org/article.pl?sid= 01/11/14/1753229&mode= nested&threshold=

Bratich, J. Z. (2002). Cultural studies, immanent war, everyday life. *Cultural Studies ↔ Critical Methodologies, 2*(1), 20-23.

Deleuze, G., & Guattari, F. (1987). *A thousand plateaus* (B. Massumi, Trans.). Minneapolis: University of Minnesota Press.

Gullo, K. (2001, December 7). Ashcroft defends anti-terror tactic. *Associated Press.* Available from http://www.washingtonpost.com/wp-dyn/articles/A7595-2001Dec7.html

Hardt, M., & Negri, A. (2000). *Empire.* Cambridge, MA: Harvard University Press.

Kiesling, E. (2001, September-October). On war without the fog. *Military Review: The Professional Journal of the U.S. Army, 81*(5), 85-87.

Martelle, S., & Tran, M. (2001, October 21). Vietnam calls O.C. group terrorists. *Los Angeles Times,* p. 1.

Massumi, B. (1993). Everywhere you want to be: Introduction to fear. In B. Massumi (Ed.), *The politics of everyday fear* (pp. 3-38). Minneapolis: University of Minnesota Press.

Jack Z. Bratich is assistant professor of communication at the University of New Hampshire.

Policing the Porous
Electronic Civil Disobedience after 9/11

19

HEIDI MARIE BRUSH

I N AN ATTEMPT TO DEFEND NATIONAL security against diffuse networks of terror, pundits of all stripes now scrutinize all porous systems—the airlines, immigration policies, the immune systems of its citizens, national borders, and indeed, the Internet. In the service of security, all that is secret, unknown, or concealed must be examined and analyzed for any hint of a threat or danger. Opposed to the stable and sedentary infrastructure of the United States, cellular organizations may emerge and flourish undetected against a mundane backdrop. Existing out in the open, in the everyday, among the mundane, terror cells threaten a security state through unknowable passages and viral transformations. Against a stable backdrop, cellular operations take up residence, achieve opaque agendas, mutate—and move on as nomads, traveling without leaving a trace.

In the spring of 2001, Osama bin Laden and Al Qaeda gained brief notoriety for the capability of waging an electronic jihad. Terror plans were apparently hidden on triple-X Web sites using a technique called steganography, or "covered writing," that allows messages to be hidden in seemingly mundane or even profane spaces. Unlike encryption, which scrambles messages, rendering them acutely detectable albeit theoretically untranslatable, steganography relies on the inherent lack of scrutiny given to unencrypted, mundane surfaces. Stego is hiding data within data, a kind of high-tech invisible ink. A cell organization posting messages on those most American of pursuits, sports and pornography, has rendered the most innocent or vacuous documents suddenly suspect.

Both steganography and encryption resist easy surveillance and regulation, as does the Internet at large, prompting security agencies to rally for more funds to track, monitor, and evaluate anyone who might be just a little . . . suspicious.

Radical political organizations both online and offline now face two new challenges as a result of the Anti-Terror Act and the move to loosen restrictions on the FBI's ability to spy on domestic political and religious organizations. Hiding out in the open, terror plans may be hatched in mosques or churches, or perhaps in an antiglobalization group, so security-minded experts opine. To be all that much more thorough, undoing restrictions on the FBI would allow a potential return to Hoover-era COINTELPRO spying on unmanageable, "problem" groups (resulting in infiltrations of nonviolent leftist groups associated with the antiwar movement, as well as more militant groups such as the Black Panthers).

The Anti-Terror Act's implementation of life in prison for computer violations (such as hacking) and the FBI's new capacities for spying on domestic organizations may at first glance suggest merely an intensification of a security state. These new policies, however, have a more collusive and cumulative consequence for radical political organizations that use the Internet for political protest, engaging in acts of Electronic Civil Disobedience (ECD). ECD is a political strategy that uses electronic techniques for the purpose of blocking information access and/or disrupting the functioning of any institution. Examples include hacking, denial of service attacks, posting electronic graffiti, and staging virtual sit-ins. ECD transforms the traditional practices of civil disobedience, such as nonviolent demonstrations focusing on economic disruption and symbolic protests, and relocates the forum of resistance from the streets onto the Internet. The EZLN Zapatistas movement is widely cited as the first implementation of ECD.

The Critical Art Ensemble's 1995 book *The Electronic Disturbance* defined "electronic resistance" and actively promoted a netwar, or ECD. Nonviolent actors such as the Zapatistas and the Electronic Disturbance Theatre have successfully engaged in ECD to achieve publicity for their cause, as well as actively disrupting the functioning of oppressive institutions. In light of the Anti-Terror Act, as well as an increased possibility of infiltration of resistant groups by law enforcement, what are the implications for actors engaged in ECD? Must nonviolent electronic political opposition come with the consequence of a lifetime in jail for protesting the WTO or NAFTA? Will denial of service attacks on corporate sites, such as Starbucks or GE, be classified as acts of terrorism?

Hakim Bey wrote of a time all too long ago when there existed "Pirate Utopias"—concealed pockets of lawlessness and bliss outside the realm of nations and maritime law. Borrowing from cyberpunk author Bruce Sterling, Bey imagined similar enclaves online as "Islands in the Net"—spaces rendered invisible to scrutiny and control made possible through encryption and steganography. Groups involved in ECD puckishly exploit these opportunities implicit in the network structure of the Internet. Must political organizations now shy away from online protest in fear of lifetime punishment for their civil disobedience? Are all cellular political organizations (such as the Zapatistas or the Black Bloc) now suspect as terrorists, rendering all of their communiqués threats to national security? Is all communication that is hidden (hidden CD tracks on a Web page) or encrypted (private e-mails) now criminally suspect?

Against the unfixed and even viral movements of Al Qaeda, the United States and its numerous three-letter agencies seek to locate an enemy without coordinates and to fix in its targets messages that cannot be seen. The messages could be anywhere, on your Web site or in my in-box. Is there nowhere left to hide?

References

Bey, H. (1995). T.A.Z. *The temporary autonomous zone, ontological anarchy, poetic terrorism*. Brooklyn, NY: Autonomedia.

Critical Art Ensemble. (1995). *The electronic disturbance*. Brooklyn, NY: Autonomedia.

Heidi Marie Brush is working toward her doctorate at the Institute of Communications Research at the University of Illinois, Urbana-Champaign.

Thank the Lord, It's a War to End All Wars . . . Or, How I Learned to Suspend Critical Judgment and Love the Bomb

20

ROBERT W. MCCHESNEY

ACK IN 1991, DURING THE GULF WAR, approximately four or five U.S. foreign wars ago for those of you keeping score at home, the late great Erwin Knoll, longtime editor of *The Progressive* magazine, was a regular panelist on the *MacNeil-Lehrer Newshour* on PBS. During a discussion of the war, one of the more conservative panelists argued that it was mandatory that the American people rally around the war effort and "support the troops." Knoll responded, "Everyone says we have to support the troops, because no one can tell us why we should be in this war."

I thought of Knoll's comments in November 2001 when I was a guest at the University of Missouri. To counter an antiwar protest on campus, several people gathered to have a prowar demonstration. Their signs said two basic things: One was the ubiquitous "Support the Troops." The other message said, "Our Troops Are Fighting to Protect Your Freedom to Protest." The first message, as Knoll keenly observed, was a bankrupt claim that any dictator or fascist could use to rally support for war. In fact, I suspect they usually do rely on that rallying cry. The second message I found profoundly ironic, in an Orwellian sense, because the Bush administration and Attorney General Ashcroft were using the war as a reason to make the greatest attack on civil liberties in the United States for generations, perhaps ever. After Bush and Ashcroft completed their handiwork, the Bill of Rights looked like Swiss cheese.

It is at moments such as these that the importance of media in a democratic society comes into focus.

In times of crisis, the challenge for journalism in a democratic society is daunting. The decision to enter war, not to mention world war, is arguably the most important any society can make. In a free society, such a decision must be made with the informed consent of the governed. Otherwise, the claim to be a democratic nation is dubious, if not fraudulent.

The degree of difficulty for journalists increases exponentially as well. Unless it is the run-of-the-mill quickie carpet bombing by a superpower of a powerless opponent, governments need active support for the war effort, both to pay for the cost of war and to provide the soldiers willing to die for the war. It has proven to be a difficult job in the United

States to enlist such popular support for war. Over the past century, the U.S. government has worked aggressively to convince the citizenry of the necessity of going to war in numerous instances. In cases such as World War I, World War II, Korea, Vietnam, and the Gulf War, the government employed sophisticated propaganda campaigns to whip the population into a suitable fury. Candidates won the presidency in 1916, 1940, and 1964 on peace platforms when the record shows they were working diligently to go to war. It was well understood within the establishment at the time—and subsequently verified in historical examinations—that the government needed to lie to gain support for its war aims. The Pentagon Papers provided the most chilling documentation imaginable of this process.

The media system, in every one of those cases, complied with government war aims. This is widely understood among U.S. journalism educators, and when we teach of these historic episodes of journalism, it tends to be with remorse and concern. This is the context for understanding the media coverage since September 11. The historical record suggests we should expect an avalanche of lies and half-truths in the service of power. Journalists, the news media, should be extremely skeptical, demanding evidence for claims, opening the door to other policy options, and asking the tough questions that nobody in power wants to address; the historical track record is emphatic in this regard.

The record is clear: Our mainstream news media have dropped the ball again. They have provided stenography to those in power, and because those in power all agree that this is a jolly good war, our news media have informed us that this is a jolly good war. Because there has been virtually no debate between the Democrats and Republicans over the proper response, the military approach has simply been offered as the only option. As National Public Radio's Cokie Roberts put it on October 8 when asked on air if there was any domestic opposition to the bombing of Afghanistan: "None that mattered."

Almost entirely absent was comment on or analysis of one of the most striking features of the war campaign, something that any credible journalist would be quick to observe were the events taking place in Russia or China or Pakistan: There are very powerful interests in the United States who greatly benefit politically and economically by the establishment of an unchecked war on terrorism. This consortium of interests can be called, to use President Eisenhower's term, the *military-industrial complex*. The war on terrorism is a gift from heaven for the military-industrial complex. It justifies vast increases in budgets and power and less accountability to Congress. It is a war that is endless, can never be won. And it is a war that the public will never have any way of monitoring because the terrorist enemy is by definition detached from governments that can be defeated.

For journalists to raise issues like these does not presuppose that they oppose government policies, merely that the policies need to be justified and explained so the support will be substantive, not ephemeral, the result of deliberation, not manipulation. Such has not been the case.

The propagandistic nature of the war coverage was made crystal clear by CNN a few weeks after the war began in Afghanistan. CNN is not only the leading U.S. cable news network, it is the leading global cable and satellite news network. The war has put CNN in a pickle. If it broadcasts the pro-U.S. pabulum it generates in the United States to international audiences, audiences react negatively. International audiences are getting a much more critical take on the war and the U.S. role in their newspapers and other media, and they will not watch CNN if it is seen as a front for the Bush administration. On the other hand, if CNN presents such critical coverage to U.S. audiences, it will outrage people in power here. CNN President Walter Isaacson solved this dilemma by authorizing CNN to provide two different versions of the war: a critical one for the global audience and a sugarcoated one for Americans. Indeed, Isaacson instructed the domestic CNN to be certain that any story that might undermine support for the U.S. war be balanced with a reminder that the war on terrorism is a good war.

In this climate, it should be no surprise that most Americans support the war, though they know next to nothing about the region we are fighting in and its history or the U.S. role in the world.

There are many morals to this story. When people in power speak in unison, one should be skeptical. When people in power wish to go to war and use patriotism and emotional appeals to quiet dissent and garner support, one's skepticism should increase exponentially. The track record is that such a war is a lie. And what James Madison wrote in 1822 is as true today as ever:

> A popular Government, without popular information, or the means of acquiring it, is but a prologue to a farce or a tragedy; or, perhaps both. Knowledge will forever govern ignorance; and a people who mean to be their own governors must arm themselves with the power which knowledge gives.

We avoid dealing with the clear political implications of Madison's statement at our peril.

Robert W. McChesney teaches communication at the University of Illinois, Urbana-Champaign.

Coming Apart at the Seam

21

DIERDRE GLENN PAUL

S O, WHAT IS THE ROLE OF the cultural studies scholar at a time like this? For this scholar at least, it is not to believe the hype.

Since September 11th, I have operated in a fugue state—a disturbed state of consciousness in which the one affected seems to perform acts in full awareness but on recovery cannot recollect the deeds. On that day, I was compelled to move beyond my own confusion and fear. After all, I felt an obligation to teach my class and function as department chairperson. What message would have been sent to students, faculty, and staff if I had failed to show, while the university required them to appear? In a similar fashion, I picked my children up early from school that day. As the day, itself, sent shock waves throughout the nation, my children needed to know that I was there for them. But as my people in the Bronx might say, my mentals was all fucked up, and they have remained that way, even until this present day.

Whereas I have always been aware of my double consciousness, defined by W.E.B. Du Bois (1903) as "ever feel[ing] one's] two-ness—an American, a Negro; two souls, two thoughts, two unreconciled strivings; two warring ideals in one dark body, whose dogged strength alone keeps it torn asunder" (p. 45), I have never before known the conflict between the disparate selves to be so great. Never before have I felt so intensely that my loyalties are torn and they may not ever be reconciled.

As I have seen American flags waving from porches and taped on the sides of cars, hear radio feature stories on proper flag etiquette, and encounter people of varying races and ethnicities sporting all the red, white, and blue merchandise that Tommy Hilfiger and Polo can muster, I wonder why I, too, don't desire to join in this celebratory moment of commonality and camaraderie?

As I sit and listen to First Lady Laura Bush and National Security Advisor Dr. Condoleeza Rice attempt to convince us, the American public, that our resulting war is partially about the liberation of Afghan women from the reign of the Taliban, I sit in a surreal haze and ask myself, What the fuck? Last I knew, charity begins at home; so possibly, Mrs. Bush and Dr. Rice might start with the liberation of American women of color from persistent cycles of poverty, domestic violence, climbing rates of HIV and AIDS infection, and disproportionate incidences of incarceration for low-level drug offenses right here on American soil!

I am a native New Yorker, and upon sight of the demolished towers, I also felt the pain of terrorism, a sense of victimization, and a connection to those killed and injured at the World Trade Center, the Pentagon, and in the air as well. Although the media have chosen to focus on the fire fighters and law enforcement personnel who gave their lives in the line of duty; the White, male airline passengers who brought down some of the hijackers; and the widows of those groups, I ponder the fate of the poor and working-class victims (many of them Black, Latino, and brown, as well as recent immigrants) who were also killed and the aftermath their families are experiencing. I also mourn for those women and men whose heroism was evident in their commitment and willingness to serve while barely making ends meet as restaurant workers, cleaning staff, physical plant workers, and clerks who kept the World Trade Center and the Pentagon operational.

But did the terror act on September 11 truly prompt the American war against terrorism? Although our loss of more than 3,000 people has been horrific and devastating, there are other factors that must be considered as we wage war. For example, the same Taliban that we are currently fighting was given $43 million by the Bush administration just 6 months prior to the writing of this piece. Did we not supply the mujahedin with blowpipe missiles in the early 1980s, so they could kill our mutual enemy at the time, the Russians (Fisk, 2001)? Or what about the blowback (a CIA code word) factor? Osama bin Laden is the "personification of blowback . . . simply defined as an operative or an operation that has turned on its creators" (Moran, 1998). In this instance and once again (as with Saddam Hussein, Manuel Noriega, and Timothy McVeigh, to name a few), the operative has turned on us—the United States.

Furthermore, is this war about avenging the death of those lost on September 11 or using barbarous military force to attenuate the American realm of political power throughout the Middle East? Finally, if it is truly a war on terrorism, is it our terrorist enemies who "slaughter populations outside American spheres of influence" (Fisk, 2001) rather than our terrorist friends that we seek to obliterate? For example, most of the September 11 hijackers have been linked to Sudan, and bin Laden is Saudi born. Yet why weren't these regions targeted in our war against terrorism as well? Is it possible that the decision has been a strategic one—these countries are too valuable to us in the oil trade?

Yet I think that this war has an even more fundamental set of questions that must be addressed. Isn't it possible that by focusing attention on an "exotic," brown, collective enemy, we may choose against questioning the premature tax rebate checks we received over the summer, prepared for dissemination prior to the planning of the budget. If focused on this murderous, brown enemy, we might ignore the increased poverty the nation is experiencing or accept the fact that there are many citizens here who are worse off since this administration took office. We might have to ponder the point that the American loss of life might just be a tangential issue as we have much more to gain (than lose) by fighting this war. President Bush desired to increase the defense budget, lead the country out of recession, and garner public support for his previously floundering presidency. Quite possibly, war room efforts have enhanced his ability to fulfill these objectives.

Another potential outcome of focusing on a collective enemy of color centers on the fact that although encouraged to place our Americanness above all else in the face of a formidable "enemy," racism and classism can still run rampant and virtually unchecked on the home front. In this fashion, very few will question the brand of patriotism that requires large numbers of Asian, Pakistani, and Arab American business owners to post flags in their windows as a way of proving their Americanness and concomitantly ensuring that they are able to remain open for business. Fewer still will challenge the glut of "Muslims-are-people-too" consciousness-raising television specials produced since September 11 or the mixed messages being put forth as John Ashcroft and our government officials simultaneously "green light" racial profiling of Muslims and Arab Americans as a national security measure. In a similar fashion and with the accompanying anthrax scare, only a select number of malcontents might ponder the fact that U.S. postal workers (many of whom are Black and Latino) have been forced to file suit for the government to effectively deal with the life-threatening infiltration of anthrax throughout their workplace, whereas government representatives were evacuated when it seeped into theirs. In a myriad of ways, if we remain focused on the enemy/outsider, we lose sight of the enemy within.

So, what is the role of the cultural studies scholar at a time like this? For this scholar at least, it is not to believe the hype. My job is to pose difficult questions and challenge standard operating procedures. My role is to ward off attempts to hoodwink me into believing that the U.S. government is fighting this war in Afghanistan to protect my freedom and avenge the death of innocent American victims by killing innocent Afghans in more instances than are recounted by the American media or that controlled by its allies. In actuality, this war just might be about saving face, bolstering a sagging economy and seemingly inept president, and embarking on a new Middle Eastern adventure, replete with the eventual "overthrow of Saddam Hussein, the destruction of the Lebanese Hezbollah, the humbling of Syria, the humiliation of Iran, [and] the reimposition of yet another fraudulent 'peace process' between Israel and the Palestinians" (Fisk, 2001). My role is like that of many cultural critics, to "present harsh truths that society would rather ignore and discredit" (Paul, 2001, p. 6).

References

Du Bois, W.E.B. (1903). *The souls of Black folks*. New York: Fawcett.

Fisk, R. (2001, September 25). *Robert Fisk: This is not a war on terror. It's a fight against America's enemies* (Independent.co.uk Argument). Available from http://argument.independent.co.uk/commentators/story.jsp?story=95825

Moran, M. (1998, August 24). *Bin Laden comes home to roost: His CIA ties are only the beginning of a woeful story* (MSNBC Opinions). Available from http://www.msnbc.com/news/190144.asp

Paul, D. G. (2001). *Life, culture, and education on the academic plantation: Womanist thought and perspective*. New York: Peter Lang.

Dierdre Glenn Paul, associate professor and chairperson of literacy and educational media at Montclair State University, is a scholar-activist, mother, and author.

9/11, Iran, and Americans' Knowledge of the U.S. Role in the World   **22**

JOE L. KINCHELOE

WHAT SCHOLARS CHOOSE TO WRITE about the September 11 attacks cannot be considered outside the context of knowledge production and the formation of the American consciousness of global politics and the nation's role in the world. As I thought about these dimensions of the September tragedies, I observed an audience member commenting about such issues on *Talkback Live* on CNN. The speaker was disturbed by what she described as the hatred of America by many countries around the world. "Why do they hate us?" she asked.

> All we have ever done is help people around the world. When there are tragedies, we are the first ones there. We mean nobody harm, we just want to live at peace with the rest of the world. None of this makes any sense to me. Why do people from other countries want to hurt the most generous and helpful nation on the face of the earth? We're the most peaceful people anywhere. I don't get it.

After a few class meetings with students following the attacks, I realized that such sentiments were not uncommon. In this context, I thought back to the opinions expressed by many Americans and by my students in the period following the Iranian hostage crisis. The sentiments of Americans at that time were very similar to the ones expressed so clearly by the woman on CNN. In response to such perspectives in the early 1980s, I was moved to write an essay raising questions about the historical relationships at work in Iran that motivated millions of Iranians to march through the streets of Teheran shouting, "Death to America." The historical insights explaining Iranian anger toward the United States are still not known by many Americans 20 years later. In light of September 11, these events take on new import as they help Americans understand one example of larger patterns of U.S. relationships with Islamic countries. They provide insight into the reasons for hatreds strong enough to motivate the viciousness of the assaults on the World Trade Center and the Pentagon.

Such issues raise profound questions for scholars of education and knowledge production in the United States. When the level of discourse about September 11 is based on presidential and TV news proclamations that we were attacked because the terrorists "hate our freedom," we understand the dimension of the problem facing us. As one White working-class man put it in a conversation with me in October 2001,

> the Muslims hate us because we're better than them and smarter than them. I'd like to kill every one of them—every man, woman, child, dog, cat, horse, and mule in Afghanistan. They are primitive people—and they don't understand anything other than raw force. I say kill 'em all.

When I asked him if he had ever thought about why many Muslims hate America so much, he told me that he didn't know and didn't care. Indeed, part of the reason many Muslims—and other peoples around the world—are so uncomfortable with the United States is for this very reason: We are so often ignorant of the problems they have with American actions in the world. If the United States was a nation secluded from the world, was not engaging in trade and commerce and political negotiations, such ignorance might be understandable. But, of course, we are not separated from the rest of the world. In fact, the United States is intimately involved on numerous levels with every other nation on earth—often in ways that do not serve the best interests of these other societies.

Returning to the Iranian hostage crisis and the Iranian revolution, I found in my research that few mainstream news magazines or TV network news programs at the time (1979–1981) ever provided a meaningful historical answer to the important question of why so many Iranians were so angry at the United States. It did not take Woodward and Bernstein to discern the post–World War II events that enraged the Iranian public. As newspapers and magazines from other parts of the world had reported on numerous occasions, and scholars of Iran both outside and inside the United States knew, the United States and Britain had staged a coup to overthrow the first democratically elected government of Iran. In 1951, Mohammed Mossadegh was elected prime minister of Iran. He immediately angered the West by initiating efforts to nationalize the primarily British-controlled oil industry. Whereas the United States in the past year and a half of the Truman administration was uncomfortable with the British plan for a coup, the Eisenhower administration eagerly supported it after the presidential inauguration of 1953. So concerned was the new administration with Mossadegh's perceived closeness with leftist factions, it worked to expand the British goals.

Two weeks after Eisenhower's inauguration, U.S. and British officials met to develop the specifics of the covert operation under the code name AJAX. The operation would rid Iran of its parliamentary government, arrest Prime Minister Mossadegh, and buttress the power of Reza Pahlavi, the shah of Iran. Though AJAX was a comedy of errors played out by inept CIA agents, it accomplished all of its goals. Even though the shah was a cowardly and weak figure, the United States and Britain provided him total support. They knew they could control him and use him both to protect their robbery of Iran's oil and position Iran as a buffer between the Soviet Union and the Persian Gulf. With Mossadegh out of the picture, the shah allowed the U.S. military and CIA to build bases in the country to intimidate and gather intelligence on the U.S.S.R. Iranians loyal to the shah were employed by the CIA to pose as communist terrorists. In this role, they harassed Muslim clerics, even bombing their homes in an effort to turn the religious community against left-wing influences.

Of course, in these actions the seeds were planted for the anti-American Iranian Islamic Revolution of 1979. If the coup and the terrorism against the Muslim clerics were not enough, Iranian life under the American-supported shah was characterized by poverty, government-sponsored terrorism against Iranian citizens, torture, and death squads. Thousands of Iranians who criticized the shah were killed under the justification of containing communist influences in the country. The official agency of state terror was called SAVAK—the shah's not-so-secret secret police. Created by the Americans to protect the shah and trained by the CIA in effective torture techniques, SAVAK helped produce what Amnesty International labeled the worst human rights record in the world during the 1950s, 1960s, and 1970s. So brutal was the force that in addition to their covert murders and tortures, they openly fired on thousands of protesting fundamentalist women, killing and wounding hundreds. No one should have been surprised when the fundamentalist revolution broke out in 1979 with the United States positioned as the target of its anger.

One feature of this tragedy that is so important for scholars of knowledge production and education involves the complicity of the American press in these activities. Reporters for U.S. wire services, newspapers, and news magazines were unquestioning participants in the CIA and other government agencies' attempts to circulate "disinformation" and perpetrate cover-ups that would facilitate the coup and the subsequent support of the shah's despotic monarchy. Reporters wrote stories about nonexistent communist plots in Iran. Critics of the shah were duplicitously labeled communist operatives. Newspapers such as *The New York Times* issued editorial warnings to other "underdeveloped countries" of the dangers faced by "fanatical leaders" similar to the "crazed" Mossadegh, if they attempted to withhold their natural resources from the United States. The shah was never criticized and was consistently referred to as a benevolent leader, a progressive reformer with great concern for his people, and a stylish politico who traveled gracefully with his beautiful wife in avant-garde international circles. Despite the overwhelming evidence of the brutality of his regime, the American press squashed stories reported in the Islamic world and beyond.

Having endured 26 years of American-financed horror, the Iranian people literally exploded in revolution at the end of the 1970s. Venting their anti-American feelings, crowds stormed the American embassy in Teheran, capturing 52 Americans. Holding them hostage for 444 days, the revolutionaries used the hostages to gain a forum for their grievances against the "Great Satan." Even then, the mainstream American press and TV news operations suppressed the story. In the quarter century since the Iranian revolution, Islamic militants from a variety of Muslim nations and organizations have pointed to the American story in Iran as just one of many examples of American terrorism directed at Muslim people. The stories of American arrogance, they tell us, are seemingly endless, as each Muslim nation has its own horror story. But even after September 11 and the questions it has raised in the consciousness of the American public, these stories are not widely known. Indeed, efforts to broadcast them are often being punished on college campuses and other public venues. And Americans still do not know what generated all the anger.

Joe L. Kincheloe is a professor of urban education at the City University of New York Graduate Center and Brooklyn College.

French Fries, Fezzes, and Minstrels
The Hollywoodization of Islam

23

SHIRLEY R. STEINBERG

Identity Construction Bullets

- I loved *Ben-Hur* and *Cleopatra*. They were long but riveting. The longest film my parents subjected me to was in 1962 when I sat through *Lawrence of Arabia (LOA)* (Spiegel, Lean, Lawrence, & Lean, 1962). It didn't take long to get the point, the rest of the show was tedious: A minor officer from England was sent to visit Prince Faisal and ended up leading an army of Arabic tribes to fight the Turks— he was a hero. Guess that was my earliest media exposure to Arabs.

- June 1968: Just down the freeway from my school, Robert Kennedy had been shot by Sirhan Sirhan, defined in the news as "a man of Jordanian descent." I loved Bobby—remember the dark and swarthy photos of the murderer, who quickly disappeared from our news limelight.

- In 1968, *Time* magazine featured a cover story on the plight of the Arab refugees. I did a speech based on the issue; I couldn't understand why the Arabic countries surrounding Israel would not let their Muslim brothers and sisters in to their homelands. I understood why the Israelis didn't make room: The country was too small and had been given to Jews. My social studies teacher didn't know anything about it.

- Four years later, just beginning a new college semester, the news hit that Israeli athletes had been kidnapped by Arab terrorists, a group known as Black September. We were glued to the television as we watched cameras cover the occupied residences; we saw shadowy figures identified as the kidnappers on the phone negotiating with authorities. Then we saw the German police shoot and kill both the terrorists and athletes on the tarmac of the Munich airport. I flew to Munich once. I assumed the tarmac was still there. No one was able to show me where it was.

- I had not visited New York City after the Twin Towers had been built. When the World Trade Center was bombed in 1993, it was shocking but very removed from my life. I had never seen the buildings. Few were killed, lots of fancy cars smashed. The news reported it was the work of Arabic terrorists. In 1994, we went to New York and scanned the World Trade Center to see where the bomb had hit. We were astounded at how huge the buildings were and how small the bomb damage had been. The buildings were obviously indestructible.

- In 1996, I was watching CNN in a hotel in San Francisco. A bomb had destroyed a federal building in Oklahoma City. The first words from the radio, TV, and papers indicated that Arabic terrorist groups had planned the mass attack. Hours later, a White man was in custody. No apology to the previously identified perps. I believe some Arab Americans complained about the erroneous accusation; the news quickly moved on to the unfolding McVeigh story.
- A network break-in to regular programming in 1997 revealed the headliner that Princess Diana had been killed in an auto accident along with her boyfriend, Dodi Fayed. Fayed was a Muslim, an Egyptian, whose wealthy father had been denied British citizenship by the queen—he also owned Harrod's of London. Continued tabloid coverage that year claimed that Diana could have been murdered to keep her from humiliating the royal family by her relationship with an undesirable man.
- September 11, 2001.

I love media. I love film, television, radio, and print. We unabashedly have several TVs in the house; they are always on. We watch movies—on tape, on television, and in the theatre. I listen to the radio 2 hours a day commuting and devour a newspaper if given the time to sit and read it. Magazines are a joy; books on tape save me on long trips. The media is also part of my vocation; it is natural for me to play with it, analyze it, and criticize it. After September 11, my pleasure became my pain as I watched each breaking news story, over and over again, on every channel—in every venue. I also knew I had to write about what I saw and heard. As I romped through my memories and the construction of my consciousness about Muslims and Arabic-speaking people, I decided to analyze how the cultural pedagogy of Hollywood had depicted these groups.

I maintain that if pedagogy involves issues of knowledge production and transmission, the shaping of values, and the construction of subjectivity, then popular culture is the most powerful pedagogical force in contemporary America. The pedagogy of popular culture is ideological, of course, in its production of commonsense assumptions about the world, its influence on our affective lives, and its role in the production of our identities and experiences (Grossberg, 1992). Movies help individuals articulate their feelings and moods that ultimately shape their behavior. Audiences employ particular images to help define their own tastes, images, styles, and identities—indeed, they are students of media and film pedagogy. Audiences often allow popular culture, vis-à-vis films, to speak for them, to provide narrative structures that help them make sense of their lives. This emotional investment by the audience can often be organized in emotional/ideological/affective alliances with other individuals, texts, and consciousness formations.

Thus, this affect mobilized by the popular culture of film provides viewers with a sense of belonging, an identification with like-minded individuals—this feeling becomes progressively more important in our fragmented society (Grossberg, 1992). Keeping in mind the complexity of the effects of film popular culture, the affect produced is different in varying historical and social contexts. With these notions in mind, I went in search of the assumptions that may have been made in the viewing of films containing Arab or Muslim characters. I did have a couple of research questions in mind: Why is it so easy for many North Americans to hate Muslims? Why are they so easy to fear and blame? With these questions, I hoped the films I viewed would shed some tentative answers and, more important to my own scholarship, ask more questions.

Selecting my films was difficult—and easy: difficult because I wanted to get a large representation of films from which to draw my data and easy because there are few popular films that contain content including Arabs or Muslims. I selected 17 films and watched and rewatched them on television or videotape. I selected movies that any modicum of my memory signaled that there was sufficient depiction of Arabs and/or Muslims to discuss. I began to view the films and scripted scenes and/or dialogue that needed reexamination. After I had gathered these data, I revisited my notes to identify themes, archetypes, and auteurship in the films. With brevity in mind, I will delineate some of my observations and findings in this article (a longer version of this article will be included in *The Miseducation of the West: Reexamining Western-Muslim Relations*) (Kincheloe, Steinberg, & Kharem, forthcoming).

Most of the films I viewed dealt with Muslim Arabs. However, *Not Without My Daughter (NWMD)* (Ufland, Ufland, & Gilbert, 1990) and *East Is East* (Udwin, Khan-Din, & O'Donnell, 1998) are films about Muslims, not Arabs. Sally Field's compelling, yet whining performance in *NWMD* dealt with an American married to an Iranian doctor who deceitfully brought his wife and daughter to his home in Iran. Sally did not want to go: "We can't go to Iran—it's much too violent." Swearing on the Koran, "Moody" promises they will be safe. After reaching Iran, greeted by a slain goat (in their honor), Sally is somewhat horrified. Cultural analysis is attempted by Sally and her spouse: "It just seems so primitive." "Beliefs seem primitive when they aren't your own." Mother and daughter became prisoners as the husband reverted to Ayotollah-generated fundamentalism. "Islam is the greatest gift I can give," assured Moody. Persian women (in full black burqahs) were yammering, scheming, whispering, and occasionally being beaten by their husbands or other available men—this was a dark, frightening, and smothering world to the former Sister Bertrille. The film was released shortly after Iranians kidnapped the American embassy employees. *NWMD* was based on a true story of one woman's experience.

East Is East (Udwin et al., 1998) is British Broadcasting Corporation–produced and deals with a lower-middle-class Pakistani man who marries a British woman. He insists on being a traditional Muslim; his wife respects that—as long as her husband doesn't catch the children carrying the statue of Jesus during the Easter parade. Not a bad looking man, Dad is devastated by his older son bailing out of his own wedding. He tries to match-make the other boys: "I'm not marrying a fucking Paki." As a father, he is overbearing in his desire to see his children as happy Muslims—he adds insult to injury as he pushes his gift of a watch with Arabic numerals on each child. They are angry when he insists they go to a school to learn the Koran. After various defeats, he begins to beat his wife and children.

I noticed that the camera angles began to change, and as the father got meaner, the character was being filmed from below the nostrils of his huge, sweating, bulbous nose—he also had yellowed, crooked teeth. He frustratingly bemoans that neighbors think he is a barbarian.

The rest of the films were about Arabs—those from Arabia (or countries divided from Arabia). With the exception of *LOA* (Spiegel et al., 1962), all films were filmed in the West. *LOA* is a dramatic (have I mentioned long?) saga about a blond, blue-eyed Englishman who, caught up in the myth of Arabia and the desert, convinces marauding rival Bedouin bands of "barbarians" to unite in their fight against the equally "barbaric" Turks. Peter O'Toole's character is a prototype to Sean Connery and Mel Gibson and is accompanied by Omar Sharif, once an enemy—now a converted sidekick. Angering the British, "Has he gone native?" Lawrence eventually leaves Arabia—naturally in better condition than he found it: "I did it. . . . Arabia is for the Arabs now. . . . Any time spent in a bed would be a waste, they are a nation of sheepskins. . . . They [the Arabs] are dirty savages. . . . Arabs are a barbarous people."

Ironically, films that were Arabic in context and content had little to do with Arabs. *Abbott and Costello Meet the Mummy* (Christie, Grant, & Lamont, 1955), *Arabesque* (1966), *Casablanca* (Wallis, Philip, Epstein, & Curtiz, 1943), *The Mummy* (Daniel, Jacks, & Sommers, 1999), *The Mummy Returns* (Jacks, Daniel, Sommers, & Underwood, 2001), *Ishtar* (May, 1987), and *The Jewel of the Nile* (Douglas, Rosenthal, Konner, & Teague, 1985) contained plots directly concerned with Arabic/Islamic themes, actors with dialogue were Western, and depending on the film, extras appeared to be Arabic. Action shots with Arabic peoples were almost exclusively shot in loud marketplaces. No heads left uncovered, the fez is an accessory of choice for comical extras. The militaristic extras (sword carrying) most often wore a kaffiyeh (couture Arafat)—several Arabs sported turbans. What struck me about the extras was the "clumping" in which they would always appear. Let me borrow from Joe Kincheloe (1997) as he described the French Fry Guys of McDonaldland: "The most compelling manifestation of conformity in McDonaldland involves the portrayal of the French Fry Guys. As the only group of citizens depicted in the Hamburger Patch, these faceless commoners are numerous but seldom seen" (p. 259).

> They intend to look, act, and think pretty much alike. Parent French Fry Guys are indistinguishable from children, and visa versa. They are so much alike that, so far, no individual French Fry Guy has emerged as a personality identifiable from the others. They resemble little mops with legs and eyes and speak in squeaky, high-pitched voices, usually in unison. They always move quickly, scurrying around in fits and starts. (McDonald's Customer Relations Center handout, 1994, p. 260)

Kincheloe (1997) went on, "As inhabitants of a McDonaldized McWorld, the French Fry Guys are content to remove themselves from the public space, emerging only for brief and frenetic acts of standardized consumption—their only act of personal assertion" (p. 260). In these films, Hollywood's French frying of Arabs leaves them to stand in clumps, to surround the action, to yell loudly in the background, and to run the market. They are incompetent in keeping their shop area organized as someone is always running through it—knocking the wares down and leaving a fist-flinging kaffiyeh-clad merchant screaming from behind.

As with Sharif in *LOA*, many of the films introduce a sidekick character for the White male lead. Loyal and faithful to death, the Tonto-ized friend is simpler, devoutly Muslim, full of Islamic platitudes and premonitions, and frightened easily. In both *Indiana Jones* (Lucas, Kazanjian, Kasdan, & Spielberg, 1981; Lucas, Marshall, Boam, & Spielberg, 1989) films, Indy is accompanied by his Egyptian pal who fears that Indy's ideas are dangerous and will create anger from Allah. He attempts to convince Indiana that he is not stupid: "Even in this part of the world we are not entirely uncivilized." Endangered at times, this minstrelized sidekick puts his hands in the air, opens his eyes widely, and shouts for safety. *Tonto* is a Spanish word for stupid or idiot.

A complete content/discourse analysis of these films introduced to me archetypes that wove throughout the weft of the films. They included the White, male leader, sent to save citizens or artifacts from the unscrupulous. Lawrence and Indiana serve as perfect Arian messiahs to these dark, mysterious Muslims. The word *barbaric* (or *barbarous, barbarian*) was used in each film. *Aladdin* (Disney Studios, 1992) opens with an overture and opening song that describes the mysterious, dark, barbaric East. Physical characteristics of the Arabs generally show bad teeth, large hooked noses, and unclean tunics and caftans and headgear that are just a tad too exaggerated. Once again, *Aladdin* does not run more than 5 minutes without describing one of the Arabic characters as "pungent." The films I viewed metaphorically included aromavision, as one could vividly smell the camel-shit-smeared, dirt-ridden, sweat-clinging clothing of Muslim characters.

The market scenes imply that Islamic countries center their cities and livelihoods on the marketplace. The Shylockization of these people is obvious in their attempts to barter and cheat consumers. Indeed, once again, in *Aladdin* (Disney Studios, 1992), the fat, toothless, dirty Arab "businessman" flings out his tablecloth and for sale sign and indicates that anything can be bought for a price. As I take in his hooked nose and sales pitch, the Semite in his character reminds me vividly that both Jews and Arabs share many of the same stereotypes: They lie, cheat, and steal.

Islamic characters are not only compared to other Semites through an analysis but to other marginalized groups. There were many, many visible comparisons to Hollywood depictions and assumptions about African Americans. Many times I was sure that the Negrofication of these characters served to show that any hated group can be exchanged with another. Exemplifying this is the language that served to incant slurs to African Americans: Sand nigger and dune coon were among the nastiest I heard in the films.

Well then, back to my questions: Why is it so easy for many North Americans to hate Muslims? Why are they so easy to fear and blame? These questions are so obviously complicated and unanswerable. However, I would maintain my contention that, indeed, popular culture is a curriculum—an overt, influential curriculum that feeds our need to consume entertainment. This Hollywood diet is not innocent; it is constructed on obsession, Otherization, fear, and most important, what sells. I hope we all are able to read the menu.

References

Arabesque. [Motion picture] (1966). Burbank, CA: Warner Bros. Studios.

Christie, H. (Producer), Grant, J. (Writer), & Lamont, C. (Director). (1955). *Abbott and Costello meet the mummy* [Motion picture]. United States: Universal Studios.

Daniel, S. (Producer), Jacks, J. (Producer), & Sommers, S. (Writer/Director). (1999). *The mummy* [Motion picture]. United States: Universal Studios.

Disney Studios (Producer). (1992). *Aladdin* [Motion picture]. United States: Disney Studios.

Douglas, M. (Producer), Rosenthal, M. (Writer), Konner, L. (Writer), & Teague, L. (Director). (1985). *The jewel of the Nile* [Motion picture]. United States: Twentieth Century Fox.

Grossberg, L. (1992). *We gotta get out of this place*. New York: Routledge.

Jacks, J. (Producer), Daniel, S. (Producer), Sommers, S. (Writer), & Underwood, R. (Director). (2001). *The mummy returns* [Motion picture]. United States: Universal Studios.

Kincheloe, J. (1997). McDonald's, power, and children: Ronald McDonald (aka Ray Kroc) does it all for you. In S. R. Steinberg & J. L. Kincheloe (Eds.), *Kinderculture: The corporate control of childhood* (pp. 249–266). Boulder, CO: Westview.

Kincheloe, J., Steinberg, S. R., & Kharem, H. *The miseducation of the west: Reexamining Western-Muslim relations*. Manuscript submitted for publication.

Lucas, G. (Producer), Kazanjian, H. (Producer), Kasdan, L. (Writer), & Spielberg, S. (Director). (1981). *Indiana Jones and the raiders of the lost ark* [Motion picture]. United States: Paramount.

Lucas, G. (Producer), Marshall, F. (Producer), Boam, J. (Writer), & Spielberg, S. (Director). (1989). *Indiana Jones and the last crusade* [Motion picture]. United States: Paramount.

May, E. (Director). (1987). *Ishtar* [Motion picture]. United States: Columbia Pictures.

Spiegel, S. (Producer), Lean, D. (Producer), Lawrence, T. E. (Writer), & Lean, D. (Director). (1962). *Lawrence of Arabia* [Motion picture]. United States: Republic Pictures.

Udwin, L. (Producer), Khan-Din, A. (Writer), & O'Donnell, D. (Director). (1998). *East is east* [Motion picture]. United Kingdom: Miramax.

Ufland, H. (Producer), Ufland, M. (Producer), & Gilbert, B. (Director). (1990). *Not without my daughter* [Motion picture]. United States: Metro-Goldwyn-Mayer.

Wallis, H. (Producer), Philip, J. (Writer), Epstein, G. (Writer), & Curtiz, M. (Director). (1943). *Casablanca* [Motion picture]. United States: Warner Bros.

Shirley R. Steinberg is an associate professor of literacy and educational media at Montclair State University.

The WTC Image Complex
A Critical View on a Culture of the Shifting Image

24

BIRGIT RICHARD

AN IMAGE NO LONGER TELLS MORE than a thousand words—images seem to offer many views from different angles. Perfectly recorded high-resolution images become enigmatic entities that are impossible to encipher. Although images show clear details, these images leave the spectator speechless, viewing the Taliban at war. The camera seems to be involved directly as the image-producing apparatus has become an active part of the battlefield and megazoom images are so close to the viewer.

We have never seen anything to equal the images of the first bombings of Kabul. In the war against Afghanistan, the United States has created nonimages. The first bombing of Kabul made TV-viewing Europe angry with CNN, who transmitted the same infrared night images already known from the Gulf War. The images of bombs over Baghdad were culturally implemented into our social memory. After 10 years, the same green sparkles reappear. War and image technologies came to a standstill with these propaganda images. Repetitive, they turn into pure nothingness and emptiness: green-colored noise. Bombs provided redundant images; it could be Baghdad again, or Kabul, we are unable to be informed by the image. We are given no information that could be transformed into knowledge about the ground war.

What does one do with these images? The images of the attack on the World Trade Center (WTC) were very clear, but the problem in reception was the preformation of memory through film imagination. This made it difficult to understand the meaning of what was seen. It is important to keep Slavoj Zizek's characterization of images in mind: They are partly situated in the subconscious in an area between the symbolic and the imaginary. It is always difficult to get certain images out of your receptory system although you may know about their possible manipulative character (Zizek, as cited in Holert, 2000, p. 27).

The aim of this destructive terrorist attack was to create a symbolic image that will remain in the subconsciousness of the West for many years. The new dimension of terror is its globality—terror has always been global—but due to the access to image, the design becomes a horrible aesthetic behind which is the killing of thousands of people. It is not only about killing and destroying but creating a monumental image of the destruction of a symbol that can leave the collective memory. This material iconoclasm leads to the unbelievable disappearance of the Twin Towers and thousands of human beings. It is paradoxical that an iconoclastic fundamentalism has created one of the strongest images that global powers have ever had to deal with. To this point, America has found no images to put against these images of destruction and collapse—images that can serve to eradicate the horrible event. The war against terror has not created strong images. America's new war and the American flag are no match for the symbolic attack. Photographers and camera operators have assisted in fulfilling a mission of the terrorists by reproducing the images of terror in real time. Terror was transformed into an aesthetic image.

The politics of visibility exist without indicating which images are covered through other images. Death and the corpses are hidden categories; the architectural destruction is shown. The aesthetic remains of the WTC do not show any traces of the thousands of dead bodies vaporized or body parts. There is no language or symbolical image for the thousands of dead bodies. The firemen are left alone with their horrible work that includes the gaze and the handling of body parts. On the other hand, the ruins of the WTC, the open wound in Manhattan, have to be plastered completely with images: crosses, angels, and photographs. This overemphasizes the basic paradigm of visual culture: Visibility does not equal transparency (Rogoff, 1999, p. 22). The unconscious metastatic production of images lacks an imagery that may be used for fueling a critical approach on the behavior of Americans and their allies. It is no longer the postmodern problem of the manipulated digital image but a concern with these politics of visibility. The images shown are not complex or multilayered; they are pure surfaces (Flusser, 1990, p. 33), with no hidden truth behind them—only images that push aside other images.

Shifting Images and Image Neighborhoods

A shifting image moves around and is connected to other images that build up clusters. Because the loop of destruction went around the world on September 11, this universe of images has to be remodeled. Now, every image visible or invisible has to find its new place in the structure. Sets of images that were accepted for decades become invisible for the moment. Shifting images do not stay at one place. Every time a new strong image appears, it brings movement into momentarily fixed images.

An image is not a firm entity. Images as representations include the attitudes of the spectators because there is no objective image to be viewed unsituated. There is not a single picture but one that must include rituals and habits composed around the reception and production. A critical analysis of the shifting image does not focus on an artist's extraordinary images. Art history has misinformed us that there is a singular image. We must include the image clusters and neighborhoods. The shifting image designs new meanings with every movement; there is no standstill in this universe. Images are characterized through their connectivity; they build knots in a rhizomatic structure. It is important to watch the movement of the images from one system to another and how they change their meanings by shifting, for example, in the case of September 11, from the art system to politics. Within the emerging networks, images crossover between social systems. As we include with the Internet, they are able to cross from one culture into another. Images are not to be bound to one specific analytical discourse.

Traditionally, different academic disciplines attempt to keep an image in or out of their systems. For example, it would be blasphemy for an art historian to purge an image from William Turner (18th century) out of the system to build up a new neighborhood with the photographs that have been made from the shell of the shattered WTC. The image clusters of Ground Zero, especially of the more artistic photographers (e.g., from the Magnum Photographers), are interesting. Their photos of the smoking remains enter into a special correspondence with the images of high art. Besides a close analysis of the formal qualities of the images, it is important to show relations between images. One does not construct analogies: A picture of the ruins of the WTC is not regarded equal to an image painted by William Turner.

New connective knots can create a cluster that can be interpreted as a sign of how a society tries to cope with its loss. The treatment of horror as an art creates symbols— transforms them into socially meaningful images. The entire WTC image cluster is so awful and strange that it begs questions. Why are images of postal workers with masks framed with the anthrax virus? Why did people in Manhattan wear masks even if they were far away from the smoldering Ground Zero? Why was a stylized accessory made from gas masks? Why does Bert from *Sesame Street* accompany Bin Laden?

The Bert and Bin Laden Story

The shifting image is globally available via the Internet. The Net is where a global image culture has concentrated its public archives. Although the destruction loop of the twin towers was originated in TV, these images were digitized and immediately put on the Net. Users could choose between countless perspectives, from professional and amateur videos and photos or screenshots from the different news channels showing the attacks on the WTC live. The Internet has established itself as a premium public storage for moving and still images that can be used by anybody with access. The shifting image is crosscultural and intersects cultures in its digitized form over the Net. A U.S. Web site uses the word *jihad* for expressing hate against the character Barney. The Web site is mistaken for an Islamic terrorist site—it is a hate page by an American. The face of Bin Laden was also immediately integrated into the western commodities cycle, which transformed him into a Halloween mask.

Shifting images move between cultures creating an Islamic pop culture that uses images of western cultures and defames them by adding their own cultural representations. The Islamic pop culture uses images for protest. To see portraits of idolized Bin Laden in a culture that is normally considered imageless by the West is strange. Posters that show Bin Laden as an Islamic hero are evidence for a popular culture that starts to work according to Western patterns of merchandising (Sterling, 2001). Different images of Bin Laden exist on posters, banners, and T-shirts throughout many countries of the Muslim world. Fan products include highly symbolic images such as the terrorist on a white horse. The terrorist also appears surrounded by a mixture of military planes and the commercial planes the terrorists flew into the WTC. There are posters with the burning Twin Towers in the background. On these images, Bin Laden looks like an Islamic action hero of the likes of Bruce Willis or Wesley Snipes in front of collapsing buildings.

From the cultural view of the West, these posters are paradoxes because they are made for an iconoclastic society (see the Hadith in Islam: "Angels do not enter a room with Figures, Images or dogs"). The availability of images on the Net may influence the way Muslim societies deal with images in general (cinemas reopening in Kabul). Considering strict Islamic restrictions, we question who will be allowed to see the images. (Females in Kabul have traditionally not been able to attend the cinema.)

Through the Internet, the images are able to cross cultures. The fundamentalists had immediate access to images of the burning Twin Towers to use them for propaganda. The digital infowar is fought with images (for the term *infowar*, see Stocker & Schöpf, 1998). Internet images do not privilege one culture; they are there for public use. After they have been picked from the Net, they may be materialized in a printed form, changed, and reproduced for profit. The availability of global images for every culture implies that there is a constant production of new meanings as images do their cross-cultural shift. The best example for this new culture of shifting image is the one that appeared first on the mailing list for Net culture and politics called nettime (www. nettime.org). It showed pro–Bin Laden protesters carrying Bin Laden posters in Bangladesh and Pakistan. The poster was a combination of images downloaded from the Net. One of the images on the poster showed Bin Laden with the character Bert from *Sesame Street*. The image originated from a hate page called "Evil Bert," where an American put Bert into companionship with dictators and terrorists—enemies to the West. The people who printed the poster got their image from the Ignacios Web site. It was discussed on the mailing list as an act of manipulation of the Western media. A posting from Diana Ozon (2001) argued that it was not manipulated. Standing against an act of digital manipulation were different photos from different agencies—different locations in Bangladesh and Pakistan that showed the same poster. How do we understand the process that placed Jim Henson's Bert on that Islamic poster and pronounced him a sibling to terrorists? A posting on nettime talks about the adoption of Bert into Muslim culture in London (Kunzru, 2001).

On American anti–Bin Laden sites, there are other variations of the poster showing Bert on the right and Barney on the left of Bin Laden. Bert, Barney, and Bin Laden have clustered between cultures. It is necessary to critically examine and inquire the field of vision. The culture of shifting image is based on uncertainties about the meaning of the singular image. One has to take a close look on image neighborhoods and clusters to unveil the different cultural discourses that run and transport these images. Researchers must question from different cultural perspectives; a critical spectatorship should take a "curious" look from the angle of the foreign culture to understand the momentary status of the nomadic image.

You Ain't Seen Nothing Yet, but Maybe Later: A Critical Focus on Shifting Images

Bert and Bin Laden show that it is impossible to keep an image in one culture as global access makes that uncontrollable. A critical culture of shifting image may ask for ways to transfer these images that say nothing into information. First, an education toward an image competence avoids a colonialization of other image cultures. An image has to be recognized and reconquered as a form of cultural knowledge and a means of participation.

Viewers need the ability to contextualize the image as active spectators to become cultur-ally competent. The aim is not find out what is the truth behind an image but to ask, Which images do others make invisible?

Image clusters have to be reframed and put into a critical discourse about how images are used to produce political and cultural meaning. This would enable a critical and non-hegemonic look at the political and social complex that infiltrates the field of vision. The image galleries of the WTC attack on the Web do not intend to provoke a critical or cu-rious gaze. The whole complex of images related to the attack does not make meaning alone. So, they have to be filled with proposals for symbolical meaning to allow people to work with the images. As active spectators, we must come to an autonomous imagi-neering against economical and political interests. It is amazing that in the case of the WTC attack, people already have found a way to deal with the event through their own image productions via the Net. Viewers are encouraged to put unknown and unusual transformation of images in public space by collecting and rearranging these images. Viewers must be included as coproducers of cultural meaning. As situated viewers, we must repopulate space through recognizing its constitutive racial and sexual obstacles (Rogoff, *The Production of Space*, 1999, p. 22). Rogoff described space as constituted out of circulating capital and that obstacles never allow us to actually see what is there. We are not asking to "see" behind the image; we are asking what other images are behind the one that is visible.

One approach would be to watch and encode the politics of visibility that deny the transparency of events because they are embedded into discourses of power. Images cover other images. Censorship is no longer the basic strategy to prevent specific images to get visible. Now, an overvisibility of a controlled imagery causes an information overload that chokes questions for the other possible images. A critique of the current image culture has to refer to this shifting image. The constant process of moving the boundaries of visibil-ity should be followed to transform these enigmatic images into cultural knowledge that may question the politics of visibility.

References

Flusser, V. (1990). *Ins Universum der technischen Bilder*. Göttingen, Germany.

Holert, T. (Ed.). (2000). *Imagineering. Visuelle Kultur + Politik der Sichtbarkeit*. Cologne, Germany: ID Press.

Kunzru, H. (2001, October 11). Message posted to nettime mailing list, archived at www.nettime.org

Ozon, D. (2001, October 10). Message posted to nettime mailing list, archived at www. nettime.org

Rogoff, I. (1999). Studying visual culture. In N. Mirzoeff (Ed.), *Visual culture reader*. New York: Rout-ledge.

Sterling, B. (2001, October 19). Bin Laden commercial products cited from *Times of India*. Message posted at www.nettime.org

Stocker, G., & Schöpf, C. (Eds.). (1998). *Infowar. Ars electronica*. New York: Springer.

Birgit Richard has been a professor for new media at the Institue for Art Education at the Johann Wolfgang Goethe, University of Frankfurt.

After 9/11—Thinking About the Global, Thinking About Postcolonial

25

CAMERON MCCARTHY

W HAT FOLLOWS IS NOT AN EXPLANATION of 9/11. For, I suspect such an effort is impossible—as futile as the effort to contain the vast waters of the turbulent sea in a teacup, to capture the sands of the beach in the cup of one's hand. What I write instead is a meditation, a set of scattered thoughts, reflections on the usefulness of postcolonial theorizing in these times, and my own biography as a postcolonial subject and educator.

If there is anyone who still resists the ideas of globalization, transnationalism, postcolonialism, and their implications for how we live with each other in the modern world, their implications for the taken-for-granted organizing categories such as nation, state, culture, identity, and Empire—the idea that we live in a deeply interconnected world in which centers and margins are unstable and are constantly being redefined, rearticulated, and reordered—then, such a person must have been awakened from his or her methodological slumber by the events of 9/11. The critical events of that day—the attacks on the World Trade Center and the Pentagon and the crescendo of the fallout attendant to these extraordinary acts—threaten to consume us all. It is striking, in the language of Michael Hardt and Antonio Negri's *Empire* (2000), how fragile modern forms of center-periphery arrangements of imperial rule are. It is striking—with the intensification of representational technologies, mass migration, the movement of economic and cultural capital across national borders, and the work of the imagination of the great masses of the people (the sorts of things that Arjun Appadurai, 1996, talked about in *Modernity at Large*)—how it is now possible to send shock waves from the margins to the epicenters of the modern life in the world we live in, and for those aftershocks and multiplier effects to sustain themselves indefinitely. Indeed, in addition to all the destabilizing effects and modulations taking place with the U.S. metropolis itself—the declaration and prosecution of war and the attendant pacification at home, the extension of the policing powers of the state, economic tremors of recession and downsizing across corporate enterprises, the daily hemorrhaging of the U.S. labor force as layoffs continue unabated—there are extraordinary ripple effects around the world. Significantly, there are perhaps unintended and unanticipated effects occurring back in the peripheries of the Third World itself. For instance, tourist economies such as those of the Caribbean and in parts of Asia have suffered untold damage. Many tourist economies have witnessed a 60% to 70% falloff in hotel bookings and the like. The World Bank has in fact warned that millions of Third World people will be thrown into deeper deprivation and displacement because of the events of 9/11. One can anticipate yet another infernal round of International Monetary Fund and World Bank interventions in Third World countries. We can now expect the increasing demands for structural adjustment packages that chip away at whatever is left of Keynesianism, Fabian socialism, or plain old welfarism in these countries. Of course, many corporations such as Nike, Starbucks, and Disney have appropriated Keynesianism, rearticulating it as an ironic substance or residue in the form of philanthropy and thereby morphing into the role of statelike promoters of ecumenical feel-good affiliation, self-help forms of involvement in community, and so forth. Disney, in fact, provides a supermodel of community of the way we are supposed to be in the form of the fabricated town, Celebration. As the state disinvests in the public sphere, corporations move in to redefine community in neoliberal terms. Organizations such as Nike's PLAY or Participate in the Lives of American Youth, the national youth organization AmeriCorps, and Teach for America are corporatized philanthropic projects aimed at redirecting the problems of America's poor away from the state back into the community and into private hands—the invisible hands of the market.

Defining Postcolonialism

Postcolonial thought can be very helpful here. Proponents such as Gyatri Spivak, Edward Said, Homi Bhabha, and Stuart Hall have engaged in a systematic reflection on center-periphery relations, the type of relations that have been severely challenged by the 9/11 attacks in the heart of global capital. Proponents of postcolonial theory have raised questions about linear models of structural integration associated with theories of cultural imperialism, world systems theory, dependency theory, and modernization studies that in whatever guise or genre had emphasized one-way models and protocols of productive and reproductive effects from metropolis to the colony. These theories of developmentalism, as I now wish to call them, had placed all life-sustaining dynamism solely in the so-called core and had accorded the Third World a very narrow set of determinations indeed—a counterfeit status—a status of what V. S. Naipaul would call the condition of "mimic men." Within this framework, the proper relationship of the metropole to the colony, after all, had been summed up in the 19th century by John Stuart Mill. In matters of practical value, the relationship between the mother country (England) and its colonies was like that "between town and country." Here, then, the social field of Third World societies had been completely leveled. And the tricky, sly, even aberrant role of the imperial symbolic (for example, national emblems, styles of dress, school songs and rituals, literature, art, ways of knowing, taste, educational exam and testing structures, and so forth) in the stratification of colonial and postcolonial social life had not been sufficiently examined or theorized. The work of symbolic capital in the constitution of the Third World middle classes and the brokering logic of the educational enterprise in mediating the class, ethnic, and gendered tensions within the postcolony had been underexplored. Furthermore, the running encounter, inventory, and register of colonizer and colonized in commodified and lived forms of life had simply been read off as a bastardized text in which the native clothed himself or herself in the uniforms of Empire and in the robes of king (I am thinking here of the cultural imperialism theories of Martin Carnoy and others).

What postcolonial theory and aesthetics (and in talking about aesthetics, I am suggesting that the artists—the writers, the painters, the musicians—were precursors to the academics and critics, that postcolonial aesthetics is a site of deep-bodied theorizing on center-periphery relations as such) point us toward is the radical cosmopolitanism and movement of ideas, bodies, notions of the good life, and what C.L.R James calls the struggle for happiness within the Third World itself, between the Third World and the metropole, and within the fractured and unintegrated spaces of the metropolis as well. There is, for example, in the language of the Guyanese novelist Wilson Harris (*Palace of the Peacock*, *Companions of the Day and Night*, and *Carnival*) a peculiar twinning of the postcolonial psyche and personality integrating the colonizer and colonized—a sense of the subtle links connecting disparate groups across the divide of history and the narratives of gain and loss. What is being argued here is that when you look at the plurality of variables and dynamics of organization, capacities, needs, interests and desires, affective relations, relations of representation and communication, and so forth—instead of, say, flows of trade—we see historically and contemporaneously that the metropole-colony relationships are very complex indeed.

Linking the Postcolonial to Debates Over School Knowledge—A Personal Story

I have been deeply informed and affected by the new theories in postcolonial aesthetics—the critique of hegemonic realism and the insistence on narrative and methodological perspectivism that released the Third World peasant and agro-proletarian subject into central semiotic movement of the novel (here, I am talking about the characters that inhabit the Macondo world of Gabriel Garcia Marques's [1970] *One Hundred Years of Solitude*, characters such as Powell in George Lamming's [1953, 1960] *Seasons of Adventure* and "G" and Thumper of his *In the Castle of My Skin*, Lucy of Jamaica Kincaid's [1990] *Lucy*, and the characters of the Cuban novelist Reinaldo Arena's [1987] *Grave Yard of the Angels*, who stop the author in the middle of the novella and ask for new roles). I enter debates over the organization of school knowledge with the whole weight of colonial history and diasporic experience on my back.

I grew up in the former British colony of Barbados in the 1960s and 1970s in a large working-class family. Like many working-class Barbadians of African descent, my parents were consigned to the working class, in part, because the British educational policy toward the colony involved a Faustian pact with the White planter-mercantile class after emancipation: To guarantee a reserve army of labor for the sugar cane plantations, working-class youth of my parents' generation were only educated to the level of elementary schooling (a source of bitter complaint for my aunt, Phyllis, who fled the colony of Barbados for Chicago with just an elementary school education and had gone on, unlike her sisters in

Barbados, to get her bachelor's degree in sociology). My mother worked for a British harbor master, and my dad was a tailor by profession —a career that he pursued after he was
a monitorial math teacher in his youth because tailoring, oddly enough, gave him more job
security and opportunity. My father successfully coached his first four children to pass the
dreaded Eleven Plus Exam that regulated transfer from elementary to secondary schooling
in the island. These exams were set in England or Scotland. Whereas we passed these quin-
tessentially British exams, the children of my mother's employer, the British harbor master, failed. Of course, this story is not unique. One is reminded here that Jean Paul Sartre
on his first attempt failed the entrance exam for the Ecole Normal Superieure, whereas his
postcolonial Other in the Department of Martinique, Aime Cesaire, would test in. Nothing is more fabulous, more fantastic, than the games of language and existence embodied
in the colonizer/colonized relationship.

For my success in the Eleven Plus Exam, I was rewarded with a scholarship to an elite
Barbadian grammar school called Combermere, well known at the time for its production
of, shall we say, nonconformists, radicals, artists, and insurgent countercultural types. The
Marxist novelist George Lamming went there. So did Edward Brathwaite, Oxford-
educated historian and poet who wrote *The History of the Voice* and won the Cuban Ministry
of Culture's Las Casas Americas prize for poetry for a collection titled *Black and Blues*. So,
too, did Austin Tom Clarke, who wrote *Growing Up Stupid Under the Union Jack* and *When He
Was Free and Young and Use to Wear Silks*. But Combermere was a high school founded in the
1650s for the education of indigent White and colored boys and had, right up until
the 1960s, a line of legendary headmasters from the metropolis, from England itself. The
last one was called Major Noot. Though Noot's own son was mentally challenged and was
not able to attend the school, Noot dedicated himself body and soul to the critical education of the children of others, largely Black Barbadian working-class youth of "promise,"
building up symbolic capital in this somewhat favored part of the periphery. At Combermere, then, I read Jane Austen, Geoffrey Chaucer, William Shakespeare, Wilfred Owen, and,
of course, T. S. Eliot, among others, for my General Certificate of Education (GCE) Cambridge Exams—set in England, sent to Barbados, marked in England, and sent back to Barbados. This was the formal diet of my Barbadian schooling, its formal curriculum, its "collection code," as Basil Bernstein (1975) in his *Class, Codes and Control* would call it. But I was
also exposed, too, in the 1970s to a different, more radicalizing, nonformal curriculum
coming in the form of popular music and the literature and images of the Black power
movement in the United States. The writings of Eldridge Cleaver (for example, *Soul on Ice*),
Rap Brown, and most important, James Baldwin. Baldwin's *Another Country*, *Giovanni's Room*,
and *Nobody Knows My Name* were particularly influential to my peers and myself at a time
when we were at the high point of adolescence and were beginning to ask the big questions
about personal identity and affiliation and human existence. As school kids, we traded
these texts as though they were priceless contraband, the alternative curriculum and a way
forward beyond the confines of a colonial schooling. But we also found in T. S. Eliot's *The
Waste Land* an extraordinary resource—a source of tropes and critique for an appraisal of
the cultural rootlessness of Barbados. And because we were so compelled by Eliot's sly use
of language, the darts and faints that seem to lurk in every line, we were emboldened by

the possession of this ironic possibility with respect to intellectual discourse and culture. We felt, through our efforts to master the ambiguity of language and the authority over meaning in Eliot, a peculiar sense of empowerment and liberation from a teacher-centered model of pedagogy associated with the colonial education model. Wilfred Owen's antiwar poems, such as "Insensibility," that depicted war as ghastly and as a place where old men sent young men to their ritualized deaths—his bitter allusion to Horace's Epicurean golden mean, "Dulce et Decorum Est Pro Patria Mori," and his relentless attention to the callous sacrifice of youth, "Tommy died pushing up the daisies"—led us to a critique of U.S. offensives in Vietnam and a healthy contempt for our own puny military in the Caribbean.

As a final coda on school days, I would leave school after completing my GCE exams in the mid-1970s and join a radical socialist group. I edited its newspaper and served as a program coordinator. Our greatest achievement was indeed the antithesis to all the classical colonial education we had received in school: We used the newspaper and other public forms, and we networked with other radical groups to mobilize Barbadians against the U.S. occupation of Barbadian soil in the form of the U.S. naval base in the northern corner of the island. Finally, in the late 1970s, the United States left.

Returning to 9/11, Fundamentalism, and the Struggle for Meaning

I say all this to say that 9/11 has somehow forced me inwards, to a place where I have no final answers, to the introspective and unstable ground of identity, origins, and nation. I now think aloud about the swath of biography in which I am wrapped, the impact of a subordinating colonial past and present on me, and the extraordinary path away from disaster, annihilation, and implacable resentment that my incorporation into the imperial order by means of a classical colonial education offered to me. The fundamentalism that saturates the agents of 9/11 is a fundamentalism more generalized in our age as globalization brings disruption and its obverse—an intense clarification of identity, origins, and nations. It is a fundamentalism that is perpetrated every day in our schools on the children of immigrants and the children of color. It is a fundamentalism deeply inscribed in the culturally monological curriculum that keeps splitting off those in the margins from the normative centers of American life. This is our misbegotten response to a globalizing world of multiplicity and difference, an Anglo-nativism that desperately tries to place the cork back into the bottle even as the genie has fled simple-minded measures of containment. What connects us all to the agents of 9/11 is this overwhelming feeling of displacement and loss of meaning and control over the fundamentals of inheritance and place. It is precisely in our moment of revulsion and terror that we find ourselves knotted together with the rest of the world and its illuminated peripheries. We are knotted together in the brave new world of out-of-place modern subjects, fettered as we are by particularism and combustible resentment, a world in which power located in the center and built on rule at a distance and strategies of divide and counter now seems peculiarly fragile, vulnerable, and distracted. Now the managers of the metropolis must reckon with the horrors that have been systematically perpetrated on the world's dispossessed beneath the gaze of U.S. sub-urban populations. They must reckon with the familiarity of horrors that are part of the everyday existence of Capetown, of Liberia, of Kingston, of Palestine. And now, God for-bid, Afghanistan.

References

Arena, R. (1987). *Grave yard of the angels*. New York: Avon.

Bernstein, B. (1975). *Class, codes and control* (Vol. 3). London: Routledge.

Carter, M. (1979). You are involved. In *Poems of resistance* (p. 44). Georgetown, Guyana: Guyana Print-ers Limited.

Kincaid, J. (1990). *Lucy*. New York: Farrar, Strauss and Giroux.

Lamming, G. (1953). *In the castle of my skin*. London: Longman.

Lamming, G. (1960). *Seasons of adventure*. London: Allison.

Marques, G. G. (1970). *One hundred years of solitude* (G. Rabasa, Trans.). New York: Harper & Row.

Cameron McCarthy teaches cultural studies in the Institute of Communications Research at the University of Illinois, Urbana-Champaign.

Working It Through
Interpretive Sociology After 9/11/01

VIRGINIA OLESEN

S OME TIME HAS PASSED SINCE the early morning of September 11, one that I now remember as the last truly tranquil moment, when sipping my cherished first cup of
coffee, the phone rings. The plumber (due to arrive shortly) shouts, agitated, "Turn
on your television, something is going on in New York." I open the tube to witness the in-
delible mind-, soul-, heart-, and gut-searing images that burn into our memories, identities, and social consciousness.

Although stunned and horrified, as the day goes by, I do not watch TV or listen endlessly to the radio. I have a lot of writing to do but cannot summon the mental energy. I
resort to the mundane to deal with myself and my churning feelings—do everyday things,
e-mail local, East Coast, and overseas friends and colleagues. I seek comfort food at our
local pub, where television transfixes the owner and waitstaff, but the chef, a refugee from
the Cambodian killing fields, is distraught.

I exchange emotions with family, friends, colleagues, students, and strangers: Fear for
and anxiety about the horror of an excessive U.S. military response and trampled civil liberties here;

Grief about those lost on the planes, at the World Trade Center, and the civilians
where bombing will surely occur;

Depression, profound depression about the nature and meaning of the events and the
future. One colleague, a workaholic, confesses, "I am only able to dawdle."

How can we interpretive social scientists interpret, never mind understand, these and
subsequent events, like the anthrax scare and what yet may come? In this crisis (if one can
use such a mild word for such profound events), fresh, unsettling events may well occur
constantly, but a strength of interpretive social science is some capacity to understand and
interpret events as they are emerging, shaping, and reshaping.

Moreover, our abundant conceptual and theoretical repertoire cannot only interpret a
wide array of topics but generate new insights (emergent symbols, definitions of emotions, new kinds of interactions—people being kindly and decent to one another, old
kinds of problems—racially and religious motivated prejudice and violence, nascent peace

movements, constructions of meanings at all levels, mass media of communication, iden-tities—the fusion of sociopolitical and sociocultural realities and the structures of every-day lives, and much more).

The larger frame is more difficult, although we also have an array of potentially use-ful tools that will need considerable refining (transformation of intentions, social worlds, social arenas, critical dramaturgy, and prophetic postpragmatism).We strain for interpre-tation: These events are far too complex to cite only religious fundamentalism; selfish do-mestic consumerism; overweening capitalism; U.S. parochialism, arrogance, and indiscre-tions; globalization; and legacies of colonial exploitation and brutality in areas before the United States was a player. We can try to interpret, but we must also apply those skills to-ward the application of our findings in realms where we have not often ventured. Much work, much difficult work lies ahead. Ambiguity, uncertainty, and complexity are now our constant companions, challenging our fundamental concepts (the future, the very possi-bility of interpretation and understanding, etc.).

Norm and Yvonna's invitation asked, "How have you worked through these issues?" I have only begun to work them through. That is a project for the rest of our lives.

Virginia Olesen is professor emerita of sociology, Department of Social and Behavioral Sciences, School of Nursing, University of California, San Francisco.

Higher Education and September 11th   27

CARY NELSON

ACADEMICS WORK TODAY IN THE AFTERMATH of a defining moment of violence, rupture, and loss. Spreading out from that center of horror—from an experience simultaneously rich and hollow, meaningful and unspeakable—are multiple possible futures whose relative probability we cannot reliably assess. We will surely contemplate in detail the character of events that will never come to pass. And events we never imagined, like the events of September 11th, will surely overtake us and displace our wisdom, our fears, and our best professional knowledge. I cannot remember another time when the future seemed so decisively unreadable, outside our control. As subjects supposed to know, academics now are merely ignorant like everyone else.

In the immediate aftermath of the attacks on the World Trade Center, officers of the American Association of University Professors put out a statement lamenting the loss of reason and decrying the reliance on violence. They noted that faculty members and institutions of higher education have special warrant to cling to reason even in times of crisis, but that reason now seemed imperiled. Reason is of course an enlightenment value itself in question. We have learned its supposed transcendence is itself contextual, that it is historically produced and contingent. Both its nature and its claim on us vary. Yet that is not to say either that reason or other enlightenment values the university has espoused, however imperfectly, are worthless or evacuated. Their local advocacy—based on their centrality to the sort of social life and public sphere we wish to sustain—remains critical.

On the other hand, writing now in December 2001, I have no insuperable problems with violence carefully targeted against global terrorist networks, whether carried out by other nations or in the manner of Israel's pursuit of Black September. I also have no objection to focused violence directed toward the leaders (but not the ordinary citizens) of the Taliban regime. But I also know such violence will coarsen and harden us nonetheless and that it carries grave risks of reprisals and deepening hatred for us across the world, let alone the certainty that innocent people will die as well. And I can hardly be confident in the Bush administration's capacity to carry out actions of which I might approve; I cannot be confident in its judgment, its competence, its values, its capacity for restraint, or its intelligence. And the excessive control of information from both here and abroad means I cannot be certain about the full range of actions the administration is already taking.

Yet as a source of alternative values in the aftermath of a national disaster, the university has not been especially impressive. Some individual faculty have been notably eloquent, whereas others have in my view been thoughtless, vulgar, unfeeling, or hollowly programmatic. At the worst, some have managed to leave the impression the United States got what it deserved, a position that is not only morally repellant but also strategically dangerous because it opened a space for a series of reactionary assaults on free speech on campus. The academic left was often too quick to opt for prepackaged explanations, certainly too quick to assume congruence between the events of September 11th and the Arab/Israeli conflict.

Yet until the crisis produced by the events of September 11th, college and university students at least had been showing significant awareness of the local and international issues making the greatest contribution to worldwide rage. Both campus living-wage campaigns and the growing movement to protest the ruthless globalization promoted by the World Trade Organization have tremendous potential to begin redressing the economic misery that underlies hopelessness across the world. These movements need to be revived and strengthened.

Universities—and cultural studies scholars especially—can also help promote a dialogue with Islam. Teach-ins have already been revived and will, one hopes, be expanded, despite their hostile reception by administrators, politicians, and conservative commentators. Some American Muslims will be willing to play key roles in the educational process, as will some foreign students from Arab countries. There is significant faculty expertise to draw on across the country. We have a role to play in pressing the country to think more deeply about religious and cultural difference and about foreign policy.

If we want to pose the broader question of what universities might do—of what roles they can and should play in the aftermath of September 11th—we might well place the vexed modern history of reason in relation to the unreadable future we face. If reason has for the cultural right seemed imperiled by postmodernism, a claim many have justly faulted, it had, we should remember, received an earlier critique in the wake of the Second World War. When reason is disarticulated from morality and decency and inclusive notions of what it means to be human, it can serve very destructive ends indeed. The rationality of segmented labor, of instrumentalized reason, and of thoroughgoing industrialization was fused with racism, nationalism, and a project of dehumanization in the death camps. Reason and the will to kill served one another well in this context. Together, they produced not only an assembly line system for murder but also the nightmare medical experiments carried out at Auschwitz.

If you want to interrogate the future of higher education in a time of crisis, I would like you to consider the possibility that Josef Mengele is alive and well on the contemporary American campus. I do not quite mean to make the lurid claim that everything he represented has returned to haunt us, but I do mean to say that university research is intermittently haunted by his legacy. Half a century ago, when the University of Rochester was injecting plutonium into human beings to see what effect it would have, it was doing so in moral company with the doctors of the death camps. And in the person of the head of Johns Hopkins Medical School, I heard part of the legacy of Josef Mengele speak to us again only this year. Johns Hopkins researchers killed a young woman by giving her a drug to mimic the effects of an asthma attack. In response to a federal investigation and questions from the press, the spokesperson for Johns Hopkins asserted that there was no need to inform her the procedure might be life threatening. Unlike Mengele, Johns Hopkins researchers did not literally seek her death, but they viewed her as a tool useable to use in pursuit of their own ends. Those who follow these issues know that thousands of uninformed or poorly informed human subjects have been used in this sort of way by faculty researchers for decades. These people were the object of a rationalized gaze that stripped them of their humanity. They were expendable.

As the university citadel of reason has gradually evolved into the campus sweat shop, this instrumentalized view of human beings has become ever more prevalent in higher education. Universities increasingly employ people without health care, without job security, without fundamental rights to due process, and at salaries below a living wage. Administrators increasingly view many of their employees as expendable. And as universities behave more and more like our most ruthlessly exploitative employers, they steadily lose any moral authority they might wield in world culture.

Perhaps it would not matter if we did not need both the university's moral and intellectual authority. But I fear that we do. Over the last half century, higher education has become the home of many of the country's critical intellectuals. They cannot speak with authority if their institutional homes are rightly perceived as honoring few if any of the enlightenment principles they claim to espouse. These include commitment to justice, fairness, decency, humanity, and community responsibility—not only as values to be taught in the classroom but also to be practiced on campus.

In some of the darker futures radiating out from New York's ground zero, we will need intellectuals who are both critical and oppositional, especially if those futures include repeated acts of terrorist violence. We do not know what the future will bring, but a number of different kinds of deadly violence are possible both here and abroad. Conservative members of Congress are already eager to restrict American rights in ways not necessary to fight terrorism, limiting judicial oversight on searches and detentions being a key example. You may be assured that not only political figures but also cultural conservatives in nongovernmental organizations will seek every advantage they can gain from further violence on American soil. Although I would not want to claim conservatives would welcome the murder of more Americans, I am confident they are already planning how to take advantage of such events should they occur. That is not to say, of course, that the American Left would not also maneuver for position in response to further terrorist attacks on American soil; it is rather to say that the Left, as usual, would be fragmented and ineffective. The Right would organize strategically to set aside its differences and act strategically. Its chance of success could be very great indeed.

A series of attacks on Americans at home would bring a much greater effort to curtail our constitutional rights. The FBI would no doubt be happy to return to its sordid history of de facto criminalization of American political dissent, all of which would be

characterized as a "threat to national security." Penetrating harmless polit
carries no personal risk; putting homegrown radicals under surveillance in...
sonnel, your budget, and your political power. From the FBI's perspective, it is easy and has
no downside. In the investigation of the September hijackings, the FBI has already shown
its willingness to arrest people on the most marginal evidence, then smear them in the
press while confirming their innocence. Arresting hundreds of innocent people and detaining them for weeks, meanwhile leaking lurid speculation about their guilt to the press,
make the FBI look vigorous but do nothing to prevent terrorism. And it undermines our
justice system in the most fundamental way.

Within a few short months of September 11th, the outlines of a national security
state are already taking shape. Its potential reach extends well beyond the war against terrorism. Its features include not only more severe restrictions on the information released
about military actions but also wholesale suppression of the historical record of past administrations. George Bush has proposed that past presidents or their chosen agents can
block all public access to much of recent presidential history. That willingness to vest
unchecked discretionary power in the hands of individuals is matched by the decision to
grant the president and the attorney general extrajudicial authority to determine the fate
of people caught up in the war against terrorism. Instead of relying on a judicial system,
we are to trust in the judgment and good will of elected or appointed officials or their
representatives. In the process, a series of familiar words and phrases is being sloppily over-
laid, vaguely applied, and willfully articulated together. Casually linked together—as concepts, warrants, and decisive values—national security, patriotism, loyalty, civilization, survival, and the war on terrorism can justify a widening denial of basic democratic rights to
a widening range of people involved in a widening range of actions. Already, Americans
seem disinclined to recognize that not only citizens but also legal residents deserve due
process. Meanwhile, selective denial of basic legal principles—exemplified in the willingness to eavesdrop on lawyer/client conversations—cannot be neatly contained with terrorism but instead will offer a model to be applied to nonviolent domestic activities.

With additional attacks, these corrupt government practices would increase still further. Shifting power over arrested people from a judicial system to individuals is a hallmark
of fascism. Meanwhile, the cultural and political demands for conformity would escalate.
Free speech could carry an increased risk of employment insecurity, not only in industry
but also for teachers without the protection of tenure. The press could further muzzle itself. And should all this come to pass, we would need universities as sites of principled opposition. Principled, alas, is precisely what higher education no longer is.

Nor will it be easy to reform higher education to meet these standards. I could point
to several forces working against us, among them the corporate values that university administrators and governing boards increasingly espouse. It is now regularly the case that
faculty committed to making the university a fair, even a model, workplace are fundamentally at odds with senior administrators, who are often devoted to the corporate
model of extracting labor at its lowest possible cost. But the regrettable truth is that many
tenured faculty are apparently perfectly happy to sustain their own salaries and benefits
through the exploitation of other campus workers. And indeed, many if not most

tenured faculty are comfortably unreflective about the economic and human practices that undergird their own privileges.

The entrepreneurial faculty member who looks out only for himself or herself is now positioned precisely to be co-opted by corporatization. We need a new breed of citizen scholars who can identify not only with institution and discipline but also with community. If such citizen scholars are to emerge in higher education, they are likely to come from the growing campus union movement, which encourages solidarity across job classifications about issues such as the need for community-wide living wages, safe workplaces, and health care. For we need not only to resist corporatization without representation, we need also to articulate an alternative vision of what a collaborative university might be like.

Universities cannot, I believe, meet the challenge posed by the events of September 11th unless they put their own houses in order. They cannot be effective sites of moral witness or political critique if they are viewed as fundamentally unfair institutions. As we turn outward toward the world, we must also turn inward to reflect on our own practices and reform them.

Meanwhile, we will continue to be haunted by images without precedent in our experience. The dissolving towers of the World Trade Center, unfurling outward in a wind of dust and flesh, scissored with falling beams of steel, exceed the possibilities for description or analysis. I visited the site at the end of October. The pile of rubble was still smoking; a doorway to hell opened up in the middle of the metropolis. Fifty and a hundred feet in the air, steel beams from the twin towers remained driven into the sides of surrounding buildings. Area shops were still closed, their goods coated with thick gray dust. And there and throughout the city, people continued to gather at makeshift memorials for the dead and the lost. The simultaneous presence of incomprehensible mass numbers with all too comprehensible individual accounts pulls us in opposite directions. And the Left in particular struggles to find consensus narratives that can sustain political community in the midst of grief. The need for interpretation in depth calls all of us in ways we could not have anticipated.

Cary Nelson is Jubilee Professor of Liberal Arts and Sciences at the University of Illinois, Urbana-Champaign.

George Bush, Apocalypse Sometime Soon, and the American Imperium

28

PETER MCLAREN

U NDER THE SIGN OF THE STARS AND STRIPES, the war against terrorism unchains the attack dogs of the New World Order in defense of civilization. In the process, the United States has crossed the threshold of militant authoritarianism and goose-stepped onto the global balcony of neofascism, befouling the Constitution along the way. As long as the nation keeps cheering, and Bush's impish jaw juts ever forward, the stench goes unnoticed.

Among the Bush administration, there is a concerted effort to meld political rhetoric and apocalyptic discourse as part of a larger politics of fear and paranoia. Like a priest of the black arts, Bush has successfully disinterred the remnants of Ronald Reagan's millenarian rhetoric from the graveyard of chiliastic fantasies, appropriated it for his own interests, and played it in public like a charm. Self-fashioning one's image through the use of messianic and millenarian tropes works best on the intended audience (in this case, the American public) when the performance is disabused of shrillness, appears uncompromising, and remains unrestrained, confident, anagogic, and sometimes allegorical. Fascist plain speak is a discursive rendering that is straightforward and unapologetic and, like an iceberg, does most of the damage beneath the surface. Bush's handlers are masters of the fascist spin, and Bush is a perfect candidate because he hardly needs any ideological persuasion to get on board the fascist bandwagon. He is the perfect host for collapsing the distinction between religious authoritarianism and politics. Bush's defense of the war on terrorism works largely through archetypal association and operates in the crucible of the structural unconscious. Bush may believe that Providence has assigned him the arduous yet glorious task of rescuing America from the satanic forces of evil, as if he, himself, were the embodiment of the generalized will and the unalloyed spirit of the American people. Evoking the role of the divine prophet who identifies with the sword arm of divine retribution, Bush reveals the eschatological undertow to the war on terrorism, perhaps most evident in his totalizing and Manichean pronouncements where he likens bin Laden and his al Qaeda chthonic warriors to absolute evil and the United States to the apogee of freedom and goodness.

One could be tempted by an easy Babylonian vengeance—the Code of Hammurabi, Lex talionis; an eye for an eye, a tooth for a tooth. It's the easy way out. It is the useless way out. It is retaliation that provokes more retaliation, an uncontrollable spiral of violence that could engulf us all. It's the U.S. retaliation against a faceless enemy that encourages and justifies Russian retaliation against Chechnya and Chinese repression against its northern ethnic groups. It's the retaliation that, like MacBeth's spot of blood, expands until it drowns all, even our sleep. (Fuentes, 2001, p. 33)

Placing a veil of righteousness over the exercise of mass destruction and the quest for geopolitical dominance (the United States is only protecting the world from those who hate freedom and who wish to destroy democracy), Bush has been accorded nearly sacerdotal status by the vast majority of the American people (that is, if we are to believe the opinion polls). I do believe that Bush is seen as offering some kind of metaphysical hope for the rebirth of the American spirit that has wasted away in a morally comatose state within what is perceived by many conservatives as the debauched interregnum of the Clinton years. Ever since the myth of America as God's chosen nation ingressed into the collective unconscious of the American people, U.S. politics has been primed for the appearance of national saviors and sinners. Without skipping an opportunistic beat, Bush has assumed the mantle of *jefe* global warlord, taken up the hammer of Thor, and is continuing to wield it recklessly, in blatant disregard for the court of world opinion. Bush appears to believe that God's elect—the American übermenschen—in their potent attempt to realize Bush *padre's* vision of making America the iron-fisted steward of a New World Order—must not be compromised by the liberal ideas of militarily (and, by association, morally) weaker allied nations. It is not as though Bush *hijo* is trying to remake the United States into a New Jerusalem. It is more likely that Bush believes unabashedly that the United States is already the New Jerusalem and must be protected by leaders ordained by the Almighty. Of course, the civilization versus chaos myth is a rewrite of the myth of White racial superiority over people of color. Instead of the echoes of Wagner, we have the music of Rocky; instead of Wotan serving as our favorite media action hero, we have Conan the American chasing Marxists through the jungles of Colombia; instead of *Triumph of the Will*, we have Fox news shots of Geraldo in Afghanistan fudging locations where certain events were supposed to have occurred (Hess, 2002, p. 4).

We need to ask ourselves how, exactly, the rhetoric of fascism works, assuming that the infrastructure for a transition to a fascist state is already in place—we have the U.S.A. Patriot Act, we have the military tribunals, we have the Office of Homeland Security, we have the necessary scapegoats, we have the Office of Strategic Influence working hand in hand with the U.S. Army's Psychological Operations Command (PSYOPS) operating domestically (actually, its operating domestically is against the law, but we know that during the Reagan administration PSYOPS staffed the Office of Public Diplomacy and planted stories in the media supporting the Contras, a move made possible by Otto Reich, now the assistant secretary of state for Western Hemisphere Affairs, and we know that a few years ago PSYOPS interns were discovered working as interns in the news division of CNN's Atlanta headquarters), we have the strongest military in the world, we have the military hawks in control of the Pentagon, and we have pummeled an evil nation into prehistory and shown that we can kill mercilessly and control the media reporting in the theater of operations, as major newspapers regularly buried stories of U.S. air strikes on civilians, such as in the case of Niazi Kala (sometimes called Qalaye Niaze), where the United Nations reported that 52 civilians were killed by the U.S. attack, including 25 children. According to the UN report, unarmed women and children were pursued and killed by American helicopters, even as they fled to shelter or tried to rescue survivors (Coen, 2002, p. 3). And we have a leader who is little more than a glorified servant of the military industrial complex, one who is able to admit this publicly and arouse little opposition. In fact, such an admission wins him the glowing admiration of the American people.

> We can recall the blindness, bordering on oligophrenia, of the U.S. government when it fed milk to vipers who responded with venom. Saddam Hussein is a product of U.S. policy to limit and fence in the triumphant and intolerant Ayatollahs of Iran. Osama bin Laden is a product of forceful U.S. diplomacy to counter the Soviet presence in Afghanistan. From Castillo Armas in Guatemala to Pinochet in Chile, it was U.S. diplomacy that imposed the bloodiest dictatorships in Latin America. In Vietnam, even though armies faced armies, the civilians were the greatest tragedies, transforming yesterday's exceptions—Guernica, Coventry, Dresden—to today's rules: the main and sometimes only victims of modern conflicts are innocent civilians. (Fuentes, 2001, p. 33)

Although Bush rhapsodizes about our "freedom and democracy" at home, the truth is that freedom and democracy have effectively been put on hold, with our Commander-in-Chief demanding: "Secure the hatch!" The Office of Homeland Security is dedicated to ensuring domestic safety; yet, at the same time, it is designed to promote what conservative scholar James M. Rhodes has called (in the context of his discussion of the Hitler movement) "ontological hysteria," summarized by Michael Grosso (1995) as follows: "Ontological hysteria consists of a prolonged fear of imminent annihilation, panic over the insecurity of existence. People experience it in disastrous, disorienting times" (p. 197). A key tactic of the Bush administration is to take advantage of this ontological terrorism, to keep the public disoriented and in a sustained feeling of dependence on Bush the Crusader to protect them. Whenever the public seems ready to let down its guard, we receive an announcement from the CIA that a terrorist attack is expected soon, perhaps in a matter of days.

The terrorist attacks—real and anticipated—have given Bush a cloak of Teflon; criticism cannot stick. All Bush has to do is make bold proclamations, bereft of complexity. The shallower the proclamations, the more profound they appear as long as they are seeped in hagiography and Biblical prophecy—well, maybe not direct Biblical prophecy but the illusion of Biblical prophecy. Apocalyptic overkill is the prophylactic gel that kills criticism on contact. The point is that it is profoundly more effective to hide complex geopolitics in the simplistic, infantilizing language of religious apocalypse and millennialist logic. Here, Manichean dualisms abound uncontested: good versus evil, civilized values versus tribal barbarism, warlords versus elected officials, and so forth. Within such a scenario, the act of critique itself is seen as intemperate. Critique is tolerated in the opinion pages of newspapers but not as editorial commentary. It can appear in local television venues with relatively small viewing audiences, but it cannot be tolerated on major televised news shows. Those who would critique a president in the midst of directing a global war against terrorism could only be seen by the public-at-large as self-interested, as a "spoiler" at best and a traitor at worst. We saw what happened to Bill Maher and Susan Sontag. And while the Pledge of Allegiance has rarely been more popular than now, I have always wondered how many U.S. citizens know that it was written in 1892 by Francis Bellamy, who was fired from his Boston ministry for his socialist beliefs and for proclaiming in his sermon that Jesus was a socialist.

Seemingly, all that Bush has to do is to remain militantly forthright: The United States has now geographically ordained a new global partnership bent on mass destruction (and therefore in need of destruction), a new axis of evil—North Korea, Iran, and Iraq—that must be terminated. You cannot name something as "evil" and then work out a compromise without you, yourself, being implicated in the very evil you ostensibly oppose. You cannot say, "America will not permit the world's most dangerous regimes to threaten us with the world's most destructive weapons" (as cited in Umansky, 2002) without backing up the threat—which is why the special operations AC-130 Spectre gunship, whose conventional weaponry since the time of the Vietnam War has been used to pulverize any and every opponent of civilization that has dared stand in its path, is now to be fitted with a laser that can bring down missiles, melt holes in aircraft, and eliminate ground radar stations. A key factor here is that it might take years to defeat an evil regime but decades to defeat an axis of evil—even with laser-equipped gunships (*Media Advisory*, 2002).

In effect, what Bush was able to do in his State of the Union Address was formalize in both temporal and spacial terms the new cold war. Of course, when you talk about an axis, there is always room for more players. For this reason, we shouldn't count China or Russia out. For the moment, they are not part of the axis, but in the arena of geopolitics, scenarios change rapidly. While Bush was touring South Korea, a U.S. soldier pointed out that an axe used to kill two American soldiers in the 1970s was now ensconced in a North Korean museum just across the border in the North. Bush responded, "No wonder I think they're evil" (Umansky, 2002). This remark was quite telling.

The fascism that is slowly settling into place is generously assisted by Attorney General John Ashcroft. Consider his recent remarks on the struggle against terrorism: "Civilized people—Muslims, Christians and Jews—all understand that the source of freedom and human dignity is the Creator" (Umansky, 2002). Ashcroft made these remarks in front of a group of Christian broadcasters. At the same event, he proclaimed, "Civilized people of all religious faiths are called to the defense of His creation. We are a nation called to defend freedom—a freedom that is not the grant of any government or document, but is our endowment from God" (Umansky, 2002). Lewis H. Lapham writes that "the country's war-making powers serve at the pleasure of people who seem more sympathetic to the religious enthusiasms of John Ashcroft than to the secular concerns of the United Nations—true believers, secure in the knowledge of their own virtue, quick to issue the writs of moral censure and to add another 40,000 names to the list of the world's evildoers" (2002, p. 9). And while our attorney general exiles Orpheus into the political hinterland by covering up the breasts of the statues located in the lobby of his workplace, he offers the wrath of Jehovah as a libidinal replacement to Christian fundamentalists embarking on their torchlit rallies and declaring that "united we stand." Recently, Vice President Dick Cheney told Orange County Republicans gathered at the Richard Nixon Library & Birthplace in Yorba Linda, California, that "the United States must accept the place of leadership given to us by history" (Pasco, 2002, p. B6). Clearly, his peace through strength message was a secular rewrite of a divine mandate to destroy the infidel. Reverend Jerry Falwell, who in the 1980s was told by President Ronald Reagan that Armageddon was fast approaching, invoked a God of vengeance and destruction when he blamed feminists, civil libertarians, abortion rights advocates, and gays and lesbians for the terrorist attacks of September 11. He echoed a belief shared by other evangelicals that divine protection is summarily withdrawn from nations who have followed in the footsteps of the inhabitants of Sodom and Gomorrah and have irredeemably become steeped in sin. To remain free of sin, the poor must remain in their natural state of acquiescence and channel dissent along non-threatening reformist paths.

Essentially, George Bush, Cheney, Ashcroft, and Falwell express similar sentiments, but Falwell has failed where the others have succeeded because their attack demonizes "them" rather than splitting "us" into an "us and them" (good Americans vs. bad Americans). Lynne Cheney can spearhead a report designed to demonize professors who speak out against civilization (read as speak out against Bush's war on terrorism), but it is unlikely that there will be serious repercussions for professors unless further terrorist attacks within the United States provoke the general population to feel more comfortable with the idea of eating their own children. If attacks recur, then clearly the stage is set to go after with more vigilance dissenters in the universities. At the present moment, because there is no mass opposition to Bush and his warlords as there was, say, to Nixon during the Vietnam War, most people are not interested in rooting out internal enemies (unless, of course, they fit the right ethnic profile). At the present time, the American public is not seeking internal scapegoats, even if some of the candidates are what the "moral majority" would regard as "perverts." For the time being, the public wants an enemy that remains "out there," one that is easily outsourced, like sweatshop labor by transnational corporations, conveniently externalized and seen as wholly Other to the values of mainstream U.S. society. We want to fight the detritus of global humanity. And anyone not willing to submit to the law of the marketplace, and the desires of its global curate in the White House, is an automatic contender for the dregs of the New World Order. Bush *hijo* believes that by challenging the interminable evil engulfing the globe, he can transform the maleficent violence of the terrorists into the sacred beneficence of America the Beautiful, promoting unanimity and the redemption of secular culture and its vile moral incohesion. Bush's behavior can be seen in the light of mimetic desire, as a reaffirmation of the spirit of the traditional values of civilization that emerges from the faultline separating the barbarians from the saved during moments of volcanic political upheaval. Bush's bombastic odes dedicated to the military machine, defining war as a way of cleansing the world of evil—an evil projected onto others, so we can have our own sins expiated—are helping to prepare the cultural cornerstone for our new surrogate victim: the Muslim. Muslims have become ritual vehicles for catharsis, purification, purgation, and exorcism. René Girard notes that "the working basis of human thought, the process of 'symbolization,' is rooted in the surrogate victim" (1977, p. 306). And while the act of generative unanimity vomited up immediately after September 11—symbolized in the phrase "United We Stand"—does not appear to be backed with the same resolve now that we have had time to engage with more digested reactions to the horror and bring to it a more critical stance (i.e., what did Bush know and when did he know it), Bush is still crafty enough to serve his potential voters what they want so much to hear: We are the world's only superpower, and that gives us the right to rewrite the rules of the game. At the helm of just states must be leaders who exemplify a religiously motivated patriotism that positions income redistribution, multilateralism, and any restraint on individual liberty as mortal enemies of the development of democracy. They must defend global capitalism as the source of freedom, even to the extent of justifying bankruptcies of corporations such as Enron as part of the survival of the fittest (even religious pundits will draw on Darwin-inspired theories if it suits their purposes). Bush and his administration are defeating democracy in their vainglorious attempt to defend it.

References

Coen, R. (2002, February). New York Times buries stories of airstrikes on civilians. *Extra! Update*, p. 3.

Fuentes, C. (2001). New reality, new legality. *El Andar*, 12(3), 33–34.

Girard, R. (1977). *Violence and the sacred* (Trans. P. Gregory). Baltimore: The Johns Hopkins University Press.

Grosso, M. (1995). *The millennium myth: Love and death at the end of time.* Wheaton, IL: Quest Books.

Hess, J. L. (2002, February). Indirect from the battlefield. *Extra! Update*, p. 4.

Lapham, C. H. (2002, May). Notebook: Deus lo volt. *Harper's Magazine*, pp. 7–9.

Media advisory: Pentagon plan is undemocratic, possibly illegal. FAIR-L (Fairness and Accuracy in Reporting, Media Analysis, Critiques, and Activism). (2002). Retrieved February 19, 2002, from fair@fair.org

Pasco, J. O. (2002, February 20). Cheney hits right notes for Nixon Library audience. *Los Angeles Times*, p. B6.

Umansky, E. (2002). Eyeing the axis. *Slate Magazine*. Retrieved February 20, 2002, from slate@slate.com

Peter McLaren is a professor in the Division of Urban Schooling, Graduate School of Education and Information Studies, University of California, Los Angeles.

"The Axis of Evil," Operation Infinite War, and Bush's Attacks on Democracy

29

DOUGLAS KELLNER

I N HIS TELEVISED STATE OF THE UNION ADDRESS on January 29, George W. Bush promised an epoch of Terror War, expanding the Bush doctrine to not only go after terrorists and those who harbor terrorist groups but to include those countries making weapons of mass destruction. Claiming that Iraq, Iran, and North Korea constituted "an axis of evil, arming to threaten the peace of the world," Bush put the "world's most dangerous regimes" on notice that he was planning to escalate the war on terror. Rattling the saber and making it clear that he was perfectly ready to wag the dog if Enron or domestic scandals and economic failures threatened his popularity, Bush put "rogue states" and terrorists everywhere on notice that he was prepared to go to war indefinitely against an array of targets in an epoch of Enduring Terror War.

As was becoming his norm, Bush's team was able to orchestrate an impressive media event with celebrities such as Hamid Karzai, interim president of Afghanistan, in the audience next to Laura Bush, along with members of U.S. military families, New York firemen, and other icons of September 11. Moreover, Bush was learning to read his teleprompter speeches with proper emphasis and pronunciation but was not able to rid himself of his tale-tell smirk, weird darting eye gestures, and increasing arrogance and self-satisfaction. He also took the occasion to announce new dangers to the United States via plans found in Afghanistan to blow up U.S. nuclear installations, public monuments, and other targets.

In fact, these documents had been found weeks before and had already been discussed in the media, so Bush was simply using the threats to legitimate his own militarist agenda and to deflect attention from his own failings at economic policy and the involvement of himself and others in his administration in the Enron scandals. Certainly, terrorism remains a threat to the United States, but to exaggerate the dangers, to escalate the war, and to engage in excessive rhetoric are arguably not the way to deal with the problem. In a round of TV interviews that preceded Bush's address, one of his advisers, Karen Hughes, claimed that Americans face dangers from up to 100,000 terrorists trained in Afghanistan and deployed worldwide. Eyes bulging and lower lip tremulous, the utterly mendacious

Hughes, who has made a career of lying for Bush, made it clear that Terror War would be a major focus of Bush administration policy. Terrorist experts were dumbfounded at the spinmistress' far-fetched fantasizing, with Stanley Bedlington, a former CIA terrorism analyst, insisting that "Al Qaeda has never had that kind of strength." Bedlington continued, "I just came back from a luncheon with about 15 specialists. If I dropped that like a rock into a stagnant pool, there would be roars of laughter" (Woodward, 2002).

Likewise, Bush's rhetoric of "evil" was becoming tiresome and worrisome to many. He used the term *evil* at least five times in his State of the Union Address and included countries such as Iran in this litany, which was itself undergoing complex domestic changes. Furthermore, what Bush did not talk about in the State of the Union speech was also significant. He did not mention Osama Bin Laden and the Al Qaeda and Taliban leadership that he had failed to apprehend. Bush did not refer to the stunning deficits that his fiscal mismanagement had produced, glossing over the reversal in 1 year from the largest surplus in U.S. history to a stunning $100 billion plus deficit (with estimates rising by the week).[1] Bush claimed that the "state of the union had never been so good," but in fact during Bush's presidency, the nation suffered one of the greatest 1-year reversals and declines in U.S. history. The U.S. economy was suffering massive unemployment, the Enron scandal was harming investor confidence and pointing to glaring problems that Bushonomics had helped produce, while the national deficit was skyrocketing.

Moreover, in his State of the Union Address, George W. Bush out-voodooed Ronald Reagan in his calls for wildly increased military spending, a jump in home security spending, large tax cuts for the wealthy, and a 9% increase in basic government programs. Bush was willing to finance this budget with a more than $100 billion deficit for 2002 and an $80 billion budget deficit for 2003. One tries to imagine the uproar this would create if the Democrats had urged such irresponsible deficit funding of the government. It was startlingly clear that the Bush administration was returning to the giant deficit spending that had seen the Reagan years double the national debt, whereas Bush I in his failed 4 years of economic mismanagement doubled the national debt once again. Every responsible economist believed that it was necessary to keep the deficit and national debt under control to ensure U.S. economic stability, but once again the Bush administration embarked on a rash and dangerous economic policy that could end in catastrophe for the U.S. and global economy.

Looked at more closely, Bush's State of the Union Address could be read as a cunning use of Terror War to push through his indefensible domestic programs such as the Star Wars missile program, his tax break and giveaway for the rich, and his social service programs that would advance a conservative agenda (i.e., people and charities would solve social problems and not government). The "evil axis" countries could be used to legitimate producing the Star Wars missile defense system that critics had claimed had not been proven workable. Although on one hand the very notion of an axis of evil suggests Bush administration geopolitical confusion and misunderstanding, on the other, it opens the way to any military intervention whatever. And by calling attention to countries that produce weapons of mass destruction, it legitimates a missile defense system that will at least allegedly protect the United States against nuclear missile attack.

Most incredible, Bush was using the Enron collapse to push his tax giveaway program and discredited pension plan. Although Bush did not mention the unmentionable name of Enron in his speech, the day after the State of the Union Bush called for pension reform in the light of the Enron collapse using the national tragedy to push his social security stock scam, telling workers that with improved investment advice and some protection, they would be better off with retirement plans in which they could choose to invest their own savings! As if the Enron scandal had not revealed the uncertainty of investment and dangers in the stock market!

The emphasis on care, compassion, sacrifice, national service, and community voluntarism in the State of the Union gave Bush credence as a compassionate conservative, as opposed to a hard-right ideologue and shameless manipulator of crisis and tragedy for his own political ends. But the emphasis on patriotism, national unity, and moral community functions to identify his party and policies with patriotism but also to identify anyone who criticized his foreign or domestic policies as "unpatriotic." Lynne Cheney, wife of U.S. Vice President Dick Cheney and a longtime cultural warrior against the Left, has been circulating texts documenting unpatriotic statements by university professors. Since September 11, Ms. Cheney had been leading an assault against dissidents to Bush administration policy on the grounds that they are not patriotic and supporting the president in a time of war and danger (Defense of Civilization Fund, 2001).[2] Stressing national unity and patriotism was thus providing a cover for suppressing dissent and difference and thus threatening to undermine U.S. democracy, revealing the dangerous antidemocracy sentiments of the Bush-Cheney gang.

Moreover, appropriating the language of "moral community" for a conservative "homeland defense" against terrorism and "an axis of evil" redefines community in conservative terms as those who identify with U.S. government policy. It also subordinates discourses of social justice, civil rights, and democracy to pulling together in the name of national unity, a move that can easily be used to suppress dissent and progressive agendas. Thus, the Bush administration is using the September 11 terrorist attacks and issues of national security to push through a right-wing agenda that is a clear and present danger to U.S. democracy as well as world peace.

Notes

1. Budget analysts noted that although it was claimed on page 396 of Bush's budget that the 2002 deficit would be $106 billion, on page 417 it is admitted that "the amount of government debt outstanding at the end of this year will rise by fully $367 billion to a new world record of $6.1 trillion" (Oliphant, 2002). When Senator Fritz Hollings confronted Bush administration budget director Mitch Daniels with this discrepancy, Daniels admitted that "we hid it but you found it." According to Oliphant (2002), the Bush administration plans to help cover the gargantuan deficit by raiding social security and Medicare.

2. Lynne Cheney and her right-wing allies had long dreamed of crushing radical voices of dissent in the university and had long waged a cultural war against their academic enemies. The conservative jihad was launched during the Reagan era when Ms. Cheney was head of the National Endowment for the Humanities, which she governed like a Taliban, rooting out all politically incorrect

policies and personnel and going after progressives in the academic world. There were some specu-lations that the U.S. Left/Right culture wars were suspended in favor of national unity against ter-rorism, but obviously Cheney and her Taliban were not going to miss a chance to go after their long-time adversaries.

References

Defense of Civilization Fund. (2001, November). *Defending civilization: How our universities are failing America and what can be done about it?* Available from www.goacta.org

Oliphant, T. (2002, February 12). *The Boston Globe.* Available from www.bostonglobe.com

Woodward, C. (2002, January 29). *Bush sketches dark portrait of the threat from terrorists* (Associated Press).

Douglas Kellner is George Kneller Chair in the Philosophy of Education at the University of California, Los Angeles.

September 11 and the Global Implications of Interpretive Inquiry

30

KENNETH J. GERGEN

I WILL NOT TREAT HERE THE FULL dimensions of my personal response to the September 11 tragedy. My aims here are not therapeutic. However, I do wish to reflect on the implications of this event for our lives as scholars and most particularly, our work within an interpretive/constructionist paradigm. But first, some Ground Zero reverberations:

> I place words to paper.
> But who shall welcome them?
> Perhaps few scholars . . .
> A handful of students—curious or daring?
> And will it be late one night, hurriedly, to capture the latest
> Or more searchingly to ensure that all is correct?
> And will the end of such efforts not be
> Yet another expansion of the realm of words,
> Endlessly circulating
> In the sealed compartments of academic self-absorption
> Safely distanced from the hard places
> Where plastic knives
> Bursting flames
> Crumbling skyscrapers
> Bodies Falling
> Thousands obliterated
> Unarticulable agony
> And a blanket of fear
> Strangulatingly spreads
> Across the globe?
> What worth my words
> Where am I, what am I
> When it comes to the hard places?

Such were my feelings for many days. It was not only difficult to write but as well to read, teach, or carry out intelligent conversation. What difference did any of this make in terms of the greater agonies ascending to global prominence? Over time, I have returned to reflect more hopefully on our efforts and most particularly the kinds of interpretivist work represented in this journal and so highly congenial with the kind of social constructionist views in which I have been immersed. Are these anything more than words on paper, invitations to more words, more paper, more comfortable insularity from the difficult challenges? Slowly I have begun to discern more positive possibilities. Consider the beliefs that for many of us drive our efforts.

The abandonment of Truth. For many of us, the point of inquiry is not to establish Truth but interpretive intelligibility. The discourse of Truth is an oppressive one. It announces that "Disagreements will not be tolerated." If we fail to agree to "the Truth," we are maligned, disparaged, barred from conversation, or eliminated. Yet the interpretivist scholar understands that there is no arrangement of words on paper that uniquely corresponds to the world as experienced. The interpretivist scholar replaces truth posits with lenses of understanding. To develop these lenses is to offer the world means of comprehending in a different way. It is to broaden the possibilities of dialogue and action.

The legitimation of "the Other." Unlike traditional social science, interpretivists do not generally seek to appropriate the "subject of research" for their own theoretical advantage. The point of research is not typically to proclaim one's own voice as superior to all others. Rather, most interpretivists attempt to give voice to the subjects of their inquiry, to enable them to speak in their own ways about what matters to them. In this way, their subjects are not reduced to objects but are given an opportunity to legitimate their modes of being within broader circles of society.

The invitation to dialogue. Because interpretivists neither seek "the last word" nor the ultimate inscription of "their own word," their research invites dialogue. The interpretivist recognizes the intelligibility of multiple realities and senses of the good and in doing so, alerts us to the necessity of "cross talk," the unfolding conversations that can bring otherwise antagonistic parties into a condition of mutual enrichment.

The appreciation of relationship. Although many interpretivists focus on individual experience, my overarching feeling is that the orientation ultimately emphasizes the importance of relationship. Even when individual experience is the center of research, illumination is in the service of enhanced relationships. Significantly, the willingness of interpretivists to experiment with multiple forms of representation is also, for me, a manifestation of relationship valuing. Each new form of report—the poem, the short story, the collage, the polyphonic document, the photograph or drawing, the multiply positioned writing, the performance—reaches a new audience and expands the possibilities for human connection.

Are the global implications of interpretivist/constructionist forms of scholarship not more promising than what our traditions have thus far served up? After all, such scholarship is itself an action in the world, not remote from the world. And if such actions can be extended—to our colleagues, our students, and to the societies of the world more generally—do we not create an alternative to the wars on Westernism, on terrorism, or alterity of any kind? Do we not foster an appreciation for multiplicity, dialogue, and relationships of mutual understanding? Our work may now represent only a candle in a vast darkness, but with enough candles and rekindled energies, we move toward the light.

Kenneth J. Gergen is the Mustin Professor of Psychology at Swarthmore College.

A Time for Butterflies and Salmon   31

WILLIAM L. MILLER

THE AIR IS BRISK and the wind is sharp and filled with the falling grief of enlightened leaves. There is one that flutters with peculiar intention. Like the dying leaves, it hovers, drifts, drops, and twists at the direction of the winds; yet it also tacks and darts, assuring its relationships to particular shrubs. In spite of the horror of September 11 and the terror of our national response, a smile of recognition removes the despair from my face. A butterfly alights upon the rubble of decaying leaves at my feet, a reminder and a metaphor of vulnerable knowing and of fragile, awesome power for change.

This vulnerable knowing, the knowing of a radicalized, interpretivist social science, is, like the butterfly, characterized by being participatory, emerging, dependent, constituted by cycles, migrations, place, development, and spurts of confused flight. It assumes the absence of utopia, perfection, or ultimate Truth but is deeply committed to the many contingent truths moving toward better life together. Like the butterfly, we seek knowledge that recognizes and informs the importance of scale and complexity and that respectfully acknowledges the unfathomable mystery and abundance of life.

Where to begin? On September 11, I waited, with many other physicians and nurses, for burned and wounded bodies. Patients and families had volunteered to go home early so that beds would be available for the care of the victims at the World Trade Center. They never came; we heard only the silent screams of thousands of souls lost in the rubble 60 miles away. We begin here. We stand in the tortured silence with the hopefulness of waiting, with the fluttering, fragile faith of the butterfly. We resist the escapist calls for revenge against the evil ones; we know the evil of such dualisms. We have a different task with evil. We must acknowledge, complicate, and stir hope into the polluted sea of evil. Evil is the arrogant poison that spews from the smokestacks and sewers of certainty and superficiality. Restoring and preserving ecological health and social justice begins in our classrooms, in our journals, in our research activities, and in our home and neighborhood lives. It is up to each of us to deconstruct the myth of evil as other and as stereotype. For me, it begins inmyclinical work as a family practitioner. Am I listening, without judgment, to the anger, the anxiety, and the faceless generalizations about evil and revenge? Am I exploring and naming, in humble partnership and with courage, the deeper sources of these feelings and voicings, the fear, the grief, the loss of control, the utter sense of helplessness? Am I complicating certainty and superficiality?

My eyes, moistened by the cold winds of late autumn and watered by the inner wells of loss, look out toward the river rushing toward the sea from which my own eyes' water came. For a moment, I imagine salmon vigorously swimming upstream. Then I remember, the salmon too are gone, not seen in this river for over a century. But they could return; salmon are still out there that remember the way. There has always been a hidden tide of history that swims upstream and keeps returning. These are the salmon of history that swim for the seventh generation with the assurance of the past but in full mindfulness of the present. Is our interpretivist science part of this tradition?

Yes, we are about deep meaning and memory, like the salmon, and about resilience and diversity and faith in emergence, like the butterflies. We represent an ancient tradition as old as life and maybe older, the tradition of the salmon. And we are local knowledge, one rooted to and complicated by place, seeking only to make our backyard a better habitat for butterflies. Our strength is in the many connections between and among the many places, the migratory routes and passages. It is time for the quiet and powerful wisdom of butterflies and salmon. Let out your wings and strengthen your fins. Let's answer the quiet call to keep growing connections and complications, to help Love grow.

Will Miller is a family physician-anthropologist and chair of the Department of Family Practice at Lehigh Valley Hospital & Health Network in Allentown, Pennsylvania.

The Heart of the Matter   32

ANTON J. KUZEL

One of the administrators interrupted our department meeting to tell us about the beginning of the events of September 11, 2001. Our discussion stopped, and we stared at a tiny black-and-white TV screen that one of our secretaries brought into the room as the second tower was struck in real time (the irony of the adjective makes me sad).

"How the hell do terrorists get on board our commercial airliners to do something like this?" I said to anyone listening. No one answered. Maybe they knew that the answer had so many layers, such complex connections. Maybe they were as stunned as I was. Maybe they thought, "Easily," but didn't want to say it out loud.

Within minutes of the attack on the Pentagon, our medical center was put on alert to receive overflow victims because we are only 100 miles away. Resident physicians and faculty from our Northern Virginia program were called into their local hospital to help. Not much extra help was needed—people were either killed, or they walked away. Most of the trauma wasn't physical.

My brother, a police officer who just retired from 30 years of service, was visiting us that week. He didn't want to watch TV, except for ESPN classics—there were no live sporting events. He didn't want to talk about what was happening.

Three days after the attack, my wife and I attended a previously scheduled concert by our local symphony orchestra. The conductor announced at the outset that the first piece on the program had been changed. They played Samuel Barber's *Adagio for Strings*. When the orchestra finished, the concert hall was silent. I recalled that the Barber *Adagio* was part of the film score for *Platoon*.

A week later, several families from our church congregation attended an interfaith service of remembrance and hope. It was held at the downtown Jewish temple and included Jewish, Muslim, Catholic, and Baptist regional leaders. There were no empty seats. The symbolism of holding this service in a Jewish temple was not lost on me given the politics attached to the terrorist attacks. Most memorable of all was when a Muslim cleric chanted a prayer for peace—in Arabic. I thought it must be the first time that a prayer in that language had ever been spoken aloud in this Jewish temple.

My work as a family physician has changed. Some of my patients were deeply affected by 9-11—one lost a relative in the second tower. Treating post-traumatic stress disorders gave way to anxiety about bioterrorism when the anthrax mailings began, and I had to relearn about a disease that I had thought typically only killed sheep. I sat with colleagues in an auditorium and watched the Center for Disease Control's live broadcast—an overview of the cutaneous, gastrointestinal, and pulmonary forms of anthrax and a summary of the current guidelines for evaluation and treatment. That day, they said not to give prophylactic antibiotics to all people reporting possible contact. I ignored that advice 2 days later when one of our patients called and told me she had received a suspicious envelope with a fine brown powder inside. At the time, I thought it odd that I consciously rejected the experts' guidelines—how unlike me. The next day a postal worker died of pulmonary anthrax, and the guidelines changed again. I didn't feel vindicated—more saddened by our limited knowledge and ability to respond. My patients are asking me if we are giving people smallpox vaccines yet.

Lines from Don Henley songs are running through my head. The stories told by the original songs were of suicide, divorce, workaholism, and other ways by which relationships are lost. Now, segments stand apart and replay with an added meaning:

> Offer up your best defense
> But this is the end
> This is the end of the innocence. (Henley & Hornsby, 1989, track I)[1]

> Lying here in the darkness
> I hear the sirens wail
> Somebody going to emergency
> Somebody's going to jail
> If you find somebody to love in this world
> You better hang on tooth and nail
> The wolf is always at the door
> . . .
> In a New York minute
> Everything can change. (Henley, Kortchmar, & Winding, 1989, track 5)[2]

> The more I know, the less I understand
> All the things I thought I knew, I'm learning again
> I've been trying to get down to the heart of the matter
> But my will gets weak, and my thoughts seem to scatter
> But I think it's about forgiveness
> Forgiveness . . . (Campbell, Henley, & Souther, 1989, track 10)[3]

Notes

1. "The End of Innocence." Words and music by Don Henley and B. R. Hornsby. © 1987, 1989 Woody Creek Music and Zappo Music. All rights administered by WB Music Corp. All rights reserved. Used by permission. Warner Bros. Publications U.S. Inc., Miami, FL 33014.

2. "New York Minutes." Words and music by Don Henley, Danny Kortchmar, and Jai Winding. ©1988, 1989 WB Music Corp., Woody Creek Music, and Dobbs Music. All rights reserved. Used by permission. Warner Bros. Publications U.S. Inc., Miami, FL 33014.

3. "The Heart of the Matter." Words and music by Don Henley, Mike Campbell, and John David Souther. ©Woody Creek Music, Wild Gator Music, and EMI April Music, Inc. All rights on behalf of Woody Creek Music administered by WB Music Corp. All rights reserved. Used by permission. Warner Bros. Publications U.S. Inc., Miami, FL 33014.

References

Campbell, M., Henley, D., & Souther, J. D. (1989). The heart of the matter [Recorded by D. Henley]. On *The end of the innocence* [CD]. Hollywood, CA: Cass County Music.

Henley, D., & Hornsby, B. (1989). The end of the innocence [Recorded by D. Henley]. On *The end of the innocence* [CD]. Hollywood, CA: Cass County Music.

Henley, D., Kortchmar, D., & Winding, J. (1989). New York minute [Recorded by D. Henley]. On *The end of the innocence* [CD]. Hollywood, CA: Cass County Music.

Anton J. Kuzel, M.D., M.H.P.E., is professor and vice chairman of the Department of Family Practice, Virginia Commonwealth University, in Richmond.

September 11, 2001   **33**
Changing the Ways of the World

MARY GERGEN

THE FLASHBULB MEMORY OF THE CENTURY
   9-11 9.1.1.   HELP!
   September 11
By whatever names . . . We all know its name.

AWEFUL: in the oldest meaning of the word: Full of awe and of dread.
The blue sky, the golden towers, the flames and the falling.
The plays and replays: searing into memory an impossible sight.
Tower 2 as it recedes—a pleated pandemonium, silent, mesmerizing,
Compellingly attracting and repelling in the same instant.

A dysphoric fairytale for our time.

A QUESTION I KEEP ASKING MYSELF that morning: Why do people hate us so much that this would happen? I really didn't understand. Do I now?
A friend and I talking: She says, "It seems that everything that could be said has been said." And I wonder if that might not be true. The words on this single morning have exceeded any other morning in the history of the world. On that first morning I resent the TV reporters . . . over and over. The same old words and pictures. Like zombies in a mental ward, they keep repeating themselves. I distain stale words. I don't want to add to the pile.

We should see sense making in progress. Perhaps we all keep on talking because we cannot rein in the tumult to make some sense. The absurdity is almost palpable.

Friends from across the globe send messages of condolences, as if a member of our family has died. Perhaps rightly, as a member of the family of nations has been mortally wounded. Nothing like this has ever happened before to us . . . not in the information age.

I take to reading poems. One strikes me as my own, not in the vision, but in the resonance of words: A woman sees a man walking as in a cloud through Grand Central Station. His dark pinstriped suit is covered in the white silvery dust of the ruin. One sleeve of his clothing is gone. His arm is bare. It is a day of ghosts; she bends to the ground and prays to a God she does not believe in.

I teach a class in social psychology, and it is held the following Monday. I give small groups of students various news clips and pieces I have taken from e-mails to read and discuss. In each group I have editorials from American papers, and I have material from other regions of the world, some that emphasize the grave assault to our identity as well as to mortal lives and some that emphasize the reasons why this might have occurred. One in particular is by a Palestinian woman who decries the bombings but who expresses her feelings about the tribulations of living under Israeli rule. I ask the students to consider how each writer makes assumptions about the nature of aggression, patriotism, terrorism, and what motivates people in their actions. I hoped they realize that there are other points of view beyond CNN. It is an attempt to bring an interpretive perspective into the room where there seems to be little space for conversational differences. But I also do not want to deny whatever reality they cling to.

Many of my colleagues describe the fearfulness of the students and their traumatic reactions to these events. I think that we elders are the truly troubled. We know better that our world had undergone a shattering, seismographic shift. They don't have the history to know. We go through various rituals of recovery, but it is for ourselves. What interpretive tools can we bring to this occasion? What words can soothe our souls?

Thousands of obituaries to print. In *The New York Times*. Each day, a new supply of tears as I read stories of teddy bears, and wedding rings, and ball games, and new beginnings ended before our eyes.

A trip to Ground Zero with a friend who was there, fleeing in the ash and smoke. The cemetery of St. Paul's where we walk is still strewn with papers that have been blasted away. One sheet clinging to a gravestone says in big bold letters, "We have a Solution to Every Problem"—oh, don't we wish.

The church is festooned with children's messages in gay color crayons. "We love you." "Thank you." "God Bless America." The workers on the site get backrubs and new clothes. This is the last day of the "recovery." Monday, the site becomes a "construction zone." The naming changes the nature of the rubble, from one of despair to one of hope.

I am waiting for the seal to crack on the seemingly unified stance regarding the curtailment of our old pre-9/11 inclinations. So far, I have not seen much resistance to the rising cries from the government for new security measures and the restrictions on civil liberties. I think of the people of Germany in another era who must have tolerated similar rulings in the name of their security. I long to hear some dissonant voices. I think I hear them in the distance. Or do I?

Where is the hope that an interpretivist social science with a value commitment to social justice might survive this onslaught of "Terror INC." on one side and modernist military experts and their supporters on the other? How might it bring new possibilities to this dire entanglement? It looks rather gloomy at the moment. Who knows what is best to do? Perhaps this is a time of reflection and reflexivity. How should we understand the dynamics of the development of a new world order discourse? Where are the leverage points for intervening with new and refashioned languages that can incorporate the desires of the people to feel safe again while averting the most strident calls for eradicating and destroying many other people and places? Patience and pragmatic insights are called on to be able to insert into public dialogue alternative forms of sense making, those that might lead to a stronger basis for reconciliation and respectful disparities among people who do not see the future of the world in the same light. There are deeper issues at stake here, even, than the restoration of calm and the serving of an "eye-for-an-eye" form of justice. If we are going to live safely and peaceably in this world, we must endeavor— each of us in our small corner of the world—to bring together in a new space those who have the influence and the wisdom to allow for the marginalized voices to be heard rather than to open the space for them to discover alternative means for gaining global attention.

There is only so long that alternative voices can be silenced in a democracy. We must not lose courage or the faith that there are better ways of living together than have so far been tried on a global scale. We must discover and support those who would go with us on this adventuresome trek. Who and where they are is uncertain. But we must not give in to despair. That road leads nowhere. Only an optimism born of our capacity to leap into a fateful future is potent. What have we got to lose? What opportunities are waiting, if we know when to jump into the flow?

Mary Gergen is professor of psychology and women's studies at Penn State University, Delaware County.

Tenets of Terror   34

KATHY CHARMAZ

IMAGES OF DESTRUCTION. American Airlines Flight 11 proceeding on course to the north tower of the World Trade Center. One tower collapsing, then the other. People fleeing. Chaos. Destruction was made immediate, real—and irrevocable. The buildings ripped open and disintegrated—in instants. So too, assumptions about the world dissolved—our world. What we assumed about daily life was turned upside down. Military might could not protect us from treacherous suicidal plots. Simple tools wreaked unthinkable damage. Economic power did not exempt us from hatred. We are not impervious to global terrorism.

In a moment's flash, a North American way of life became undependable, unpredictable. The morning of September 11 awakened us from the dream of reason—American reason. The events crashed on us and with them, the American dream that our reasoning reigned throughout the world and guided the course of history. Myths of safety, security, personal invulnerability, and collective invincibility disintegrated with the falling of the Towers. What would come of the power wrested in the attacks and countered by subsequent American military actions? Would this elusive war realign old alliances, rewrite world opinion, and reverse economic arrangements? With the dawning of the 21st century had life taken ominous new form? Would these events mark the end of the American century, as we had known it, more effectively than any calendar?

When I looked around me what did I see? Sadness. Grief. Loss. Overwhelming loss. Loss of a sense of personal invulnerability—of immortality. Loss of the significance of immediate pursuits. And loss of naive optimism.

When I talked with students, they voiced their struggle to comprehend the unfolding realities and to understand their place in a changed world. They talked of the sudden meaninglessness of commodities and competition. They looked for solace within their families and religious faiths. They hoped for rapid resolution and an end to violence. Yet the hush of silence was also discernible. Some thoughts and feelings remained unspoken but were mirrored in students' serious faces, reflected in sorrowful eyes. One student's silent thoughts etched questions on his face. A week before September 11, I had read silent questions on his face but then about the course, its requirements, and challenges. After September 11, his face again revealed unasked questions—this time with stifled fears. The questions in his eyes now revealed deeper thoughts—of life and death, meaning and motive—and an unpredictable present and uncertain future.

Like my students, perhaps many of us stand between speech and silence on collective grief and loss. We too feel the loss and try to make sense of terror and death. We too speak of palpable uncertainty and take silent refuge in routine realities. Yet as interpretive social scientists, we can contribute to the shape of the world to come. The path may not be easy, but the work remains essential. It calls us out of our universities and takes us into the world. Although we may study individuals, we must attend anew to how cultural context, historical location, and social position are played out within their lives. We bring an open-ended worldview and sense of wonder to our studies as well as epistemologies and methods. Thus, the possibility exists of transcending the boundaries of culture, place, and time to bring new understandings of and to the world. We can move back through centuries and forward into unanticipated futures.

Interpretive social scientists have special tools to study processes that shape social life: We can define implicit actions and discern tacit meanings.

Specifically, how might interpretive social scientists offer new voices of reason? Some ideas come to mind. Communications scholars might explore the battle of words for controlling images in the media. Does the rhetoric of patriotism mystify the politics of power dripped in oil? Symbolic interactionists can observe the development and change of meanings and actions—of nations, leaders, and ordinary citizens. Which actions give rise to escalated reactions? How does religious fundamentalism of the Eastern world collide with that of the Western? Historians can trace alliances and allegiances and the scars of conflicts past. How might a people with a long view of history view a nation that looks to individual futures, not collective memories or futures? Ethnographers could study customs enacted in daily life and embedded in tradition. What ancient loyalties and lasting hostilities spawn collusion and conspiracies? What does terrorism mean in war-torn villages among a starving people?

Collectively, interpretive social scientists can offer understandings that can inform social policy. With hope, skills, and perseverance, let us work to make our dream of reason a reality.

Kathy Charmaz is professor of sociology and coordinator of the Faculty Writing Program at Sonoma State University.

Alone and Together
A Reflection for *Qualitative Inquiry* on the Terror Attack

DAVYDD J. GREENWOOD

Spain, October 6–11, 2001

SEPTEMBER 11 LEFT ME, like most of us, in a vulnerable emotional and intellectual state. My reactions to these events, like everyone else's, were colored by my own life experiences. I found myself lurching through personal flashbacks to cataclysmic events in my own life: meeting my father for the first time I could remember when he returned as a stranger from World War II, collapsing in grief in my car outside the post office at Grinnell College on learning of the assassination of John F. Kennedy, getting my high school yearbook and seeing the absent names of friends who died in Vietnam because they did not go to college, and the surreal morning of the first terrorist assassination in the Spanish Basque Country in 1968, which took place very near where I, with my young family, had just started to do fieldwork.

I felt deeply alone because I knew how idiosyncratic most of my memories were. I soon found I could barely watch the endless so-called "news" programs because of the banality of the reporting and the constant repetition of the pictures. I felt put upon. I wanted the tragedy to belong to me in my own way without so much media interference. It was fine to share the pictures, some of the grief, and the outrage, but the experience was MINE and I resented feeling that my memory was being manipulated and programmed into collective reactions. Perhaps this is partly because I have always had a gut aversion to the conformity of crowds and imperious demands for unity.

But with time, I found a way to understand the repetitious language of "terror," "war," "nation," "flag," and "innocence" that had followed these horrible events. Although such concepts still do not attract me, I now realize better that building this collective response has much to do with putting a name and face on the unspeakable and incomprehensible. It reduces the chaos that threatens to turn the meanings of our lives into nonsense into a narrative that makes some kind of sense, even if it be malign and satanic. And it is clear that having some kind of shared sense may well be preferable to having a world that makes no sense at all.

So, when I hear the commonplace that Americans have "come together" because of the tragedy, it probably has a peculiar meaning for me. We have come together for a moment because we have collectively realized the triviality of our daily concerns, the vulnerability of our lives, and the meaninglessness of so much we take for granted. So I think the marathon reporting and image repetition was less a coming together than an attempt to nullify the searing nonsensical reality of these events, a reality that we momentarily and dangerously experienced uniquely and individually and that threatened all of our grip on the world.

As a person who builds theory from practice, I found that unlike many of the reporters and some of my colleagues and students, I was anxious to reestablish daily routines and to move my feet (and eventually my heart) back onto some kind of solid ground by recreating that ground again through personal action one foot in front of the other even though the road ahead could not be seen. I also believe that there is a politics in doing this that is deeper than flags and pep talks. I learned long ago in the Spanish Basque Country that insisting that life goes on is a meaningful weapon against terrorists. There is a kind of heroism and patriotism in going on with daily life against pulls of meaninglessness, blame, and revenge.

I felt trivial and selfish in this reaction, but as my action research seminar with a group of undergraduates and graduates at Cornell began on Wednesday, September 12, I realized that most of my students were struggling the same way and wanted to share their experiences without losing the right to have them be entirely their own. At the same time, I was nervous because I feared that my younger students, who mainly have grown up in a period of unprecedented peace and prosperity, would be unable to cope with this. That was a foolish underestimate of the sort older people are prone to. Instead, I learned something from these young people that inspired and comforted me.

Despite their lack of experience with tragedies like this, their immediate reactions were caring, intelligent, and focused. Beyond expressing their obvious grief and fear, they proved instantly to be very smart about avoiding dangerous reactions. On September 12, they were already articulating their fear of a U.S. overreaction, of massive militarization, of the suppression of civil rights, of prejudice against foreigners, and the rise of a fear of the "other" in general. They understood immediately that "America" was not under attack but that global civility, democracy, and freedom were. They apparently see more clearly than many of their elders. I felt lucky to be with them that day and in the following days.

The conversation I am reporting took place in a course on action research, an approach to research designed to provide a democratic alternative to socially disengaged and self-regarding academic social science. Suddenly that "noble" project seemed trivial, and we all felt for a while that nothing that we could hope to do would be significant enough to affect such massive world events. But we opted to continue doing what we can do best as professors and students in the hope that, paraphrasing Chris Argyris, we can increase the likelihood of unlikely but liberating outcomes. Alone and together, one foot in front of the other. . . .

Davydd James Greenwood is the Goldwin Smith Professor of Anthropology and director of the Institute for European Studies at Cornell University.

Educating Students from Abroad
Possibilities for Peace and Research

SHULAMIT REINHARZ

A FEW DAYS BEFORE THE TERRORIST attack on Washington, D.C., and the World Trade Center, there was bloodshed in Israel and what is now called Palestine (Gaza and the West Bank). Although these were acts of completely different magnitude, they were interconnected in several ways. For example, a rumor was spread throughout the Arab world that Israeli intelligence (the Mosad) perpetrated the attack on the World Trade Center. Osama bin Laden frequently condemns Israel and America in the same breath. Americans were killed in the attacks in Israel and in the United States. Israeli standards of security are now sought for U.S. airports. And Palestinian youngsters celebrated the success of the terrorists in achieving their goals in both cases. Children were involved in all these cases—children lost parents, lost their own lives, became refugees, celebrated, were recruited into war.

During that time, a public relations company seeking speakers available to appear on a televised talk show gave a station representative my name. Although I did receive a follow-up call, I was not invited to be one of the television guests. I think my lack of invitation stemmed from the fact that when asked what my "angle" was, I said I would like to talk about *positive steps* that might be taken to reduce the antagonism.

The positive step I had in mind was to invite sizable numbers of Palestinian children to receive an American education focusing on issues of democracy. My idea is that young people should have a chance to form a different life from those of their parents. I also believe that people from any area will probably resonate well to the ideas of religious freedom and self-expression that are available in this country. My expectation has always been that whatever the nature of the "war" that the United States will fight against the Taliban or terrorism, the United States will emerge the victor. And then the United States will begin the economic rehabilitation of the countries in which it has fought (similar to what the United States did with the Marshall Plan and in Vietnam). Is it possible to carry out this economic/educational rehabilitation plan in advance?

Is teaching people about collective decision making compatible with a variety of religions and cultures? Will people from other societies allow their children to be reeducated in the United States? What does it mean for a child to receive an education that upholds values different from those in his or her home country? Many people involved in higher education think that "study abroad" is beneficial to U.S. students. Can we develop a "study abroad" program for youngsters in grade school or high school so that we can bring about change in young people? Can U.S. schools take on these functions?

I do not believe that dialogue and open education can solve all problems, but I do believe that dialogue and education do allow people to see each other as people who can plan activities that are mutually beneficial. I also believe that in the case of the Palestinians and the Israelis, the two groups share so much that if enmity could be reduced, the two sides could achieve great things and would even enjoy each other. We have tried a few such programs at my university, with wonderful results in most cases.

What does interpretive social science have to do with these musings? Two things. First, we need to describe the process of transformation that occurs when people are immersed in cultures other than their own. How does it happen that individuals change—what are the manifestations of change? And second, we should trace the erosion of negative stereotypes as that erosion does occur. Anthropologist Ruth Benedict was engaged in a similar project to reduce American stereotypes about the Japanese people (see Caffrey, 1989).

If it is true that there are 11,000 revolutionary terrorists worldwide organized in clandestine cells, willing to die while carrying out missions of destruction, it will be nearly impossible to eliminate the threat they pose to the United States by ordinary means. We may be able to demonstrate that it is possible to convert or cool out the enemy through subtle means of attractive reeducation and relocation.

Reference

Caffrey, M. (1989). *Benedict: Stranger in This Land*. Austin: University of Texas Press.

Shulamit Reinharz is Jacob Potofsky Professor of Sociology at Brandeis University.

LIVING IN THE PRESENT

III

STACEYANN CHIN

for Christopher Conti

Allegiance

In the fall of 1990
I let go of my virginity
The Desert Storm blasting loud from his 13 inch TV
of course it was summer there
Kingston sweltering
sweat collecting in my navel trembling
in the face of the unknown

I wondered then
if the explosions were for me
or the little people on the blue screen
far away from my pleasure
they were pictured small
boys with metal rods pointing to where they suspect America
might be

Today I make love to a young girl
the sound of this New War everywhere
wonder what we will lose this time

This time
I was visiting
home for when it began
bright
silver bombs bursting clouds

buildings
the victims
everything looks small on cable TV

I don't know
maybe the boys in Kuwait lived
maybe only their dreams died in the gulf that year

But I will never be that girl again
slow turning beneath his hands

I am a woman now.

Flags

My little brother walks home with a kid from Afghanistan
my brother doesn't know
what the kid from Afghanistan thinks about the war
but everyone knows has family at home
he knows he likes the Mets more
than he likes the Yankees
I'm not sure what kind of passport he has
but they both go to IS-53
and he likes being a freshman there

This war will take years
we are told
nothing more concerns us
we are told

These boys will be men when it is over

Staceyann Chin moved from Jamaica to New York in the summer of 1997, discovered performance poetry in 1998, and now is a disciple of the spoken word movement.

Thoughts Beyond Fear

38

LOIS WEIS

September 11, 2001

9:10 a.m.

MY SISTER CALLS. KATHI HAD DINNER with Jim last night. He is staying at the World Trade Center hotel and has a 9 a.m. meeting. We don't know what floor the meeting is on.

I am gripped by fear as we try to find out where Jim's meeting is. All circuits are busy. His office in Atlanta is closed. My sister assures me that Jim is resourceful—that he will get out. I keep looking at the falling buildings and know that no one at the top will get out alive. And we don't know where his meeting is.

I spend the day glued to the phone and the television. My hands shake as I call the high school my two daughters attend to tell them about their uncle. Pink slips are floating through the school as parents call the office and alert the school as to missing relatives. All students are called into the auditorium —many, including my ninth-grade daughter, are sobbing. I can't reach my husband to tell him about my brother. Tears soak my face and my clothes as I experience the powerlessness that so many experience on a daily basis all over the world. I feel connected to all and connected to none. I am deeply scared.

3:30 p.m.

Kathi calls. Jim is out, standing in midtown where he walked after the collapse of the buildings. I thank God that we are blessed—that at least in my little corner of the world my family and friends are safe. I fall to the ground, both in gratitude and in fear. My tears flow as I wrap my quilt around me.

October 2

The days and weeks go by. How can this happen? Knowing that nations around the world are victimized by globalization helps me not at all. I fear for all of us. I grieve for those who lost loved ones; I grieve for the children—for their loss of innocence, for the moment that will never go away in the lives of so many.

Our interpretivist social science speaks little to such tragedy but speaks volumes to our space as social activists. More than others we gather the data that touches people's lives. We get so close as we cry with those who have been hit, beaten until bloody, trashed, frisked, pushed up against walls, and misnamed—those whose humanity and dignity have been stripped and robbed. Amid the horrific tragedy of September 11, let us not be blind to atrocities in our own country. This tragedy should make us look inward as well as outward, taking as a starting point the tragic lives of individuals who daily survive at the margins in the United States. We feel their pain—the pain that seeps through the very pores of our own society. The pain that both energizes and destroys. I collapse at a conference. I cannot act as ventriloquist for one more beaten woman; the hurt sears my soul as I attempt to put out there the smashed spirit that litters the American poor and working class—the spirit that matches my own as an affluent woman in America but one who knows full well the terror of smarting in pain.

Out of the depths of our pain we must hold on to our responsibilities. To not mince words as we represent ourselves and others in our work. To not paper over and attempt to explain away that which can have no explanation or excuse. For an engaged activist research agenda can tolerate nothing that is fundamentally wrong. And we cannot and should not be lulled by the drug of objectivity or deconstructionism, nodding off as we pick apart categories and refuse to name atrocities, simultaneously letting those in pain burn, we afraid to name any wrongdoing for fear of being labeled modernist or, perhaps worse, politically engaged. We get close, and that closeness touches chords within our heart and our soul that match those of the people with whom we work. We need to continually be mindful of inscribing in the social science literature vengeful and hateful apologetics for the status quo. But in so doing, we need to remember that some behavior is plain wrong and must be labeled as such as we work toward a more just and equitable society. We cannot shirk our responsibilities as intellectuals by hiding behind the cloak of overly meek or inward-looking social science, whether quantitative or interpretivist. We touch other people's lives. We know and share their pain. We know what contributes to it. The tragedy of September 11 should make us remember that we have our part to play in hearing those who speak to us and that we must continue to engage in conversation and action around leaving the world a better place than when we first met it. As we author the written edifices that honor the memory of those with whom we speak and work, we need call the atrocities—those that break the soul of the parents and children who entrust us with their stories and their lives.

The whole world is but a narrow bridge, but the essence of it all is not to be afraid to walk, to hold hands and walk it together (Nachman of Bratslav). Let us grab hands and use our research voice to leave the world a better place than when we first met it.

Lois Weis is professor of sociology of education at the University of Buffalo, State University of New York.

Love Survives

39

ARTHUR P. BOCHNER

WHEN THE CALL COMES, I'm on the road, somewhere near Macon, Georgia, on my way home from vacation. I'd been staying near Smokey Mountain National Park for the month of August, a respite from the humid Florida summer. My partner, Carolyn, answers my cell phone.

"Yes, this is his number," she says, sounding concerned.

"Who is it?" I interrupt, my heart racing. Only my family and my mother's caregivers would call me on a Saturday on my cell phone. This can't be good.

"Well he can't talk now because he's driving, but we'll take the next exit and he'll call you right back." Carolyn ignores my intrusion, turns off the phone, then says, "That was Susanna. She wants to talk to you about your mom."

"Did she sound upset?" I ask. "What's wrong?"

"I don't have the details," she replies. "Just try to stay calm. You can call her back as soon as we get off the highway."

The exit is only four or five miles down the road, but it seems like an eternity. Carolyn doesn't say anything, which makes me more certain that something ominous is going on. As we drive, I recall the e-mail I received the night before from Susanna. "The infection on your mother's foot is slowly healing," she wrote. "Otherwise I haven't noticed any acute changes in her condition." But then she added, "Your mom is very quiet. She may be waiting for you to come and visit." Suddenly, these words feel very menacing and I am angry with myself for not paying closer attention. But what could I have done from 600 miles away last night?

We exit on one of those deserted side roads in South Georgia that resembles a scene from *The Twilight Zone*—a road from nowhere to nowhere. In the field of tall grass behind the truck stop, Carolyn walks our four dogs while I make calls to Susanna, the geriatric care manager, and Carol, Mom's CNA.

"I don't want to alarm you, but I'm very worried about your mother," Susanna says. "She's just not speaking, and her head tilts to the left. She can't control it. I think she's waiting for you, Art." Afterward, Suzanne's words hang in the air. "She's waiting for you, Art." A chill runs up my spine. Why didn't she just say it? Mom's dying, isn't she?

Carol, the CNA, is direct and to the point. "Get here as soon as you can if you want to see your mom again. She's fading fast. I think she's just holding on to see you."

When Carolyn and I arrive at the nursing home 6 hours later, I am shocked by what I see. At the end of July, I had pushed Mom around in her wheelchair. Although she'd been losing weight, she still appeared stout and lively. She may have been confused, but she was talkative, engaged, and alert. Now she lies quietly in bed. Her face looks skeletal, and she is weak, frail, and immobile.

"Hi, Mom, it's Art," I say, leaning over the rail of her bed and clasping her hand. "Do you know who I am?" She starts to say "Yes," but the word doesn't come out. Instead she nods her head. Later she mouths a few words faintly. She doesn't appear to have the strength to speak even if she were able to form words. Carol brings her in a milkshake, reminding me that Mom can only eat pureed food and take in liquids.

"Are you comfortable, Mom?" I ask, wanting to be sure she's not in pain. She nods her head and I feel relieved.

"You love Art, don't you Minnie?" Carol, the CNA, asks in a tone of voice reserved for talking to babies.

"Yes," Mom answers, in an audible voice this time, her eyes staring directly into mine.

When I stand up or move around the room, Mom's eyes follow me. The whole night, whenever she is awake, she never stops looking at me. Her brow furrows and she appears to be frightened and confused. I sit close to her and rest my head on the bed near her arm, clasping her hand in mine. I try to hide the terror I feel. Where is the articulate, clever, witty mother of my youth? Who is this woman occupying my mother's body who feels and smells like Mom?

When she sleeps, her breathing is shallow, even with oxygen in her nose. Although she struggles repeatedly to talk to me, she can form only a few words. She is primarily a body now. Carolyn comforts me, squeezing my hand and hugging me when I start to sob. I try to hold back the tears, but I can't. At that moment, I had no idea how many tears I would shed over the next 3 weeks.

Ten days later, on my way to see Mom, I take Carolyn to the airport for her trip to see her mother, who is rehabbing in a nursing home in Virginia. I drive across the causeway and stop for breakfast at a family-owned restaurant a couple miles from the nursing home. When the waitress comes over to take my order, I have my head buried in the sports page of the *St. Petersburg Times*. Abruptly, she says, "Did you hear that a plane just crashed into the World Trade Center?" "No," I reply, looking up at her.

"They think it was a plane that went off course, but I bet it was terrorists."

I hear the sound of the TV behind the counter but see that no one is watching it. I eat my breakfast quickly, glancing at the TV but not really taking it in.

"There's been a second crash into the World Trade Center," my waitress announces when she brings my check. "I told you it was terrorists," she adds emphatically.

I pay for breakfast and leave the restaurant quickly, noting all the people now huddled around the TV. In the van, I tune to the radio reports. They portend a grave situation, although Bryant Gumbel cautions about drawing conclusions too swiftly, in the name of objectivity. "Remember Oklahoma City," he reminds.

As I pull into the nursing home, I make a call to my brother, Mel, on my cell phone. He lives in TriBeCa about 10 blocks from the World Trade Center. He answers on the first ring.

"Mel, I just heard about the crashes. Is everyone all right there?"

"Oh, Art," he says in a choked voice, "it's so horrendous. Lizbeth and I were editing a manuscript at the kitchen table when we heard the sound of a plane flying low over our building. That never happens. So we went down to the street, and we could see the first plane, the tail was just hanging out of the building, swinging back and forth, and the top of the building was smoking. My God, do you know how many people are in there? And our kids had just left for school. We don't know how we're going to get them."

"Are they okay?" I restrain the mounting fear I'm feeling as I try to take in the shocking magnitude of these details. I'm standing outside the van now shivering in spite of the hot Florida sunshine.

"We think they are. They're several miles away, but at opposite ends of the city."

"I'm just glad you are all safe."

"I better go, Art. I want to see what they're saying on TV."

I feel relieved that Mel is safe, but his description of the burning Towers scares me in an unfamiliar way. I feel as if I'm suffocating when I think of all the people in the building who are dead or dying. But I have nothing to compare this experience to but movies. I'm ashamed that I have this perverse desire to see more of what's happening on TV.

I run into the nursing home and enter Mom's room. I lean over the railing of her bed and kiss her. When I tell her about the crashes, her eyes follow me, but she stares blankly and does not respond. The TV is tuned to an old Western movie. I flip obsessively through the channels until I hit CNN. The voice says, "We're going to take you now to our reporter at the Pentagon, where there has just been news of an explosion." The picture shows a fire burning and black smoke enveloping part of the building. The reporter continues, "We're now getting reports that the flights of the hijacked planes originated at Logan in Boston and at Dulles."

Dulles! The word slaps me into reality. My god, Carolyn's plane is heading for Dulles. I have to do something. What? Nothing feels safe at the moment. I feel helpless. I want to be with Carolyn, not here.

"All planes in the air have been ordered to land at the nearest airport," the CNN reporter announces. "America is under attack. America is on high alert." I can think only of Carolyn, not the big picture. At the moment, she's the one thing I'm sure of—or unsure of. She anchors my world. At least her plane's not going to Dulles. But where is she? What if there are terrorists on her plane?

Frantic, I dial my travel agent to see if she can tell me where Carolyn's plane will land. "Kelly, I need your help." I shout into the phone. "My wife, Carolyn, is in the air. I need to know where her plane is going to land." She responds calmly, inquiring about the flight information. Before she can get the information off her computer, we get disconnected. I dial again and again but get busy signals each time. Finally, she gets through to me.

"The computer shows that plane will be landing in Charlotte at 10:25." I see on my watch that it's 10:05. I walk in and out of the nursing home entrance, adrenaline shooting through me. I pace across the corridor, aware that people are watching me. It's the longest 20 minutes of my life. I try to reach Carolyn's older brother in Luray, where she was headed. Carolyn's younger brother died in a plane crash, and I'm concerned her whole family is thinking the worst. The cell phone won't connect, so I try the pay phone. It won't connect either. I dial over and over. Damn it, nothing ever works when you need it. I've got to get out of here.

I head for the causeway, driving like a madman. I keep trying to reach Carolyn on the cell phone. I keep saying "Carolyn Ellis" into the voice recognition receiver. Over and over and over again. I want to shout her name so she'll hear me, but when I do I get, "Please repeat the name." Damn technology. "Please, please, let her answer," I say softly. If I can only hear her voice, I'll know she's all right and we're going to survive this. Suddenly, halfway across the causeway, I hear a voice that sounds very far away on the other end of the phone.

"Hello."

"Carolyn, Carolyn," I scream into the phone. "Oh, thank God it's you. Are you all right?"

"I'm okay," she reassures. Her voice is calm, but she sounds breathless, as though she's rushing.

"Are you in Charlotte?"

"Yes. We just landed. They're opening the door now. But how did you know?" She sounds different—more formal—as if she's not reacting emotionally.

"I called the travel agent."

"Where are you?"

"I'm on the causeway, driving back from the nursing home." "Carolyn," I say, raising my voice, "get out of the airport. Do it now."

"I will. I'm headed out. . . . " The phone clicks off.

I'm unable to reach Carolyn again until I arrive home. By this time, she's at a rental car agency, about to head out for Virginia.

"I felt so out of control," I say, choking up. "It seemed like planes were going down right and left. I don't know what I'd do if I lost you."

"You won't, I'm fine," she says. Her voice trails off as if she's distracted. I realize, then, how different her situation is from mine. She has to make all these decisions. While my emotions are raw as I stand here helplessly, she's in problem-solving mode. How little she must know about what's going on, I think.

"I guess you haven't heard any of the details."

"Not very many."

"People were jumping from the top floors of the building. There were thousands of people in there, and police, and firemen. And then the buildings collapsed with no warning, like the time our rafts pancaked on the Colorado River. You could see people running through this ball of smoke and ash, screaming, and trying to dodge the falling debris. Mass chaos. You can't imagine the horror. Our lives are never going to be the same. . . . "

"Oh, it sounds awful," she says. Then, "Art, I have to go. I'm pulling out of the parking lot now."

"Call me every hour," I demand.

"I will. I love you," she says, and then the phone clicks off.

I feel my body shaking and wipe away the tears streaming down my face. I take out the bottle of malt scotch that I bought 15 years ago and turn on the TV.

Three days later, sitting in the dark, I feel as if the world is coming to an end. The wind howls fiercely in the aftermath of the tropical storm that drifted slowly through Tampa last night bringing 12 inches of rain. Down the block, an old oak tree felled by the storm leans on the power line. I have no water or electricity. No TV to watch; no light to read by. Carolyn is still in Virginia, 1,500 miles away—out of reach. I can't get to my critically ill mother today because the causeway is closed due to the storm. She hasn't been able to talk or move for 2 weeks now. They say she had "a major event"; I suspect she had a stroke. My four dogs nestle close to me as I lay on the couch in the darkness. Frightened by the unfamiliar sound of the wailing winds, two of them shake nervously. They move closer, trying to hide under me. They want me to protect them, make them feel safe. They do not know how vulnerable and scared I feel. Or do they? I hold them tighter to me—for me.

I sense that the whole world is teetering on the edge of oblivion. The thought terrifies me. I try to regain a calmer state by reminding myself that this is how it is supposed to feel when you're in the middle of an epiphany. Theory doesn't comfort me. It seems beside the point.

Feeling lightheaded, I close my eyes. My mind races with cinematic images and emblems. I see the faces and forms of the dead, a rainbow of ethnicity and social class: CEOs in suits and ties; brokers in rolled-up shirtsleeves; police, firemen, and security guards in uniforms; chefs, waiters, receptionists, janitors, clerks, and mailroom workers—the men and women of everyday life. A bicycle daredevil, a mountaineer, a trivia expert, an expectant father, a dancer, a woodsman, a humorist, a classical musician. Americans, Mexican Americans, Chinese Americans, Ethiopian Americans, Italian Americans, African Americans, Albanians, Cubans, Russians, Australians, Brits. Their eyes close. Death levels the field.

The film rolls. Other faces appear. The mothers, husbands, wives, and children of the missing. Their minds know the odds are against them, but their hearts refuse to give up. There's still time—hope. They post photos of the disappeared at the entrances of hospitals, on scorched trees and charred buildings. Bereft of a body, they resist the rituals of grief— for now. My eyes follow them as they walk through the haze near Ground Zero. I feel as if I'm watching surreal images in a Buñuel film, then I realize this is true. These aren't special effects. Those aren't actors. This isn't a script. What I see is an image of hell—the thick white ash covering the streets and the cars, the trucks, and the bodies of emergency personnel; the scattered pages of stock reports and desk calendars blowing across the streets; the fragments of broken glass and burned up wires; the rescue workers carrying body bags and wearing nose masks to tolerate the stench of decomposing flesh and burning debris; the fear and terror on the faces of the bystanders. Watching them, I wonder what they're thinking. "That could have been me." "How did it feel to die in there?" "Why did they do this to us?" "Will I ever feel safe again?" "I want to kill the terrorists."

Another scene. Everyone looks enraged, their faces red with anger. They raise their fists and stick out their chests. They pledge their allegiance to America and their readiness to fight for freedom. They want to strike back, avenge this horror, blow them—the enemy—off the face of the earth. They shout their resolve to do what needs to be done. They speak of killing, not healing, of winning the war, not achieving social justice. Retaliation is justice, they imply. The warmongers find their justification in the thousands of innocent civilians who have been killed. The generals come into focus now, making their military calculations and strategic plans. They tell us to prepare for a long war, a different kind of war, an unconventional war, a difficult war. The "enemy" is not a state but a web of cells devoid of boundaries, a cellular opponent whose strategy involves the use of credit cards, airline tickets, and rental cars and whose main weapon is the reign of terror. In the background is the echo of our president's voice, "Evildoers, cowards, you're with us or you're against us, it's the bad guys versus the good guys, we'll smoke them out of their holes, we'll dry up the swamps in which they live." A voice off screen defiantly asks, "How will we know when we've won?" Silence. Another rejoins, "Where will the battlefield be?" Silence. "If we kill innocent civilians, how are we better than them?" Silence. "How will we know when it's over?" Silence. Fade out.

Fade in. I see bin Laden enter the scene. He stands in front of a cave, sand blowing in the wind across his cape. He says America is a snake. He will cut off the head of the snake. He warns that America will never again feel safe. In a quiet voice, he spews his wrath at our policies and our morals. America defends evil regimes that would be overthrown if the snake did not guard them. America offends the Muslim holy sites. America intrudes on Islamic soil. America's mores—our movies, our music, our cultural products—defile the canons of Muslim faith. He says he is not afraid of American might. There is no shelter from his terror. It is America who kills innocent civilians. American infidels.

I am frightened by this image and of the words bin Laden speaks. Then I recall that Mohamed Atta drank alcohol, played video games, and frequented strip clubs the week before he carried out the master plan. Foad Ajami (2001), a renowned Middle Eastern scholar, appears on the screen. "It is not so simple," he says. "Contradictions abound. New freedoms trying to exist in tandem with old theologies. Yearning and repression. Atta's generation in Egypt is tormented by the glamour and temptations of the West. They came so close to modernity and then the rug was pulled from under them. If your dreams and temptations are thwarted, your hatred grows, and you blame those who have intruded on your world. Taking them down becomes your mission. When you feel humiliated, you respond with wrath."

A light shines in my face, waking me from my reverie. The power is back on. A shower of light into the confusion. The movie didn't end, it stopped before we got to the moral of the story, where the narrator sums up, tells you what it means, ties up the loose ends. I want the happy ending. The one where war is averted and safety restored. In the final scene, a new generation of moderate and liberal Islamic leaders preach understanding, not hate, and Islamic children join new Islamic social movements that protest terror, worship freedom, promote education, respect and honor women, and demand freedom of expression. Middle Eastern countries are governed by democratic leaders. Their citizens participate actively in governance and show tolerance for differences of faith. There is no hunger, no despair, no hatred. I blink. My eyes open. The blank TV screen stares back at me.

I'm sitting on the floor beside Mom's bed, holding her hand, looking into those piercing eyes that never look away from me. It's been 20 days, and Mom's still hanging in. "I think she needs your permission to die," the hospice nurse told me yesterday. Initially, that sounded like psychobabble, but then I realized how much I'd been clinging to Mom. I've learned to be in the silence. When I feed her, touch her, and caress her, a warmth circulates through me that I've never felt before. I feel needed. Her eyes tell me she loves me. She wants me here. She doesn't look scared, the way she did the first night I returned. The muscles in her face are relaxed. It's as if she feels at home here for the first time. In the quiet of our eye contact, I've learned that without silence, words would be meaningless; without listening, speaking loses its capacity to heal; without empathy, fear becomes consuming.

As I look into Mom's eyes one more time, it occurs to me that the blank stare has disappeared. Dementia notwithstanding, she knows I'm here. I feel it. I see it. I know it. How can I let her go now, when it's been so long since I felt she really was here? What do you say to somebody who is leaving you forever? I think of all the children who never got to say goodbye to the parent who didn't come home on September 11. And their parents. And my siblings who aren't here, although they could be. Then I think of those calls from the people in the World Trade Center and on the hijacked planes who knew they were about to die (Veale, 2001). "I love you, take care of the children." "Darling, the building was hit with something. I don't know if I'm going to get out. But I love you very much. Bye." "I'm on the plane and it's hijacked and it doesn't look good. I just want you to know that I love you and I hope to see you again. . . . Know that I love you and no matter what, I'll see you again." "I love you a thousand times over and over and over again. I love Emmy [too]. . . . Whatever decisions you make in your life, I need you to be happy, and I will respect any decisions that you make." "I love you, Mommy, goodbye."

As I kneel beside Mom, my head resting beside her shoulder, I suddenly realize several hours have passed while we've been here connecting through the silence. I look into her eyes, knowing she is listening. I clear my throat, fighting back the tears. "Mom, I think it's time to go. This is no life for you. I'll miss you, Mom. I love you so much and I'm so grateful for all you've done for me. Mel and Reeta and I are closer than we've ever been, and we're all happy in our careers and in our marriages. You don't have to worry about us. We'll be fine. I love you, Mom." I kiss Mom on the lips, then on the forehead and leave. For the first time, I don't say, "See you tomorrow."

Mom died the next day. I haven't been across the causeway since.

Thousands died on September 11, and they died for real; but thousands died together, and therefore something lived. The most important, if distressing, images to emerge from those hours are not the raging towers or of the vacuum where they once stood; it is the shots of people falling from the ledges and in particular, of two people jumping in tandem. It is impossible to tell from the blur what age or sex these two are, nor does that matter. What matters is the one thing we can see for sure: They are falling hand in hand. Think of Philip Larkin's poem about the stone figures carved on an English tomb and the "sharp tender shock" of noticing that they are holding hands. The final line of the poem has become a celebrated condolence, and last Tuesday—in uncounted ways, in final phone calls, in the joined hands of that couple, in circumstances that Hollywood should no longer try to match—it was proved true all over again, and in so doing, it calmly conquered the loathing and rage in which the crime was conceived. 'What will survive of us is love' (Lane, 2001, p. 80).

REFERENCES

Ajami, F. (2001, October 7). Nowhere man. *The New York Times Magazine*, pp. 19–20.

Lane, A. (2001, September 24). This is not a movie. *The New Yorker*, 79–80.

Veale, S. (2001, September 16). Voices from above: "I love you, Mommy, goodbye." *The New York Times*, Section 4, p. 7.

Arthur P. Bochner is a professor of communication and codirector of the Institute for Interpretive Human Studies at the University of South Florida.

Take No Chances

40

CAROLYN ELLIS

"**Y**OUR BAGS ARE LIGHT. That's good." The dark-complected, clean-shaven, 40-ish-looking man scurries around the Royal Cab to load my small, soft-sided bag and laptop backpack. I nod in appreciation as I talk on my cell phone, which has become my lifeline during the last week. "I am at the rental car agency in Richmond now," I explain into the phone. "The taxi is here to take me to the airport. I must go."

"Take no chances," my husband Art implores, resisting my attempt to end the conversation.

"Don't worry. I'll be careful." I hang up and get into the backseat of the cab.

"I lost my suitcase," I reply once I am settled. "When I went to visit my mother to help her return home from a stay in a nursing home, she gave me this small bag and a few of her clothes."

"It'll be easier to get on the plane," the man says, "faster without so many bags."

"Will they let me take my things on the plane?"

"I don't think so. That's what I heard on TV."

"I was on a plane Tuesday morning," I say. Noting the man's Middle Eastern appearance, I wait to see how he will respond.

"If you see a group of Muslim-looking men together, turn and head in the other direction," my husband, worried that I was flying home to Tampa alone, had instructed on the phone. "If they're getting on your flight, don't get on. Take no chances."

"I doubt I'll be the only person watching out for Muslim men," I had replied.

"I guess you're right," he acknowledged. "Just take no chances. Be a good ethnographer. Pay attention to your surroundings."

"I haven't been able to talk for 3 days," the dark-complected man says now, as he pulls into traffic. "I am so distressed. I can't sleep. Nothing."

"It's awful," I acknowledge, not knowing how to talk about the terrorist attacks in New York and Washington that occurred almost a week ago now.

The man continues talking, seeming to have a running dialogue in his head. "It's bad for me in three ways. I am Middle Eastern, I am a Jordanian, and I'm a Muslim. But I'm also an *American*," he says with emphasis.

The word *Muslim* makes me flinch slightly. Yes, I thought he was Muslim. He's brave to say so. Normally I would not have thought about his being Muslim, and we likely would have had a lively conversation about what his home country is like. I listen to his words. He speaks of bin Laden, Israel, Jordan, Palestine; their relations, wars, and conflicts. I listen, nod, and shake my head. My feelings are jumbled. I am slightly apprehensive. Numb still and fatalistic. Yet I have a strong desire to communicate with him. Unexplainably, I feel excited. He doesn't seem threatening or like my enemy. But probably some of the hijackers didn't either, I think. *Take no chances, my husband had said.* How does he feel, other than distressed? Do I dare ask him?

"I have two sons. They are in Jordan with my wife, who is English," he offers, speaking intensely, in a quick cadence with few pauses. "She's there because she needed help from my parents with the children. But my family is too far away now. They are scared for me. Every day my wife calls and the first thing she says is, 'Are you safe?' They were supposed to come here next month. Now they won't. Too dangerous." I think of how frightened Art and I were to be apart during the attack. We too call every day now, many times, encouraging each other to *take no chances*. I feel a kindred spirit with this man's wife.

"In Jordan, my wife wears a *hijab*, the traditional head covering. She asked me how she should dress and I told her. She put on the veil and asked me how I liked it. 'It is beautiful,' I said. Everyone wears it there," he explains, sounding apologetic, "even those who visit. She chooses to wear it." I cannot imagine experiencing the world in and through a veil. I wonder if this veil covers his wife's eyes as well as her head and neck.

"My sons ask me what it means to be a Muslim. They hear on TV that the terrorists were Muslim men. They know I am a Muslim man. They ask for explanations. How do I explain?" His question sounds rhetorical.

"What do you say?" I ask, interrupting.

"What?" he asks, turning again to look at me. He pauses. "I tell them these men are not Muslims like I am. It is not the same. But that is not enough."

Quickly he asserts, "Good Muslims don't go to stripper bars." I wait for him to say that good Muslims don't kill people, but he doesn't.

"Muslims died in the World Trade Center," he does say, "along with all the others. I've visited the World Trade Center with my brother who is a general in the Jordanian army. It could have been my family on those planes."

"Have other Americans acted badly toward you?" I ask.

"No, no they haven't. My American friends, they have called and reassured me. They are worried. So are my Muslim friends. We met last night, all Muslims, and we talked and we cried. A woman from a church came to speak to us. She cried and we all cried. I cry a lot. I wear dark glasses," he says, turning around and taking them off, "because I never know when I will cry." His eyes are red and sad, very sad. "Can you imagine us all crying together?"

"Yes, yes I can. I cry a lot too. Your story makes me cry now," I say. He turns again, looks at my wet eyes, and then continues talking.

I think about the feelings I had after the initial attacks. On Tuesday, after my plane scheduled for Dulles was diverted to Charlotte, I rented a car and listened to National Public Radio all the way to my mother's house in rural northern Virginia. The revenge talk resonated with me. *Blow 'um off the face of the earth,* I had felt momentarily. I don't know who "um" was exactly, but the picture in my mind was of dark-skinned men with turbans, long robes, and beards. The feeling didn't last long, but it was strong and interrupted briefly the void of hopelessness, fear, and vulnerability that overcame me.

"I'm 40," the man continues. "I came to America because I wanted prosperity and security. I wanted to be safe."

"Like the rest of us," I say.

"To be safe, that is most important. The Americans, they argue over who should be president. But it doesn't matter if it is Bush or Gore, just that there should be someone and we should be safe."

"I watch the news a lot. I've lived with the idea of bin Laden for years," he continues. "I don't know how much Middle Eastern history you know, but . . . " Without waiting for an answer, the man launches into the history of Jordan-Israel relationships. I have trouble following until, "My friends in Jordan, they hate Jews," he says. I cringe, thinking of my dark-complected Jewish husband and my own identification with Judaism. My husband had said that Jews in Israel were worried they would be blamed for this. Might there be violence against Jews here? Could my own bearded husband be mistaken for a Middle Eastern man?

Wondering the same, a few days later my husband will suggest shaving the beard he has had for more than a decade. I run my fingers lovingly through his soft salt-and-pepper facial hair and think that might be for the best. Take no chances.

"I lived with Jews in England," the man says, and I relax a bit. "I got along with them fine. If you treat them right, they'll treat you right. I dated a Jewish woman for 3 years. We would have married, but she said the children must be raised Jewish. I couldn't do that so we broke up."

"My husband is Jewish," I reveal hesitantly. He acknowledges what I say with a nod and continues talking about Middle Eastern history. I examine his demeanor, how he speaks, the emotion in his words, and wonder what living in America will be like for him now. I look closely. Did the terrorists look and act like him? What if he's a fake? What if he really hates all Americans? What if he means me harm? I shake my head. Don't let yourself even think that, I reprimand. What kind of world would it be if we let ourselves think like that? His pain seems authentic. Trust your feelings, I tell myself.

Take no chances, my husband had said.

"I love America," he suddenly says. "I'm loyal to this country."

"Are you worried about prejudice?" I ask.

"No, I'm not. When people yell slurs at me, I pretend I don't hear. I don't get upset."

"That's probably the best way to react," I say. What must it feel like to have experienced this as a tragedy and now to feel blamed for it? What about Muslims who lost loved ones? Is the feeling similar, on another level, to being considered a suspect by the police after your child is murdered?

I think of how African Americans often have had to pretend to ignore prejudice. Now American Blacks and Whites are on the same side of this crisis. No worry this week about young Black men and crime. No headlines or op-ed articles about "fixing" Black-White relations. The category "us" suddenly has gotten bigger and more diverse, but the line between this "us" and "them" feels ominous and sinister. Will Muslims take the place of African Americans in our class system? "They're not yelling at you, you know," I say in defense of "us" and to make him feel better. "They're yelling at a symbol." Does that make him feel better or worse?

"I know that. And I won't respond unless someone tries to do me harm, then I'll defend myself. But that's all."

"I love this country," he says again. "I pay my taxes because I am proud to be an American. I always make sure I pay them to the penny because, well, because I'm a stranger and that means they might look more closely at me and I never want them asking me for more."

"Do you understand the terrorists?" I ask.

"I understand them all right. They want everyone to look like them, to think like them, to act like them. And if you don't, they want to kill you. There are extremist groups in the United States too, you know."

"Certainly," I agree, a picture of White survivalists forming in my mind.

Blow 'um off the face of the earth, I hear in my mind. *Take no chances.*

We arrive at the airport 3 hours before my flight. The driver hurries around to open the door. "This is good, very light," he says, taking my small bag. "Now people won't rush to the airport at the last minute. This has been a wake-up call."

"Yes," I say, as he offers a hand. I check the meter and pay him: $29 for the fare and $3 for a tip.

When he reaches in his pocket for change, I put my hand on his arm, "No, it's for you." I wish then I had given him more.

"Thank you. I never forget tips that Americans give me." Does he mean now or always?

"Good luck to you," I reply. "Let's hope for better times ahead." Sometimes cliches are the best we can do.

I face him and look directly into his eyes and he into mine. I push my lap top backpack that hangs off one shoulder toward my back. Without thinking, I put my arms around his neck. He gently places his hands around my waist, my head falls on his shoulder, his head bows over mine. We hold onto each other for several moments and we cry.

Take chances, I think as I pick up my suitcase and head into the airport.

"I've read your story. It's on the counter," my husband Art says a few days later as he prepares to go visit his mother, who is critically ill after suffering an apparent stroke. When nothing more is forthcoming, I ask, "Do you like it?"

"It's about an important issue," he replies. "But the story is not as emotional as other pieces you have written."

"I wondered if it was a bit flat," I say. "But, you know, this whole experience has been somewhat numbing; there was a feeling of shock last week. An unreality. Like a dream. At the same time, this has been one of the most emotionally intense times of my life. I cried often while watching television, experiencing other peoples' losses and then thinking about the impending loss of our two moms and my fear of losing you. I've felt tremendous love from and for the people in my life. I feel all that even now."

"I feel the same. But I'm not sure that juxtaposition of vulnerability and fear with love comes through in the story. At least not for me. I don't come off sounding very good," he says, his hand on the doorknob. "I sound like I hate all Muslims."

"And I sound suspicious of all Muslims," I say.

"To understand what I said to you and the refrain in your head would take contextualizing our conversations. I mean, you were getting on a plane less than a week after the attack, for God's sake. I had just gone through the experience of your being on a plane during the attack. I was scared to death I was never going to see you again. I'd just watched this PBS interview with Bob Woodward, who warned of further attacks soon. He said that Americans needed to be watchful of their surroundings."

"Which meant at that time being watchful of Muslims," I say.

"I guess," Art responds thoughtfully. "Anyway, he frightened me. I immediately thought of you, of the danger you might be in. Still, I'm ashamed that I reacted in a way that seemed so categorical."

"We both did," I admit. "But we've tempered those categorical impulses now and become more sensitive to the political, social, and personal costs of thinking and acting that way."

"Some of our saddest moments this week have come from reading about Muslim Americans' experiences with discrimination and hate crimes," Art says.

"The tension in the story revolves around these issues: How can we be watchful and cautious without singling out and discriminating against a particular group of people?" I offer.

"I think the tension in the story concerns our living in fear," Art suggests.

"Living in fear yet choosing to follow our instincts about the people we meet. We have to put caring about our fellow human beings above our suspicions and fear, as I did with the cab driver," I respond.

"But can we trust those instincts now?" Art asks.

"That's the question. And what might happen if we trust and care for the wrong people at the wrong time. That's certainly a reasonable impulse given how loving toward our friends and families we're feeling after our loss," I ponder. "Even toward strangers," I add.

"Maybe that's why it's easier for some people to respond in anger to what has happened. Maybe anger helps temporarily, as it did for you in the story, with the feelings of vulnerability. I know I've never felt this vulnerable before. I really don't know how to make these feelings go away."

"Or if they should. It's hard to know how to feel now as individuals or as a country, much less what to do about these perplexing issues. What do we do?"

Just then Art's cell phone rings. He signals to me that it's his mother's hospice nurse. As he hurries out the door, I answer my own question. "Take chances," I say quietly.

Carolyn Ellis is a professor of communication and sociology in the Department of Communication at the University of South Florida.

Show Me a Sign   41

IVAN BRADY

T
HERE IS HOPE IN BELIEVING that the bottom line of human nature is ultimately one of sociability, not social pathology. We know that resource sharing contracts in scope with prolonged deprivation and that human relationships which might be maintained in less troubled times tend to get sloughed off under such conditions. Accordion-like, the overall pattern includes and excludes people and groups variously in expanding and contracting ranges of cooperation and solidarity, and it is driven by perceptions of relative resource advantage, if not by an interest in survival itself. We've seen this kind of movement in fine grain in our villages and towns and in relations between nations as private interests and political economies slip from good to bad, rich to poor, and back again. We've also seen a reaction to changing environmental circumstances that seeks to expand against cultural difference in wars of ideological and territorial aggrandizement, all of which are fueled by intolerance by definition. But what does this say about us as a species? About our prospects for living up to the name "human" in the process of managing our relations with others? Looking a little closer at ourselves under extreme conditions can provide some answers. What happens in the individual extreme when all the strategic resource chips are down, when people know in their deprivations that they are past the point of no return, when they believe that they have no chance of resurrecting a life path that would sustain them? There is evidence to suggest that what happens is not a Hobbesian war of all against all, every man (and woman) for himself in an all out grasp for the last bread crumbs, as fearful folklore and underinformed social science would have it. In the end, we are social animals.

   We know that the grisly facts revealed to the liberators of Auschwitz and other concentration camps at the end of World War II included human beings gassed to death in ovens—victims of hate and cruelty beyond any sense of credibility. We also know that some of them climbed on each other's backs in an effort to escape the confines of their murderous smotherings and that some of them clawed hard enough on the walls to embed their fingernails in the concrete. But that wasn't the end of it. At some point, resignation to their horrible fate set in and a sign emerged, a generalizable item, I think, a symbol of triumph of the human spirit drawn out of the psyche in desperation and left for us like a text to be read in a twisted pile of dead men, women, and children. Many chose to die in a final physical embrace, entwining family and strangers alike. I take that as poignant and enduring evidence that we can matter to each other, irrespective of who we are, even (or especially) under the direst of circumstances. The ultimate concerns of life transcend what separates us as cultures, combine us in one big mirror image as a species. We could find this thought and organize it in our societies if only we knew how to look—if only we had words to impose the idea indelibly on ourselves, to remember it in images that flare eternally in the conversations we have about others and differences, particularly when troubled times circle us up around the bonfires of our lives.

Much of the prospect for knowing or acting on this larger sense of humanity is lost to consciousness in the ordinary run of cultures and competitions for space, food, and the certainties that meaningful and satisfying lives must conform to the values of your own cultural beliefs. That's the balance point of life today, and there is nothing in our current global repertoire of behaviors and persuasions to keep that pattern from devolving into dangerously competitive relationships, as we saw on September 11 in the viciously culture-bound attacks on New York City and the Pentagon—a fireball of hate and anger exploded in the face of trust. America showed another side of self-interest as it moved to embrace its own in the wake of this tragedy and began to build a levee of heroic strength, high-risk relief, and soothing words to stem the tide of outrage and tears. Although retracted in scope from a global perspective and mostly unrecognized in the wrenching national pain of the moment, the prospect for global humanity known and cherished was insinuated in that resurrected solidarity. The blow knocked the wind out of most of the world. The pain was human, not just American, and thoughts of commonalities were showing up in word and gesture everywhere, including Ground Zero. Some unlucky souls in the tower attacks realized that they were trapped above blazing holes of concrete, steel, airplane fuel, and annihilating smudge and smoke that blocked all passages of escape. They chose to jump to a certain death rather than face a terrifying immolation. Hope for the species flickered again briefly in a tiny sign on the way down. Some of the jumpers were holding hands. I don't know what you call that in anthropology. I don't know how to teach its deeper meaning to terrorists or the Taliban. I only know that it has to be said and that we have reason to hear it, all of us.

Torn Shawl

Isle of Man, September 11, 2001

Shawl of yours
            Knitted vee
        Draped over a chill
        Love scented in wool
        Clambering on rocks
        Uphill from the sea

Hand of yours
    Redemption
   Soft touches smoothing
   Shredded commitments
   Shared shivers of fear
   Until healing's begun
Heart of yours
    Hearth aglow
   Palms fanning embers
   Honey mead plumbed
   Nourishment drained
   Straight into my soul
Flesh of yours
    Moist perfume
   Red orchids unfolding
   Rapture and rhythm
   Rising bright as the sun
   On splayed winter dunes
Death of yours
    Blackened stone
   Hard ink on my compass
   Dark blood in my brain
   Heart weavings rendered
   On seabeds of bone

Pipers

New York City, September 18, 2001

Dear Grandfather,

We saw the parade today
The men wore plaid skirts
Like our school uniforms

They marched in small steps

   Step   Step   Step

All in a row

   Step   Step   Step

The music didn't breathe
It just kept coming out

High notes and low

High and low again

> *Amaaazing grace*
> *How sweet the sound. . .*

Step   Step   Step

Many people were crying

The pipers acted like they were doing
What they always did when people were sad

I will never forget them

I wonder if I will ever see them again

Love,

Marianne

Ivan Brady is distinguished teaching professor and chair of anthropology at the SUNY Oswego.

A Walk in the Olive Grove   42

WILLIAM G. TIERNEY

> The freedom which we enjoy in our democratic government extends
> also to our ordinary life. We throw open our city to the world, and
> never by alien acts exclude foreigners from an opportunity of
> learning or observing although the eyes of an enemy may
> occasionally profit by our liberality.
>
> —PERICLES, THE FUNERAL ORATION

IN 1975 I GRADUATED FROM TUFTS UNIVERSITY, cut my shoulder-length hair, and
headed to Morocco to begin a 2-year stint in the Peace Corps. I had few preconcep-
tions about what Morocco and Islam would be like, but in keeping with most 21-
year-olds, I suppose, I thought I knew myself pretty well. One lesson I learned in Morocco
was how little I knew and how much I had to learn.

After 10 weeks of language training, we left for our assignments. With a combination
of hubris, idealism, romanticism, and foolishness, I had asked to be placed by myself in a
mountain town that was a day's journey from the trappings of modernity. I arrived in
Tahala after two train rides, a third-class bus, and a final hike into town.

Tahala was a Berber village nestled in the Atlas Mountains in central Morocco. They
had just started a high school and I was to be the first foreign teacher—a ninth-grade English teacher. The Peace Corps administrators had advised us to find someone to tutor us in
Arabic, and admittedly, I needed someone desperately. I have never been good at learning a
foreign language, and after 10 weeks I was able to mumble a few phrases using the present
tense, but I stumbled whenever I had to speak in the past, and the future tense got conveyed
by my motioning with my hands as I muttered phrases in the present tense hoping my lis-
teners understood. "I am leaving my bags in Fez yesterday," was one of my first language for-
ays with my principal. "I go to Fez tomorrow. I return in two nights. But I teach today."

Because I was the only foreigner in Tahala, and an American as well, I was an object of
intense curiosity. Many of my fellow teachers had studied in the town up the road where

there had been French teachers, but an American was something new. Children especially were astonished by me. When I went to market to buy a kilo of potatoes for the luncheon soup, a mob of children followed me waiting to hear me blurt out my Americanized Arabic.

Although by the end of my stay my Arabic had improved and I had learned how to function in a society where I was constantly watched with a mixture of amusement and astonishment, during those first months in Tahala I have never felt so alone or grown so much.

We encounter difference in different ways. The easiest response is often the reflexive one: I know what's right, and those who are different from me are wrong. Men who love men in a heterosexual culture are immoral, objects to be condemned. People whose skin is not white in an Anglo society must have some flaw. Those who are disabled are freaks of nature; perhaps they deserve pity—because they are different from the abled. If I do not have to confront those who are different from me, then I might fall back on a comfortable relativism where the other's culture is not right or wrong, just different. Such relativism is made more difficult on an individual level when I must live in the foreign culture, and it is more anguishing on a national level when those who are different from "us" employ terror to try and destroy us. We then revert to reflexive responses.

Those first months in Morocco, I had a wealth of similarly reflexive judgments. Sexual relations between men and women were topsy-turvy, making a mockery of everything I had just learned was good and just in my college classes. The pacifism I had articulated so clearly in working against the Vietnam War seemed out of place in a society where everyone seemed to shout at one another. Even my definition of what was "fair" was challenged in a society where one had to bargain for everything—even potatoes. Why did I have to pay 25 cents more for a pound of potatoes from the same merchant than the woman who preceded me? The merchants, I felt, cheated me because I was a foreigner.

I lived in a small apartment where there was electricity for a few hours a day. I had been told there was a shower, but the landlord had neglected to tell me that it was a cold-water tap that was above the squatter toilet, and the water worked only for an hour at dawn. He too had not been fair. I spent a great of time in that apartment puzzling out what was right and what was wrong and who was I.

Soon after I arrived, there was a knock at the door and I swung it open to meet Nezmi. He wore what I came to see was his standard clothing: a light brown *djelaba* that was soiled at the edges and old black shoes with holes in the tops. He was a small, rotund man with a tightly clipped black beard and intense brown eyes. I remember most clearly his laugh and his smile.

When I opened the door he grabbed my hands and offered the standard greeting: "*Salem Ali-kum*—the peace of Allah be with you." Even with my neophyte's language skills I was able to respond in turn: "*Ali-kum Salem*—and the peace of Allah be with you."

He kept holding my hands and laughed slightly as he told me that he had heard I wanted an Arabic teacher. "I will teach you," he said. "We will be friends. Let's take a walk."

Nezmi taught me Arabic by taking me on walks in the foothills of the Atlas Mountains above town. As was standard custom in Morocco, he often held my hand as we walked, and the initial curiosity of the villagers gave way to a sense of normalcy as they saw Nezmi walking with his American. Although Nezmi was only a few years older than I, I always treated him more like a respected elder. We do not have a good equivalent in English for what Nezmi was; his life centered on studying the Koran although he was neither our version of a minister nor a monk. He usually kept to himself, although when we walked children often ran to him and kissed his hand.

"We are very different, William," he began that first day so many years ago. "Do you like us?"

I forget my response, but I recall my many conversations with him revolving around his initial question. He spoke quietly and corrected my numerous grammatical mistakes, but he kept asking me what I liked and didn't like and how Morocco was different from my version of America.

He always arrived unannounced, but he developed a habit of coming toward the end of the day, and we would walk to an olive grove above Tahala to watch the sun begin to set. The last time I saw Nezmi we took what had become our familiar path to the olive garden and we sat quietly against a tree watching the sun's demise.

"Allah has given us many blessings, William," he said. "This day. Our friendship."

"Praise Allah," I responded. My Arabic had improved in the year I had lived in Tahala so that I now was able to speak in the present, past, and future tenses, and Nezmi was departing for a Koranic school in the south.

"I am sad you are leaving, my teacher," I said, and he laughed at my formality, that I called him my teacher.

"When you go home to your family, William, try to remember the teachings of Allah. You are a Christian, but remember Allah's truths: Evil occurs when we forget. Always try to learn. The suffering of the world is from those who neither remember nor learn."

Pericles's oration and the madness of a handful of men show the dangers that exist when we throw open our city to the world. Nezmi's orations showed me the joys that arise when I am able to avail my selves to opportunities of learning and observing that same world.

William G. Tierney is the Wilbur-Kieffer Professor of Higher Education at the University of Southern California.

From Sea to Shining Sea
Stories, Counterstories, and the Discourse of Patriotism

43

GERARDO R. LÓPEZ

IN THE DAYS FOLLOWING THE WTC/Pentagon/Pennsylvania catastrophe, I have seen an enormous outpouring of American patriotism, national goodwill, and public spirit from all corners of the globe. As the nation and the world nervously await for survivors to be pulled from the wreckage by heroic and courageous service workers, as we collectively mourn the lives of those lost in this horrible tragedy, and as we try to sort out the many emotions we feel as a result of this incident, the American flag has taken on new and significant meaning in the public discourse. I have seen the flag on everything from buttons, lapel pins, earrings, ribbons, T-shirts, stickers, ties, and vehicle antennas. Indeed, as Americans search for a common symbol of allegiance to bring them together during these troubled times, they have found such a symbol in the American flag as well as in patriotic songs and anthems.

Interestingly, during these times, I've also witnessed some very problematic incidents, not only in my hometown of Columbia (MO) but across the nation as well. Acts of hate, racism, rancor, scorn, and admonition—targeted mainly at Muslim citizens, people of Arab descent, and the entire Middle Eastern community (and often, Indian and Southeast Asian communities as well)—have paralleled this rise in American nationalism. Sadly, the construction of an American "national identity" has been built on the evilization of the Islamic and/or Middle Eastern "Other."

As the national media delivers images of an America "under attack," messages are delivered into homes—both overtly and subtly—of "extremist Arabs" and their hatred of everything American. Even the president suggests "they" hate "us" because of what America stands for: "a democratically elected government . . . our freedom of religion, our freedom of speech, our freedom to vote and assemble and disagree with each other" (Bush, 2001). Although such an explanation may sound appealing to many living in the United States, let us not forget the fact that U.S. international policy has not exactly been laissez-faire. America has many enemies, and common sense should tell us there is more to this story than a mere hatred of American democracy.

The point of this discussion, however, is not to judge American foreign policy. Neither is it to provide a simplistic explanation of why people would ruthlessly murder thousands of innocent people and terrorize a nation. My point is that the messages we receive in the media, the stock stories (Delgado, 1995) about this crime and the people behind it that are universally accepted as truths, are constantly filtered into our daily consciousness. And whereas acts of terrorism are never acceptable under any circumstance, the larger American public (and the world) receives messages that position American values and mores as neutral while Osama Bin Laden—and by extension, fundamentalist Islamic groups—are positioned as "radical extremists."

While the American public sifts through Congressional renditions of "God Bless America" and Grammy-Award-winning versions of "America the Beautiful," and as images of fallen towers and fallen heroes crisscross the airways directly from "Ground Zero"—I often wonder what message is sinking in and whether this discourse serves to "bring us together" or to solidify and reinforce subliminal fears of the Muslim and/or Middle Eastern Other:

> **"Oh beautiful, for spacious skies . . . "**
>
> *One day after the attack, an Arab American graduate student from our university found a cup of blood in his mailbox. The word "RAGHEAD" was painted in blood on a piece of his mail.*
>
> **"For amber waves of grain . . . "**
>
> *Osama's Coffee Zone, a local coffee house in Columbia, Missouri—owned and operated by a naturalized U.S. citizen born in Jordan who happens to share the same first name as the suspected terrorist—found his glass door covered with spit when he opened for business 2 days after the attacks.*
>
> **"For purple mountains majesty . . . "**
>
> *Two female students from Turkey were "silently harassed" by a group of White male students outside a university building 6 days after the attack. One of the males made a "gun gesture" with his hand and pretended to shoot the girls. Another male was overheard whispering the words "fucken terrorists" as they walked away.*
>
> **"Above the fruited plain!"**
>
> *A flyer was anonymously posted on the door of my department's copy room the day after President Bush delivered his address to the Joint Session of Congress. The flyer warned that "Arabs are going feel the wrath of America."*

What we've observed in the past 10 days is not unusual or aberrant. In fact, critical race theorists such as Derrick Bell, Richard Delgado, Patricia Williams, Juan Perea, and Mari Matsuda have consistently stated that racism and ethnocentrism are alive and well in this country and will probably never be eradicated because the law and other juridical apparatuses normalize racism by circulating stock stories and sanitized understandings of events. What are not circulated are the counterstories (Delgado, 1995) that undergird these same incidents: stories that are not told, stories that rub against our most fundamental understanding of reality, stories that reveal the underbelly of American society—the hate crimes, the scapegoating, the vilification and denigration of anything "un-American."

In short, the national sentiment expressed toward Arabs and Muslims under the guise of "American patriotism" isn't anything new. In fact, such hatred has reared its ugly head in the past: It happened to the Irish of the 1850s, the Germans during WWI, the Japanese during WWII, the Mexicans during Operation Wetback, and the Russians during the Cold

War. In fact, the very definition of what and who is an "American" has shifted as different "outgroups" become "ingroups" when the situation and historical circumstances change.

America is indeed wounded, but our wounds are far deeper and more pervasive than the physical and emotional wounds made by terrorists on September 11. Perhaps in these sad times, it is better for us to do some introspection and ask ourselves what is an American and who is (and who is not) included when we wave the American flag and sing songs of what makes America so beautiful.

References

Bush, G. W. (2001). *Presidential address to joint session of Congress*. Retrieved September 20, 2001, from http://www.whitehouse.gov/news/releases/2001/09/20010920- 8.html

Delgado, R. (1995). Legal storytelling: Storytelling for oppositionists and others: A plea for narrative. In R. Delgado (Ed.), *Critical race theory: The cutting edge* (pp. 64–74). Philadelphia: Temple University Press.

Gerardo R. López is an assistant professor in the Department of Educational Leadership and Policy Analysis at the University of Missouri–Columbia.

Fieldnotes from Our War Zone
Living in America During the
Aftermath of September Eleventh

44

H. L. GOODALL JR.

W HEN THE FIRST NEWS FLASH about an airplane hitting theWorld Trade Center broke over the airwaves, I had just handed over my only pair of progressive lenses to an unknown eyeglass technician at a local optical shop.
Without my glasses on, I am nearly blind. My unassisted vision has dipped below 20-
800, and I have severe astigmatism, which renders the empirical world past the tip of
my nose largely incoherent. There are also psychological dimensions to being without my
glasses, even for the few minutes it usually takes to adjust the frames.

I become aware of my own vulnerability in ways that border on the paranoid. I cannot see anything or anyone clearly, and because what I do see is little more than areas of
fuzzy color punctuated aurally by voices attached to structures of various sizes and shapes
that with my glasses I know as human beings but without them appear more as geometric
possibilities, I tend to close in on myself, pulling my six-foot-two-inch frame into the
smallest space possible, as if bracing for an imminent attack.

"Come! Look at this!" commanded a mildly accented Middle Eastern male voice from
the rear of the store. His voice was so persuasive that everyone moved in that general direction except me. I didn't dare risk it. I have learned from years of bumps and bruises and
falls in my own home when I venture from my own bed to a known bathroom in the night
that I am far better off not moving anywhere without my eyeglasses. Given that I no longer
possessed them and given that the man whom I had handed them over to was now in the
rear of the store with everyone else, I felt especially alone and even more vulnerable. So I
didn't move.

Instead, I listened. What I heard was the curious, prolonged absence of language in the
rhetorical form of a collective stunned silence. After that I heard an "Oooh," in the form
we reserve for a commingling of surprise and empathy, and then a low grunt of the sort
men use when a particularly hard tackle has occurred on a key player during a football
game. And then, the odd silence returned again. Whatever it was that captured their attention on what I would later learn was a small color television in the break room had the
effect of reducing five or six previously social, talkative people stone-cold quiet.

I had no idea what it was that was causing this reaction, but I knew it could not be good. Whatever they were seeing was either unutterable or ineffable. My paranoia increased proportionately. Finally, able to stand my aloneness no longer, I edged my way along the countertop to the door of the break room and inquired as politely as I could about what they were seeing on the screen. I think it was about this time that I heard the announcer say something about a plane that had crashed into one of the twin towers of the World Trade Center, someone else reported that a man on the street said it was a small plane, but someone else reported that it was a jet airliner. There was some confusion.

I still couldn't see anything. Everyone's eyes were on the small television screen. No one spoke. We were all still listening. I moved into the room and blurted out, "I can't see a thing without my glasses." I tried to sound lighthearted about it, as if this were simply an inconvenience to me rather than a matter of some urgency, which, by now, I was feeling this gathering situation to be.

The short man who had my glasses in his hand said, "Oh, sorry" and immediately handed them back to me.

I put them on and took a deep breath. I blinked and then looked up, then down again at the screen.

That was when the second plane hit the World Trade Center.

Now I understood the silence. Which is to say that now I understood nothing but knew that everything had changed.

I came in for a simple adjustment to the frames of my eyeglasses, but it was clear to me—as it was clear to everyone standing in that small room and to most people watching the same horrific scene everywhere—that what we were seeing was a still unutterable change in how the world works and that what we were experiencing was the as yet ineffable shift of our lives because of it.

I forgot about getting my frames adjusted. I ran to my car, found my cell phone, and called my wife. She had been watching the same images on the screen. We talked about what we should do, as this undefined madness was clearly intended for us to take personally, and the mediated repetition of the images ensured that every one of us, everywhere, got that message in no uncertain terms.

But what *are* we supposed to do when something like this happens?

There were the obvious family-checking phone calls to make, our son's school to check out, echoing thoughts from old movies about stocks of food, water, whiskey, and gasoline. There were our jobs too. Now that this nation was clearly under siege, are we still supposed to show up for work?

The reports kept coming in, now one about another missing plane that may be headed toward Washington, then another about possible terrorist attacks in major cities, then another one, somehow the weight of it even heavier, about another plane that had just crashed into the Pentagon.

The Pentagon? My god! That was a symbol that could not be under-read as a sign. Perhaps World War III had begun. At least, that's what I thought. Then dismissed. Then thought all over again. My American childhood during the 1950s and 1960s had prepared me for a sudden eruption of this particular storyline, had left a permanent dark inscription on my soul about the cruel inevitability of another World War.

Again: What are *we* supposed to do?

I went to the office. I realized the irony of this decision but also knew that I bore the responsibilities of a department head in a state-assisted university system that held firm bureaucratic lines of authority. If University of North Carolina at Greensboro makes a decision—about closing, about fortifying the campus, about whatever—I was the one on the front lines paid to carry it out.

I drove onto campus and saw that nothing much had changed. Perhaps there were fewer cars and pedestrians but perhaps not. I glanced at my wristwatch and saw that we were between periods, so no class changes were in progress. Fewer persons on the streets were at best ambiguous signs. I parked my car and entered Ferguson Building. I listened for voices in the building, but there were none. I walked down the long hallway toward the Communication Department suite of offices and saw only a handful of students, all of them engaged in reading normally or talking normally among themselves.

It was as if they didn't know yet, and for a long moment I wondered if it was my duty to tell them. I decided against it on the grounds that inciting panic was never a good thing. Besides, what did I really know? Only that the media was reporting a series of terrorist attacks on the United States. Saying that sentence aloud itself sounded absurd. It spoke of life as we have come to know it fictionally on film screens, in television dramas, in the plots of Tom Clancy. Even though I had seen the World Trade Centers attacked, even though I heard reports of the attack on the Pentagon, and even though I heard rumors of missing airplanes over American airspace, I still didn't want to say those words aloud.

I heard myself saying exactly that anyway. I spoke those words to our departmental secretary, to our undergraduate assistant, and to three faculty members who were otherwise engaged in work in the quiet space of their own offices. I felt my body tense while I spoke those words and felt my stomach muscles tighten and heard myself repeat the news several times, but I still didn't believe it.

Collectively we then experienced a small comedy of academic proportions, which is to say it was a small but highly ironic comedy indeed. We are a Communication Department, but we had no television set that could receive a cable signal. Furthermore, our computers tried to log on to CNN online, then ABC News Online, even NPR online, but to no avail. The Internet was either jammed with traffic, or it too had been the subject of an attack. Either way, we in the Communication Department found ourselves without an available channel.

Fortunately, our departmental secretary, Janice Smith, remembered that we had stored an ancient black-and-white 12-inch television set in the old janitor's closet. She found it, found that it still had attached rabbit ears, and plugged it in. It worked! We could only receive two very local stations, but at least we had news! We gathered around it, students and faculty and staff, huddled together against whatever would come.

That was when the first of the twin towers collapsed.

Then the second tower collapsed.

I thought I had known the feeling of horror until that moment. I thought I knew it earlier this very morning, in fact, when I saw the image of the second airplane crash into the second of the Trade Center towers, but I had not really known it. I still had hope then, hope for survivors, hope for the building itself. I had known a quiet stillness of the heart that may have been a precursor of the horror we were now bearing witness to, but I had not known the sheer hopeless reality of this full, silent, deadening of the spirit that descended into and around us, this quick eclipse of the human soul, this all-powerful evil awfulness.

Some of us wept openly, some of us continued to stare at the screen, perhaps thinking that in one of the continuous replays there would be some kind reversal of events or better, that this whole thing had been a mediated test of some national security system and that nothing so bad had actually happened. Or failing that, maybe one of us was waiting for a superhero to emerge from the smoky ruins and go after the evildoers, just like in any one of a hundred movies we have all seen and cheered, where the images of mass destruction do little more than inspire us to consume more overpriced popcorn and Coca-Colas, see ourselves in the hero's role, imagine ourselves saving the world.

None of us, at least none of us who lived in that heroic image of whom we would be, seemed to be answering this call. The president was unseen but rumored to be in the air somewhere over Louisiana. The vice president was in the White House but had a weak heart. Military leaders were either out of the country or unavailable for comment. The FBI antiterrorist team was attending a convention in California. Former President Clinton was down under in far-away Australia. Al Gore, well, the last we saw of him he had grown a beard but beyond that, who knew?

This horror show was happening in front of us. Continuing to happen in front of us. It was continuing to happen live and on television in front of us but it was definitely not live television in the familiar ways we had come to know live television. We were a Communication Department, and we should know something about all of this, something useful if not even theoretically complete, but we didn't.

All we knew was that we were at war on American soil.

That we were Americans.

And that what we were seeing on television wasn't at all TV. It was history.

The history that we too are characters in.

My father was a diplomat in the Eisenhower administration who ran agents deep into Central and Eastern Europe using F. Scott Fitzgerald's *The Great Gatsby* and *The Holy Bible* as his only codebook.

My father was a patriot, a Purple-Hearted, Air-Medalled, Presidential Citationed 100% disabled American War veteran who by the age of 23 had survived being a bombardier who was shot down twice in a B-17 and who had also survived a resultant recovery in a German prisoner-of-war camp. He believed mightily if not entirely blindly in God, Country, and the American Way of Life well into the late 1960s when those values didn't work quite as well for him or for our country anymore. Nevertheless, the one thing he made me promise him—swear to him on the family Bible—when I left for college in 1970 was that I would not become a Communist.

Imagine all of the other things he could have made me promise not to do in college in 1970. Or not to become in life. But no. In his mind, in his heart, Communism was the one unspeakable evil unleashed on the world, and it was our solemn duty as democratic-loving citizens of these United States to oppose, deny, fight against, and eventually, to overcome it. My father died in 1977 at the age of 54 of Legionnaire's disease, so he never saw the triumph of democracy over Communism, nor was he able to witness the tearing down of the Berlin Wall, nor would he live to see what I have lived to see in the wake of September 11, which is the partnership of the former Soviet Union with the United States of America against terrorism.

I'm not sure he would have believed it. I'm not sure he *could* have believed it.

I'm not sure I believe it either.

My father had a major role in the evacuation of American and British citizens from the Suez during the first crisis there in 1956. Beyond that diplomatic role, he had very little personal knowledge of the Middle East or the Near East or of Asia. He felt that it was unwise to support Israel in any other way except as a land- and air-based resource of potential use against the Soviets, but this was a fairly common view in the State Department during the Eisenhower administration. If he ever thought about the Arab world, I never knew it. But he was a career man at State, and a posting to an Arab nation had about the same promotional clout as a posting to anywhere in Southeast Asia, which is to say that such postings were considered hardships and were not meted out to the best or the brightest candidates.

Think about that, won't you? I know I have.

In many ways, my father was very much like his country. Diplomatically, he resided most comfortably in London, Rome, and Washington, but he maintained bachelor apartments in Paris and in West Berlin. He, like his country, taught his children to respect our flag, to obey our parents, to honor our servicemen and women, to get a good education so that you can earn a good living, to read our Bible, and to prepare for the eventuality of World War.

That he, nor for that matter I, never saw the interconnected complicitness of those values in the political construction of the world now seems amazing. But I grew up in a world and at a time that was amazing on so many levels. Amazing in its possibilities, its dreams, its atrocities, its delusions, and its deep self-deceptions.

I was one of those towheaded children whom you see in 1950s news clips hiding beneath a school desk during nuclear alerts. I was one of those children whose sixth-grade field trip was a visit to a nuclear silo, where we were encouraged to touch the tall missiles while wearing radiation badges that would supposedly glow if something went irrevocably wrong. I was also one of those children who grew up with Marine Corps bodyguards, a father who lived a life I knew nothing about, a mother who suffered a nervous breakdown when my father's seemingly well-ordered life fell apart. I was a child who—because of and despite these things—grew up to be a young man who at 25, at the dispensation of my father's last will and testament, was given a key to a safety deposit box in Western Maryland and where there later I discovered my father's true-life diary in a gun-metal gray box with a heavy coffin-like lid.

Beneath that diary was a well-worn, heavily marked-up copy of the Scribner's Library paperback edition of *The Great Gatsby*.

Possibilities, dreams. Gatsby's own take and my father's, at least for a while.

Atrocities, delusions. Nick Carroway's narrative and to some extent, my own.

Self-deception. Maybe we all share this one, for it speaks to our international arrogance and ignorance, born not so much out of malice toward others or even a lack of tolerance for differences that do, indeed, divide us, but moreover, like the fundamental flaw at the heart of this great American history that all of us are writing, that all of us are characters in, it emerges from our own hard-won but privileged carelessness.

We *are* a careless people.

We too often mistake our open generosity for enough.

Somewhere I learned to read the twin towers of the World Trade Center as the vertical lines in an American dollar sign. Someone, some semiotician, must have taught me to read them like that. Probably as a result of that lesson I understand that in many places around the world, those twin towers stood not as generous, benevolent emblems of our economic strength in the world but as the twin symbols of power and arrogance that controlled the economic interests of the world.

But this is not a war merely about symbols.

It is a war about people, as all wars ultimately are. It is about the nearly 3,000 human victims of the former Trade Center's collapse, the 189 civilian and military dead at the Pentagon, the 45 souls lost in the crash—at 450 miles per hour—of United Flight 93 in Pennsylvania.

It is also about the untold millions of people who have died of starvation, poor health care, political violence, and of simply having been born to a lifetime of poverty and despair somewhere in the world that remains largely unseen and unnoticed by those of us who do not share their all too common fate.

Once again, in light of the events of 9/11, thinking about wars that are about people, we all face Doestoevsky's question: "What shall we do?"

Ideas are supposed to help answer that question. But this is also a war about ideas—contradictory ideas—that have brought us into this war and that define opposing interests in its resolution and outcome. "What shall we do?" depends on what we think has been done and should be done, and very clearly there are very different answers to that one.

It is not a simple task, sorting out ideas. Perhaps this is why our first response is to revert to symbols. Symbols give us something to rally around because they are strategically ambiguous enough to empower local definitions that if closely examined or publicly debated would reveal precisely those differences that we don't seem to have the resources to sort out.

That is why I wasn't surprised to see American flags blossom on every street in our town, on every available bumper, on people's shirts and blouses, on envelopes, desktops, computer screens, packages, fast-food containers, neckties, belt buckles, guitar cases, coffee mugs, and so on. Our flag is a symbol of unspeakable unity with the ideas of freedom, of democracy, and undeniably, of capitalism. Wearing it, displaying it, even cutting a paper version of it out of the local newspaper and taping it onto a window or door—all of these acts communicate a commonality of agreement about large ideas—philosophical principles—that under any other circumstances are used as resources for articulating alternative perspectives on how best to conduct our national experiment.

But not right now.

Right now, flying the American flag is a symbol of unity and a sign of support for what our president has now officially named a War on Terrorism. I don't think in my lifetime I have witnessed such a public display of patriotism. Certainly I have never participated as actively in one. Born during the ill-named Korean conflict and a soldier in what Norman Mailer called "The Army of the Potomac" in my opposition to the War in Vietnam, I grew up proud of the flag but aware of its ability as a symbol to be abused by those in power; used for questionable and unlawful political ends; claimed by racists, sexists, and the always heavily armed ignorant as their own. I never once delighted in seeing it burned or ravaged but understand our Bill of Rights to allow for it because I do believe that the cure for bad ideas is the freedom to express those and better ideas.

The only flag my little family owns is the one that covered my father's coffin. It is a sacred flag to us. My father fought for it and in no uncertain terms died because of having fought for it. He loved it and honored it, and in the very end it alone covered and I hope quieted the pain in his war-broken body and war-tortured mind. So when we discussed bringing our flag, my father's flag, down from the attic and flying it in front of our house, I had very mixed emotions.

We decided not to. The first reason we gave to each other was that it was a very large flag and we had no flagpole. Then we reasoned that hanging it from the upstairs window wouldn't be appropriate somehow. Finally we agreed to go out and buy another flag and allow this one, this sacred one, to remain where it was, both as a material object in the attic as well as in our memories.

But there were no flags to purchase anywhere in our town. They had already been consumed by others quicker to the task than we were. The fact of this immediate consumption made me smile even as it saddened me. Americans are better at consuming than anyone else on the planet earth. Our president had even encouraged us to consume to demonstrate our patriotism, and if we had any doubt about this war on terrorism being also a war in favor of consumer capitalism, after that speech we had no doubts about it at all. In many ways, the freedom to consume—now the obligation to consume—has become a large part of the American Way of Life. Not having a purchased flag on display in front of our mortgaged home, not having a newly store bought flag sticker emblazoning the rear windows and bumpers of our highly polished upscale cars, not having a tri-colored flag pin to decorate our red, white, and blue clothing—well, my wife and I felt a little conspicuous for our failure to consume as well as patriotically underdressed when out in public, at least for the first few days.

It didn't take long for the ugly side of misplaced American patriotism and flagsmanship to show itself. On our campus, a Lebanese student was physically attacked by a roaming pack of wild boys intent on revenge against anyone who looked like she or he might be from the Middle East. One of our graduate students, a lovely young woman from India, was questioned loudly, rudely, in public by three rednecks about what country she came from. Afraid for her life, she told them she was Hispanic. She hated the fact that she had lied about her heritage but suddenly realized that her life in America would never be the same. Two nights later she and her friend Abu, a rug merchant from Pakistan, were accosted by a car full of drunks spitting hate at them.

No real American abides these acts of cruel ignorance.

No American patriot dies defending these twisted expressions of the freedom of speech.

No American flag should ever be waved over this mean trespass.

But these physical acts, these explosions of raw emotions, this new American life of ours under the mediated watch of unfolding unambiguous uncertainties, all of us rightly or wrongly wanting to do something to make it go away, again raises the big question: What *are* we supposed to do?

War is incoherence.

War is what happens when we stop making sense.

I don't know what we are supposed to do.

Osama bin Laden. Al Qaida. Anthrax. Smallpox. Cipro. Suitcase nukes. Crop dusters. The Taliban. Islam. Jihad. The Northern Alliance. A whole new language of warfare. What can we learn? What should we believe?

Just beneath the surface: How much of what we are seeing on TV is real? How much is the camera's easy indulgence of available hate and fear? How much of how we are making sense of this war is being evoked out of the depth narratives of hate and fear, and how much of it is a reasonable deduction based on accurate media representations?

On TV we see Arabs and Muslims openly hating us.

Osama bin Laden again. The Taliban again.

On TV we do *not* see Arabs and Muslims who *aren't* openly hating us. Peaceful streets do not make the news.

Our president, George W. Bush, Jr., addresses the nation on television. Thank God he looks good! He is *inspiring*. He has a plan. America will lead the international war on terrorism, and we will not stop until this war is won.

We are, as a nation, for awhile, relieved.

Then: Anthrax found in a tabloid media outlet in Florida, then in mainstream media centers in New York. Is there a tie to the terrorists? Anthrax is found in post offices in New Jersey. Anthrax is found in the Hart Senate Office Building in D.C. Anthrax found in the post office that serves Congressional offices. By early November, there are four people dead from anthrax and over 32,000 people on daily doses of Cipro although only 5,000 of them really need it.

We are told not to take Cipro unless we really need it.

But how would we know we need it until it may be too late?

We are told to take flu shots this year. Take them *now*. Anthrax and smallpox start out by mimicking the flu. That's why.

We find out that the Hart Senate Office Building will never be declared totally safe. We are told that officials believe we all have to learn to live with an "acceptable level of risk."

What is an acceptable level of risk?

There is a rumor of smallpox somewhere. What bright boy, what bean counter in Washington *ever* decided to end inoculations against this deadly killer? I know it was back in 1977, but my dear God, that was still during the Cold War and Russians were still our enemies and they maintained a stockpile of the virus! What were we thinking?

We are repeatedly told that this will be a long war. A very long war. We are talking *years*. Many years. No one knows how many years exactly, which means that there is no end in sight.

The sights are all on television, where there is also no end in sight. What we are seeing is that we are bombing a godforsaken land named Afghanistan. Nightly. Then daily and nightly. The bombs are called "smart bombs," and we are shown detailed diagrams of how they seek to destroy only those targets they have been taught to seek to destroy.

But sometimes they miss their targets. Smart bombs gone wrong. How is that?

A former Soviet general who led attacks on Afghanistan for a decade tells the cameras that the only thing you accomplish by bombing is "a rearranging of rocks." We learn that the Northern Alliance, which may or may not be trusted, which may or may not be a band of thugs, which may or may not win this war on the ground if given enough support by the United States, typically uses horses to launch raids against Taliban tanks. We are supplying horses to them as well as guns, food, ammunition, and relentless air support.

Another former Soviet general says that Americans should "iron their mail" to kill anthrax, but this advice is quickly discounted by scientists who point out that the mail would probably catch fire before it killed the anthrax spores, which require temperatures in excess of 300 degrees, or direct sunlight, to be rendered harmless.

Current thinking in Washington and at the Centers for Disease Control in Atlanta suspects that the anthrax problem has nothing to do with the Taliban or Osama bin Laden. It may be the work of an ordinary person with some knowledge of chemicals, post offices in New Jersey, and a deeply held grudge against specific persons in government. The FBI offers a profile of a loner, with mood swings, who has been in the area of Trenton and/or Baltimore-Washington recently.

Is this the best the FBI can do?

A news report is issued that announces a critical need for foreign language speakers to volunteer for the CIA and FBI. Specifically, they need people with some knowledge of the many dialects in the Arab world. Recruiters are dispatched to colleges to search for talent. Another report explains that because the CIA was downsized and its field operations cut back, we have almost no local knowledge or contacts in the Arab world. Retirees volunteer to come back into service of their countries. Money is approved to build up field operations again, but the forecast for any real payoff is expressed in years, not months or even days.

Thousands of people are shown marching and protesting against the war in the always crowded streets of Pakistan, Saudi Arabia, Turkey, England. There is a new peace movement growing in these United States. Columnists and pundits debate. Some want an all-out campaign with ground soldiers and missiles and tanks and occupation of Afghanistan and maybe even Iraq; others say we need to heed the lessons learned by the former Soviet Union; still others say we ought to treat bin Laden and the international web of terrorists as criminals, not as cause for a large-scale military action. In our local papers, people write in support of peace and are attacked by those who read their words as signs of national weakness. I think: How can anyone be against peace?

But terrorists are. No doubt about that. No doubt that the Taliban and Osama bin Laden want evil American people, we infidels, dead. I am reminded of Don, a guy I knew who was in the Navy in WW II. One perfect summer afternoon he told me that he knew he was in a war when the first Japanese Zero opened fire on his gunnery station aboard his destroyer in the Pacific. Up until that time, war was abstract, he said. As I look at the coverage of the Taliban spokesperson on MSNBC, I think I know what Don meant. I think: This man, this group, wants *to kill me*.

I wonder how many men, loyal to the Taliban cause, sworn to Osama bin Laden, live in America? Or in North Carolina? Greensboro? Or even close by . . . .

We are suddenly alerted about a possible terrorist attack in the next few days. Don't know what, don't know where. We don't ask why anymore.

I begin to fear the news. What new threat will I hear on NPR, CNN, MSNBC? What television program will be interrupted by a government official saying that something horrible is being planned for us, the National Guard has been called out, and that all Americans should take reasonable precautions?

What is a reasonable precaution?

The softly labeled "clean-up" at Ground Zero in lower Manhattan continues hour by hour, day by day, month by month. Our universally acclaimed national heroes, the firefighters and police, show increasing signs of fatigue. Depression. Sadness. We see that too. But we don't say anything. I'm not sure we know *how* to say anything about it. Nobody knows what to say to or about a fatigued hero.

The bombs we are dropping on Afghanistan are now called "daisy cutters." They weigh 15,000 pounds, are dropped out of the rear cargo door of MC-130s by parachute. They detonate above ground and destroy everything within a 70-yard radius above and below the earth. "Everything" is a military spokesperson's soft symbol too, a polite way for talking heads and government officials to avoid saying "people," or "plants," or "animals," or "the possibility of vegetation for years to come." My guess is that we—it's not a "they" anymore, is it?—*we* are dropping daisy cutters on Afghanistan to collapse the underground tunnels and arms caches, burying alive anyone hiding there. My guess is also that by showing us what daisy cutters can do, we are demonstrating that we will stop at nothing—*nothing*—to win this war.

We are told that the only bomb in existence that is more powerful, more awful, more devastating than a daisy cutter is a nuclear device. Device is a soft symbol too. Nuclear is not.

I do not fail to interpret this symbol—nuclear—as a sign. But I do not want to. I am reminded of my father again, who told me that I should get the best education I could because it was the one thing nobody can take away from you. True, Dad, but it is also something that you can't get away from either.

Texts, images, nerves, silences, fear, names, and fragments, the continuing incoherence of war.

I am in the parking lot across the street from our gym talking to my artist pal Mike. Mike is a figurative painter with enormous talent, just on the threshold of a big career. We are waiting for the end to a surprise fire drill that caught even the staff unprepared. Apparently someone working on the air conditioning tripped the switch accidentally, but these days, well, any alarm is cause for alarm.

Everyday life gets interrupted by lived metaphors for war.

Mike says, "Maybe if bin Laden had been able to see a good therapist once a week when he was a kid, or given Prozac a few years ago, none of this would have happened." It occurs to me that my wife voiced a similar diagnosis, although she interprets bin Laden's destructive actions in a more Freudian way, seeing him as a victim of his own father's neglect. All this warfare is twisted masculine revenge in the form of a global attention-getter.

Maybe they are right. Or maybe they are just trying to make sensible the incoherence that makes war by naming causes. As if naming causes gives us control over the course of this collective historical narrative. As if naming causes and offering cures inoculates us against what we fear is all too possible.

Narrative Cipro.

But I am interested in the fact that lately I've been in a lot of conversations like this one. I've also received a lot of e-mail with cartoon attachments depicting the madness of bin Laden, the Taliban, and suicide bombers, each fragment diagnosing some cause for the world as we now live in it, each text or visual offering a narrative cure that often is delivered with an explosive, vengeful punch line. For bin Laden, there is a narrative in cultural circulation that pronounces him as suffering from mental illness, his supposed madness an explanation for the madness we all share. Other explanations narratively package ends that we Americans, we New Testament Christians, can appreciate. For example, in one widely distributed cartoon scene, suicide bombers expecting their lot of 50 virgins at the gates of Paradise are instead confronted with a large, looming Satan and the awaiting flames of a Christian version of Hell.

Telling a story is inherently a search and a desire for an ending. A thematically coherent ending. Perhaps even a just ending.

But we tell stories to search for endings nonetheless.

The narrative search for endings is rhetorically tied to understanding beginnings, and every episode—every text, every fragment, every visual image—that moves us from beginnings to endings in the language of transformation is the architectonic journey of form.

We tell ourselves stories of war to transform what is incoherent into a recognizable pattern, to find amid the chaos that is our lives some sensible form.

Which is to say that we tell ourselves stories of war to end those stories.

Wanting it so doesn't make it so.

We cannot end this war by telling a story about ending this war. Oh, but I wish we could. I'm not willing to say that stories don't have powers in the world, I know better. We are, after all, fighting a war that is about the power of stories to shape the world and the rightful consequences of a particular interpretation of those powerful stories. Think of the stories of Islam, of Christianity, of Judaism, of Capitalism, of History, of Destiny, of Freedom. Think of stories of cultural domination and of resistance to forms of domination. Think of the distinction between freedom fighters and terrorists, of America the Beautiful and of America the Powerful. In some very important ways, the power of stories in the world is part of the lesson we should be learning because it is certainly part of the challenge we are facing as civilized people.

Terrorism is an attack on our story, this American story, the story we offer to the world. It is a story that we Americans see as being about freedom, democracy, equality, individuality, and wealth. But ours is not a universal interpretation. Our freedoms are read as signs of irresponsibility, our democracy and equality viewed as arrogant insults, our individuality evil, and our wealth the rotten core of the apple that spoils the rest of the world's harvest. Interpreting America's story that way, as an American contradiction that is dangerous when loosed upon the world, makes terrorism not only possible, it constructs an oppositional storyline that makes terrorism inevitable. For terrorism, before it is an act, is a story too.

A powerful one.

It is a story—an old one at that—about righting the wrongs of the world, about giving over one's self to a cause greater than one's self, and it is about answering a call to duty that may well result in sacrificing one's life. This is the story of all revolutions, if not all armies, and it is the plot common to heroic epics. It is what we send human beings to war for.

It is also a powerful antistory about the forceful interruption of someone else's peaceful storyline, someone else's plan for their life. The instrument of this interruption has always been an act of unspeakable violence, whether the weapon of choice was a knife, sword, pistol, cannon, or an airplane dropping the ultimatum was delivered, the antistory has always been a way of attempting to change the course of someone else's story *irrevocably*. No one can ever be the same after a terrorist attack. No one can ever live as if it hasn't happened or regain the innocence that is now gone.

I think mostly these days about our children.

How do they make sense of all this incoherence, these disruptions, this pervasive if often unspoken fear of the future? I look at our child, our fine son, 11 years old, a tall, good-looking kid with a smile on his face and a skateboard tucked under his arm, heading out the door to play with his neighborhood pals. In some ways, on the surfaces of our lives, it is as if nothing has happened. Kid, skateboard, neighborhood, pals. Beneath those surfaces, though, I know a child who has had something taken away from him that I cannot replace, not even with love, even though that is the best of all that I have. He doesn't ask about the war anymore, just accepts it as a fact of his everyday life. That too lingers below his surfaces and works inside of him in ways I cannot name or change, and yet, I know this rude fact shapes and defines his life.

Yesterday I was asked to give what has become my annual talk to the fourth grade in my son's elementary school. My talk is about World War II, not because I am an expert on the subject but simply because I am genetically linked to it by way of my father's story, which one of the fourth-grade teachers heard about, which led to the invitation, which is why I go there. Also, I have his medals, overheads of a B-17, and some maps of Europe during that time.

I begin by asking the students if they knew when World War II started, and this year, as in years past, they tell me December 7, 1941. I tell them that is true for *our* country but not for Europe. I tell them that a world war requires a global perspective, not just a local one. I explain about Hitler's rise to power in Germany, Mussolini in Italy, and the invasion of Austria, Poland, and France. I use the overheads to show the progression of Axis forces, and I talk about the heroic role played by Great Britain, the French underground, the freedom fighters in Sicily and Northern Africa.

I wonder what they are really hearing. What they are comparing my words to.

I then tell the family story about my father, the high school baseball player turned aviator, his participation in D-Day, culminating in my largely reconstructed and cleaned up account of his last flight over France when he was shot down and taken prisoner by the Germans. I always tell the class that he was treated well by the Germans, mostly because he learned to speak German in high school and they could understand each other. Usually I then go back to the maps and talk about the Allied advance across Europe and bring the story to a satisfying conclusion with the formal surrender of Germany on May 8, 1945.

But this year, a 10-year-old girl interrupted me—politely, using only a raised hand—and asked me a disarming question: "Did your father have a good life after that?"

I looked at her. She was a young girl. What should I tell her? Certainly not the whole truth, that my father's wounds led to a lifetime of drug use and alcoholism, that he woke up at night screaming in terror as he vividly relived his airplane, on fire, falling from the skies, his paralyzed body unable to do anything but accept whatever would happen next. Nor that he died at age 54 a broken man. Or that I never really knew him.

No, I didn't want to share those thoughts, those facts. So instead I did what adults do when confronted by hard questions we don't want to answer posed by children. I asked her a question: "Why do you ask that?" I offered, as softly as I knew how to.

"My daddy is flying a plane in the war against terrorism," she replied. "I want to know how it will be for him, you know, when he comes back."

I can only hope now that what I told her comes true. I told her a story with a happy ending, a just ending, an ending I never knew but have imagined for myself, and for my father, a million times.

This too is what terrorism has done to us. It has made little girls and boys ask unanswerable questions about unspeakable things. And these questions they ask are also only the surfaces.

I don't think my eyesight has improved since September 11, but I do see at least some things much more clearly now.

I see that in this life there is no time to waste. It seems like such a simple sentiment, but I tell you it is profound to live this way. There are times when I wonder how I ever lived any other way, but then I laugh. This is the same truth realized by all survivors regardless of their war zone: survivors of Pearl Harbor, of Hiroshima, of Korea, of Vietnam, of Bosnia, of Ethiopia, of the Persian Gulf; of cancer, heart disease, car crashes, rape, incest, trauma, and loss. It is also the same truth realized by all survivors of terrorism worldwide—Palestine, Israel, Iraq, Iran, Japan, Brazil, Honduras, Mexico, Northern Ireland, Great Britain, France, Germany, Italy, Africa, Russia, China, Cambodia—must I go on?

All Americans join this international storyline with the simple recognition that we too are survivors of terrorism. We are the survivors of September 11, 2001.

It could have been us.

There is no time to waste.

Our lives have been redefined in relation to this day, and it is our job to respond to it with our lifetimes. The responses we make—however we choose to do that—will become part of the unfolding story of history, nothing less. Those responses will determine how we live and how we die; how our children will make sense not only of these events but also of our personal role in responding to them, our contribution to the ongoing storyline. Finally, how we respond to September 11 is about the direction and moral content of that American story, the lessons it offers to the world about our country, ourselves, and our civilization.

Bombs and missiles and tanks and guns are tragically unfortunate but necessary parts of our story, but not the main part, nor I hope in the end, the most important part. How we learn again to live, and to live better with each other, and to live differently in the world—that will be America's great contribution to the epic story of life on this blue earth.

H. L. Goodall Jr. is professor and head of the Department of Communication at the University of North Carolina at Greensboro.

What Kind of Mother . . . ? An Ethnographic Short Story

45

KAREN SCOTT-HOY

> How dreadful it will be in those days for pregnant women and
> nursing mothers!
>
> —MATT. 24:19

A TEAR TRICKLES DOWN MY CHEEK as I breathe deeply, trying desperately to hold onto this moment; to treasure this time of gentleness, of love, in a day that has been full of horror and pain. As I nurse him, my youngest son's head leans against my chest. His breathing has slowed, and his body becomes heavy in my arms. Fear has left his body for a while. I tuck him into his bed and place his favorite toy alongside him. Automatically, his arm reaches for it and draws it to him, helping him to feel secure and safe. I bend and kiss him gently. We sing our prayer together. At the end he adds, "Please be with the people in America who are sad. . . . Amen. Goodnight Mum," he drawls sleepily.

Silently, I add my prayer for other would-be terrorists, the people of the Middle East, and for what I fear will occur.

What kind of mother prays for terrorists?

"Goodnight sweetheart. Sweet dreams," I reply, although I wonder if that will be possible for anyone tonight, for the world seems a very different, troubled place.

Quietly slipping from the room, I am confronted by a disarming thought. Perhaps the world is not really such a different place; it has just become a less secure place for my family, friends, and me, people in the Western world. Perhaps I am just beginning to understand, to feel, to experience what millions of others in this world live with and through every day. Could it be that the world in which I felt so secure and safe was always an illusion?

I join my older sons in the lounge, where the atmosphere is strained and tense as it has been since the first images of the terrorist attacks on New York and the Pentagon were beamed around the world. Embedded in my mind are the words of the radio announcer on the early morning news and the strain in his voice as he declined to wish

Figure 1: Nursing Mothers

early risers the usual "Good morning," for, as he said, "there was nothing 'good' about this morning."

From that moment I had tuned into television reports, in a state of disbelief and shock. "This is like a movie," says Alex. "It doesn't seem real."

"Yes, it is," I agree.

I realize, like many others here in Australia, most of what my sons know about America and Americans is gleaned through watching movies and television, just as many Americans only know about Australia from watching *Crocodile Dundee*. Maybe that is why although I see the images and hear the reports, I am finding it so hard to believe, to take in what has happened. In the back of my mind, hope lingers that it is not real, that it has been manufactured or misunderstood like *War of the Worlds*; or maybe I have been conditioned to hope for that Hollywood action hero to somehow rise from the rumble and put everything right.

What kind of mother struggles to tell the difference between fact and fiction, between truth and twaddle?

"Unfortunately, it is real. And it won't have a happy ending," I mumble out loud.

"It's on every channel," Alex says, flicking from station to station.

"I know."

At first I was unsure about letting the children watch the endless reports, but it was on every channel, and so they watched with me. How odd that I should think of stopping them from watching these reports as many of the action movies they had watched were more violent, more destructive. It must be something to do with the fact that this is real.

"How do you feel when you see that?" I ask as the video of the plane flying into the second tower is screened repeatedly.

"It's weird," Alex replies.

I want to ask what's weird, the notion that someone would fly a plane full of people into a building, or the feeling it gives you watching it, but don't, because "it's weird" seems to sum up how I feel too. I wonder if watching movies has desensitized us to senseless acts of violence and suffering, or if it's just impossible for us to feel anything other than "weird," as the implications of what we are seeing are too overwhelming to deal with right now.

What kind of mother exposes her children to such violence and pain in the name of entertainment?

I've been to "The States," to use the Australian expression, several times, and I've shared the hospitality and friendship of its citizens. My nephew lives in New York. He was my first thought this morning as Australians woke to hear what had happened overnight. He is safe, for now. I have e-mailed other friends to say I am thinking of and praying for them. I don't know what else to do.

I am scheduled to travel to Atlanta next month, and I have been so looking forward to being with friends and attending the National Communication Association convention. As a person and an independent scholar, I value those times immensely as they enable me to sustain my passion and continue my work. The States are part of my real world, not just my world of entertainment.

As if reading my thoughts, my oldest son looks away from the screen and asks, "Will you still go?"

All day I have been trying to find an answer to that question. I don't want to let terrorism change my life or intimidate me. I want to be defiant. I want to be strong. I want to be close to the people I love, not half a world away. Tears fill my eyes. I want to go.

What kind of mother even contemplates leaving her children at a time like this?

I look at Lachlan and see the fear in his eyes. I say what he wants to hear.

"I don't think so."

He looks relieved and turns back to the screen.

It is now late at night here, early morning in New York. I listen intently as people are interviewed, not because I want to be a voyeur, but because I want to share the burden and understand the pain. Being so far away where life carries on pretty much as usual, I am frightened I might forget for a moment what has happened. I feel somehow that hearing the people's stories will help me make sense of what I see and feel.

A young, fair-haired woman nursing a child is being interviewed. Her dirty face is strained and tear streaked, her eyes seem vacant and withdrawn. Her clothes are covered with dust. The child has in her hand a picture. In large letters is printed the word *MISS-ING*. I blink hard to clear my blurring vision. The tears roll down my face.

What kind of mother takes her child into a place of such devastation?

I have spent the day calculating the risk of being killed by or involved in a terrorist attack; that mother and child have calculated the chances of survival, of a miracle, of finding hope in the face of hopelessness. I see how she clutches her child. I know how I have struggled here to answer my children's questions, how much harder must it be for her? How do you explain what has happened to a child? Behind her I notice a wall covered with sheets similar to the one her child is holding. There are so many. Having lost a loved one like that, how could you ever say "goodbye" to someone again?

I switch off the television but not the faces, the stories, or the pain.

As the early morning spring sunshine fills the room, I turn the page of the newspaper. "An attack on America is an attack on us." "Australians stand with the U.S. in the War against Terrorism." "Australia pledges troops. . . . " At sixteen, my eldest son is too young to be drafted, but I feel afraid. I recall how young Australian men—some just sixteen—lied about their age to go and fight in 1914. A cold shiver runs down my spine.

What kind of mother sends her sons to war?

On the opposite page, photographs of Osama bin Laden and the hijackers are featured. I wonder how their mothers are feeling, if the mothers' faith is as unshakable as that of their sons. Are they proud of their sons or do they wonder where they went wrong? Dealing with the death of your child seems to me tragic enough, but to know that he was the cause of so many other deaths—I cannot even begin to imagine what that would feel like.

What kind of mother raises sons full of hate and able to kill others?

In this moment, I am reminded of my Eurocentric, Christian worldview. Of course, I cannot understand, until I am prepared to hear their stories, to listen to what they have to say, to try to suspend my judgments. I see that for some, these acts are perceived to be part of a "holy" war: a war seeking "to make someone pay," to right wrongs. They are acts deeply embedded in and intricately interconnected with the suffering, pain, and power associated with colonialism and oppression, capitalism and poverty, racism and power relations.

Comfortably seated in my kitchen, reading the newspaper and sipping my morning coffee, I realize I hold a position of privilege. Momentarily, I find myself reflecting on this privilege and see that how I live my life may also constitute part of the problem now facing the world; a problem posed—some would say "a wake-up call" delivered—by men prepared to die and kill to make their point.

What kind of mother raises her sons to die for what they believe in?

I have taught my children to stand up for what they think is right. My children have been taught that it's not just what we do, the stategies we employ, that are important but the motivation or meaning we attach to our actions. We talk about what we perceive as injustice in the world and ways we can help make the world a better place. These decisions are commonplace and part of our everyday lives, from simple actions such as recycling rubbish, to making financial commitments to international aid agencies, or our practical hands-on involvement in primary eyecare in the small island nation of Vanuatu in the Southwest Pacific.

Looking back at the photographs of the hijackers, I peer deeply into the eyes of the terrorists trying to see—I don't know what—maybe evidence of evil lurking. I don't see it. They look like anybody looks in their driver's license or I.D. photo. I recall the number of times I have laughed at the "hardened" appearance of friends or relatives in these "mug shots." How can I recognize good and evil? Would I recognize a terrorist if I met one?

I think back to a personal safety campaign—"Stranger Danger"—conducted in our local primary school in response to an increasing number of child molestations and kidnappings. I realize it's been a long time since I offered a ride to a hitchhiker or allowed my child to sit and talk with a stranger without watching them like a hawk. My world has changed, not only dramatically as on September 11 but also subtly over a longer period; I just haven't taken the time to notice before. I have allowed "Stranger Danger," fear, and distrust to infiltrate my life and change my behavior.

What kind of mother teaches her children these things?

I turn the page and look down at the photograph of an Afghan mother clutching her child. She is one of many Middle Eastern asylum seekers coming to Australia in boatloads from Indonesia. As I view photographs of Afghanistan and hear stories of unseaworthy boats, of enormous amounts of money paid to corrupt officials and people smugglers, of the horror in their homeland, I wonder if I would have the strength to endure what she has.

What kind of mother smuggles her child out of her homeland?

For some time, these asylum seekers have been viewed by many Australians with suspicion and concern; however, since September 11, they have been perceived as boatloads of potential "sleepers." Images of a sneaky, conniving, manipulative, and coercive people are burned into the minds of an already uneasy public, fueled by media reports of piracy, refusal to leave naval vessels, lack of I.D. papers, hunger strikes and riots, and mothers throwing their children into the sea.

What kind of mother throws her child into the sea?

Some people argue compassion has given way to fear. Others argue that rational thought must win over irrational desires of "do-gooders," and still others argue that the crisis is not about humanitarian concerns, terrorism, or international goodwill but about shutting down a bad business: the business of people smuggling. "There are legal ways of entering Australia, of applying for asylum, these people are 'queue jumpers'," says one article. "Desperate people in need of compassion," reads another, "Australia is a multicultural country and richer for it," reports still another.

What kind of mothers do we want in our country?

As I look across at the opposite page of the newspaper, I see that The Wiggles, a popular children's group, are going ahead with their tour to The States. They say it wasn't an easy decision, especially for those with families, but that they must support their fans.

I wonder how you make that choice: fans or families, colleagues or kids? What will these mothers, their wives, tell their children if daddy doesn't come home?

Underneath is a report that the Australian Kangaroos rugby team has cancelled its tour because of safety concerns. They are accused of being pathetic wimps.

As I read that, I flinch.

What kind of mother gives into terrorism, cancels her trip, and stays home with her children?

Looking up from the newspaper, I notice Vaughan sitting on the grass in the sun. As I watch, he moves the brightly colored toy cars from place to place, lunging back and forth using the terraced garden, ablaze with spring colors to create different levels. I can hear his chattering and what sounds like singing.

Leaving the newspaper on the table, I make my way outside into the garden.

"That looks like fun!" I exclaim as I approach. "What's happening?"

"The terrorists have just blown up the tourist center and the fire trucks are coming."

I am taken aback at his reply. "Didn't I just hear you singing?"

"No, that was the siren!" he replies.

I smile, but no words will come. I want to scream, to cry out against his loss of innocence. I want singing not sirens. I want the world to be filled with fairy tales with happy endings. I want good to triumph over evil. I want to be able to meet people and invite them into my home without fear or suspicion. I want to feel safe, to be able to travel to see my friends and colleagues and know that I will come home. I don't want my child playing with terrorists.

Then, as I stop and listen, I realize he is working through and making sense of what has happened in his world through this story, this game. Perhaps if I join in I will find some answers too. I sit beside him. The grass feels cool and still a little damp from the dew. The sun is warm, and the scent of lavender fills the air.

"Can I join you?" I ask.

"Yes. You can be the hospital and look after the sick people," he replies.

"Okay."

He drives over the ambulances.

"What do I do?" I ask.

"Oh. You know . . . what you always do to make things better."

For a moment I am unsure, caught off guard.

Then I grab him and hold him close to me. We roll over on the grass as I kiss him on the cheek and he shrieks with delight.

"This is what I do to make it better," I laugh.

Karen Scott-Hoy is currently associated with the Centre for Research in Education, Equity and Work at the University of South Australia.

Poetry

46

TRACY K. LEWIS

September 11

What but a coup
of gravity was this,
the Big Apple free-falling
to confirm an axiom of Newton
and Frost: something there is
that loves not walls nor human
travail, up is a hard
clawing against weight
and wind, and down,
an instant's effortless plummet
on the plumb line
that ends at Earth's core?
And so a hand darted
from shadows and pushed,
and the edifice fell,
and dust coated the world.
Yet we are they
for whom up is a code
in the flesh, a calling
not to be refused, so
that something will ascend
from the slag-heap of martyrs
and mortar to lift again
its face in air
and say, "We live, we are."

Untitled

Not the frauds of flag and anthem,
but a simple bodily striving
through our common air
is what makes them my brothers,
these fallen.
That cabbies, bankers,
hookers, cops, waiters and firemen
labored in the ether I likewise breathe
is what calls me
from my cocoon of skin
to this rare oneness
with those who I am not.
Now fingers of that selfsame air
pinch their ashes from the places where they fell,
and our lungs inhale
memories of who they were
and harbingers of what we will become.

Tracy K. Lewis is the coordinator of the Spanish program at the State University of New York at Oswego.

Happy

47

PATRICIA GEIST MARTIN

"**H**APPY IS GONE!**"** MAKENNA, my eight-year-old daughter, yelled in her high-pitched voice of surprise as we pulled into our driveway.

"No, really? Are you sure?" I ask softly, feeling already the shock and devastation I hear in my daughter's voice.

It was dark. The flash of the car's headlights had already passed by the planter where our life-size scarecrow, Happy, stood guarding our house since October 1. After pulling into the garage, we both jumped out of the car to inspect the scene of the crime. Sure enough. No Happy. And no stake that held Happy in place in front of the cobwebs, ghosts, and spiders decorating the front of our house.

"Who would do this?" Makenna whispered. "Why?" "How could they do this?" "Did they take anything else?" "Why?" The questions streamed out with hardly a breath in between as tears began to well up in her eyes.

Later, we discover that along with Happy, our U.S. flag was missing. My husband, J. C., and I try to calm Makenna's fears that someone might return to steal other things by telling her that it was probably a teenage prank.

That night at bedtime, she is still struggling with the "whys" and "how could theys," and so I try once again to explain.

"Makenna, remember this feeling of loss you are having right now when you are a teenager. Imagine that you are with a group of friends and they say, 'See that scarecrow there. Let's see if you can get it.' "

"I dare you," Makenna chimes in with a devilish grin.

"Yeah, that's right, it is probably a dare. And you run as fast as you can, grab it and run back to your friends and say, 'I got it. I got it.' "

By this time, Makenna is laughing and smiling and I am thinking, "Thank goodness, that worked."

Only a moment later, her laughter stops abruptly and her eyes and mouth form a very serious look as she proclaims, "It's still not right!"

"I know, I know," I say as I rub her back and feel with her deeply what it means to face this form of violation for the very first time.

In the morning, I wake up to find her dutifully making colorful illustrated signs that she insists we put up all around the neighborhood.

So the two of us walked, talked, stapled, and taped ten signs to telephone poles, just in case the pranksters threw Happy in the bushes and someone found her.

Figure 1

But no one has called.

Makenna told me in a questioning voice that "we should put an announcement on the Internet to find our missing 'Happy.' "

She asked J. C. in a telling voice, "Daddy, do you think this might have anything to do with the terrorists?"

The answers don't come easily these days.

So the very next day we picked out a new scarecrow.

Makenna named her "Happier."

Patricia Geist Martin is a professor in the School of Communication at San Diego State University.

9/11, Who Are We? 48

JAMES JOSEPH SCHEURICH
University of Texas at Austin

WHAT IS IT TO BE HUMAN? What is Humanity? Who is my neighbor? These are the questions that arrive with me, my green tea, and my lightweight laptop at my old oakwood breakfast table. i am alone, awake before anyone else, watching out the window three grackles argue loudly (my anthropomorphic interpretation, of course) from my very nice housebome.

[helpushelpme]

If you have ever been around grackles, though, you will know what i mean. These aves class creatures (order, Passeriformes; family, Fringillidae; genus, *Quiscalus*) are not pretty, romantic birds, the ones nature poets or zen monks commonly take up as lovely metaphors, the ones that make you thrill at nature or godess gift, Darwinian or not, for original beauty. But this poesy i undertake here is not pretty, romantic, or lovely, and perhaps grackles are the right bird, the proper metaphor. They are usually seen as ugly, irritating, loud, mostly unloved.

Norman and Yvonna e-mailed me, as they did many others, asking me to respond to 9/11. i didn't respond to the first call, but i began to think about it. The second time they e-mailed, just recently, i decided to throw my hat in the ring. This is my hat; you are the ring.

9/11 terror fear death, its larger global context, a sometimes murderous U.S. policy now and past, the hatred unto death actions against the U.S., the "war" in Afghanistan—these are not pretty poetry. These are death, bombing, bullet holes, suffering, grenades, land mines, real, ugly, degrading. Loved ones gone, Afghans, Americans, Arabs, leaving a horrible aching sobbing hole one really never overcomes or gets past grieving forever. oftenleavingfeardespairhatred?

[doiyouweknowwhatloveis]

my loved ones, especially my children who are going to school far from me, i worry about them the most, them, going to war, being on a hijacked plane, them, getting anthrax, becoming caught in some insanity somewhere, i have bought them maps and told them to put them in the trunks of their cars; i have looked up and told them the closest quickest roads to get out of their cities and into the countryside; they are patiently accepting of my parent worries; i imagine fear they can't get home and i can't get my arms around them.

These other loved ones of someone else, of my neighbors (of mine?) those in and those not in the towers and Pentagon. They are firepeople, police, everyday people, rich poor, women men, gay straight, different races countries religions. & my other neighbors; they are collateral damage in Afghanistan; they are Taliban, U.S. soldiers, all caught in torturous hell, recognized or not. gendered war games, mainly played by men, men here, men there, men everywhere, but constantly persistently unrelentingly, with no-voice women and children as always many victims. children, adults, all around the world, this country too, dying, suffering, intended unintended abused ignored unknown, in wars, in famine, can't afford care for curable diseases, despicable shelter, lacking love, dying, suffering for race, for global class system, gender, sexual orientation, disabilities, language, culture, and . . . leaving fear&hatred&despair?

The theories, the explanations, analyses; it is their fault, our fault; we are evil, they are evil. left right center tells us what to think who to blame how to understand these days of our lives. They are all so sure so complete so total. who is my our their enemy? = who is my our their neighbor?

[saveussaveourselveswearefullofhatredignoranceavoidancewhereislovewhatisit]

i am a rich white american; i can go to bed, wake up, drink green tea, have solace, safety, luxurious peace, talk about grackles, possess protection, joy, love, write words, successfully seek connection, support. i wasn't in the towers, nor were my loved ones; i am not in Afghanistan on any side, nor were my loved ones; i am not dying or suffering; i have enormous, yes, really enormous, wealth, privilege, space, time, pleasure, peace, love and loved ones friends colleagues who have the same.

but. still. we—all of they and i and you—are all Humanity. Aren't we? Aren't all of them our/my sisters and brothers, our/my neighbors to be loved like one loves oneself? The right, the left, the Taliban, the Christian capitalists, the Palestinians, Dr. Condoleezza Rice, the skin heads, wee children, the Israelis, Saddam, Turkish women fasting & dying for justice, bin Ladin, Mother Teresa, the war lords, the gang lords, Nelson Mandela, young lovers, drug dealers, Afghani women, Catholic priests, all of them, individual & group, aren't they all my neighbors that I must love as myself? Can i even say this, though? Aren't these words still just pretty birds? i have so much and thus the balance, the equity, is so far,, far,,, far,,,, gone that even to say the word, equity, rings hollow, undermines itself, mocks me, mocks you. These words are lies. They are false. i am false. i know not love. i am a liar. i am the problem.

[pleasehelpusweknownotwhatwedo]

While no zero-sum "reality," all that i have, the benefits, the privileges, the toys, the luxury, these surely have some careful measure of intimate correlation to the severe lack of equity, the severe avoidance of, distance from, the pain, the pain of my sisters and brothers, of my sisters and brothers, the am i truly not sobbing cannot stop sobbing, why am i not fearing the death of love, grieving foreveryellingscreaminggoingtotallyinsane?

MYSISTERS&BROTHERS MYNEIGHBORS AREDYING SUFFERING WITHOUTJUSTICE RIGHTNOW ALLDAY CONTINOUSLY eachsecond everymoment herethere everywhere myside theirside noside leavinghatredfeardespair?

Surely, it is insane that one child (what if it were one of my beloved children?), one person—let alone, literally millions, right now, this moment—is hungry, is suffering from a disease that can be cured, is dying because of humanity prejudices, can't get shelter, peace, support, love., while i have so much,,,, while i have so much. spiritually, why am i NOT deeply, totally, completely in love with all my neighbors as myself?

[pleasehelpus]

Who am i, then, to cast a drama a reckoning a fantasy called research or science? Who am i to direct, choose the characters, block out the action, signal the interpretation, the meaning? What tricky game am i up to? What charade, what sham, hustle, what con is research, science, me?

Can i call for love, more love? Can i call for spirituality, mine yours ours, at all? Can i call myself yourself ourselves a ChristianMuslimCherokeeBuddhistHinduJewHopi, a Lover of the Great Spirit—a human?

Can i justify me, my writing, research, my work, these words? i think not. i think i am a liar. i am not crying. i am a propagandist. i do not love my neighbor. i am a social scientist. stop reading my words. Stop. i am a liar. Stop reading. i lie. S T O P no

James Joseph Scheurich is an associate professor in educational administration at the University of Texas at Austin.

The Death of Ordinariness
Living, Learning, and Relating in the Age of Anxiety

49

CHRISTOPHER N. POULOS

The Age of Anxiety

ON SEPTEMBER 11, 2001, something died.
It wasn't just people.
On September 11, 2001, ordinariness died.

On September 12, a day into this shattering, shivering ordeal, I get up, as if everything is normal. I shake my head, wondering if I have been dreaming. I turn on the television, just to see if it really happened. News reports only; no breaks, no commercials. It happened all right.

As I drive to work, a tear wells up, seemingly out of nowhere. I wonder, What will happen to us? What will be the fate of the soul of humanity?

As I drive along in light traffic, on my way to the office, I ponder this new world we have been thrust into. Will the grief one day subside, as I know it has in the past? Will anxiety quicken and thicken until we can no longer stand it? What will we do, now that our president's plane has landed and America has been called into action? What exactly will we sow in the world, now that we have reaped this horror?

I wonder. . . .

"I'm shocked out of my shoes," my neighbor said.

"Speechless," said another.

"Scared to death," a third.

"Pissed," said another.

I remember other times in my lifetime when we felt this way. When thinking about events like these, we place ourselves in a story.

Where were you when JFK was shot?

I was five years old, but I remember clearly the crowd around the television in my house, one of the few TVs owned by the students at the seminary where my dad was studying.

How about Martin?

RFK?

John?

An ordinary January day, 1986. . . . I am standing at work, reading a report indicating how busy we are. This is my second corporate job out of college. I am a floor supervisor in a busy customer service call center. A light that helps us track how many calls are coming in flashes frenetically on the wall, showing more than a hundred calls holding. Phones ring; service representatives answer. And then, suddenly, all is stone cold still, eerily quiet. No ringing, no flashing. Heads "prairie dog" up from the cubicles. What's going on? And then a manager appears, tells us, "The Challenger exploded on take-off. We're setting up a television in the break room." She leaves. We stand, staring around at one another, struck mute, horrified.

Remember the first World Trade Center disaster?

Oklahoma City?

Columbine?

Where were you?

What's your story?

In every case I can think of, that great machine, the purveyor of news and entertainment and story that came into our homes—became the center of many homes in the 1950s—draws us under its spell. We seek the TV the way cave dwellers must have sought the campfire, the way Linus searches for his blanket on wash day.

Security. Story. Sense.

This time, as the shock gradually dissipates, we begin talking: family, friends, neighbors, colleagues. Stories unfold, as they did on those other fateful, horrifying days.

I have a friend who was in the Capitol building when the Pentagon was hit. He was set to testify before a congressional committee. Suddenly, hundreds of people were being evacuated from every government building in the area. But for many, there was no designated place to go to. My friend was simply told to "get as far away from the center of town as possible." He emerged to gridlock on the streets of Washington and to no available cabs anyway. So he and several others walked-jogged-ran, ties flapping in the wind, to Georgetown. They huddled in a corner pub, watched events unfold on CNN.

As the days go by, we swap stories, and we begin to talk about what it all means. It seems to many of us—to me and my friends and my colleagues and my neighbors—that we stand at a turning point in human history. We are in a new era. The threshold to this new era began to be constructed as the great wars of the twentieth century—the world wars and the cold war—unfolded. But those wars were comprehensible. We knew our enemy; we had a foe we could identify. Then came Vietnam, and comprehension began to slip. Now comes the "war on terror." This "war" and our foe are hard to define. Ambiguity rules.

On September 11, 2001, as the towers collapsed, ordinariness itself collapsed. We Americans were all stunned, lost; our human finitude—the fragile ephemerality of life itself—was suddenly "in our face." Our ordinary lives, and the sense of security our ordinary daily routines bring us, have, in a blinding flash and a searing explosion, been vaporized. What had been a comfortable, perhaps even complacent, existence, was, in that flash, morphed into a painful puzzle. In the interruption, we searched for something that would help us make sense. But what we found was a strange new world, a fragmented world of hurt and anger and pain, of sadness and questioning and fear!

We were thrust into something no one among us wanted but all had to accept. Anxiety descended like a dark cloud. In the weeks since, it has been hard to fend off despair, with daily reports of possible targets, anthrax scares and various threats, FBI warnings, talk of war and terror filling the air.

I have heard several symbolic interpretations of the structure of the now vanished World Trade Center since it fell. One is that they formed the vertical bars of a dollar sign, that this attack was thus an attack on the Almighty Dollar. Another is that they stood, simply and starkly, as the gateway to the American Dream, a dream of unprecedented, audacious, and freewheeling prosperity. And a third: That if you tilted your head sideways, they looked like an "equal" sign, representing the grand notions of equality—equal access, equal opportunity, equal freedoms—that underpin the American Dream.

I am not sure what to make of these interpretations.

I only know that, where those towers stood, there is now a (symbolic?) hole, wider and deeper than the buildings were. And I know that, somewhere in the rubble partially filling the hole are the dust and ashes that were once thousands of living, breathing human beings.

I know that there are an awful lot of children who no longer have fathers or mothers.

I know of many mothers and fathers who have lived through the unthinkable. No one believes that they should or will outlive their children, much less that they should or will endure the unspeakable horror of facing the senseless, brutal murder of their children.

I know that there are siblings and grandparents and cousins and dear, dear friends who are lost to us all.

I also know that symbols have sprouted like wildflowers in the North Carolina spring. Antenna flags are de rigeur. Red, white, and blue . . . even Christmas lights have taken on these patriotic hues. Ribbons and songs and banners and billboards . . . all attempts to make response possible, to make sense out of nonsense, to resurrect a shred of hope from the pit of Ground Zero Despair.

Our ordinary old world has been shattered. Beyond the ordinary ambiguity of postmodernity, we now live in the age of extraordinary anxiety. And with the death of the ordinary, we find ourselves examining our taken-for granted assumptions about life on this planet.

We Americans have, until September, lived in a privileged space in the life-world. We have taken our prosperity, our strength, our safety, our security, and our ordinary workaday lives, as givens. While the rest of the world has lived with terrorism for many long years, we have largely ignored the growing threat, shielding ourselves from the stark realities of discontent among those who do not share our privilege.

Now we find ourselves in need of new ways of navigating and negotiating our world. What should we do now? How should we face the threat? And how, exactly, should we respond to our president's suggestion that we calmly return to the business at hand? How do we live out our (no longer ordinary) daily lives and their roles, all the while fully aware of the ever-present danger and the anxiety that danger provokes?

Anxiety and Response

I wake up trembling. At first, I think the ground is shaking. I have never lived in an active earthquake zone, but my first thought is that an earthquake must be happening. It feels as if the earth is shaking. But I quickly realize it's just me. I am shaking, a tear streaming down my cheek.

Bad dream. Really bad dream.

It's usually just a brief flash, invading my consciousness, often at the end of another, seemingly unrelated dream. Then a cold sweat breaks out around my neck, and I awake, shivering.

And then I stand up to face another day.

As the early morning fog slowly lifts, I remember parts of the dream. I am standing, looking out the window of a tall building. It reminds me of my old 24th-floor office in downtown Denver. As I gaze out at the peaceful mountains in the distance, I spot an airplane. Suddenly, the plane turns toward me, and I realize it is aiming at me. I jump out of bed, look out my bedroom window, pondering, shivering, searching for an airplane.

Anxious, fearful, shaken.

It is more than two months now since that September day when the earth shook, but I find I cannot shake the feeling of impending doom.

I had a physical exam the other day. For the first time, I have a blood pressure reading in the "high" range.

The doctor says one word: "Anxiety." He lifts his voice a little as he pronounces the final syllable of the word. Is it a question? "Anxiety?" The ambiguity there makes me anxious.

So I have twin gifts arising from the ashes of the twin towers. There is blood pressure. And there are the dreams, always the dreams.

I am haunted by my dreams.

My wife Sue has a different form of anxiety response. Every night at midnight she rises, frustrated in her attempts to find sleep, and sits on the couch watching CNN. How can anyone sleep through this? Even as I am haunted by the gifts of my sleeping unconscious, she is haunted by the impossibility of sleep. She finally turns in around 4 a.m., only to rise to meet the day two hours later. The effects of sleep deprivation are starting to show as she loses track of daily tasks, suffers short-term memory loss, and responds curtly to other humans she encounters. Her doctor said it too: "Anxiety?"

In early October, almost exactly one month after the tragedy, Sue flew through Chicago on her way to Denver. As the plane took off from O'Hare, it turned over Lake Michigan and followed the Chicago skyline, passing not too far from the Sears Tower. That tower had a new meaning that day, as she gripped the armrest. "All I see is water and buildings"—the quote echoed in her mind. Apparently, a passenger on one of those fateful New York flights left a desperate message on her home answering machine moments before the plane was engulfed in flames. And there was Sue, a month later, flying over water, near buildings. These days, once-ordinary events take on extraordinary meanings.

And now anxiety arises, daily, just as we do. But we must remember: Anxiety is anything but ordinary. Anxiety is an interruption, a shattering of our routines, a disruption. Anxiety is a force that disrupts daily life and causes us to reorient ourselves to our world. Now we are reoriented, to what once was an ordinary date on a calendar: 9/11.

Every day, as I try to recover the ordinary—as I eat, work out, shower, write, teach, talk, sleep—at some point my mind travels back to 9/11.

Interruption, uncertainty, anxiety. . . . I stood, frozen, in front of the television in my office, watching the horror reproduced. Time and again since that day, the image of the plane going into the tower has been played. The image is etched into my memory forever. In one reel, a man is sitting in the foreground, enjoying his morning latte. He looks up, yells, and runs, as flames erase people.

Ordinary time/routine/progress was shattered that day as the towers of ordinariness and routine crumbled. Anxiety has intruded. We are in its grip. For a time, we were frozen in our tracks, stuck, mute, horrified. Then, slowly, we gathered ourselves and tried to go on. I have wanted to shake off the anxiety, wanted to just be "normal" again. And yet, there is a certain force, a power to that anxiety—a force that has begun, over time, to present me with a new set of possibilities.

In the tradition of existential phenomenology, anxiety serves as a turning point. The interruption occurs, and choices appear. In a flash, as the realization of human finitude descends into everyday awareness, the ultimate choice confronts me: Despair or Faith, Sickness or Health, Death or Life. I am filled with anxiety, even (sometimes) dread.

And yet, anxiety may not represent a force to be avoided or eliminated. Seeking a therapeutic solution is, though certainly applauded by our culture, called into question. It is not therapy per se that we need.

It's not that therapy is bad. It's just that therapy cannot accomplish what we might be tempted to ask of it—that it relieve the anxiety permanently. And there is another danger in putting too much stock in a therapeutic "solution." That danger lies in the possibility of self-absorption at a time when we may need to be other-oriented.

But there is something else, too—something that may be a gift or a byproduct of therapy but that operates beneath the surface of "cure." Anxiety calls for healing and creation and possibility, not cure.

That's the gift of the mad Dane Kierkegaard: the leap beyond Despair . . . into possibility!

Possibility! Ah! I think I understand! Or do I? Wait? What, exactly, is possibility? Is it not the opening that beckons to us, that calls us to go on, even in the face of Despair? Is it not the Infinity that awaits us as we author (coauthor?) a life? Is it not what Paul Tillich called "the courage to be" in spite of/in response to the anxiety that threatens to engulf and overwhelm us?

What gives me "possibility" in my life? For many in this stream of thinking —most notably, perhaps, Kierkegaard (1980), Marcel (1960), and Tillich (1952)—possibility is evoked in the world of human community.

Community and Family

On September 12, 2001, we gather at the fountain of my university, to commemorate, to give voice to a community response to the tragic events of 9/11. A fine Carolina-blue sky belies the cloud of dusty-smoky angst that has descended upon us. Hundreds of us encircle our protected campus centerspace. We stand together, quietly, wondering what will come next. We come together, uncertain of what we need, but knowing nonetheless that coming together is necessary. We could not not come together. There are some things in life that simply must be done. Faculty members, administrators, and students speak publicly and reverently about our shock, our grief, our dismay, and our hopes for the future. As we quietly return to our offices and our classrooms, not one of us knows what will come next. Yet, somehow, we know that the work we are doing here still matters, that teaching and learning must continue.

And we know this: We do it together, because that is the only way to do it that makes sense. We gather to teach and to learn, to explore our human commonality, our alterity, our knowledge, and our possibility.

I think it is the people in my life who offer me an opening to possibility. Anxiety intrudes . . . and I search for relation.

On the day of the attacks, my first instinct was to gather with my family. As soon as we could, we met in my mom's kitchen. And we all told our stories of the day. We told our stories because we had to; we are story-making animals.

We spoke our lives into Being during those moments around the kitchen table. We spoke of where we were when we first learned of the horror. We tried, collectively, to make sense of it all. To tell our stories seemed so natural, so right. So we sat together, spinning our tales, reaching for that special understanding that is the gift of the story.

A key part of our common human story is this: family. The family has a structure that gives us life and love and community and communication. That structure gives us rules and roles and ways of seeing ourselves that no other social structure gives. In our culture—in this newly-reunited/nervous/proud/sad/defiant United States of America—that structure in all its forms and all its varied definitions is somehow at the center of who we are.

Late on the afternoon of September 12, I walk through the front door of our new home. It is good to be home. We have lived here for six weeks, just long enough for me to start feeling comfortable in my new job as assistant professor at the University of North Carolina at Greensboro. And now this. We have left our long-time community in Denver behind us for now. As I enter this place that is now my home, I ponder how hard it is to build community in a new place. After twenty years in Denver, we had people we could rely on. We belonged. We were connected. It is hard to leave that behind, and try, somehow, to re-create it in a new place. And now this. How to build community in a shattered world?

I find Sue, standing in the kitchen, staring into the soup she is cooking. She does that when she's anxious. When all else fails, cook soup. A tear trickles down her cheek as she turns, sensing my presence. She doesn't speak, but she moves toward me. We embrace. I offer her my caress, as she offers hers. We will get through this, together. And we know: This is the meaning of family. We are deeply related.

Family. . . . I find myself thinking about it a lot these days. What is the essence of family? What does it mean?

When my sons were born, now some years ago, I was first to hold them. Speaking of interruption, of disruption, and anxiety. . . . .

Both were "emergency" births, one a caesarian, the other a "distressed" child-in-crisis. In each case, I was present to cut the cord, which had, until that moment, given them life.

And when I looked upon their faces, I was transformed. There is no other experience like this one, no other moment in life so compelling. When I looked upon their faces—in that brief moment when the first spark passed between us—I knew. I knew I would sacrifice all else that I know or care about or own or feel for the sake of this One Other. I was ecstatic. In those moments, I witnessed the birth of possibility anew.

And on that strangely surreal afternoon years later, on the day we have come to refer to as *the day after*—on September 12, 2001—my son Eli, now age 10, walked into his room and closed the door. In the period of about an hour, he constructed a weapon. The technology consists of a sheath, worn across his back at a diagonal angle, and a white stick, about three feet in length and made of oak, fitted into the sheath. The stick can be drawn, ninja-like, for use as a club or a spear or a sword. He now rides his foot-propelled scooter up and down the street in front of our house, weapon slung across his back, ready, patrolling, protecting. He does this daily, as soon as he returns home from school. He has not said a word. Maybe he is trying to do something to fend off the anxiety, or at least to put anxiety to use.

He needs to help, to feel power, to make a move, to respond . . . he needs to make a difference. He needs to *matter*.

What should I, as father, do? I am his father, yet I, too, am lost. I do not know what to do for him, how to comfort him, how to help him make sense of the senseless. How do you explain to a ten-year-old something you have no explanation for? What to say, and how?

And yet, there is less ambiguity here than in some relationships; as we move about within the life-worlds shared by small children, we may rely on time-tested roles. The child seeks some comfort; I, as father, offer my love unconditionally. I am ever aware of encroaching anxiety; I hesitate to increase it with my children. Rather, I am their "rock," the steady one who can offer, if not certainty, at least some sense of stability and protection in an anxiety engulfed world. I do not know if I am doing the right thing. I only know that I must answer the call that issues forth from the very presence of my children in Being. I only know that, in that call, at least in this instance, I hear a plea for love-as-embrace. So I embrace my children, and my wife, often. I embrace my family, and I am grateful for their presence in my life.

Drawn into communicating, we are often speechless. And yet, we respond to each other, speaking with the words of the body, with gestures of love and caring and connection. Sometimes that is all we have.

And I keep a close eye on them. Eli enters the house, crying. I look him in the eye, and we hold that gaze for a moment. We have always been close; we know each other well. Both of us are scared. We hug each other, tightly, knowing and not knowing, gripped by anxiety and, at the same time, transcending it, if only momentarily, with love.

Whatever happens, we know this: The love flowing between us is powerful. Maybe it is enough. Surely, it is all we have.

And this: Perhaps anxiety has its limits, and we have met them.

On September 15, we gather at Eli's school for a community-building potluck supper. At the end of the evening, as we walk up the hill toward our cars to head home, a single airplane streaks across the sunset-fired Carolina sky. We all pause, hushed, in awe. A kid points, says, "Hey, look! The first airplane!" The first airplane to fly out of our little airport since that horrible, black Tuesday.

On another day, Eli and I take a bike ride. After a few miles, we sit down on a bench, resting. Words flow forth. Eli starts talking about his feelings of anxiety, about the horror of terrorism, about how the bullies at his school have escalated their acts since September 11, about how the bullies are like terrorists.

And I wonder: How should I respond, how should I comfort him, how should I take my stand in this extraordinary moment?

As father, I stand in a special place in his life. So I call his school and I intervene. At the very least, he should feel as safe as possible in this crazy world. I may not be able to stop the terrorists, but I can do something to stop the bullies at my son's school. So I call the principal of his school and set into motion a chain of communicative events that leads to the end of the silent reign of terror on the playground.

To Teach?

Anxiety. Again: September 11, 2001. I stand before my Persuasion in Western Culture class. I am, for the first time in my career, struck mute. I stand, arms at my sides, silent for a full minute. Although this is a rhetoric class—and the acts of terror which had sent me reeling just a short time ago were clearly rhetorical-symbolic—I find myself at a loss, unable to be truly responsive, incapable of making a single content point or of drawing any sort of meaningful relationship between our study of rhetoric and events out in the world. The anxiety—the deep uncertainty, the dread—are simply too intense. I find myself tilting toward silent Despair.

So, as eloquence fails me, I haltingly tell my students the news. I do not know what to say. "Something horrible has happened," I say. Then I simply offer the minimal information I have gleaned from early, somewhat sketchy news reports, hastily retrieved from the small television in my office. A student flees the room, tears streaming down her cheeks.[1] Questions—but few answers—hum about the large lecture hall for about fifteen minutes.

Then, 170 people fall silent. There is little more to say. We do not yet know what questions to ask. How do you even frame a dialogue about something that is unlike anything in your previous experience? I reach for the analogues, but I cannot see them right now. How much context do you need before you can discuss the "text"? At the suggestion of several students, many of whom want to go out and learn more, others of whom want to call their families or gather with friends, I dismiss class, but offer to hang around to talk if people want.

A few students mill about the front of the room. One, an Iranian girl, asks me, "Should I be getting in my car and driving out of this country?" A sophisticated question for this suddenly shocked and uncharacteristically inarticulate Ph.D. to try to answer. I babble some attempt at comfort. Another student chimes in, "I don't think you have to worry." The Iranian girl does not look reassured.[2] We talk aimlessly for a few minutes, most of us just wanting to be in the company of fellow humans, I think. I open my office to those who want to learn more from the television. As the day wears on, I find myself needing to retreat and connect with my family. I leave campus, engulfed by a hazy cloud of confusion and emptiness.

The next day, as the time for my Relational Communication class approaches, I find myself unable to concentrate on the day's lesson. I begin to ask myself some simple but compelling questions: What is the point of my life in the academy? Why am I a scholar-teacher? How might I draw on our collective anxiety and answer what my friend Michael Hyde calls the "call of conscience?"

My students must be asking some questions, too. What will come next? Will we go to war? Will I be drafted? Will/did someone I know and love die?

So, one day after the horror, I open up class by offering the opportunity to simply engage in unstructured dialogue about the anxiety we are experiencing. The dialogue is both solemn and active, engaged and engaging. As we try to make sense of what has happened, emotions run high. We probe and we question; inquiry and a genuine search for understanding are the guiding forces this day. Questioning is the center, but the center does not hold.

Shock, dismay, outrage, fear; we are mostly numb, often silent, sometimes angry, truly sad. Gradually, amid all these contradictory feelings, a desire to do something to help emerges.[3] And, as we continue our search, ideas and questions fill the air, but few definitive answers.

We search for analogues in our prior collective experience, to see if we can make sense. Terror: Oklahoma City, Columbine, the previous bombings at the World Trade Center . . . all are horrific, but all fall short. The magnitude of this attack is staggering, overwhelming the analogues. And those earlier events seem so remote, so small, so *ordinary*, by comparison.

We sense that this time is different, that something has ended, that something else has surely begun. But it is clear that our limited experience, our limited sense of context, limits our inquiry. Still, we press on.

All we can do is inquire . . . and interpret. Some students take an immediately patriotic stand; others wonder and question and explore; still others are thoughtfully self-critical.

"Have I personally done enough to thwart violence in this world?" one asks.

"Maybe we should try to figure out why they hate us so much," chimes in another. The effect of that simple remark is electric.[4]

And then, just as I think we are succeeding in our quest to make sense of this anxiety-bind we have been thrown into, my students surprise me. They ask me to move on—to get back to the study at hand, to continue with our examination of relational communication, and to leave the collective tragedy we are suffering behind for a bit.

What should I do? How can I help to transform this decisive "retreat" into an important moment? Should I challenge the retreat? Or should I honor it? I agonize for a moment.

But I also understand why, perhaps, we all need some distance. We need to retreat. We are on anxiety overload.

We have met the limits of anxiety.

We have met the limits of anxiety, and those limits are us.

We have had all we can stand, for now.

At the outer limits of anxiety, we need the comfort of routine.

Still, this leads me to wonder how to answer the call of conscience that I hear as I stand before the students as "teacher." What to do, how to engage?

I have noticed, over the years, that often my students seek to define, to contain, to categorize learning:

"Will this be on the test?"

"What will the test be like?"

"Will you give us the answers before the test?"

"How much of this do we have to know?"

"I missed class the other day—did I miss anything important?"

These questions rise up out of something—anxiety perhaps. Fending off anxiety, we engage the drive for the definite, for predictability, for routine.

And I wonder: Am I called to reduce anxiety, or to help put it to good use? Perhaps I, as teacher, should embrace the moment. What is a teacher, really? Am I a purveyor of information? Or am I called to lead a community of learners across a dangerous, anxiety-filled threshold?

After many years as a student myself, I know one thing: Coming to know is an act that requires change, a process that, by its very nature, creates anxiety. So I think that to teach from a space of compassion, responsibility, and commitment, I must draw on the existential anxiety we all share. We move toward knowing via the energy of anxiety, compassion, and the commitment to share our lives, our thoughts, our feelings, our questions, our desires, our interpretations, our dreams, our questions . . . always questions.

As a learning-questioning community, we move, together, beyond anxiety; we spring into new worlds of relating.

Fortuitously, perhaps, the announced subject of class that day is "communicative competence." So we weave together the contours of competence with our understanding of the communicative moments that are unfolding in response to these events that have so violently disrupted our ordinary understandings of communication and its place in our life-world. We speak of the relative rhetorical competence of the communicators whose primary symbolic act was to destroy. We speak of how we might respond appropriately and competently to the challenge that has been set for us by these Others who have interrupted our lives.

Return

December 11, 2001. 8:46 a.m. The nation pauses for a moment of silent remembrance. We mark this occasion with silence because sometimes words fail us, because sometimes silence is the most appropriate response, because sometimes we must go back to the silence that struck us in the beginning.

Silent shock, silent grief, silent reverence.

But silence only goes so far, only comforts us for a time.

So we humans begin to speak and to listen, to connect and to relate. We always return to each other. We find some help in each other.

There is, it seems, in human life, an eternal, perennial return to origins. The origin of social life is, perhaps, that in relating we fend off the paralyzing force of anxiety. In relating, we find the heart to go on.

Back we go, then, to the beginning.

Together.

Know this: The anxiety that has disrupted our lives from September 11 onward is, though perhaps shockingly fresh and particularly intense, not a new experience.

The truth is that living and learning and relating produce anxiety. By their very nature, these most fundamental human endeavors disrupt our routines, our understandings, and our relationships.

We change.

We do not know what lies before us. We never do.

So we live with anxiety: Uncertainty, disruption, loss of stability.

So, perhaps, we must embrace the anxiety of Being. At the very least, acting out of such a commitment, we cannot help but bring about a measure of change in our collective orientation to the matters at hand.

Perhaps we learn to live in an Age of Anxiety by going toward it, by leaping into the anxious universe of possibility—the infinity that stands beyond the ordinary, the everyday, the taken-for-granted.

Perhaps we must just walk forward, head on, into the new worlds that erupt in encounter, in living, in learning, in relating.

And perhaps we learn to live in this new age by engaging new ways of relating to others, especially to those others who are strangers to us.

Perhaps we had better learn how to relate in new ways to these others who see us as the enemy.

Perhaps we had better learn a bit about Islam and its followers.

Perhaps we had better, as my student suggested, try to figure out why some people hate us enough to want us dead.

Perhaps we had better learn how to speak and to listen across chasms of difference.

Life itself—despite our best efforts to control the uncertainty—is anarchic, disruptive, unpredictable.

But perhaps—and this represents our best hope for the future—anxiety can also serve as the fire in the crucible that lights the spark of our collective creativity.

Perhaps together we can plunge headlong into the Age of Anxiety and forge new ways of relating that will bring an end to the horror.

Perhaps together we can, at last, embrace "the courage to be."

Perhaps. . . .

Notes

1. I later learned that this student's aunt worked in the World Trade Center. Thankfully, she survived.

2. Two days later, she told me her employer was "reevaluating" her employment. She is suffering; I do not know what to say. So I listen. Eventually, she decides to seek counseling, as her problems, it turns out, are large and overwhelming.

3. One student stood and made an impassioned plea for donations; already, she was thinking of the children of slain office workers in New York and had organized a small campaign to buy a small

measure of comfort for these kids. In one day, she collected more than five hundred dollars; by the next day, a shipment of teddy bears was on its way to New York.

4. A young Jewish student stormed angrily out of the room at this moment: The remark apparently was interpreted as a strike at U.S. foreign policy toward Israel. It was all too easy to dismiss his reaction as hotheaded; it takes a little deeper examination to come to understand it; it takes even deeper probing to come to understand the multiple layers of truths contained in this little burst of dissensus. In any event, it lit the fire of classroom dialogue.

References

Kierkegaard, S. (1980). *The sickness unto death* (H. V. Hong & E. H. Hong, Trans.). Princeton, NJ: Princeton University Press.

Marcel, G. (1960). *The mystery of being*. Chicago: Regnery, Gateway.

Tillich, P. (1952). *The courage to be*. New Haven, CT: Yale University Press.

Christopher N. Poulos is an assistant professor of communication at the University of North Carolina at Greensboro.

Democracy and the Politics of Terrorism   **50**
Community, Fear, and
the Suppression of Dissent

HENRY A. GIROUX

F IVE MONTHS AFTER THE HORRIFIC terrorist attacks on the Pentagon and the World Trade Center, President George Bush announced in his State of the Union Address on January 29, 2002, that the "war against terror is only just beginning" and that if other governments exhibit timidity in the face of terror, America will act without them. Claiming that the security of the nation was his first priority, Bush not only proclaimed a war without end but suggested that the United States would act unilaterally throughout the world to enforce what he called "our responsibility to fight freedom's fight." Appealing to what he described as a resurgent sense of unity and community in the country, Bush announced that American citizens were no longer willing to simply live their lives devoted to material pursuits and a "feel good" attitude. According to Bush, in the aftermath of the events of September 11th, America had been reborn with a renewed sense of patriotism, community, and public spiritedness. Painting the United States as a beacon of civilization, Bush urged Americans to perform voluntary acts of public service, be alert for signs of potential terrorism at home, support massive increases in the military budget, endorse an energy policy that involves more drilling for oil, accept a huge tax cut for the rich and major corporations, and tolerate the suspensions of some basic civil liberties and freedoms, especially those granting more power to the police, FBI, CIA, and other security forces.

Although Bush and his associates are quick to remind the American people that much has changed in the United States since September 11th, almost nothing has been said about what has not changed. I am referring to the aggressive attempts on the part of many liberal and conservative politicians to undermine those public spaces that encourage informed debate, promote a remorseless drive to privatization, and invoke patriotism as a cloak for carrying out a reactionary economic and political agenda on the domestic front while simultaneously cultivating an arrogant self-righteousness in foreign affairs in which the United States positions itself uncritically on the side of purity, goodness, and freedom, whereas its opposition is equated with the forces of absolute evil.

As a wartime president, Bush enjoys incredibly high popular ratings, but beneath the inflated ratings and the president's call for unity, there is a disturbing appeal to modes of community and patriotism buttressed by moral absolutes in which the discourse of evil, terrorism, and security works to stifle dissent, empty democracy of any substance, and exile politics "to the space occupied by those discontented with the West, and dispossessed by it" (Hesse & Sayyid, 2001, p. 3). Shamelessly pandering to the fever of emergency and the economy of fear, President Bush and his administrative cohorts are rewriting the rhetoric of community so as to remove it from the realm of politics and democracy. In doing so, Bush and his followers are not only concentrating their political power, they are pushing through harsh policies and regressive measures that cut basic services and public assistance for the poor, offer school children more standardized testing but do not guarantee them decent health care and adequate food, sacrifice American democracy and individual autonomy for the promise of domestic security, and allocate resources and tax breaks to the rich through the airline bailout and retroactive tax cuts. Under the auspices of a belligerent nationalism and militarism, community is constructed "through shared fears rather than shared responsibilities," and the strongest appeals to civic discourse are focused primarily on military defense, civil order, and domestic security (Anton, 2000, p. 29). Within the rhetoric and culture of shared fears, patriotism becomes synonymous with an uncritical acceptance of governmental authority and a discourse "that encourages ignorance as it overrides real politics, real history, and moral issues" (Said, 2002). The longing for community seems so desperate in the United States, steeped as it is in the ethic of neoliberalism with its utter disregard for public life, democratic public spheres, and moral responsibility, that in such ruthless times any invocation of community seems nourishing, even when the term is invoked to demand an "unconditional loyalty and treats everything short of such loyalty as an act of unforgivable treason" (Bauman, 2001, p. 4). How can any notion of democratic community or critical citizenship be embraced through the rhetoric of a debased patriotism that is outraged by dissent in the streets? What notion of community allows Peter Beinart, editor of *The New Republic*, to wrap himself in the flag of patriotism and moral absolutism while excoriating those who are critical of Bush policies? He wrote, "This nation is now at war. And in such an environment, domestic political dissent is immoral without a prior statement of national solidarity, a choosing of sides" (as cited in Lapham, 2002, p. 7). Charges of unpatriotic dissent are not restricted to either protesters in the streets or to those academics who incurred the wrath of Lynne Cheney's American Council of Trustees and Alumni for not responding with due Americanist fervor to the terrorist attacks of September 11th. It was also applied to Senate Majority Leader Tom Daschle when he offered a mild critique of President Bush's plan to launch what appears to be a never ending war against terrorism. Trent Lott, the Republican leader, responded with a crude rebuke, suggesting that Daschle had no right to criticize President Bush "while we are fighting our war on terrorism." Community in this instance demands not courage, dialogue, and responsibility but silence and complicity.

Eric Hobsbawm (1994) has observed that "never was the word 'community' used more indiscriminately and emptily than in the decades when communities in the sociological sense became hard to find in real life" (p. 428). Maybe it is the absence of viable communities organized around democratic values and basic freedoms that accounts for the way in which the language of community has currently "degraded into the currency of propaganda" (Lapham, 2002, p. 8). How else can one explain the outrage exhibited by the dominant media against anyone who seems to question, among other things, the U.S. support of friendly dictatorships, including Afghanistan and Saudi Arabia, and the PATRIOT Act with its suppression of civil liberties or even suggest the need for a serious discussion about how U.S. foreign policy contributes to the poverty, despair, and hopelessness throughout the world that offers terrorist nihilism the opportunity "to thrive in the rich soil of exclusion and victimhood" (George, 2002, p. 12). Actual democratic communities are completely at odds with a smug self-righteousness that refuses to make a distinction between explaining events and justifying them. As Judith Butler (2002) pointed out,

> To ask how certain political and social actions come into being, such as the recent terrorist attack on the U.S., and even to identify a set of causes, is not the same as locating the source of the responsibility for those actions, or indeed, paralyzing our capacity to make ethical judgments on what is right or wrong . . . but it does ask the U.S. to assume a different kind of responsibility for producing more egalitarian global conditions for equality, sovereignty, and the egalitarian redistribution of resources. (pp. 8, 16)

Such questions do not suggest that the United States is responsible for the acts of terrorism that took place on September 11th. On the contrary, they perform the obligatory work of politics by attempting to situate individual acts of responsibility within those broader sets of conditions that give rise to individual acts of terrorism while simultaneously asking how the United States can intervene more productively in global politics to produce conditions that undercut rather than reinforce the breeding grounds for such terrorism. At the same time, such questions suggest that the exercise of massive power cannot be removed from the exercise of politics and ethics, and such a recognition demands a measure of accountability to be responsible for the consequences of our actions as one of the most powerful countries in the world. As Jerome Binde (2000) observed, "Being able to act also means being able to answer for our actions, to be responsible" (p. 57).

The rhetoric of terrorism is important not only because it operates on many registers to both inflict human misery and call into question the delicate balance of freedom and security crucial to any democratic society, but also because it carries with it an enormous sense of urgency that often redefines community against its most democratic possibilities and realized forms. Rising from the ashes of impoverishment and religious fundamentalism, terrorism, at its worst, evokes a culture of fear, unquestioning loyalty, and a narrow definition of security from those who treat it as a pathology rather than as a politics. In part, this is evident in Bush's "war against terrorism," which, fueled by calls for public sacrifice, appears to exhaust itself in a discourse of moral absolutes and public acts of denunciation. This all-embracing policy of antiterrorism depoliticizes politics by always locating it outside of the realm of power and strips community of democratic values by defining it almost exclusively through attempts to stamp out what a former counterterror expert in the Reagan administration calls "corrupt habits of mind that are still lingering around, somewhere" (Ledeen, as cited in Valentine, 2001). The militarizing of community and the perpetuation of a harsh culture of fear and insecurity not only result in the narrowing of community and the ongoing appeal to jingoistic forms of patriotism to divert the public from addressing a number of pressing domestic and foreign issues, they also result in the increasing suppression of dissent and what Anthony Lewis (2002) has rightly called the growing escalation of concentrated, unaccountable political power that threatens the very foundation of democracy in the United States.

At the core of Bush's notion of community and hyper-patriotism is a notion of temporality that detaches itself from a sense of public deliberation, critical citizenship, and civic engagement. Jerome Binde (2000) referred to this view of temporality as "emergency time" and described it as a "world governed by short-term efficacy," which under the imperatives of utter necessity and pragmatism eschews long-term appraisals and gives precedence to the "logic of 'just in time' at the expense of any forward-looking deliberation" (p. 52). According to Binde, emergency time opens the way for what he called "the tyranny of emergency." He explained,

> Emergency is a direct means of response which leaves no time for either analysis, forecasting, or prevention. It is an immediate protective reflex rather than a sober quest for long-term solutions. It neglects the fact that situations have to be put in perspective and that future events need to be anticipated. Devising any durable response to human problem . . . requires looking at a situation from a distance and thinking in terms of the future. (p. 52)

Lacking any reference to democratic collective aims, the appeal to emergency time both shrinks the horizon of meanings and removes the application of governmental power from the fields of ethical and political responsibility. Emergency time defines community against its democratic possibilities, detaching it from those conditions that prepare citizens to deliberate collectively about the future and the role they must play in creating and shaping the conditions for them to have some say in how it might unfold. Under such conditions, cynical reason replaces reasoned debate with the one-way gaze of power, and popular resistance to the "war" is dismissed as "a demagoguery of the streets, while dictators are offered up to us as responsible representatives of their countries" (Hesse & Sayyid, 2001, p. 3). But emergency time in the context of Bush's "war against terrorism" also rejects the radical secularism at the heart of substantive democracies in favor of a religious vocabulary. The metaphysics of religious discourse dispenses with the task of critically engaging and translating the elaborate web of historical, social, and political factors that underscore and give meaning to the broader explanations for terrorism. Instead, the complexity of politics dissolves into the language of "crusades," "infidels," "goodness," and "evil." Under such conditions, as Steven Lukes and Nadia Urbinati (2001) pointed out,

> a rhetoric of emergency has arisen in which a Manichean impulse is given free range, in which "our" (American? Western?) values are seen as threatened by an enemy that is seen as the incarnation of evil and variously identified as "fundamentalist" and "Islamist" as embodied in Al-Quaida and personified by Osama bin Laden. (p. 1)

It is the displacement of politics and the weakening of democratic public spaces that allow for religious ideology and excess to define the basis of community, civic engagement, and the domain of the social. Against this notion of emergency time, educators, cultural workers, and others need to posit a notion of public time. According to democratic theorist Cornelius Castoriadis (1991), public time represents "the emergence of a dimension where the collectivity can inspect its own past as the result *of its own actions*, and where an indeterminate future opens up as domain for its activities" (pp. 113-114). For Castoriadis, public time puts into question established institutions and dominant authority. Rather than maintaining a passive attitude toward power, public time demands and encourages forms of political agency based on a passion for self-governing, actions informed by critical judgment, and a passion for linking responsibility and social transformation. Public time renders governmental power explicit, and in doing so, it rejects the language of religious rituals and the abrogation of the conditions necessary for the assumption of basic freedoms and rights. Moreover, public time considers civic education the basis, if not the essential dimension, of justice because it provides individuals with the skills, knowledge, and passions to talk back to power while simultaneously emphasizing both the necessity to question what accompanies viable forms of political agency and the assumption of public responsibility through active participation in the very process of governing. Against Bush's disregard for public discussion of his policies, his fetish for secrecy, his clamoring for a notion of patriotism that is synonymous with a mindless conformity, and his flaunting of presidential power, public time gives credence to a notion of democracy that calls for the "creation of unlimited interrogation in all domains" of public life. Democratic politics and viable notions of community are created and affirmed when public spaces are created that enable individuals and social movements to exercise power over the institutions and forces that govern their lives. Under such conditions, politics is not relegated to the domain of the Other as a form of pathology but is central to what it means to build vibrant public spheres and democratic communities (Castoriadis, 1997).

What has become clear both in Bush's State of the Union Address and in the policies enacted by his administration is that there is no discourse for recognizing the obligations a democratic society has to pay its debts to past generations and fulfill its obligations to future generations. His tax cuts privilege the commercial interests of the rich over public responsibilities to the poor, the elderly, the environment, and the children. His call for military tribunals for trying noncitizens, his detaining of more than 1,200 Arabs and Muslims for extended periods in secrecy, and his willingness to undermine the basic constitutional freedoms and rights by enhancing the power of the police and other enforcement groups pose a grave threat to those civil liberties that are fundamental to a democracy. Edward Said (2002) argued more specifically that

> Bush and his compliant Congress have suppressed or abrogated or abridged whole sections of the First, Fourth, Fifth and Eighth Amendments, instituted legal procedures that give individuals no recourse either to a proper defense or a fair trail, that allow secret searches, eavesdropping, detention without limit, and, given the treatment of the prisoners at Guantanamo Bay, that allow the US executive branch to abduct prisoners, detain them indefinitely, decide unilaterally whether or not they are prisoners of war and whether or not the Geneva Conventions apply to them—which is not a decision to be taken by individual countries.

Most important, Bush's "war against terrorism" camouflages how democracy is being undermined through its relentless attempts to depoliticize politics itself. What began as the demonization of political Islam has now been extended into the demonization of politics itself as Bush and his cohorts put forth policies that attempt to erase the possibility of imagining a democratic future, the democratic space of the social, the meaning of democratic community, or the practices that anchor democratic life. As Hesse and Sayyid (2001) insightfully observed,

> Through such processes, politics seems exiled. While the centre is reoccupied by a naturalised world order, politics is proscribed from the domain of order itself. Paradoxically, cynical reason becomes a dominant ideology within an apparently post-ideological West. In a Western world apparently deprived of political alternatives to corporate capitalism, neoliberalism and global social inequalities, what once passed for politics has been exclusively transposed to the space occupied by those discontented with the West, and dispossessed by it. (p. 3)

By depoliticizing politics, the "war on terrorism" becomes both an empty abstraction and a strategic diversion—empty because terrorism cannot be either understood or addressed through the discourse of moral absolutes and religious fervor. Militarism does not get at the root of terrorism; it simply expands the breeding grounds for the conditions that give rise to it. Military interventions may overthrow governments controlled by radical fanatics such as the Taliban, but they do not address those global conditions in which poverty thrives, thousands of children die every day from starvation or preventable diseases, 250 million are compelled to work under harsh conditions, or some 840 million adults are without adequate shelter and access to health care (Pogge, 2000). As long as such inequalities exist, resistance will emerge and terrorism will be the order of the day. Not only is this a problem that will not be solved by dropping thousands of bombs on poor countries (with or without accompanying packets of food), it also suggests rethinking how U.S. policies actually contribute to these conditions through their support of military dictatorships, their unilateral disregard for international coalitions, and their ongoing support for the ruthless policies of global neoliberalism. The rhetoric of "antiterrorism" cleanses Bush and his cohorts of the obligations of political and ethical responsibility on a global level by ignoring the complex bonds that tie the rich and the powerful to the poor and the powerless. Such ties cannot be explained through the language of a rabid nationalism, hyped-up patriotism, or religious zeal. As Judith Butler (2002) pointed out, fatuous moralism is no substitute for assuming responsibility for one's actions in the world. She wrote,

> Moralistic denunciation provides immediate gratification, and even has the effect of temporarily cleansing the speaker of all proximity to guilt through the act of self-righteous denunciation itself. But is this the same as responsibility, understood as taking stock of our world, and participating in its social transformation in such a way that non-violent, cooperative, egalitarian international relations remain the guiding ideal? (p. 19)

Moralism may offer Bush and his cohorts the ground of innocence, but it does nothing to further the dynamics of democracy or civic engagement and may, as John Edgar Wideman (2002) suggested, even serve to "terrorize" those Americans it claims it is benefiting.

By launching a phony war [Bush] is managing to avoid the scrutiny a first-term, skin of its teeth presidency deserves. Instead, he's terrorizing Americans into believing that we require a wartime leader wielding unquestioned emergency powers. Beneath the drumbeat belligerence of his demands for national unity, if you listen you'll hear the bullying, the self-serving, the hollowness, of his appeals to patriotism. Listen carefully and you'll also hear what he's not saying: that we need, in a democracy full of contradictions and unresolved divisions, opposition voices. (p. 38)

If Wideman is correct, and I think he is, then Bush's innocent posturing wrapped in the righteousness of the rhetoric of antiterrorism also provides a massive diversion from addressing those political issues at the heart of what it means to measure the reality against the promise of a substantive democracy. Bush commits us to the dark world of emergency time, a world divided between good and evil, one in which "issues of democracy, civil comity and social justice—let alone nuance, complexity and interdependence simply vanish" (Barber, 2002, p. 17). In the name of "fighting freedom's fight," he constructs a world view in which the growing gap between the rich and the poor is ignored, massive unemployment is disregarded, the war against youth marginalized by class and color does not exist, poverty and racial injustice become invisible, the folly of attacking the public sector is passed over, the shameful growth of the prison-industrial complex is overlooked, Enron is easily forgotten, and threats to the environment evaporate.

Bush's notion of community depoliticizes politics and makes a sham of civic complexity and responsibility. If we are to challenge his policies, progressives need to reclaim a notion of politics that embraces a notion of public time, one that fosters civic engagement and public intelligence. This means at the least creating the conditions for rendering governmental authority accountable for its actions while also mobilizing the conditions for citizens to reclaim the power necessary to shape the regimes of power and politics that influence their lives on a daily basis. The greatest struggle Americans face is not terrorism but a struggle on behalf of justice, freedom, and democracy for all of the citizens of the globe. This is not going to take place, as Bush's policies will tragically affirm, by shutting down democracy, eliminating its most cherished rights and freedoms, and deriding communities of dissent. On the contrary, the struggle for democracy has to be understood through politics, not moralism, and if politics is to be reclaimed as the center of individual and social agency, it will have to be motivated not by the culture of fear but by a passion for civic engagement and ethical responsibility, and the promise of a realizable democracy.

References

Anton, A. (2000). Public goods as commonstock: Notes on the receding commons. In A. Anton, M. Fisk, & N. Holmstrom (Eds.), *Not for sale: In defense of public goods* (pp. 3–41). Boulder, CO: Westview.

Barber, B. R. (2002, January 21). Beyond jihad vs. Mcworld: On terrorism and the new democratic realism. *The Nation*, p. 17.

Bauman, Z. (2001). *Community: Seeking safety in an insecure world*. Cambridge, UK: Polity.

Binde, J. (2000). Toward an ethic of the future. *Public Culture*, 12(1), 51–72.

Butler, J. (2002). Explanation and exoneration, or what we can hear. *Theory & Event*, 5(4), 1–21.

Castoriadis, C. (1991). The Greek polis and the creation of democracy. In D. A. Curtis (Ed.), *Philosophy, politics, autonomy: Essays in political philosophy*. New York: Oxford University Press.

Castoriadis, C. (1997, May). The crisis of the identification process. *Thesis Eleven*, 49, 85–98.

George, S. (2002, February 18). Another world is possible. *The Nation*, p. 12.

Hesse, B., & Sayyid, S. (2001, November 28). A war against politics. *Open Democracy*, p. 3. Available from openDemocracy@opendemocracy.net

Hobsbawm, E. (1994). *The age of extremes*. London: Michael Joseph.

Lapham, L. H. (2002, January). American jihad. *Harper's Magazine*, pp. 7–9.

Lewis, A. (2002, August 9). Taking our liberties. *The New York Times*, p. A27.

Lukes, S., & Urbinati, N. (2001,November 27). Words matter. *Open Democracy*, p. 1. Available from openDemocracy@opendemocracy.net

Pogge, T. W. (2000, Fall). The moral demands of global justice. *Dissent*, pp. 37–43.

Said, E. (2002, March 5). Thoughts about America. *Counterpunch*. Available from www.counterpunch.org/saidamerica.html

Valentine, D. (2001, November 8). Homeland insecurity. *Counterpunch*. Available from www.counterpunch.org/homeland1.html

Wideman, J. E. (2002, March). Whose war. *Harper's Magazine*, pp. 33–38.

Henry A. Giroux is the Waterbury Chair Professor of Education at Penn State University.

It's Your World, I'm Just Trying to Explain It   51
Understanding Our Epistemological and
Methodological Challenges

GLORIA LADSON-BILLINGS

I PRESUME THAT ONE OF THE REASONS I have been invited to speak to the Qualitative Inquiry Special Interest Group is the fact that I contributed a chapter to the 2nd edition of the *Handbook of Qualitative Research*. But perhaps if the program planners realized I came kicking and screaming into that assignment they may have thought twice about the invitation. When Norman Denzin first approached me about contributing a chapter to the *Handbook* my first response was an unequivocal "no." I explained to him that I had just accepted the editorship of the *American Educational Research Journal*, I was a member of my university's athletic board, I was woefully late on several major writing projects, and I was attempting to have some semblance of a life. There just was no room in my schedule for another major writing task. But Norman was wise in the way those who have endured the academy almost always are. He suggested that I take a look at the current chapter he was asking me to replace and then get back to him. I went back and re-read that chapter and while it was indeed a good chapter, I knew that there was something else I wanted to say. Thus, my ego led me into yet another challenge for which I had no time.

But, even the writing of that chapter entitled "Racialized discourses and ethnic epistemologies" takes on a different set of meanings in our current socio-political context. The events of September 11, 2001, have colored almost all public discourse in this country. There is no way to ignore it or minimize the way it has shaped the material and symbolic world we inhabit. But, this shaping of our world is a perfect example of what this talk is about. First, let me be clear, nothing can excuse the horrific acts perpetrated against the people in the World Trade Center, the Pentagon, and the three airplanes that were highjacked and turned into weapons. But, how we have shaped that event and the subsequent public conversation are perfect examples of the epistemic panic (Gordon, 1997) I tried to capture in the *Handbook* chapter.

There are three epistemological themes that were made manifest as a result of the attack. One theme is that of defining humanity. The second theme is that of defining importance, and the third theme is that of determining the future. In this discussion I will attempt to draw parallels between these themes and the knowledge construction process that governs the academy.

From the very moment of the attack the official rhetoric told us we were dealing with madmen, lunatics, and evildoers. We also learned that there were two choices available to us—either to be with "us" or to be with the "terrorists," and clearly, since the terrorists were "deranged" fanatics, the only humanity available was that which was associated with the moral, civilized "us." Next the images that accompanied the "them" were from a pre-modern era. Without the trappings of the West—modern dress, daily conveniences, and reason-governed institutions—configuring the "them" as other than human was fairly simple. Such an us-them paradigm makes sense in a Cold War reality. However, in a new world configuration, such binaries are useless. According to Huntingdon (1996) in his book, *The Clash of Civilizations*, affinities are less related to nation-states and more related to cultural or civilizational ties. Thus, the lack of humanity we have ascribed to those who are half a world away is also mapped onto those who share their cultural and/or religious ties. Americans of Muslim, Arab, and/or Middle Eastern descent no longer can lay claim to the same humanity as those of us wrapped in this new national "we."

The creation of the inhuman "them" is a very old ontological strategy. Indeed, my *Handbook* chapter is about the way the Enlightenment thinkers defined humanity—as those for whom knowledge was first scientific and second absolutely knowable and truthful. The human is he (and he is deliberate and definitive here) who understands that "natural science could be summarized by its laws and employs an experimental method to seek truth (Ladson-Billings, 2000). Thus, those who subscribed to an epistemology that conjoined the seen and unseen, the flesh and the spirit, this world and the next were either religious fanatics (if they were white) or primitive, unevolved, and not yet human. Yet scholars like Ani (1994) suggests that if you "rob the universe of its richness, deny the significance of the symbolic, simplify phenomena until it becomes mere object, [then] you have a knowable quantity. Here begins and ends the European epistemological mode" (p. 29).

Now it is important to be clear that there is nothing wrong with this mode of thinking. What is wrong is the imposition of this mode on all people and the dismissal of modes of thought that conflict with it as untrue, biased, ideological, and/or superstitious. The real challenge of this current era is to understand as Geertz (1983) pointed out that all cultures are local—not universal. And, as Pandian (1985) further elaborates that the Judeo-Christian culture of the west is a local culture, not a universal, transcendent, supra-culture under which all others must be subordinated. However, the combination of opportunity, economics, military might, and technology have afforded the West unique and powerful influences in the world—first through the industrial age and the rapid manufacturing capabilities, and next through the information age where ideas, symbols, and whole cultural systems can be transported and inserted into other cultural systems in an instant. Scholar Sylvia Wynter (1992) cites Eritrean ethnologist Asmarom Legesse in pointing out that:

> As Westernized scholars, we invariably see the "models of the universe" native to this specific "local culture" (even if one that is now secularized and globalized), as if they were models of an in-itself reality. So rather than being aware of the fact that we too conceptualize and

know our social reality *through* the prescriptive categories of a "local" world view, we have come to believe that the knowledge we have of our social reality is a *supra-cultural* rather than a culture-specific order of knowledge. (pp. 8-9)

Today we continue to grapple with a cultural logic locked in binaries. It understands dichotomy and opposition and has little room for complexity. It cannot hold two competing thoughts at once and imposes on us a "regime of truth" that makes it impossible to confer humanity on anyone outside of its system of thought and mode of behavior. Stanley Fish (2001) in his *New York Times* editorial following the September 11 attacks, points out that like Edward Said we must reject "false universals." He further asserts:

How many times have we heard these new mantras: "we have seen the face of evil"; "these are irrational madmen"; "we are at war against international terrorism." Each is at once inaccurate and unhelpful. We have not seen the face of evil; we have seen the face of an enemy who comes at us with a full roster of grievances, goals and strategies. If we reduce that enemy to "evil," we conjure up a shape-shifting demon, a wild-card moral anarchist beyond our comprehension and therefore beyond the reach of any counterstrategies.

Fish's point is that without an understanding of the basic humanity of an opponent, there is no opportunity for worthy confrontation and real resolution to our problems. Rather, we continue to chase ghosts, always presuming the other to be without reason, rights, or rationale.

The second theme is one of determining importance. Over and over people in this country describe the world as pre–September 11 and post–September 11. Yes, this is a significant date, for now, but it takes history to determine whether or not it will become a teleological fault line. For me time and chronology can be divided in an infinite number of combinations—pre–April 4, 1968 (assassination of MLK) and post–April 4, 1968, pre-summer of 1963 and post-summer of 1963 (bombing of the little girls in the Birmingham church), pre-summer of 1955 and post-summer of 1955 (murder of Emmett Till). Each of these events made *me* feel less safe, less secure, less able to lay claim to any notion of myself as American. But, now I am learning that September 11 is the dividing line I must use if I am ever to claim "real" citizenship. All other notions of what is or is not important become subjugated to this new indicator that is reinscribed in every newspaper, every broadcast, and every popular media outlet. For instance, on December 20, 2001, we learned that the economy of Argentina was collapsing. There was rioting and looting in the streets and the president had announced his resignation. On the *CBS Nightly News* that evening, Dan Rather devoted almost all of his coverage to the 100-day "anniversary" of 9-11. We learned that Liberty Island was reopening to the public (but not the Statue of Liberty itself), the government had come up with a plan for compensating the victims of the attacks, and the Pentagon was being rebuilt. The story about Argentina's literal collapse was inserted on the 2-minute "world wrap" section of the news. This is a glaring example of how our "local culture" creates significance and insignificance. September 11 as a declared date of significance negates all others in the same way 1066, 1492, 1776, and December 7, 1941, are supposed to stand in high relief against all other dates, times, places.

A friend and colleague, Hassimi Miaga, has developed a sociocultural chronology we use with pre-service students, in which he examined a series of events that occurred at the same time. For example, in 1492 his chronology states:

After 800 years of occupation by Africans, the edict of expulsion forced thousands of African Muslims (Moors) and Jews to flee Spain. Sonni Ali Beer, the great Malian conquerer, died. Columbus made his way to the Americas and the Renaissance began in Europe.

All of these things were happening simultaneously and their importance was specific to the people who were directly impacted. This is not meant to minimize the arrival of Europeans in the Americas so much as it is to place it in the context of a variety of human events. The dominance of European or Western science and technologies has made Western worldviews the valued worldviews. Again, my Malian friend shared with me that growing up in Mali he sang a song that swore allegiance to "our ancestors the Gauls," and his school calendar included a Christmas holiday for a Muslim nation with built-in snow days in a country that does not experience snow.

Thus, our penchant for fixing a point in time as *the* point in time for everyone to reverence reflects our continued misunderstanding of the ways our epistemological biases shape the realm of possibilities for everyone.

The third theme that has devolved from September 11 is that of determining the future. This theme is more interesting because it is imbedded in a national narrative that we all realize is a persistent myth. In this narrative, we say something like, "We'll never be the same because of what happened to us on September 11." Actually, that would be a comforting thought—that we would never be the same. Unfortunately, this notion of a differently oriented America is one that will not materialize. No sooner than the events of September 11 sunk in, the nation took up a rhetoric about the need to place Americans of Arab/Middle Eastern descent under strict surveillance and to restrict their freedom. There have been a number of proposals aimed at curtailing civil liberties—military tribunals instead of civilian courts, restricting access to presidential papers, coercion of national loyalty. These kinds of things reflect not how we are different, but rather how easily we retreat to old patterns of behaviors and old discourses that almost always lead to bad results. The same kinds of responses were apparent after Pearl Harbor. The difficult issue is that we are more likely to be exactly like we were (and even more so, if that is possible) because of September 11. Before the attack, the very concept of an American was being contested. It was a fluid concept that was being made and remade in a myriad of ways. In some places it included a variety of language groups—English, Spanish, French Creole, Vietnamese, Hmong. In other places it included a variety of religious practices. In still other places it included race, class, gender, sexuality, and ability differences. However, it was not a settled or definitive concept. Soon after September 11 who and what constituted an American became a fixed and rigid image. And, that concept has little room for dissent or challenge. I fear there will be a retreat to nativist and parochial thinking about who we are and who or what the "other" is.

A local example of this narrow construction of "American" and "patriot" came into play in Madison, Wisconsin—the place some call the last bastion of communism in the

Western world. Well before the events of September 11, some state legislator inserted a rider into the upcoming state budget agreement. This rider required all schools in the state to have students recite the Pledge of Allegiance or sing the National Anthem every day. Typically, such rulings would have little or no impact on Madison schools. However, after September 11 the newspapers constantly reminded the public of the new state requirement. When the pledge/anthem edict went into effect, several parents from the elementary school with the most international student body appealed to the school board about the coercive nature of the ruling. Three of the five board members present at that meeting voted to have the district play the National Anthem only. Their decision set off a firestorm. Before long, Madison's "anti-American," radical, left-leaning sentiments were made fodder for conservative voices throughout the country. Specifically, the decision was the topic of Rush Limbaugh's radio program and had city officials fearful that conferences and other business interests would desert Madison. Before long a recall effort was put into motion and a special school board meeting was held at the largest high school auditorium. Over 1,000 people showed up at the school board meeting. People stood up singing the anthem and reciting the pledge. Although speakers were given only 3 minutes to share their views, the school board meeting lasted until 3 a.m. Two of the school board members rescinded their votes. One stood firm. Hate and vitriol spewed out of the mouths of the audience members. One man, a local radio "shock jock," told the newly elected Hmong member of the board to "go back to Vietnam!"

After some discussion, the recall proponents decided to just try to recall the one board member who refused to change his vote since the other two members would be standing for reelection in the spring anyway. In the meantime, one of the local newspapers (that generally supported the recall folks) did a feature on the school board member. He was a former English teacher in the district and devotes his free time to assisting non-English speaking immigrants with acquiring English so that they can prepare for the citizenship examination. In the article, he was quoted as saying that he would never change his vote about the Pledge because you could not coerce people to be patriotic. "Patriotism is what you do, not what you say."

The current end of this story is that the recall movement failed to garner the 30,000 plus signatures and the democratic process allows the duly elected school board member to remain in office. But think about what this has meant to the community. A school district that has an abysmal track record educating black and Latino students cannot get anyone to a board meeting on the achievement needs of students of color, but not saying the Pledge brings people from miles around. The attack has not made us different; it has made us predictably more like ourselves.

What This Means for Research

The ability to define humanity, to determine significance or importance, and to determine the future has an important impact on research and scholarship. Not too long ago a colleague attended a meeting where the president of a major philanthropic foundation commented, " I don't know why we keep receiving all of these critical theory proposals. We're not going to fund any of them." The attitude of the funder is shocking, not because the funder has predetermined what s/he will fund—foundations do that all the time. But, it is the basis for this decision. This funder has mapped out the epistemological landscape and decided what is worth knowing. I think we could agree that if a funder decided that s/he was willing only to fund mathematics or science related proposals, that is his/her privilege. We might disagree with this strategy but at least we could understand the funder's position on prioritizing what to fund. However, when a foundation decides that an entire epistemological stance is illegitimate, it is not merely stating a priority but rather determining what does and does not count as knowledge.

In my own work, I have used critical race theory to explicate new epistemological perspectives on inequity and social injustice in education. Although some might consider a "racial" theory an essentialized approach to analysis and interpretation of social phenomena, critical race theory actually attempts to make plain the racialized context of public and private spheres in our society. It functions as a useful rubric for understanding the taken-for-granted privileges and inequities that are built into our society. It employs narratives and counter-narratives to add context and complexity to the microaggressions people of color experience daily.

Critical race theory asserts that racism is normal, not aberrant, in U.S. society and because it is so ingrained in our society it looks ordinary and natural to people in the culture. Indeed, my students who are most taken aback by racism tend to be my international students because the racism seems so evident and explicit. U.S. students of color have grown accustomed to the exclusions, the surveillance, and the inequities.

Critical race theory often takes the form of storytelling, "in which writers analyze the myths, presuppositions, and received wisdoms that make up the common culture about race" (Delgado, 1995, p. xiv). This means that CRT understands that our social world is not fixed, rather it is something we construct with words, stories, and silences. But, we need not cave in to social arrangements that are unjust; we can write against them.

CRT calls for deeply contextualized understandings of social phenomena. Unlike the positivist tendency to strip down and sterilize social and cultural issues into distinct component parts, critical race theorists insist on providing a context to make sense of what transpires, to fully elaborate a story, and make evident complexity.

CRT is informed by a notion of "interest-convergence," a concept developed by Derrick Bell. It argues that white elites will tolerate or encourage racial advances for people of color only when they also promote white self-interest. So, if you examine legislative and judicial changes such as affirmative action or school desegregation, you can see that the ultimate payoff went to whites. In the case of affirmative action, the figures are clear that the biggest benefactors were white women and since white women typically live in white families, the benefits accrue to entire white communities. In the case of school desegregation, the proliferation of magnet programs, school desegregation workshops, courses, etc., all created work opportunities that often went to whites. Indeed, as Foster reports, the greatest casualties of school desegregation were black teachers and administrators.

Critical race theorists are willing to try out new forms of writing and thought. Some are postmodernists, some use biography and autobiography, stories and counter-stories.

Others have been experimenting with humor, satire, and narrative analysis "to reveal the circular, self-serving nature of particular legal doctrines or rules."

CRT represents a space of both theoretical and epistemological liberation. It offers an opportunity to challenge the taken-for-granted theories and concepts that govern our disciplines and circumscribe our thinking. I would never suggest that CRT is the only way to theorize the racialized subject. I would never suggest that it is the only way to make sense of the ongoing inequity and social injustice that shape our society. Believe it or not I might be the first to say that if you are working with thousands of data points, you may want to quickly reach into your methodological tool kit for multiple regressions or structural equation modeling. But I ask that you reach with full knowledge of what those tools can and cannot do. I ask that you step back to look on what epistemological ground you have planted your feet. I ask you to recognize what the "truths" your epistemology illuminates and what "truths" are simultaneously occluded by it. I ask you to keep open the possibilities of limitless thinking and innovation. I ask you to remember that in a society structured by dominance and subordination, it's someone else's world, we just try to explain it.

References

Ani, M. (1994). *Yurugu: An African-centered critique of European cultural thought and behavior.* Trenton, NJ: Africa World Press.

Delgado, R. (ed.). (1995). *Critical race theory: The cutting edge.* Philadelphia: Temple University Press.

Fish, S. (2001, October 15). Condemnation without absolutes. *New York Times* (opinion).

Geertz, C. (1983). *Local knowledge: Further essays in interpretive anthropology.* New York: Basic Books.

Gordon, E. (1997). Task force on the role and future of minorities–American Educational Research Association, *Educational Researcher,* April, pp. 44–52.

Ladson-Billings, G. (2000). Racialized discourses and ethnic epistemologies. In N. Denzin & Y. Lincoln (eds.). *Handbook of qualitative research.* 2nd ed. Thousand Oaks, CA: Sage.

Note

Wynter, S. (1992). *The challenge to our episteme: The case of the California textbook controversy.* Paper presented at the annual meeting of the American Educational Research Association, San Francisco, CA.

9/11 and the Poetics of Complicity **52**
A Love Poem for a Hurt Nation

STEPHEN JOHN HARTNETT

I N MY INITIAL, STUNNED THINKING about the terrorist strikes, I stumbled again and again not only on my utter unpreparedness to make sense of what happened but also, perhaps even more frightening, on latent assumptions about national exceptionalism, race, class, religion, and the use of armed force. I thus found myself wondering along with Rachel Blau DuPlessis (1996), "How in the world did ideology get in my head, locked so firm?" (p. 34). Even while organizing and participating in various political responses to the War on Terrorism, I found myself struggling to make sense of the relationships among overarching critical-theoretical stabs at understanding, rapidly changing political scenarios, and my immediate personal sense of confusion and loss. Thus, like DuPlessis and fellow *Cultural Studies* ↔ *Critical Methodologies* contributors Patricia Ticineto Clough (2002) and Laurel Richardson (2002), I found myself acknowledging with a new urgency both the fragility of human existence and my deep implication in and complicity with many of the structures of oppression, obfuscation, and obliteration highlighted by both the terrorist attacks and the resulting "war."

In my confusion regarding how to approach these questions, I recalled Kenneth Ames's (1985) suggestion that

> as long as we can maintain a sense of being startled by what we see, even an inclination to believe we have stumbled onto truly weird behavior, we have a better sense of appreciating how a phenomenon actually functions in our culture. (p. 9)

My contribution to this issue of *Cultural Studies* ↔ *Critical Methodologies* seeks to embody Ames's sense of wonder and DuPlessis's sense of confusion by creating a montage of stunned witness and reflection. By merging the citational style typical of academic work with the evocative power of poetry, with this combination rendered in fragmentary observations marked by broken lines indicating jumps in time and space, the poem that follows strives to render the swirling, boggling, yet nonetheless narrative structure of my grappling with 9/11. Italicized passages indicate quotations, which are referenced in the end notes to the article.

In addition to these methodological observations, I should note that I strive below to situate my thoughts within a historical framework that refuses to grant 9/11 its much bal-lyhooed status as a world-changing event of unprecedented proportions. For although the acts of 9/11 were indeed unparalleled in terms of the immediacy and spectacularity of their violence, the background to them and the subsequent U.S. response to them are both utterly familiar. As Michael Hardt and Antonio Negri (2000) argued in a cynical yet in-sightful phrase in *Empire*, "interventions are always exceptional even though they arise con-tinually" (p. 38). One of the many representational dilemmas of 9/11, then, is to honor its brutal exceptionality, its standing as earth-shakingly "weird behavior," while situating it within its banal familiarity, its place within deep historical narratives so well known to everyone on the left that we sometimes forget how important they actually are for influ-encing our present crises.

I. Terrors

destruction impossible to imagine
    no electricity little water
      one phone for every 500 people

3 percent of girls in school
    one-in-twelve women
    dies in childbirth

life expectancy forty-four
    leaving me five bodies
    in the cracked fields

where no crops grow
    traversed by *700,000 fighters*[1]
    hoping to die in battle

as last month's allies
    slaughter each other
    in the *barren mountains*

around Gardez where Saifullah
    and Padsha Kahn Zadran
    send thousands of men

into *twelve hour battles*
    their commander shouting
    I'll fire and fire and fire
    All night and all day
    until I bring this
    To a finish[2]

meaning everyone dead
        as 600 U.S. troops
spread the violence to

the forsaken Philippine
        island of Basilan where
        our new partners in the war

        on terrorism are brutally out of
                control running *death squads*
        while battling the Abu Sayyaf

supposed allies of Al Qaeda
        just another *dirty war*
        our boys training *murderers*

and torturers in the art of
        executions and disappearances[3]
        using the war on terrorism

        as an excuse to reclaim
        Subic Bay Naval Station
        the Philippine *real estate*

for monitoring China
        Washington greasing the
        wheels with *$4.6 billion*

in military and economic
        aid buying *access* for
        permanent overflight rights[4]

that's $4,600,000,000
        of our tax money
        not for education

not for health care
        not for housing
but the American way

defended from *30,000 feet*
        by *pilotless Predator drones*
        laser-guided *AC-130 gunships*

CBU-87s spreading bomblets
        filling the fields with yellow
        prizes for the curious

spared the brutal majesty of
    Joint Direct Attack Munitions
$20,000 2,000 pound bombs

courtesy of *Boeing* guided
    by the *satellite-based*
Global Positioning System[5]

the technology of death
    celebrated in the press
as American ingenuity

conquering the world
    with better minds
God-like intelligence[6]

yet *Qaeda still able*
    To strike the U.S.
Head of C.I.A. Says[7]

meaning *wars without end*[8]
    claiming human rights
to crush uncooperative

Iraq the next target
    Hussein must be overthrown
Senior Officials say

smugly naming invasion
    as *regime change* pursued
in *a variety of options*[9]

all forgetting history's nagging
    reminder overwhelming military
superiority does not translate

into security Mastery of
    the known world does
not confer peace of mind[10]

which perhaps explains *The*
    Office of Strategic Influence
planting news items disinformation

and other covert operations
    designed by The Rendon Group
the *consulting firm* that lied

about slaughtered children
in Kuwaiti hospitals
turning a war for oil

into a human rights
campaign paid *$100,000*
a month for waging[11]

secret information warfare
the Pentagon calls it
managing information[12]

turning death into a
13-part reality series
on ABC primetime

filmed by Mr. War
Jerry Bruckheimer
producer of *Pearl Harbor*

Black Hawk Down
films the brass love for
promoting its war effort[13]

the nation thus hypnotized
Hollywood and the Pentagon
turning the faraway

into the familiar
the deadly into the kind
They make slaughter

and call it peace[14]

II. Home Fronts

celebrate democracy in action
the free exchange of ideas
via mass-produced form letters

Senator Richard Durbin
lackey waterboy puppet
chirping the party line

no choice but to
use military force to
promote democracy

human rights and
    economic development
via *commonsense provisions*

like *updating wiretaps*
    and surveillance laws[15]
standing to cheer

His Fraudulency's chant
    Our cause is just Our
war is only beginning

for *the axis of evil*
    calls us nobly forth
to fight freedom's fight[16]

His Fraudulency's challenge
    delighted the old guard
in revolutionary Tehran

where *millions of Iranians*
    launched *dirgelike chants*
Death to America!

liberal reforms stalled
    extremists ascendant
the old terror revived

in a nation filled with
    a *resurgence of disgust*
with America—Death to[17]

Bush! prodding poking
    The Anger of the Damned
their *crushing humiliation*[18]

feeding photogenic rage
    produced to explain
the next round of bombings

the *axis of evil* but a wish-list
    for a perpetual war economy
$379 billion for 2003

    largest increase in Pentagon
        spending in twenty years
    but *less than 10%* slotted

for *domestic security* proving[19]
   the War on Terrorism
is a red-herring an excuse

for unencumbered Empire
   the end of checks-and-balances
the end of civil liberties[20]

   John Ashcroft channeling McCarthy
       before the Senate Judiciary Committee
   on 6 December 2001 claiming

questioning the government
  only aids terrorists for it
erodes our national unity

and diminishes our resolve[21]
     beware the living dead
   Fenno rising from his grave

Gazette of the Unites States
     wrinkled in his Federalist hands
   attacking Jefferson and Franklin

blustering once again
    He that is not for
us is against us![22]

1798 another witch-hunt
    Jacobins stalking the land
   the Federalist Boston *Centinel*

ranting whatever *American*
    opposes the administration
   is an anarchist and a traitor[23]

like the wobblies in 1917
    165 arrested for "espionage"
   in 1920 over four-thousand

foreigners deported without trial
    one Wobbly asking in court
   how in hell do you expect

a man to be patriotic?[24]
    Senator Norris warning[25]
   We are going into war

Upon the command
    of gold We are about
to Put the dollar sign

On the American flag
    the Senate erupting
Treason! Treason! [26]

Wilson's war lackeys all
    proud like Bush's today
wearing flag pins proving

loyalty courage honor save
    Senator La Follette as ever[27]
the voice of reason justice

the Progressives' champion
    farmer lawyer activist
skewering the bosses

no pin no war no treason
    arms folded no handshake
following Wilson's declaration[28]

    La Follette knew
        Mother Jones Knew
    Eugene Debs knew

as we know as well
    suffocating phony patriotism[29]
feeds no one

heals no one
    teaches no one
brings no peace

the brave then as now
    refusing the majesty of war
chanting praying singing

Another world is possible[30]

III. Complicity

I'm tempted to resort to Karma
    to explain the madness of
a world turned upside down

where even nature appears
      stunned angry malicious
   as in Central Mexico where

freak storms freeze the sky
      sending 270 million butterflies
   plummeting to death[31]

    while in the mean streets
         hoopsters dream of soaring
      in *$200 Nike Jordan XVIIs*

    as Spike Lee manufactures
         the legitimacy of cool
      for a *$10 million advertising*

campaign to teach youngsters[32]
      to cherish commodities
   to worship the superficial

    while New York's finest
         arrive *with several vans*
      for midnight sweeps

    clearing Fifth Avenue
         of the homeless sleeping
      outside the shelter

the Presbyterian Church
      offering food cots showers
   for *28 to 35 people a night*[33]

local merchants complain
      such kindness compromises
   window-shopping pleasure

    I walked that Avenue
         every day last summer
      tramping from 108th

    down Broadway to 81st
         across to Central Park West
      where Sycamores shade

    Teddy's giant finger
         pointing to genocide
      from the granite steps

of the Museum of Natural
    History where kids run in
circles stunned by dinosaurs

the size of houses cutting
    through the Park's joyous
fields of play music lovers

walking arm in arm
    pushing baby carriages
Living Arts on the bench

emerging at Fifth and 57th
    where taxis limos carriages
jostle for the Plaza's royalty

pausing to wonder at wealth
    so obscene it's boggling
before hustling to the Library

where Tilden Lenox Astor
    carved in the marble foyer
speak of aristocratic glory

yet I worship each day
    their democratic vision
embodied in this gift

this most holy of places
    where the rich and poor
study shoulder to shoulder

amazed by the ease of luxury
    propped open store doors
offer blasts of air-conditioned

relief from the sticky heat
    everyone so beautiful
I felt like a bum

until passing the Church
    to talk with the forgotten
their rage festering

beneath tattered blankets
    sunburned leathery skin
piss-stained cardboard

as the beautiful people
    cell phones chirping
deals dates destinies

> double lattés in hand
> >curse their entreaties
> >to *help if you can*
>
> and one wonders
> >standing there ashamed
> >how could you not
>
> >fear *the rot*
> >>*at the heart*
> >*in the sick*
>
> >*fat veins of America*[34]
> >>how could you not
> >>love it as well
>
> >my people my park
> >>my towers crushed
> >>my neighbors dead
>
> >my library my nation
> >>*We hold these truths*
> >>how could you not
>
> >>love it as well

Notes

1. "Building the Peace" (2002, p. 3).
2. Burns (2002, p. A13); see Onishi (2001).
3. Kristof (2002).
4. Bonner (2002).
5. Schmitt and Dao (2001).
6. See Mitchell (2000).
7. Risen (2002).
8. "Endless War Budget" (2002).
9. Gordon and Sanger (2002).
10. Ignatieff (2002, p. 4).
11. Dao and Schmitt (2002).
12. Dao (2002b).
13. Barringer (2002).
14. Tacitus (as cited in Hardt & Negri, 2000, p. 3).
15. Senator Richard Durbin (personal communication to Brett Kaplan, January 15, 2002).
16. "Text of President Bush's State of the Union Address to Congress" (2002, p. A22).
17. MacFarquhar (2002).
18. Pamuk (2001).
19. Dao (2002b, p. A21).
20. See Dworkin (2002).

21. "Excerpts from Attorney General's Testimony" (2001, p. B6).
22. As cited in Smith (1956, p. 15).
23. As cited in Smith (1956, p. 178).
24. As cited in Zinn (1980, p. 364).
25. Senator George Norris of Nebraska.
26. As cited in Kennedy (1980, p. 21).
27. Senator Robert La Follette of Wisconsin.
28. See Kennedy (1980, p. 15).
29. George (2002, p. 11).
30. George (2002, p. 13); and see Cooper (2002).
31. Yoon (2002).
32. "New Air Jordans" (2002).
33. Fritsch (2001).
34. Snyder (1974, p. 18).

References

Ames, K. (1985). Introduction. In A. Axelrod (Ed.), *The colonial revival in America* (pp. 1–14). New York: Norton.

Barringer, F. (2002, February 21). Reality TV about G.I.s on war duty. *The New York Times*, p. A13.

Bonner, R. (2002, March 4). U.S. and Philippine governments revive old relationship. *The New York Times*, p. A11.

Building the peace. (2002, February 11). The Nation, p. 3.

Burns, J. (2002, January 31). Fighting erupts in Afghan city as warlords compete for power. *The New York Times*, pp. A1, A13.

Clough, P. T. (2002). Posts post September 11. *Cultural Studies ↔ Critical Methodologies*, 2(1), 15–17.

Cooper, M. (2002, March 11). From protest to politics: A report from Porto Alegre. *The Nation*, pp. 11–16.

Dao, J. (2002a, February 21). New agency will not lie, top Pentagon officials say. *The New York Times*, p. A12.

Dao, J. (2002b, February 13). Warm reaction to bigger Pentagon budgets. *The New York Times*, p. A21.

Dao, J., & Schmitt, E. (2002, February 19). Pentagon readies efforts to sway sentiment abroad. *The New York Times*, pp. A1, A10.

DuPlessis, R. B. (1996). Manifests. *Diacritics: A Review of Contemporary Criticism*, 26(3/4), 31–35.

Dworkin, R. (2002, February 28). The threat to patriotism. *The New York Review of Books*, pp. 44–49.

Endless war budget. (2002, March 11). *The Nation*, p. 3.

Excerpts from attorney general's testimony before Senate Judiciary Committee. (2001, December 7). *The New York Times*, p. B6.

Fritsch, J. (2001, December 18). Church suit seeks to stop police from ejecting homeless from its property. *The New York Times*, p. A17.

George, S. (2002, February 18). Another world is possible. *The Nation*, pp. 11–13.

Gordon, M., & Sanger, D. (2002, February 13). Powell says U.S. is weighing ways to topple Hussein. *The New York Times*, pp. A1, A14.

Hardt, M., & Negri, A. (2000). *Empire*. Cambridge, MA: Harvard University Press.

Ignatieff, M. (2002, February 28). Barbarians at the gate? *The New York Review of Books*, pp. 4–6.

Kennedy, D. (1980). *Over here: The First World War and American society*. New York: Oxford University Press.

Kristof, N. D. (2002, February 12). Sleeping with terrorists. *The New York Times*, p. A27.

MacFarquhar, N. (2002, February 12). Millions in Iran rally against the U.S. *The New York Times*, pp. A1, A10.

Mitchell, G. (2000). Placebo defense: Operation desert mirage? The rhetoric of patriot missile accuracy in the 1991 Persian Gulf War. *Quarterly Journal of Speech*, 86(2), 121–145.

New Air Jordans hit stratosphere in price. (2002, February 3). *The New York Times*, p. 2.

Onishi, N. (2001, December 28). Afghan warlords and bandits are back in business. *The New York Times*, pp. B1, B3.

Pamuk, O. (2001, November 15). The anger of the damned. *The New York Review of Books*, p. 12.

Richardson, L. (2002). Small world. *Cultural Studies ↔ Critical Methodologies*, 2(1), 24–26.

Risen, J. (2002, February 7). Qaeda still able to strike U.S., head of C.I.A. says. *Cultural Studies ↔ Critical Methodologies*, pp. A1, A10.

Schmitt, E., & Dao, J. (2001, December 24). Use of pinpoint airpower comes of age in new war. *Cultural Studies ↔ Critical Methodologies*, pp. B1, B3.

Smith, J. M. (1956). *Freedom's fetters: The alien and sedition laws and American civil liberties*. Ithaca, NY: Cornell University Press.

Snyder, G. (1974). Front lines. In *Turtle Island* (p. 18). New York: New Directions Press.

Text of President Bush's State of the Union Address to Congress. (2002, January 30). *The New York Times*, p. A22.

Yoon, C. K. (2002, February 12). Storm in Mexico devastates monarch butterfly colonies. *The New York Times*, pp. A1, A5.

Zinn, H. (1980). *A people's history of the United States*. New York: Perennial.

Stephen John Hartnett is an assistant professor of speech communication at the University of Illinois.

Afterword
Marching Orders for a Divided Nation, Renewed Commitment for an Engaged Social Science

WE HAVE TRIED TO SHOW, with this collection of work from profoundly engaged social scientists, the range of expression from a particular set of people: engaged social scientists, clinicians, poets, communication experts, autoethnographers and biographers. Throughout this collection are central themes which recur again and again—a sense of mourning, not just for our lost sense of security and safety, but also for a nation befuddled by the savagery of attacks on nonmilitary and civilian targets. A sense of bewilderment that rules of engagement we (somewhat naively) believed to be widely shared—military attacks on military targets only—are not only not shared, but they are spurned with disdain. The sense that we somehow have gone very, very wrong in our relations with some parts of the remainder of the world, and perhaps, we do not know how to "fix" it—for Americans are the original "fix-it," "can-do" handymen of the geopolitical shop floor. Many of us do not know how to fix it, because we do not fully understand what is broken, or how it came to fall into a state of disrepair. We suspect, deep in our generous, if clumsy, national heart, that we have done something wrong; we are not certain what it might be, or how we can, in effect, apologize and make it better.

Those are the voices heard in this volume. Against those voices, and in an insistent chant, has appeared a bifurcation of the discourse around the tragedies of September 11, 2001. This other voice in the bifurcated discourse is the "official" voice of Washington, especially of a president and a cabinet who have unilaterally declared war on an enemy who dissolves into the fog of mountains in lands far, far away. We are at war with Osama bin Laden. No, we are at war with the Taliban, which is believed to be sheltering bin Laden. Well, perhaps we are really quite unhappy with Pakistan, where bin Laden might have slipped over the border. No, we may be at war with Iraq, where Saddam Hussein might be creating weapons of mass destruction and biological warfare, and where some of the money which supports international terrorism might be, even now, being laundered. If we could only just arrange the assassination of Saddam Hussein, then we might restore some sense of security to our own borders. Is this not correct?

Against this official declaration of a state of permanent siege, permanent war, a discourse of resistance, a discourse of dissent, a discourse of civil civic disagreement, stands counterpoised but threatened. The ability of ordinary citizens, as well as public intellectuals such as academics, to express reservations about the prosecution of warfare and bombing in Afghanistan has been severely curtailed in the wake of public speeches by Lynne Cheney and others. In Lynne Cheney's speeches, she cites academics who express reservations about the war in Afghanistan, names them (along with their institutions), and draws perilously close to labeling such dissenters as traitors and treasonous.

We do well to mourn as much for our vanishing civil liberties and right of assembly and dissent as for the loss of life which occurred on September 11. The moves to squash dissent regarding the war in Afghanistan—through such congressional initiatives as the declaration of Loyalty Day, the P.A.T.R.I.O.T. Act, the unilateral declaration that suspected terrorists will be tried in closed and secret military tribunals, the imprisoning of Arab Americans and Muslim Americans, on grounds no more substantive than they are of Arab descent or Islamic religious beliefs, without recourse to any of the safeguards normally provided to citizens under our Constitution—is sufficient to strike terror in the hearts of ordinary citizens. To academics, professionals and public intellectuals, long accustomed to the liberties of "academic freedom" and the prerogatives of freedom of speech and civic debate, all of these moves signal losses far greater, in substance and in import, than the loss of the World Trade Center towers, the Pentagon and Flight 93, however horrific and devastating those losses are.

The pressure to squash dissent regarding the war in Afghanistan—which many suspect is not being waged against bin Laden, who proves a fiercely elusive target, but rather against the Taliban and other anti-American forces in that country—to portray patriotism as absolute loyalty to the "war on terrorism" and fealty to the administration's initiatives, is itself creating a backlash. David Broder, a regular (and well-respected) columnist for the *Washington Post*, writes that while on tour with Democratic presidential hopefuls, he began to hear the same questions, over and over again, across the country. An astute political analyst, Broder concludes that "what I heard convinces me that the nine-month moratorium on dissent from Bush's war on terrorism is coming to an end" (*Bryan-College Station Eagle*, July 3, 2002). Many of the questions posed to Vermont Governor Howard Dean, Broder reports, "involved not just the war itself, but its effects on personal liberty and political dissent" (July 3, 2002, A8). That evaporating moratorium on dissent, coupled with genuine alarm regarding the moves to abridge personal liberties (often focused on Attorney General John Ashcroft, but equally likely the responsibility of other voices in the president's advisors as well), and the growing suspicion that we have no genuine target of this "war," no real means of combating a set of techniques rather than a belligerent nation, has led to concern about what might profitably be done.

Clearly, no one group of individuals, no one profession, can do it all. But as social scientists, are there roles which make our work meaningful? Are there activities in which we might engage which will serve both to enhance democratic ends, and at the same time, resist the rapid encroachment on personal freedoms which have been the hallmark of this nation for nearly three hundred years? We believe so. As social scientists, there are two critical roles for us to play.

As teachers, we have an obligation to raise the stakes on critical thinking in our own classrooms. We cannot afford the stubborn refusal we sometimes encounter from students who prefer their own comfortable worlds to confrontation with other, startlingly different, worldviews. September 11, if it taught us nothing else, taught us that "diversity" and "multiculturalism"—long viewed as radical ideas in some quarters (D'Souza, 1991; Bloom, 1987)—are useful, but now weak and superceded terms for a radically reconfigured world (Hunter, 1991; Bérubé and Nelson, 1995) which needs to think in terms of geopolitical relations and systemic economic and political repression and oppression. Our legacy to our students, in the final analysis, has to be the legacy of the tragedies of September 11: a heightened awareness of our citizenship as contingent, in part, on achieving the rights of free and open citizenship for the global community of which we are a part.

Our second critical role, as social scientists and public intellectuals, will be to keep alive not only dissent—when we disagree with policies which make the world a less safe place, as in the recent proposals to consider using tactical nuclear weapons in Iraq and perhaps Afghanistan—but also the idea of dissent as a constitutional right. Put another way, dissent serves both to continue political pressure against an amorphous but increasingly dangerous "war on terrorism," and also to reinforce its peaceful use as a uniquely American right.

We see this book as a small part of that dissent, both against a regime of policies raining terror on a starving and displaced population, millions of which have probably not seen hide nor hair of bin Laden, and against the encroachments against civil liberties increasingly pressed on ourselves domestically. We hope that it will be read as both a hymn of mourning—a comradeship of grief with all of those who lost loved ones—and a call to arms on behalf of civil and political dissent.

Notes

1. And even as this is being written (19 June 2002), the world press is asking who knew what and when and why were there not steps taken to prevent what happened on 11 September 2001.

2. Each piece initially appeared in one of the two journals we edit or coedit, *Qualitative Inquiry and Cultural Studies* ↔ *Critical Methodologies*. We are grateful to Sage Publications and Catherine Rossbach for expediting the appearance of these pieces in this book.

3. Because the events of 9/11 unfolded so quickly (see appendix A), on the table of contents for each essay we list the date it was recived in our offices.

4. When such occurred, journals and newsletters presented suggestions concerning how a particular discipline (e.g., sociology) could speak to the causes and meanings of terrorism, or hate crime, or responses to disaster. See the two articles in *footnotes*, 2002, 2002 (cited below), but also see Applegate (2001), Jackson (2002), *Feminist Media Studies* (2002); Harpham (2002), Mitchell (2002); Silvers and Epstein (2002); Andrews and Cole (2002); also Chomsky (2001). For a criticism of how the academy responded to 9/11 see Jackson (2002), and also American Council of Trustees and Alumni (2001); and on threats to academic freedom *New York Times* (2002).

References

Altheide, David. 2002. "Communication as a Power in Peter Hall's Work." *Studies in Symbolic Interaction* 25: 34–46.

American Council of Trustees and Alumni. 2001. *Defending Civilization: How Our Universities Are Failing America and What Can Be Done about It.* Washington, D.C.: American Council of Trustees and Alumni.

Andrews, David L., and C. L. Cole. 2002. "The Nation Reconsidered." *Journal of Sport & Social Issues* 26: 1–2.

Applegate, James. 2001. "The Tragedy of Hate: The Need for Engaged Communication Scholars." *Spectra* 37 (November): 2–3

Arsmitage, John. 2002. "State of Emergency: An Introduction." *Theory, Culture & Society* (Special issue on 9/11) 6: 1–19

Baudrillard, Jean. 1988. *America.* London: Verso.

———. 2001. "The Spirit of Terrorism." *Le Monde*, 2/11/01. <http://www.lemonde.fr/article/0,5987,3232--239354-,00.html>

Bérubé, Michael, and Cary Nelson. 1995. *Higher Education under Fire: Politics, Economics and the Crisis of the Humanities.* New York: Routledge.

Bloom, Allan. 1987. *The Closing of the American Mind: How Higher Education Has Failed Democracy and Impoverished the Souls of Today's Students.* New York: Simon and Schuster.

Broder, David. 2002. "Signs That Support of War Is Waning." *Bryan-College Station Eagle*, July 3, A8.

Chomsky, Noam. 2001. *9-11.* New York: Seven Stories Press.

Cockburn, Alexander. 2001. "Faceless Cowards?" *The Nation* 1 (October): 8.

Critical Inquiry. 2002. Special Issue, 9/11.

D'Souza, Dinesh. (1991). *Illiberal Education: The Politics of Race and Sex on Campus.* New York: The Free Press.

Dworkin, Ronald. 2002. "The Threat to Patriotism." *New York Review of Books* (28 February): 44–49.

"Feminist Media Studies Responses to September 11." *Feminist Media Studies* 2, 1: 291–324.

Friedman, Thomas L. 2002. "A Failure to Imagine." *New York Times.* Sunday, 19 May, Op-Ed: 15.

Giroux, Henry. 2000a. *Impure Acts: The Practical Politics of Cultural Studies.* New York: Routledge.

———. 2000b. *Stealing Innocence: Corporate Culture's War on Children.* New York: Palgrave.

Hall, Stuart, Chas Critcher, Tony Jefferson, John Clarke, and Brian Roberts. 1978. *Policing the Crisis: Mugging the State, and Law and Order.* New York: Holmes and Meier.

Harpham, Geoffrey Galt. 2002. "Symbolic Terror." *Critical Inquiry* 28: 573–579.

Hunter, James Davison. 1991. *Culture Wars: The Struggle to Define America.* New York: Basic Books.

Jackson, Jean E. 2002. "ACTA Report Criticizes Professors." *Anthropology News* (March): 7.

Judt, Tony. 2002. "America and the War." Pp. 15–30 in Robert B. Silvers and Barbara Epstein (eds.), *Striking Terror: America's New War.* New York: New York Review Books.

Kellner, Douglas. 1989. *Critical Theory, Marxism and Modernity.* Baltimore: Johns Hopkins University Press.

Kincheloe, Joe L., and Peter McLaren. 2000. "Rethinking Critical Theory and Qualitative Research." Pp. 279–314 in Norman K. Denzin and Yvonna S. Lincoln (eds.), *Handbook of Qualitative Research*, 2nd ed. Thousand Oaks, CA: Sage.

Kittridge, William. 1987. *Owning It All.* San Francisco: Murray House.

Massing, Michael. 2002. "Think Tank." *New York Times*, May 4 (Saturday): A17.

McChesney, Robert W. 2000. *Rich Media, Poor Democracy.* Urbana: University of Illinois Press.

Mitchell, W. J. T. 2002. "911: Criticism and Crisis." *Critical Inquiry* 28: 567–573.

"National Science Foundation Awards Post 9/11 Attack Grants." 2002, November: *footnotes* 29, no. 8: 2.

Nelson, Cary, and Dilip Parameshwar. 1996. "Cultural Studies and the Politics of Disciplinarity." Pp. 1–19 in C. Nelson and D. Parameshwar (eds.), *Displinarity and Dissent in Cultural Studies.* New York: Routledge.

New York Times. 2002. "Editorial: Protecting Speech on Campus." 27 January (Sunday): 12.

Redburn, Tom. 2002. "The Week That Was: The Enron Debacle Follows a Now Established Format for Scandal." *New York Times* Sunday, 20 January: 24.

Said, Edward. 2001. "Backlash and Backtrack." *al-Abram*, weekly on-line edition, September 27-October 3.

Schell, Jonathan. 2001. "A Hole in the World." *The Nation* I (October): 4–6.

Silvers, Robert B., and Barbara Epstein (eds.), 2002. *Striking Terror: America's New War*. New York: New York Review Books.

"Social Sciences Turn Expertise to Terrorism and 9-11; an ASA Priority for 2002 Annual Meeting, Too." 2002. February: *footnotes*, 30, no. 2: 2, 8.

Tierney, John. 2001. "Fantasies of Vengeance Fed by Fury." *New York Times*, 18 September: A24.

Appendix A
Post-9/11 Timeline

Date

Sept. 11: Hijacked airliners crash in N.Y.C., at Pentagon, in Pennsylvania.

Sept. 11: Wal-Mart reports nationwide sales of U.S. flags up 1,800 percent over a year ago; ammunition purchases rise 100 percent.

Sept. 12: President Bush delivers televised national address from Oval Office.

Sept. 12: H. CON. RES. 224:
Expressing the sense of the Congress that, as a symbol of solidarity following the terrorist attacks on the United States on September 11, 2001, every United States citizen is encouraged to display the flag of the United States.

Sept. 13: H. J. RES. 63:
Declaring that a state of war exists between the United States and any entity determined by the President to have planned, carried out, or otherwise supported the attacks against the United States on September 11, 2001, and authorizing the President to use United States Armed Forces and all other necessary resources of the United States Government against any such entity in order to bring the conflict to a successful termination.

Sept. 14: President Bush visits Ground Zero in New York City in response to chants of *USA! USA!*

Sept. 15: Bush tells U.S.: "We're at war," names Osama bin Laden "prime suspect."

Sept. 17: Bush declares that the U.S. will launch a crusade against a "new kind of evil."

Sept. 20: Bush creates cabinet-level Office of Homeland Security.

Sept. 20: Bush orders the deployment of warplanes, ships, equipment and personnel to the Persian Gulf and Afghanistan theater.

Sept. 20: Bush declares a war on terrorism, but Congress never votes on the War Powers Act.

Sept. 20: In a speech before Congress, Bush warns the Taliban to turn over all terrorists in Afghanistan.

Sept. 21: Congress approves $15 billion federal aid package for U.S. airline industry.

Sept. 21: Pop culture celebrity superstars stage telethon (*America: A Tribute to Heroes*) to raise money for victims of Sept. 11 attacks; stars include Tom Cruise, Julia Roberts, Robert De Niro, Bruce Springsteen, Stevie Wonder and Celine Dion.

Sept. 21: Taliban rejects Bush's ultimatium and vows to continue to protect Osama bin Laden and the Al Qaeda terror network even if that provoked war.

Sept. 27: Bush authorizes National Guard troops for airport security.

Sept. 27: FBI releases names of hijackers.

Oct. 5: First of five anthrax deaths.

Oct. 5: Britain's Tony Blair lays out the most detailed U.S.-supported evidence linking Sept. 11 hijackers to the bin Laden network.

Oct. 7: U.S. opens first air assault against Afghanistan with cruise missiles. Bush declares, "I gave them fair warning."

Oct. 13: Anthrax scares ripple across the nation.

Oct. 19: U.S. ground forces battle for first time in Afghanistan.

Oct. 26: Bush signs a terrorism bill that he calls an "essential step in defeating terrorism, while protecting the constitutional rights of all Americans."

Oct. 28: U.S. Patriot Act implemented.

Oct. 30: For the second time in a month the FBI issues an alert warning Americans that it had credible evidence to believe there could be new terrorist attacks.

Nov. 7: First full month of war in Afghanistan.

Nov. 7: Bush urges other nations to join war on terrorism.

Nov. 8: A report attacking criticisms of the war on terrorism is issued by the Americal Council of Trustees and Alumni: "Defending Civilization: How Our Universities Are Failing America and What Can Be Done about It."

Nov. 14: Bush issues controversial War Tribunal order.

Nov. 16: FBI reports that they found no evidence indicating that any of the roughly 1,200 people arrested in the U.S. played a part in the suicide hijacking plot of Sept. 11.

Nov. 28: First American dies in Afghanistan.

Dec. 6: Afghans sign an accord to create a multiethnic government.

Dec. 8: Formal ground war draws to an end.

Jan. 10: U.S. military cargo plane leaves Afghanistan with the first twenty Taliban and Al Qaeda prisoners to be transferred to Guantanamo Bay, Cuba.

Jan. 29: In State of Union address, Bush characterizes Iraq, Iran and North Korea as the Axis of Evil. Bush expands war on terror to include the Axis of Evil. Bush calls for creation of USA Freedom Corps.

Feb. 9 : Bush administration begins serious planning for a campaign against Saddam Hussein.

Feb. 11: Pentagon commits 650 soldiers to help Philippine government track down and defeat Abu Sayyaf, an Islamic grouip with possible links to Osama bin Laden.

Feb. 27: Pentagon flirts with a high-level office to influence public sentiment abroad.

Mar. 7: National Guard begins phased withdrawal through May of airport security-duty.

Mar. 7: Flight 93 National Memorial Act (introduced in House, but since signed into law) to authorize a national memorial to commemorate the passengers and crew of Flight 93 who, on September 11, 2001, courageously gave their lives by thwarting a planned attack on our nation's Capital.

Mar. 10: A new organization, headed by William Bennett, Americans For Victory Over Terrorism, is announced.

Mar. 11: President unveils September 11 postage stamp.

Mar. 12: Homeland Security Advisory System: Ridge announces the color-coded advisory system.

Mar. 12: Cheney sent to the Middle East.

Mar. 20: Military Tribunal Authorization Act of 2002 (introduced in House, but since signed into law) to authorize the president to establish military tribunals to try the terrorists responsible for the September 11, 2001, attacks against the United States, and for other purposes.

Mar. 21: Homeland Security Council Executive Order: Executive Order Establishing the President's Homeland Security Advisory Council and Senior Advisory Committees for Homeland Security.

April 4: Bush announces Colin Powell will be sent to the Middle East.

April 9: Defense Budget Restoration Act (introduced in House) to authorize the appropriation of the $10,000,000,000 reserve fund within the national defense budget function for activities to prosecute the war on terrorism.

April 30: Bush joins with Congress in legally proclaiming May 1 as Loyalty Day.

May 3: Bush restores nondiscriminatory trade treatment to the products of Afghanistan by proclamation.

May 7: President Bush meets with Prime Minister Sharon.

May 14: President signs Border Security and Visa Entry Reform Act.

May 24: Senators call for creation of an independent counsel to investigate America's intelligence agencies and their conduct before and after 9/11.

May 31: Last steel beam is removed from WTC.

Appendix
September 11 Web Resources

Research & Reference Resources, Events of September 11, 2001
http://www.freepint.com/gary/91101.html

September 11 Web Archhive
http://september11.archive.org/

Legislation Related to the Attack of September 11, 2001
http://thomas.loc.gov/home/terrorleg.htm

Faith and Values—9/11 Remembered (Religious responses to 9/11)
http://www.faithandvalues.com/channels/september-11.asp?source=google

International and U.S.A. News from September 11, 2001, and the next 111 days of 2001
http://www.september11news.com/

The September 11th Fund
http://www.uwnyc.org/sep11/

The Avalon Project at the Yale Law School: September 11, 2001: Attack on America
http://www.yale.edu/lawweb/avalon/sept_11/sept_11.htm

The September 11 Digital Archive: Saving the Histories of September 11, 2001
http://911digitalarchive.org/

The Nation—September 11, 2001
http://www.thenation.com/special/wtc/index.mhtml

The National Security Archive September 11 Sourcebooks
http://www.gwu.edu/~nsarchiv/NSAEBB/sept11/

Media Map—September 11 Journalists' Resources
http://www.mediamap.com/Sept11.asp

Human Rights Watch—September 11 and Its Aftermath
http://www.hrw.org/campaigns/september11/

University of Arizona September 11 Resources
http://www.u.arizona.edu/ic/humanities/september11/pages/

C-Span—September 11 Video Archive
http://www.c-span.org/terrorism/

After September 11—Images from Ground Zero
http://www.911exhibit.state.gov/

Guardian—Timeline of 9/11 Recovery Operation
http://www.guardian.co.uk/uslatest/story/0,1282,-1772349,00.html

White House September 11 pages
http://www.whitehouse.gov/president/september11/01.html

Anti-Defamation League's Pages on Voices about September 11 (Commentary from a wide variety of groups, from civil rights groups to extremist organizations)
http://www.adl.org/terrorism_america/saying_092001.asp

Indy Media—9/11: Peace & Justice
http://www.indymedia.org/peace/

Crank Dot Net—9/11 Conspiracy Theories
http://www.crank.net/911.html

Douglas Kellner—BlogLeft: Critical Interventions
http://www.gseis.ucla.edu/courses/ed253a/blogger.php

Research Buzz—9/11 Links
http://www.researchbuzz.com/911/

About the Editors

Norman Denzin is professor of sociology and communications at the University of Illinois at Urbana-Champaign. He is co-editor of *The Handbook of Qualitative Research*, 2nd ed., co-editor of *Qualitative Inquiry*, editor of *Cultural Studies—Critical Methodologies*, and series editor of *Studies in Symbolic Interaction*.

Yvonna Lincoln is professor of higher education and human resource development at the Texas A&M University. She is the co-author of *Effective Evaluation, Naturalistic Inquiry*, and *Fourth Generation Evaluation*, the editor of *Organizational Theory* and *Inquiry*, the co-editor of the newly-released *Handbook of Qualitative Research*, 2nd ed., and co-editor of the international journal, *Qualitative Inquiry*.

Credits

"One Face in the Crowd," "Aftermath"
Mary Weems, Qualitative Inquiry, Volume 8 Number 2
pp. 135–136, copyright © 2002 Sage Publications
Reprinted by Permission of Sage Publications, Inc.

"Posts Post September 11"
Patricia T. Clough, Cultural Studies↔Critical Methodologies, Volume 2 Number 1
pp. 15–17, copyright © 2002 Sage Publications
Reprinted by Permission of Sage Publications, Inc.

"The Mourning After"
Michelle Fine, Qualitative Inquiry, Volume 8 Number 2
pp. 137–145, copyright © 2002 Sage Publications
Reprinted by Permission of Sage Publications, Inc.

"Grief in an Appalachian Register"
Yvonna Lincoln, Qualitative Inquiry, Volume 8 Number 2
pp. 146–149, copyright © 2002 Sage Publications
Reprinted by Permission of Sage Publications, Inc.

"Listening to the Heartbeat of New York: Writings on the Wall"
Joanne Robertson, Qualitative Inquiry, Volume 9 Number 1
Forthcoming from Sage Publications

"Relationships–Responsibilities, Once Removed and Ever Connected"
Karen Staller, Qualitative Inquiry, Volume 9 Number 1
Forthcoming from Sage Publications

"Some Thoughts on Recovery"
Greg Dimitriadis, Qualitative Inquiry, Volume 8 Number 2
pp. 146–149, copyright © 2002 Sage Publications
Reprinted by Permission of Sage Publications, Inc.

"What Is Over? Ruminations from One Who Has Already Lived through Another September 11"
Angharad Valdivia, Cultural Studies↔Critical Methodologies, Volume 2 Number 3
pp. 354–358, copyright © 2002 Sage Publications
Reprinted by Permission of Sage Publications, Inc.

"What Will We Tell the Children?"
Norman K. Denzin, Cultural Studies↔Critical Methodologies, Volume 2, Number 20
pp. 214–216, copyright © 2002 Sage Publications
Reprinted by Permission of Sage Publications, Inc.

"Small World"
Laurel Richardson, Cultural Studies↔Critical Methodologies, Volume 2 Number 3
pp. 354–358, copyright © 2002 Sage Publications
Reprinted by Permission of Sage Publications, Inc.

"Week Four"
Norman K. Denzin, Qualitative Inquiry, Volume 8 Number 2
pp. 199–202, copyright © 2002 Sage Publications
Reprinted by Permission of Sage Publications, Inc.